E. Smith

Toynbee

and

History

CONTRIBUTORS

Wayne Altree

Sir Ernest Barker

Geoffrey Barraclough

W. den Boer

George Catlin

Rushton Coulborn

Christopher Dawson

Abba Eban

Edward Fiess

Pieter Geyl

Walter Kaufmann

Hans Kohn

Tangye Lean

H. Michell

Hans J. Morgenthau

Lewis Mumford

G. J. Renier

Frederick Robin

Jan Romein

Pitirim Sorokin

O. H. K. Spate

Lawrence Stone

A. J. P. Taylor

Kenneth W. Thompson

Arnold J. Toynbee

Hugh Trevor-Roper

Linus Walker

W. H. Walsh

Gotthold Weil

Toynbee and History

Critical Essays and Reviews

Edited by

M. F. ASHLEY MONTAGU

An Extending Horizons Book

PORTER SARGENT PUBLISHER
BOSTON 8, MASS.

EDITOR'S FOREWORD

Arnold J. Toynbee's *A Study of History* is undoubtedly the most widely known work of contemporary historical scholarship. In the United States alone—in which country the work has made its widest appeal—more than seven thousand sets of the ten-volume edition had been sold by the end of 1955. The masterly one-volume abridgement of the first six volumes by Somervell, which appeared in 1947, was a Book-of-the-Month Club selection, and through that outlet sold considerably over one hundred thousand copies, while the Oxford University Press has sold almost two hundred thousand copies. There have been innumerable discussions of Toynbee's work in the press, in periodicals, over radio and television, not to mention countless lectures and seminars. Through the agency of all these media Toynbee has himself actively assisted in the diffusion of his views.

It can therefore be said, without exaggeration, that of its kind Toynbee's *A Study of History* constitutes one of the most famous and most widely discussed books of its time. That time extends from the year 1934, when the first three volumes were published, through 1939 when volumes IV-VI were published, through 1954 when volumes VII-X made their appearance, to the reaches of the next generation or more, which will doubtless develop into the period of exegesis or hermeneutical criticism of the Toynbeean canon.

Toynbee is already, and will be for some time to come, a power in the world to reckon with. It is the impression of some students of the human scene that that power has been neither adequately understood nor sufficiently estimated. Whether this be so or not, it is generally agreed that the influence which Toynbee's *A Study of History* has already exercised, and is likely to continue to exercise, cannot be overlooked; indeed, it is inescapable.

There is scarcely an aspect of the life of man in the modern or in the ancient world which Toynbee's monumental work does not touch upon. Toynbee's erudition, acknowledged by all, is so vast and convoluted that among those who read him

> ... the wonder grows
> That one small head can carry all he knows.

For most of Toynbee's readers that wonder assumes the form of admiration and something verging upon awe. Toynbee's achievement is of staggering proportions. Ten volumes (with two more

vii

promised), 6,290 pages, 3,150,000 words, 332 pages of index with 19,000 entries, the magisterial third-person style, the prodromic periods, the Greek elegiacs, the Latinisms, the neologisms, the sonorities of sensuous and esoteric names, the sinuosities of the author's thought, the prodigious show of learning, and not least the experience and authority of the creator of *A Study of History,* combine to produce an overwhelming effect. The general reader concludes the book with the feeling that he has read something great and wonderful.

However, if he is critically minded, he wonders how sound it all is. To anyone who is in any way professionally concerned with the history of man, the question is frequently put by such readers: "What do you think of Toynbee?" There is a genuine interest in knowing to what extent the book presents a sound analysis of history.

It is scarcely possible that there is anyone living who, from the matrix of his own knowledge, could deliver an authoritative verdict on the work as a whole—such polymaths are no longer among us. But in the many special fields which have been harvested to supply grist for Toynbee's *Study,* there are a number of distinguished workers. By gathering together their views and criticisms of Toynbee's particular treatment of their own fields, some approach may be made to a balanced and well-considered judgment on *A Study of History.* It is such an approach which the present volume attempts.

In addition to the views and criticisms of the experts, and not less valuable, are the insights into Toynbee's work provided by literary critics and humanists. Their opinions, it is hoped, are adequately represented in the present volume.

It has been urged by some that the value of Toynbee's work does not rest so much upon its empirical accuracy as upon the insights and carefully considered judgments of an exceedingly well-informed mind—"one schooled by action as well as reading—concerning an immense range of matters bearing upon the present plight and probable future of humanity."[1] It has also been suggested that scholars are on shaky grounds when they criticise Toynbee for forsaking the severe and restraining grooves of academic discipline for the more expansive groves of Intuition and Prophecy. The scholars may succeed in avoiding the smaller errors but fail to achieve the grander vision of the Magister.

---

[1] Arthur Bestor, in a review of Toynbee's last four volumes in *The Progressive,* December 1954, p. 32.

Toynbee claims to have applied the empirical method to the study of history. This claim has been disputed by his fellow-historians. Much else is in dispute. The views and criticisms of the experts being set before him, the reader will, it is believed, be in a position to draw his own conclusions concerning the soundness and value of Toynbee's work.

The editor's function has been to bring this gathering of experts and scholars together within the covers of a single volume, and to present their contributions in the form in which they were originally published. Three of the contributions appear for the first time in English: namely, Professor W. de Boer's "Toynbee and Classical History," which originally appeared in Dutch in the journal *De Gids* in October, 1948; Professor Jan Romein's "Reason and Religion"—hitherto unpublished—which represents the introduction spoken by Professor Romein when Toynbee lectured at the Hague in 1954; and Mr. Wayne Altree's "Toynbee and Chinese History," which represents a revised version of a paper which originally appeared in German in *Saeculum* in 1955 (Vol. 6, pp. 10-34).

It has already been stated that the editorial practice has been to reprint each contribution exactly as it appeared in its original form, except that misprints and "writing" errors have been silently corrected—the latter always at the request of the author. Details relating to the original publication are given at the foot of the page of each contribution.

In a volume of this kind a certain amount of repetition is unavoidable. Each writer offers a summary of what Toynbee attempts to do, and makes that summary in his own way. In so doing each writer affords something of a new view of Toynbee's achievement. Hence, the editor has considered it desirable in the author's and the reader's interest to retain these summaries.

The reader will, of course, distinguish for himself those pieces which deal with the first six volumes only, those which review the last four volumes, and those which are devoted to the ten volumes of *A Study of History*.

Largely for reasons of space it has not been possible to include in the present volume a number of excellent critical essays and reviews on various aspects of Toynbee's work. The editor expresses his regrets to the authors, and the hope that if this book meets with any success it may be possible to include their work in a future edition.

While more extended acknowledgement is made elsewhere in

these pages, it is a great pleasure to be able to thank here the authors and publishers who by their kindness and ready cooperation made this volume possible. Special thanks are due to Mr. Fon W. Boardman, Jr., and the Oxford University Press, publisher of Toynbee's *A Study of History,* for unfailing courtesy and invaluable assistance. To Professor Pieter Geyl, of the University of Utrecht, the editor is indebted for many kindnesses, and finally, thanks are due to the publisher, Extending Horizons Books, particularly Mr. F. Porter Sargent and Mr. E. Nelson Hayes, for their sympathetic interest in this work.

Princeton, N. J.   M. F. ASHLEY MONTAGU

CONTENTS

CONTRIBUTORS

Wayne Altree, has lived in the Far East and studied Chinese history at the universities of Hong Kong, Hawaii, and Harvard

Sir Ernest Barker, Lately Professor of Political Science at Cambridge University

Geoffrey Barraclough, Professor of History at the University of Liverpool

W. den Boer, Professor of Ancient History at the University of Leyden

George Catlin, Lately Professor of Politics at Cornell University

Rushton Coulborn, Professor of History at Atlanta University

Christopher Dawson, Historian and Writer; Gifford Lecturer, 1947-48

Abba Eban, Ambassador of Israel to the United States

Edward Fiess, Instructor, Department of English, Brooklyn College

Pieter Geyl, Professor of History at the University of Utrecht

Walter Kaufmann, Associate Professor of Philosophy at Princeton University

Hans Kohn, Professor of History at the City College of New York

Tangye Lean, Assistant Director of External Broadcasting, British Broadcasting Corporation

H. Michell, Lately Professor of Political Economy, McMaster University

Hans J. Morgenthau, Professor of Political Science at the University of Chicago

Lewis Mumford, Humanist, city and regional planner, and writer

G. J. Renier, Professor of Dutch History and Institutions at the University of London

Frederick Robin, Editor of *The Reporter,* New York, N. Y.

Jan Romein, Professor of Modern and Theoretical History at the University of Amsterdam

Pitirim A. Sorokin, Professor Emeritus of Sociology at Harvard University

O. H. K. Spate, Professor of Geography at the Australian National University

Lawrence Stone, Lecturer in Modern History, Wadham College, Oxford University

A. J. P. Taylor, Fellow and Tutor in Modern History, Magdalen College, Oxford University

Kenneth W. Thompson, Assistant Director, The Social Sciences, The Rockefeller Foundation, New York, N. Y.

Arnold J. Toynbee, Director of Studies in the Royal Institute of International Affairs, and Research Professor of International History at the University of London

Hugh Trevor-Roper, Christ Church, Oxford University

Linus Walker, Dominican House of Studies, Washington, D. C.

W. H. Walsh, Professor of History, Merton College, Oxford University

Gotthold Weil, Professor of Arabic and Turkish Philology at the University of Jerusalem

ACKNOWLEDGMENTS

The courtesy of the following authors, publishers, journals and copyright holders in permitting the use of copyrighted material is herewith gratefully acknowledged:

Arnold J. Toynbee and the Oxford University Press, Arnold J. Toynbee and the Royal Institute of International Affairs, Mr. Tangye Lean, Professor G. N. Renier and The Beacon Press, Sir Ernest Barker and the Royal Institute of International Affairs, *The Times* (London), Mr. Lawrence Stone and *The Spectator*, Mr. A. J. P. Taylor, and *The New Statesman and Nation*, Mr. Hugh Trevor-Roper and *The Sunday Times*, Mr. Lewis Mumford and the *New Republic*, Professor Rushton Coulborn and the University of Chicago Press, Professor George Catlin and *The Political Science Quarterly*, Professor Pitirim A. Sorokin and the *Journal of Modern History*, Professor Kenneth W. Thompson and the University of Chicago Press, Professor W. den Boer and *De Gids*, Professor O. H. K. Spate and the University of Melbourne, Professor Walter Kaufmann and *Partisan Review*, Dr. Frederick E. Robin and the American Jewish Committee, Linus Walker, O.P., and *The Thomist*, Professor Jan Romein, Professor Hans Kohn and *The Christian Register*, Professor Pieter Geyl and the Philosophical Library, Professor Edward Fiess and *The Journal of the History of Ideas*, Professor Arnold J. Toynbee and *The Journal of the History of Ideas*, Mr. Abba Eban and the Israeli Library of Information; Professor Hans J. Morgenthau and *Encounter*, Professor H. Michell and the Royal Society of Canada, Mr. W. H. Walsh and *The Times* (London), and Professor Gotthold Weil and *Middle Eastern Affairs*.

Toynbee

and

History

A STUDY OF HISTORY

WHAT I AM TRYING TO DO*

ARNOLD TOYNBEE

Since 1927 I have been writing *A Study of History* side by side with the Chatham House *Survey of International Affairs* that my wife and I began to write in 1924. I could not, I believe, have done either piece of work if I had not been doing the other at the same time. A survey of current affairs on a world-wide scale can be made only against a background of world-history; and a study of world-history would have no life in it if it left out the history of the writer's own lifetime, for one's contemporaries are the only people whom one can ever catch alive. An historian in our generation must study Gandhi and Lenin and Atatürk and F. D. Roosevelt if he is to have any hope of bringing Hammurabi and Ikhnataon and Amos and the Buddha back to life for himself and for his readers.

The particular generation into which I was born happens to be a revolutionary one. In less than one lifetime the face of the World has changed almost out of recognition, and the West's position in the World has undergone the greatest change of all. So, if one has been following the course of World affairs since 1914, one is bound to have gained, from this alone, a good deal of new knowledge about history; and, meanwhile, the forty years that have seen this new chapter of history writing itself have also seen the Orientalists and the archaeologists recovering for us other chapters of history that had been either forgotten completely or had been remembered only in a few shreds and tatters of tradition. In our day the Minoan Civilization has risen from its grave below the Graeco-Roman Civilization; the Shang Culture in China from below the classical Chinese Civilization; the Indus Culture from below Aryan India; the Hittite Civilization from below the Asia Minor known to Herodotus; and at the same time our picture of the Sumerian and Egyptian Civilizations, and of the pre-Columbian Civilizations in the New World, has been quite transformed by the new knowledge that the excavator's spade has brought to light here too. This rediscovery of the rather less recent past, together with the portentous events of our own day, has given us a wealth of new historical information. Our vision of the history of Mankind, since the rise of the earliest known civilizations about 5,000 years ago, has been enormously enlarged and has also been brought into much deeper

International Affairs, vol. 31, 1955, pp.1-4.

focus; and, since curiosity is one of the characteristics of human nature, we find ourselves moved, in our time, to take a new look at the face of history as a whole. This is the origin of my book *A Study of History*. It is one person's impression of history in the new light in which we can now see it; and of course a number of other people have been tempted, by the same opportunity, to take their look and form their impressions. Each of these individual views will show the new picture in a different perspective; and, since it has only lately become possible to take this panoramic view of history, the first attempts (of which mine is one) are sure to be revised and corrected and superseded as time goes on and as more people turn their minds to this exciting intellectual enterprise.

There is, though, one negative observation that will, I believe, continue to hold good. As soon as one looks at the new panorama of history, one sees that it bursts the bounds of the current framework within which our Western historians have been doing their work for the last 250 years. This Late Modern Western view of history was a reflection of the temporary situation during the Late Modern Age. From the failure of the second Ottoman siege of Vienna in 1683 down to the outbreak of the first world war in 1914, Western Europe dominated the rest of the World, while the West European middle class dominated the rest of the population of Western Europe. During that brief and abnormal period of history, the World was being managed by a Western European middle-class oligarchy which could afford to be small because it was uncommonly able and sensible. Under this dispensation 'the lower classes', 'the colonials', and 'the natives' did not count; though, between them, they accounted for all but a tiny minority of the human race; and this state of the historical facts set the pattern for the Western historians of that age.

The traditional pattern in the West down to the end of the seventeenth century had been the Israelite pattern, which Christendom and Islam had taken over with modifications in their own favour. In this Jewish-Christian-Muslim view, history had appeared to be an act of God beginning at the Creation and destined to end in the Last Judgement, while Israel (or Christendom or Islam) had been singled out as being the people chosen by God for carrying out His purposes. The last great Western exponent of this Jewish-Christian-Muslim pattern of history had been Bishop Bossuet. His eighteenth-century successors made the Late Modern Western pattern of history, on which we have been working since Bossuet's death, by cutting God out of the picture and dealing with the Christian Church as the Church had dealt with Israel. Bossuet's successors appropriated the role of being 'the Chosen People' from the Christian Church, as the Church had appropriated it from

Israel; and they transferred this role, partly to 'Europe', but mainly to the particular West European nation to which a particular historian happened to belong: to France, Britain, Italy, Spain, and so on, as the case might be. This eighteenth-century Western view of history as a movement in a straight line, leading up to a twentieth-century 'Europe', 'Britain', or 'Nicaragua', instead of leading up to a future Last Judgement, simply cannot take in the new panorama that the twentieth century has now opened out before our eyes. In that antiquated Late Modern Western picture there is no room at all for China or India, and hardly any room even for Russia or America. And where are we to find in it so much as a niche for the Mayans or for the Hittites? In the light of our new knowledge, we are compelled to discard this pattern, as our eighteenth-century predecessors discarded Bossuet's. Once again, we have to look at history with new eyes, as our eighteenth-century predecessors did.

The histories of all the civilizations that have now come to light cannot be arranged in a single series leading up to the present state of any one living civilization or any one living nation. Instead of the beanstalk pattern of history, we have to draw for ourselves a tree pattern, in which the civilizations rise, like so many branches, side by side; and this pattern is suggested by the most important feature in the history of the Modern Age. In this age our Western Civilization has collided with all the other surviving civilizations all over the face of the planet—with the Islamic civilization, with the Hindu, with the Chinese, with the Aztec, and so on,—and we can take a comparative view of the effects of these simultaneous collisions upon the parties to them. This comparative treatment can be extended to the whole of history; and it is, in fact, the method of the human sciences: the theory of knowledge, psychology, anthropology, sociology, economics. The human sciences like the natural sciences, make a comparative study of their data in order to discover the structure of the facts and the events; and I believe that here the historians ought to take their cue from the scientists. The academic division between history and the social sciences is an accidental one which is an obstacle to the progress of understanding. We need to break down the traditional partition, and to throw history and the social sciences together into a single comprehensive study of human affairs.

In a study of human affairs the first thing now to be done is to explore how far we can carry, in this field, the scientific method of investigating 'laws', regularities, uniformities, recurrences. Some Western historians in the post-Bossuet age have denied that there are any regularities in the course of human affairs and have declared, with evident sincerity, that they have no such patterns in their own minds. Yet the use made by these very historians of such patterns as 'Europe' and 'Britain' shows that they are mistaken in their belief about the nature of their own mental operations. A pattern is still there; it is, as we have seen, the classical Jewish-Christian-Muslim pattern thinly disguised in secular modern dress. The difference between these post-Christian Western historians and their Christian predecessors is that the moderns do not allow themselves to be aware of the pattern in their minds, whereas Bossuet, Eusebius, and Saint Augustine were fully conscious of it. If one cannot think without mental patterns—and, in my belief, one cannot—it is better to know what they are; for a pattern of which one is unconscious is a pattern that holds one at its mercy.

One of my aims in *A Study of History* has been to try out the scientific approach to human affairs and to test how far it will carry us. Of course, no one would seriously contend that there are no patterns at all in historical thought, for thought itself is a mental pattern, and no historian could think one thought or write one line without using such mental patterns as 'society', 'state', 'church', 'war', 'battle', and 'man'. The real question at issue is not whether mental patterns exist but whether they cover the whole field of human affairs or only part of it; and my own belief is that there are some things in human affairs that have no pattern because they are not subject to scientific laws. One such thing, I believe, is an encounter between two or more human beings. I believe that the outcome of such an encounter would not be predictable, even if we had a complete knowledge of all the antecedent facts. I also think that the poetry and the prophetic vision that well up out of the subconscious depths of the human soul are not amenable to law. I think, in fact, that here we are in the presence of genuine acts of creation, in which something new is brought into existence; and this leads us back towards the Biblical view of history which was accepted in the West from the fourth century till the end of the seventeenth.

More than twenty-seven years have now passed since I began to make my first notes for *A Study of History,* and I am conscious that, during these years, my outlook has changed. As I have gone on, Religion has come, once again, to take the central place in my picture of the Universe. Yet I have not returned to the religious outlook in which I was brought up. I was brought up to believe that Christianity was a unique revelation of the whole truth. I have now come to believe that all the historic religions and philosophies are partial revelations of the truth in one or other of its aspects. In particular, I believe that Buddhism and Hinduism have a lesson to teach Christianity, Islam, and Judaism in the 'one world' into which we are now being carried by 'the annihilation of distance'. Unlike the Judaic religions, the Indian religions are not exclusive.

They allow for the possibility that there may be alternative approaches to the mystery of Existence; and this seems to me more likely to be the truth than the rival claims of Judaism, Christianity, and Islam to be unique and final revelations. This Indian standpoint is the one from which the last four volumes of my book have been written. For each of us, the easiest approach to the mystery of the Universe is, no doubt, his ancestral religion; but this does not mean that he ought to rule out the other approaches that the other religions offer. If one can enter into these, as well as into one's own, it is gain, not loss.

This book is now behind me; but even the longest books is only one piece of action, and, though the book is finished, the subject is perennial. As I write these words, I seem to catch the faint sound of the busy archaeologist's trowel, as he deftly uncovers new layers of buried civilizations in Bucklersbury and Beyce Sultan and Palenque. Meanwhile, the critical current chapter of the history of our own world runs on; and, all the time, the psychologists are digging down deeper in the new dimension that they have added, in our lifetime, to the study of human affairs. A student of history will never find himself out of work, so long as he keeps his wits.

A STUDY OF HISTORY

WHAT THE BOOK IS FOR: HOW THE BOOK TOOK SHAPE*

ARNOLD TOYNBEE

HOW THE BOOK TOOK SHAPE

How did the plan of *A Study of History* take shape? The gist of it must have been in my mind by 1920, because I made my first deliberate attempt at writing it that summer. The first essay came to nothing, and no wonder; for I had tried to cast it in the form of a commentary on the second chorus—'That uncanny creature Man'—in Sophocles' *Antigone*. This false start was owing to an education in the Greek and Latin classics. Yet, without that education, I should never have had the idea at all; for what set me off was a sudden realization, after the outbreak of the First World War, that our world was just then entering on an experience that the Greek World had been through in the Peloponnesian War. That flash of perception had suggested to me that there must be some sense in which Greek history was not 'ancient' but was contemporary with ours, and this would mean that Greek history and our history could be laid out side by side and compared with one another. But why had my classical education made me interested in the historical approach to the Greek Civilization in preference to the literary approach or the philosophical? This is a question which I can answer with certainty. It was because my Mother was an historian, and because she had fired me with her own love of History. Greek history was not particularly her line, but it had to be my line if I was to combine the love of History that I had been given by her with the Greek and Latin education that was still the staple at Winchester when I went to school there. So the germ of the idea of this book was planted in the writer's mind by his Mother at a very early stage in his own mental history.

My second shot at planning the book was made on the 17th September, 1921, in the train between Adrianople and Nish, and this time I succeeded; for, by the end of that day, I had written down, on half a sheet of paper, a list of about a dozen headings; and these headings stand, with very little change, as the titles of the thirteen parts of the book, now published in ten volumes. This time I had not deliberately set myself to make the plan. I had

---

*Pamphlet written by Professor Toynbee upon the completion of the last four volumes of *A Study of History,* and issued by the Oxford University Press.

8

spent the day looking out of the railway carriage window, and the plan that I had jotted down at the end of the day had seemed to come of itself. If this partly accounts for my success this time, another reason for it is that I now also found a way into my subject. I got it from an Irish philosopher in California, F. J. Teggart, and Teggart had got it from Turgot. That great eighteenth-century man of genius had seen that, if one wanted to make a comparative study of History, one ought to start by trying to account for the local differences in the cultures of the living societies, and to work back into the past from this problem in the world of one's own day.

I now had my plan, but it was not until 1927-8 that I was ready to translate this plan into detailed notes for a book. I had to wait and work, because it was obvious that a comparative study of civilizations could not be based just on a comparison of the one into which I had been born with the one in which I had been educated. An acquaintance with Western history and Graeco-Roman history was not nearly enough for my purpose; and, though, by this time, Byzantine history and Islamic history had already risen above my horizon, I had to start from the beginning in learning the rudiments of the histories of India, China, Japan, and the pre-Columbian civilizations of Mexico and Peru. Meanwhile the archaeologists had been coming to my help by bringing back to light a number of buried and forgotten civilizations—the Shang culture in China, the Indus culture in Pakistan, the Minoan in the Aegean—but it was quite a task even just to keep track of all this pricelessly valuable new knowledge.

The notes for the whole book, which I wrote at last in 1927-8, were voluminous, but they never set hard. When after a journey round Asia in 1929, I began to write the book, the notes changed and developed as I went on. Volume vi, bringing me to the end of Part V, was published 41 days before the outbreak of the Second World War in 1939, and for the next seven or eight years I was wholly occupied with war-work, while the notes for Parts VI-XIII lay in safe-keeping in New York. If I had not had these original notes on my table when I started to write the rest of the book in the summer of 1947, I could never have finished the job; but, if these now twenty-years-old notes had not once again turned fluid, as, once again, they did, I could never have finished the job either; for at this stage large batches of the notes had to change almost out of recognition under the solvents of new knowledge and new experience. I should, indeed, have been unfit to finish the job if, in 1954, I had still seen History with just the same eyes as in 1927-8. But, in spite of these changes in detail, the plan made in 1921 still held firm; and this has been fortunate, as it has saved the book from losing its original unity.

WHAT THE BOOK IS FOR

The only good reason for writing a book is because one's wish to write it is a master passion. The wish has to be masterful because the work is tormenting, as every writer finds. One writes for fun, but this fun is also hard labour. Of course, this does not mean that one's work has no purpose. A strong desire implies the presence of a strong purpose inspiring it—even though the latent purpose may not crystallize into consciousness till the work is well under way.

One of my purposes in writing *A Study of History* has been to throw my infinitesimal weight into the balance in which the historian's interest and activity is distributed between the study of History in detail and the study of it as a whole. In my belief, there is no fundamental or irreconcilable opposition between these two sides of an historian's work. One cannot be a historian without both taking general views and verifying particular facts. But each individual and each generation is apt to throw more weight into one of these two complementary scales of the historian's balance than into the other. The balance is always fluctuating and is therefore always needing to be readjusted; and, in the generation in which I happen to have been born, most Western historians have been throwing most of their weight into the study of details. They have been exploring the vast surviving archives of the local governments of our Western World, and they have therefore been apt to see History mainly as the documentary history of Western national states. This has been a valuable and admirable enterprise, and no historian who was in his senses could think of saying about it: 'We have done what we ought not to have done'. It might, though, perhaps be said of my generation of Western historians with more justice that 'we have left undone those things which we ought to have done'. As far back as I can remember, I have always felt that many of my seniors and contemporaries have become prisoners of the documentary wealth which they have opened up. It has been a generation in which historians have had keener eyes for the trees than for the wood; and, since the righting of the balance—on whatever side it may need righting at the moment—is a job that has perpetually to be done, I have felt a vocation to do something, in my own work, to help to bring the wood back into focus. This has been one of the purposes of the present book.

The need for re-directing our attention to a general view of History has also been borne in upon me by other things that have been happening in our time. While the students of medieval and modern Western history have been opening up our Western archives, the Orientalists have been winning new knowledge about the other living civilizations, and the archaeologists new knowledge about civilizations that had not merely been 'dead' but had been forgotten for centuries. All these different intellectual activities have been making magnificent additions to our stock of historical knowledge in detail, but they have been going their separate ways without much reference to one another. Why not try to bring them together? Why not try to take a synoptic view of all the civilizations that have been brought into our ken by the separate achievements of the archaeologists, the Orientalists, and the archivists? To make a shot at this synoptic view is another of the purposes of this book.

And then, lastly, there is a practical purpose which I have very much at heart. While, in the field of historical study, the archivists, Orientalists, and archaeologists have still been working almost out of touch with one another, in the field of practical life the World has suddenly been linked up into a single world-wide society by the technicians' feat of 'annihilating distance'. Civilizations which have developed very diverse traditions and diverse ways of life during the centuries for which they have been living in isolation have now suddenly been brought within point-blank range of one another. Their atomic missiles are now poised head to head, while their minds and hearts are still poles apart. We are all aware how dangerous this situation is for Mankind; we shall want to do anything within our power to ease it; and an historian has one thing that he can do. He can help his fellow men of different civilizations to become more familiar with one another, and, in consequence, less afraid of one another and less hostile to one another, by helping them to understand and appreciate one another's histories and to see in these local and partial stories a common achievement and common possession of the whole human family. In an age of atomic weapons and supersonic guided missiles, Mankind must become one family or destroy itself. And it *is* one family; it always *has* been one family in the making. This is the vision which one sees when one focusses one's gaze on the whole world today. I do believe that a synoptic view of History is one of the World's present practical needs. And I therefore also believe that any early work in this field will have proved its worth if it is rapidly superseded, as a host of fresh workers pours in to gather up the harvest. If this were to happen to my book, I should feel that it had succeeded beyond all my expectations.

A STUDY OF TOYNBEE*

TANGYE LEAN

The author of a great book often takes a more obvious physical imprint from his thought than Arnold Toynbee has done. By the end of the last war his lean and distinguished appearance might have classed him as one of those elder officials of the Foreign Office in whom acquaintance with policy has heightened reserve into a dominant character trait. His geniality in conversation, and the smile of his grey-green eyes, had a touch of unreality; underneath seemed to lie something like foreboding, or at least anxiety of the kind which had slightly disordered his sparse white hair. But if the visitor had left his impressions at that, he would have been unable to account for the subtle and pervasive current of strength running unexpectedly through him to wake his finely shaped hands into clear, incisive gestures. And if our visitor left the Foreign Office with an afterthought about Arnold Toynbee's hands, he might suddenly have realized that they were an artist's hands, or perhaps even a prophet's—and that would, probably, have been the end of his attempt to form a coherent picture.

Born eleven years before the end of the nineteenth century, Arnold Toynbee grew up in an atmosphere which had the authority of permanence. The Bible, the study of history, and the classics were its foundations. Gibbon contributed if not urbanity, at least a certain sense of breadth and ease. Toynbee won a scholarship to Winchester, where he read the classical set-pieces, including Thucydides, with the concentration and lack of disturbing insight that set-pieces demand. By now he had learned to express his feelings in Greek elegiac verse, and from Winchester he won a classical scholarship to Balliol. In Edwardian Oxford he extended his reading, solidified his landmarks, and won the appropriate degree for classical examinations passed with orthodox brilliance. To this his College added a Fellowship; but before he took it up on the eve of the first world war he had two important experiences.

The year in which Toynbee graduated saw the works of Bergson, delayed by translation, sweep into Oxford in an abrupt and surprising flood. They came to Toynbee's own intellectual world 'with the force', he has said, 'of a revelation'. And what was revealing was not simply the intelligibility of a universe dissected with French clarity and Jewish intuition: Bergson claims that there are two automatic distortions in our thinking about life: we protect ourselves from the continuously disintegrating and re-forming flux

*Horizon, (London), January 1947, pp. 24-55.

which is its reality by isolating out the 'present moment' and static 'periods' from the past. The habit has been forced on humanity by preoccupation with a bare living to be earned from the rearrangement of dead objects. But the consequent mechanical 'cramp' of minds which have successfully tackled the material world with a technique of isolation and abstraction is misplaced in considering life itself, where to be realistic we need the help of evolution, psychology and our deepest intuitions.

Bergson points in fact to chasms of assumption beneath the floor of the nineteenth century; his philosophy gives Toynbee his first coherent picture of impermanence, and spreads out later like a kind of dye in his mind, influencing his sense of values, suggesting clues for further research, colouring even his style of exposition. If direct quotations from *L'Evolution Créatrice* itself are rare twenty, or thirty, or forty years later in *A Study of History,* it is because the book has fused into the whole structure of Toynbee's thought.

At the end of 1911—he was now twenty-two—he went for a nine-month tour of Greece, travelling on foot in Crete and the Athos Peninsula, as well as among the inland areas. Once, as he turned the corner of a mountain at the eastern end of Crete, he stumbled on the ruins of an eighteenth-century villa built by a Venetian grandee just before the hold of Venice on the island gave way to the Turks'. Analysing the strange sensation he had as he successfully 'placed' the building, he realized that although this was a piece of modern western architecture, built here by western hands, it seemed precisely as dead, as remote less than two centuries after its demise, as the Minoan palaces at Cnossos and Phaestus which he had been inspecting a few days previously. So 'thalassocrats', he reflected in his Anglo-Greek terminology, shared death in common when separated by three thousand years, and verses ran through his head—as verses and classifications regularly jostle for position in him at moments of historical emotion. For mortality was here at its most impressive when over a vast period,

> in due time, one by one,
> Some with lives that came to nothing, some with deeds as well undone,
> Death came tacitly and took them where they never see the sun.

But Browning had by now brought nineteenth-century England to his mind, aligning a third 'thalassocracy' with the others; for if Venice had managed to keep her grip on Crete for four and a half centuries, that was at any rate longer than his own country had yet ruled over the earliest of her dominions. Toynbee felt a chill in the atmosphere of his baroque ruin; it was a *memento mori* for Britannia as much as for the Doge and Minos.

He had to be back at Oxford for the Michaemas Term, but there was time to bring with him more than the tremendous confirmation which first-hand experience of a culture always gives to its admiring student. The conversations he overheard in Greek cafés about the foreign policy of Sir Edward Grey gave him the beginnings of a sense of political relativity; and as he watched the Balkans lining up for war (he was himself arrested as a spy for crossing a viaduct), as he saw the Austro-Hungarian Imperial Army dawdling in uniforms cut to the mode of 1848 and dyed with the blacks and ethereal blue of the Quattrocento, he again felt a hint below the surface of the changes prepared by time.

Back in the quietness of Balliol, he took up his Fellowship, specialized in Ancient History, and a year later married a daughter of Gilbert Murray. In another year the war had broken out, and he left his studies for the long immersion of five years practical work for the Government. Editing a Blue Book under the direction of Lord Bryce, working on Turkish affairs in one Intelligence Department after another—this kind of experience, shared since then by so many intellectuals, had its profound effect on Toynbee, but was less immediately decisive than the fact of the war.

It was in March 1918, as the Third and Fifth British Armies were cut down by fifty German divisions, that the sense of an impending collapse of Western civilization reached its height; and now Thucydides and Lucretius, whom he constantly re-read, were big with a meaning that he had not seen when they were academic texts. So war in the fifth century B.C. had 'eaten away the margins of ordinary life'; so Lucretius, writing more than a century after Hannibal's invasion, knew precisely the emotional defence of the individual confronted by a succession of mass offensives:

Nil igitur mors est ad nos neque pertinet hilum.

'I shall never forget', he writes in 1921, 'how those lines kept running in my head.' And the thought that had begun to form in him outside the Venetian grandee's villa in Crete took a more definite shape. In the historians of the nineteenth century there must have been something radically inaccurate—their vision of history as a single track mounting, with dips and loops, but mounting purposefully to the heights on which we lived, must have been as distorted by unreflecting egotism as accounts of the solar system before Galileo and Copernicus, or of zoology before Darwin. An enormous, unperceived 'egocentric illusion' had been at work, feeding on industrial and democratic assumptions less obvious to ourselves, but quite as misleading as the military and administrative bias of the Latin historians or the pyramid-Pharaonic horizon of the Egyptians. And if, almost overnight, Thucydides and Lucretius could be recognized as contemporaries instead of ancestors rigidified in a remote point of time, did not this open up the possibility of a revolutionary and more complex approach to history?

But one more turn was needed to the screw prising up the foundations of a nineteenth-century education before Toynbee would face the task which a break-up would impose on him personally. First the smoke of war had to clear, and that process seemed to be happening in the optimism of the Peace Conference as it assembled in Paris with himself buried in the Middle East Section of the British Delegation. In a more desolate sense, but perhaps more lucidly than anywhere else (with the possible exception of Spengler's *Decline of the West,* which Toynbee had not yet read) the smoke of war had already cleared in Valéry's post-war essays.[1] Here, with a poet's brevity and the immaculate logic of a mathematician, we are shown the culture of the West as doomed liner from which we can see the wrecks of previous vessels scattered on the ocean floor, and see them no longer with the blasé curiosity of sightseers but as passengers on a sister-ship whose sirens have just announced that we shall join them.

A curious and lovable detail which we must notice in Toynbee's mind at this turning point is his devotion to maps and time-tables. There are maps showing exactly where he found himself in Greece and Turkey between January and September 1921, or setting out

---

[1]The opening passage of *Variété* invites comparison with some sentences in Toynbee's survey *The World After the Peace Conference*: Nous autresm civilisations, nous savons maintenant que nous sommes mortelles. Nous avions entendu parler de mondes disparus tout entiers, d'empires coulés à pic avec tous leurs hommes et tous leurs engins . . . Nous appercevions à travers l'épaisseur de l'histoire les fantômes d'immenses navires qui furent chargés de richesse et d'espirit. *Nous ne pouvions pas les compter.* Mais ces naufrages après tout n'étaient pas notre affaire. Elam, Ninive, Babylone étaient de beaux noms vagues et la ruine totale de ces mondes avait aussi peu de signification pour nous que leur existence même. Mais France, Angleterre, Russie, ce seraient aussi de beaux noms. Lusitania aussi est un beau nom. Et nous voyons maintenant que l'abîme de l'historie est assez grand pour tout le monde. (*Variété,* by Paul Valéry (Claude Aveline, Paris; 1926. The essay was first published in the *Athenaeum,* in April 1919, pp. 5-6).

In 1914 educated persons in the West were, of course, aware that other great civilizations had gone down to destruction. The fall of the Roman Empire was the familiar background of Western Society itself; and for a century past, the enterprise of Western archaeologists had been bringing to light, in Egypt, Mesopotamia, Crete, Central Asia, and Yucatan, the magnificent remains of civilizations so utterly cut off that their scripts had become extinct and their very names forgotten . . . the general proposition that not only individuals but societies are mortal might be admitted by the rational Western intellect, but how could this apply in practice to the apparently triumphant vitality of Western civilization on the eve of war? . . . By January 1920 the picture had changed. (*The World After the Peace Conference,* by Arnold J. Toynbee (Oxford University Press; 1924), pp. 87-8.)

on a smaller scale his journey to Japan *via* Constantinople and back by the trans-Siberian railway. Psychologists would diagnose this as a defence, like the learning of foreign languages, against a threatened loss of security, and they would no doubt make this diagnosis the more confidently on noting his behaviour at (say) 12 a.m. on January 1930, at Omsk. Here and at that moment he takes out his pocket-map with a greater need of support than in England (where his habit is still dogged enough to incur the ridicule of his family), for he finds against his hopes that Omsk is actually further east than Bombay, and to argue, as he does, that the degrees of latitude 'are paraded in less open order' in the north than at the Equator, is a comfort which deadens but quite fails to cure the disorder he feels at still being in the wilderness eight days from his goal of Victoria Station.

We need not pursue other examples of Toynbee's resort to maps to imagine his reaction on seeing, whether through Valéry or his own sufficiently prepared eyes, this vision of a doomed liner listing towards the hulks of earlier wrecks. *Nous ne pouvions les compter,* writes Valéry, we *were* unable to count them; but thanks to an industrious generation of archaeologists the count had now become possible. That was, of course, the least of the possibilities in this situation that struck Toynbee. What was needed after a count was a reconstruction of the courses before shipwreck, an analysis of the crucial errors which sent them down, a sorting to discover whether it was the same kind of reef they had all struck. A chart of this kind could do two things: it could give an indication, but perhaps no more, of the point in our own course which we had reached; more certainly by ringing round the fatal errors, it could tell us what corrections to make to our course—if there was still time to make any—before we joined the forerunners who had gone blindly down.

It is fair to present the genesis of *A Study of History* in this purposive light. Besides being a man of his generation impatient at the sterilities of the detached academician, Toynbee is profoundly a moralist and Christian, determined in a crisis to help his fellow men. One can see this peeping through the reserve of his private life when, for instance, as a young man investigating the minorities crisis in the Near East, he struggles on the Yalova jetty south of Constantinople for the lives of refugees from Greek terrorism, moved beyond bearing by that typical atrocity of our age, the official order which drags a family into separation from its father or husband. Faced by the more massive threat of a collapse in civilization, his desire is to save his fellow-men alive if possible, and to save their souls if it is not.

He differs rather unexpectedly from many scholars who have

mastered a mass of facts, for the process of mastery gives insight into trends which shape the material, and the more concentration is focused on these trends the more completely does the specialist believe in their power, until he is forced to the conclusion that they are all-powerful and his universe an automatic mechanism. The attitude finds its climax in Spengler's statement that the collapse of the West 'is obligatory and insusceptible of modification . . . our choice is between willing this and willing nothing at all'. But in Toynbee an opposite tendency can be traced.[2] As a young man, enthusiastic at discovering patterns common to the Hellenic world and our own, he is inclined to believe them inevitable, to hint even at the possibility of a morphology of civilizations (which is what Spengler produces). On reflection and after research Toynbee becomes cautious; he recognizes the virtual impossibility of prediction in human affairs—even though he remains tempted to try it; he learns from the psychologists that 'cures', which amount to restorations of freedom, are achieved by a conscious recognition and mastery of tendencies which control the neurotic only in so far as they are unrecognized by him. Above all, as his personal religion gains strength, which it appears to do in the six published volumes of *A Study of History,* he insists on the freedom of the human soul to decide its own destiny. Today it is no longer caution which dominates Toynbee, but a positive demand that we should accept responsibility for the fate of our civilization. In religious terms, his function in handing a map to the ship's company on the eve of disaster is to give them more clearly their freedom of choice.

At the age of thirty-three, as he jotted down the plan of the book on half a sheet of notepaper, Toynbee realized that it could scarcely work out at less than two million words, or about twice the length of *The Decline and Fall of the Roman Empire,* which took Gibbon twenty years. With the research into the data of the known civilizations, he might with the utmost determination hope to finish it in his old age, sometime in the nineteen fifties, assuming always that catastrope had not overtaken us. There were other personal problems, such as a living to be earned for his family, and a reputa-

---

[2]1921 (Article on History in *The Legacy of Greece*): 'Societies like individuals are living creatures, and may therefore be expected to exhibit the same phenomena'.
    1939 (*A Study of History,* vol. IV): '. . . societies are not, in fact, living organisms in any sense . . .' (summarizing conclusions already reached in vol. III, 1934).
    In the three volumes of *A Study of History,* published in 1934, Toynbee's 'social laws' are expounded less tentatively and with fewer reservations than in the volumes published in 1939. In the latter the word 'law' is scarcely ever used in this context without quotation marks.

tion to be lost—no negligible sacrifice—among orthodox historians who would feel themselves challenged by the undermining of their traditions.

A further difficulty almost doubled the effect of the rest. Just as his thought, as we noticed in Crete, is profoundly imbued with a relativity which demands concentration at the same moment on two or more points widely separated in time, so in his life from the first world war onwards we find alternating activities and interests which have needed superb co-ordination to prevent a collapse from overloading. In an article in *The Nation and Athenaeum* in 1929, he describes a hunt in Tokyo for the top hat which was *de rigeur* for the Imperial Chrysanthemum Party. His pursuit culminates in the necessity of intercepting an unknown man with hatboxes, who would enter the hotel by any one of three separate doors through which continuous streams of people were already passing. It was a problem which might have flustered the smoothest of detectives, but Toynbee decides

> to take up a position from which the outside three-quarters of either eye divergently commanded each of the two side doors, leaving the two inner quarters to converge upon the central entrance (a contorted but effective kind of squint); and there I waited, more intent and alert than a tiger awaiting its prey . . .

With later complications, which are as inevitable as his success, this solution gets him his top hat, and is not dissimilar either in technique or drive, from his pursuit of truth.

Toynbee has used three separate 'eyes' to find the data for *A Study of History*. The first, a traveller's eye, has contributed little direct material; very few of the hints quoted in this note on Toynbee's development can be found in *A Study of History,* which the naive reader overlooking one or two references might take for the work of a scholar-recluse. In fact, the sense of live bone and tissue which Toynbee conveys in a dozen different civilizations could only be given by someone who had spent several years in contact with them; nor, if he had remained in the West, could he have shed so completely the perspective of his fellow historians who see little more than Egypt and 'the Unchanging East' beyond our own civilization and its ancestors. Toynbee has spent most time in Greece, studying the Hellenic, and in Turkey the Ottoman Societies; but he has also managed a bird's-eye view of the Near East generally for (according to his classification) the Islamic, Syriac, Iranic, Babylonic and Hittite Societies; he has travelled in Crete on foot among the faint shadows of the Minoan Society, visited Japan, Korea and China for the Far Eastern Society, India for the Hindu Society, and most cursorily of all, Russia for the Old Orthodox Christian Society. Articles written at high pressure in the trains have helped to pay his passage.

His second 'eye', which he did not allow to droop, gave him automatically as a member of the Western Society a view of a civilization still living out some phase of its existence. Since the first world war ejected him from Oxford to survey the contemporary scene, he has done this continuously from choice, editing and largely writing with his own hand the massive annual volumes of *The Survey of International Affairs* for Chatham House, and publishing several minor studies on particular areas of international relations which interested him.

On his return from the Paris Peace Conference of 1946, which concluded his second long bout of war work, he began the editorship of a history of the second world war. The writing-up of all this material has already been considerably longer than *A Study of History,* but the use of it as a measuring rod against which other societies can be laid was essential to Toynbee's method.

There has been a third 'eye' and this, researching directly into the fabric of a score of civilizations other than our own, must have borne a greater strain than its colleagues. One is overcome sometimes in reading *A Study of History* by a kind of defensive dizziness which is not so much intellectual confusion, because Toynbee writes with clarity, as the fatigue of a sightseer who is in need of a rest from revelations which come too thick and fast. To select this material Toynbee must have had to be selective, to pick his way where the indications unmistakably led, and his determination must have had to be all the greater while holding two professorships, first in Byzantine and Modern Greek Language, Literature and History, and then in International History, as Research Professor, at London University. At the same time he has worked as Director of Studies at Chatham House.

But in its essentially individual nature, Toynbee's masterpiece is a contrast to the 'joint-stock' products, encyclopaedias and Cambridge Histories, which have been the work of many hands, and when all allowance has been made for the devotion of his wife and other helpers, the mere making of this book suggests that it will live as an example of human endurance and achievement stretched, on its particular plane, to the limit. If we take the crucial difficulty —the sheer length and scope to which at the age of thirty-three he decides to sacrifice his life—what unnerves us is that it is self-imposed. Toynbee has a diviner's intuition of his own strength; he accepts burdens which he can carry, but only just carry; it is the virtually impossible that seduces him. 'To spin straw into gold thread,' he protests, 'to separate grain from chaff without a winnowing fan, and all the other impossible demands that are made upon the ingenuity of the heroines in fairy-stories, would not be more difficult than the task that now confronted me.' The task here was to acquire the top hat for the Chrysanthemum Party, but it might have been the establishment of Mr. Nair's trans-desert bus service to Baghdad, or the goal of Constantinople considered from a Ford on an ox-track of the Great Balkan: provided only that it is pos-sible, he will start bravely out, apprehensive of failure ('Would the poor thing ever start up? And should we lose our way and not have the energy to find it again?'), but as secretly exultant as when in footnotes to the first volume of *A Study of History*, he refers ahead to sections more than a million words before they have been written.

We must notice, too, that while Toynbee welcomes a burden which he himself accepts at the risk of breaking his back, he takes prompt avoiding action from the blind external threat. Thus he accepts the calculable risks attached to the writing of his master-piece, but discreetly, at the Munich Conference of 1938, sends the notes for the unwritten volumes to New York.

We conclude that the enormous difficulties to which Toynbee submits himself play a positive, 'enabling' role; they liberate his creative power. But we cannot leave them at that. As a Christian, he is deeply aware of the significance of suffering in the New Testa-ment, but again as a Christian he would not accept as complete an account of it which limited the consequent Redemption to indi-vidual terms or even to the earthly fate of a civilization. St. Augus-tine, who began to write *De Civitate Dei* after the sack of Rome by Alaric, and died while the Vandals encircled the walls of Hippo around him, was the instrument of something greater than himself; for personalities, in Toynbee's view, who have 'succeeded in attain-ing self-determination through self-mastery find in the act that they cannot live and cannot die unto themselves'; however impos-sible their mission—even if it is to convert a species to a new way of life, which would mean the creation of movement where, by definition, there is a halt—they cannot rest until they have achieved the purpose for which they were sent into the world.

We can now proceed to analyse *A Study of History*,[3] but with the rider that a book of this length, planned to its own proportions, must inevitably dissolve in summary to an echo blurred by absence of complexity and depth—thereby sadly illustrating one of Toyn-bee's 'laws' on the effects of the diffusion of culture.

---

[3] At the writing of this essay, more than a third of *A Study of History* was still in note form. Volumes I to III had been first published in 1934 and volumes IV to VI in 1939. A version in one volume, abridged by D. C. Somervell and revised by Arnold J. Toynbee, was due from the Oxford Uni-versity Press shortly.

*   *   *

The screen has enlarged and become immense; that is our impression if we come in the middle. Around the standard-sized screen the darkness has been chased back in all directions at once, revealing live areas where we had known at most a name. The camera chooses, perhaps from the conventional high road of history, a significant detail like the drawing of a sword, holds it in close-up, and then another detail of the same species, and then another—a Pope takes the sword, a Spartan, an Assyrian, a Manchu; as the reel unwinds we notice that this repeated act is pregnant with events we had perhaps half suspected but failed, within our limited field of sight, to recognize with certainty. We realize next that this is not simply an instructional film which deals with unrelated facts 'of general interest'—it has a plot: the destiny of civilizations, their birth, growth, breakdown and collapse.

However unprovocatively one might choose to describe a method of historical exposition like this (and Toynbee does not fight shy of the word 'scenario'), the dismay of conservative historians would be assured. We have already noticed in watching the growth of Toynbee's mind his break with certain fundamental traditions of contemporary historicism; we must now give his reasons for three more immediate breaks which, added to the rest, distinguish the technique we have just been witnessing from what we may call the straight historical film. The size of screen we have been used to is the National size (the titles, *A History of the English People, A History of the United States, A History of France, The Italian Renaissance*), but this concept 'National', which has come, symptomatically, to mean a standard product, is unsuited in its restrictive and vainglorious effects to the study of history, as we see at once if we reduce it to the scale of, say, Portugal or Belgium, for these small states are, like ours, simply the interdependent members of a particular civilization and cannot be considered in isolation, even in their larger sizes. The revolutionary screen is therefore essential, if only to keep in perspective the egocentric illusions of modern nationalism.

A second novelty is subject-matter transcending the familiar periods of historicism, such as the wars of Napoleon and the Ptolemaic Dynasties, with State archives and other plentiful sources of evidence. Now these established periods have, in fact, been so arbitrarily chosen, are so remote even from utilitarian considerations of the obvious kind, that we may suspect the scholar has not first asked himself (in Toynbee's wording): 'Is Ptolemaic Egypt the most interesting and important phenomenon in the particular age of the particular society to which it belonged?', but instead and without noticing the colour he takes from his industrial surroundings: 'What is the richest mine of unworked material in this field?' But it is, of course, intolerable that our historical research should be governed, like our industry, by the amount and disposition of raw materials; we should choose according to its importance and our need of enlightenment.

Finally, the Toynbee scenario is startling in its abandonment of the pre-relativist time-scale where the story unfolded on a single plane—an arrangement which forbade an act of Napoleon's, for instance, to be seriously compared with another of Tiglath-Pileser's, or the mental attitude of the conquistadores. But here the cinema metaphor is on Toynbee's side, for it is plainly (in the cinema just as much as in modern science) at least as strange to restrict ourselves to a single time-scale and thus automatically exclude from view any event outside a fictitious 'mainstream of Civilization', as if there had been only one civilization. Toynbee protests that some of the most important stages in history have been left unexplored in this way—the universal state of the Guptas in India, for example, and the fate of the Syriac Society after it had performed the momentous act of fertilizing the proletariat of the Hellenic Society with Christianity. And in reply, finally, to the objection that the facts of history are unique events which cannot be compared, Toynbee grants they are unique in many respects, but insists they are comparable in so far as they are members of a class; anthropology, for instance, is dependent on such limited comparisons. And Toynbee caps his argument with a charming analogy. Insurance firms, which deal in the lives of unique human beings, succeed in making a profit from their comparative study of events within a civilization, and scholars need not hestitate 'in this adventure, at any rate', to scorn the businessman's lead.

Taking for granted the peculiarities of Toynbee's screen, let us watch it give an over-all view of the position now reached by social Man. In front of us is a precipice whose sheer rock offers no respite to climbers except a ledge, with figures already lying on it. These prostrate figures, classified as primitive societies, are usually dismissed as torpid by nature, but more probably they are exhausted from the prodigious climb by which a small minority out of innumerable thousands reached the ledge alive from a lower ledge occupied by Sub-man. From this successful minority, a handful which we may now call civilized societies have already started to climb up again to the next ledge out of sight overhead; all we know about this further point is that it represents the mutation where Man becomes Superman, or in religious terms a communion of Saints. We know, too, that the distance so far achieved is a minute fraction of the climb. We can see this in perspective by remembering that primitive Man began to climb out from the animal world some 300,000 years ago, where as civilizations have only been organizing themselves for 6,000 years, and in that time their mortality has been so high at the same rate (if we take Sir James Jeans's estimate of the habitable duration of the world) we can forsee the birth and death of 1,743,000,000 civilizations. However disturbing such a figure may seem to believers in a single 'Civilization' (and it is perhaps meant to annoy them), there is a close relation between it and dangers of the precipice. The rock face presents the same threat to civilizations as it did to primitive societies: a mistake will send them crashing to their death, but so, too, will an attempt to retrace their steps, or to rest. When once a society has started out, it has no choice but to collapse or reach the ledge above.

With the reservation that archaeologists may yet produce new candidates, and with some hesitation as to the extent of certain civilizations, Toynbee identifies twenty-six as having been born alive, in addition to four which miscarried. Of these twenty-six, no fewer than sixteen are already dead and can be seen on the rock face as more or less fragmentary skeletons; three more (the Esquimaux, Polynesians, and Nomads) may be dismissed as arrested civilizations which are pinned to the precipice, by a special kind of misjudgment, in a state of life-in-death; and this leaves (if we combine the two distinguishable Orthodox Christian Societies into one, and similarly include the Far Eastern Society in China with its offshoot in Japan) a total of only five surviving societies:

> The Modern Western Society.
> The Orthodox Christian Society (adding South-East Europe to Russia).
> The Islamic Society.
> The Hindu Society.
> The Far Eastern Society (including Korea and Japan with China).

We must notice that all the climbers left in the field are descendants of earlier civilizations (the first two, the twins of the Graeco-Roman 'Hellenic Society', are already in the third generation, since the Hellenic Society was itself the offspring of an earlier Minoan civilization). But when we look closer at these relatively young athletes, we find four of them so far gone in decay that their death is a predictable certainty; there remains only the Western Society whose fate is in doubt.[4]

---

[4]The Soviet Union and its international revolutionary pretensions are reduced in this perspective to a final phase in the distintegration of the Orthodox Christian Society after infection by Western Marxism. The fate of Communism is, in Toynbee's view, likely to be that of other religious move-

The volumes of *A Study of History* are now given over to detailed examination of the societies' actions at every crucial turn in their climb or collapse. The major headings, 'Genesis', 'Growth', 'Breakdown', 'Disintegration', each bring with them conclusions based on empirical surveys of behaviour, and a pattern gradually emerges of a 'type-history' of civilization which sheds light on our own predicament. The pattern is surrounded by every kind of reservation, and we should constantly keep in the background of our minds Toynbee's refusal, in spite of his vivid metaphors, to consider civilizations as 'living organisms'—the individuals who compose them are the only living organisms, and the civilizations themselves no more, objectively, than 'the common ground between the respective fields of activity of a number of individual beings'.

We are faced at the outset by the problem of explaining why the figures on the ledge have ever woken from their sleep to face the dangers above them. The principles generally used in explanation are Race and Environment, but neither here nor at any point in the decadence are these solutions acceptable to Toynbee, at bottom, because he declines to see psychical differentiation explained by a set of differences in a non-psychical field. He has no difficulty in mobilizing modern scientific knowledge and his own relativist sense of humour against the Race Theory. A Kaffir servant-girl used to faint in the presence of some friends of his who were staying in South Africa; alarmed, they consulted an older servant who explained: 'The fact is, she has come straight from her village . . . and she isn't quite used to the white people's smell. But don't you worry . . . we all used to faint at first, but now we have quite got over it . . .' Moreover, purity of smell or of race is an unpromising solution in view of the evolutionary success of mongrels. Similarly with environment; the evidence that by itself it can be the determining principle is misleading, even when physical environment is closely involved as, for instance, in the genesis of Egyptian civilization.

Toynbee's own conclusion is that a special type of conflict is responsible, that the primitive society (embodying a passive principle) only emerges from its torpor when it is challenged by another, negative principle. Mythology explains the creative social act in just these terms with the story of Adam and Eve whom the Serpent successfully challenges to abandon the paradisiac 'food-gathering phase" of primitive Man although a perfect integration had been

ments which have turned militant in the same way, such as Maccabeanism and Sikhism. Beginning as a panacea for all mankind, they become imprisoned for effective purposes within the frontiers of a parochial state, are degraded into 'a local variety of Nationalism', and gradually see the state which has captured them assimilate itself to the standard type of (in our world) increasingly totalitarian state-pattern.

achieved on that level; Job and Faust similarly emerge from an ordeal of testing by Satan to a higher plane than they would have reached without it. In the language of Chinese mythology, a passive Yin-state is transformed into Yang-activity. The vent is psychological, it is a victory in the soul which can be seen even more clearly in the birth of 'related' or descendant civilizations which emerge (in response to an exclusively human challenge) from the body of a society in disintegration. But the Egyptian example, an 'unrelated' civilization born of a climatic challenge, is clear enough.

The primitive communities who lived on wild game and plant-life in North Africa, when it had a temperate climate, chose various ways out at the end of the European Ice Age, when the atmosphere dried up and with it their food supplies. The escape chosen by some was to plunge south into the rich tropical monsoon belt; but others chose to go east to the Nile, which was water indeed, but so formidable a wilderness that it seemed a forlorn hope to those who shied away. The communities who stayed had a double task, not only to settle on new ground, but to achieve a new way of life, to become cultivators instead of 'food-gatherers'. The scene for this necessary process was a continuous forest of uncontrolled and apparently uncontrollable papyrus swamps whose giant stems allowed only wild boards, hippopotami and crocodiles to pass. Here, within a few centuries, the civilization of Egypt had emerged, the effective response to a tremendous challenge; and Toynbee switches us away from Egyptian irrigation systems, literature and higher religion to watch, some hundreds of miles to the south in the present day, the descendants of the 'sluggish and unambitious' communities who chose the tropical escape—a series of squatting totem clans, the Dinka, still ruled over by rain-makers who are ceremonially killed before old age. 'Just so,' he comments, 'some five or six thousand years ago, the fathers of the Egyptian civilization (perhaps accompanied by the forefathers of the Dinka . . . before the parting of their ways) were squatting on the edge of the jungle-swamp which at that time occupied the Lower Nile Valley and the Delta.'

The stimulation of conditions of pressure has its counterpart in the demoralization which sets in under conditions of ease. Biologically these reactions can be seen in the vigour of the pollarded willow and the lanky growth of one which has never felt the axe. In the Bible the Lord 'scourgeth every son whom He receiveth'; and in Homer, it is not when confronting the Cyclops or Scylla and Charybdis that Odysseus comes nearest to failure, but on the lotus-eaters' island, in Circe's parlour and with Calypso. And this fundamental principle which is discerned by biology and mythology in the individual can be found not only decisively influencing the birth of civilizations, but pulsating more or less strongly, with more or less resulting achievement, throughout their existence. Bearing in mind that failures to respond with success at all are always in the majority in history as in evolution, we see from a survey of human achievement that 'hard' countries stimulate while 'soft' countries demoralize (notice 'Attic Salt' but 'Boeotian Swine'), new ground is more promising (and incidentally more productive of epic poetry) than old, military blows and pressures stimulate both counteraction (Rome-Carthage, France-Germany) and the regular polarization of political power at a threatened frontier. But there is a limit, of course, beyond which the severity of a challenge becomes inimical. The figures pinned alive to the face of the rock made the mistake of accepting too great a challenge; balked by a projection in the precipice, they performed the *tour de force* of levering themselves out over it, and had no further strength to move. Thus the Arrested civilizations weather away in immobility—the Nomads paralyzed by the all-out effort to keep in touch with their 'flocks', the Polynesians by challenging great distances of sea with no better weapon than a canoe; the Esquimeaux by the problem of sustaining life below zero. In scientific terminology, 'the most stimulating challenge is to be found in a mean between a deficiency of severity and an excess of it.'

While the working of 'Challenge and Response' clearly plays an essential role in this analysis of the growth of a civilization, it cannot by itself provide a criterion of growth. This is readily assumed by egocentric optimists of our Western Society (which now envelops every remaining civilization in the world), to be the extent of a civilization's command over its human environment, or its 'size'. But as soon as we remove the problem from its subjective context in the present and ask whether the Syriac and Hellenic civilizations, for instance, were more dynamic than the Indic or the Sinic because their expansive power was greater, we suspect that the question is absurd. Under empirical study of societies in their final stages of disintegration, the expansive tendency emerges as a general symptom of decline, automatically entailing a loss in qualitative terms; it is a disease,

> an elephantiasis or fatty growth; a running to stalk or a running to seed; the malady of the reptiles, who turned huge on the eve of being surpassed by the mammals; or the malady of Goliath who grew to gigantic stature in order to succumb to David; or the malady of the ponderous Spanish galleons which were routed by an English mosquito-fleet.

The reason for the expansion of a society as it expires becomes clear when we analyse the process by which it absorbs another. The 'social rays' a civilization emits are of three kinds, economic, political and cultural, with varying speeds and intensities of penetration.

In the growth period the rays given off are fused as harmoniously together as the elements of the society itself, and accordingly the infection of others is slow (as slow as the penetration of the cultural ray, which is the slowest but most complete in its effect); in decline, as a society rigidifies into hostile elements, so the rays given off are diffracted, and penetrate at the speed of the fastest ray, the economic.

But if size is no criterion, is not increasing technical command of the environment a proof of growth? Should we not, with Procopius after the wars of Justinian, criticize 'people who . . . persist in an open-mouthed adulation of antiquity and refuse to admit the superiority of modern inventions'? The answer is provided by the usual empirical survey, but most spectacularly by the Assyrian Society and by the Hellenic itself, where an arrest or setback in civilization was invariably accompanied by an improvement in the art of war. The most that can be said for technical progress is that advance in its own sphere is shown by 'etherialization', and increase in simplicity and subtlety, illustrated in the introduction of the alphabet in writing, or in our own society by the change-over from steam to oil, from telegraphy to telephony. Translated into biological terms, this criterion of growth would apply to the little 'theriomorphs', the ancestral mammals of H. G. Wells, fluently adapting themselves to problems which defeated the reptiles. In individual and social terms the criterion becomes the presence or absence of self-determination. Thus in a crucial response, from which the mainstream of Hellenic civilization flowed, the challenge produced by over-population in the Greek States was met by Athens with the specialization of her own internal agriculture and manufacture for export. Corinth and Chalcis had already responded to the pressure by overseas colonization, Sparta by attacking her neighbours; and while Corinth and Chalcis simply reproduced themselves abroad and Sparta crippled herself by the strain of militarism, Athens developed internally. Her economic innovations called into being new classes, and in response to this further challenge Athenian statesmen made a series of adjustments to her political institutions which flowered in democracy. The growth of Athens, by this criterion, took place in an interval between the first two centuries of Greek expansion and the later outburst under Alexander, culminating at last in the enormity of the Roman Empire.

Growth is thus a process in which challenges, arising thick and fast from an originally successful response, are solved more and more internally; creative minorities 'withdraw', as Athens withdrew in the early centuries, to return later with an appropriate solution which is copied by other members of the society. These minorities may be 'penalized', they may be forced to withdraw, like Thucydides in the Peloponnesian War, or Machiavelli from Florence at the end of the intensive Italian Renaissance, or the Quakers and other Nonconformists from England at the Restoration—or they may go voluntarily, like Moses on Sinai or Plato's Philosopher Kings, but 'the return is the essence of the whole movement', however reluctantly it may be undertaken.

Their solutions, if they are brought back to a society which is still in growth, are followed, by the few to whom their message leaps as a spark, and by the mass process of mimesis which persuaded even animals to listen to the music of Orpheus. A growing society is thus like a walker, whose first leg, as it leaves the ground, is the creative minority, and whose back leg, the uncreative majority, continues to support the body until the moment has come, with the return to earth of the front leg, to imitate the forward movement. To sustain the process an *élan* is necessary, which we may call Promethean because the conservatism of society opposes it as obstinately as Zeus did.

The nature of breakdown now becomes clearer. If the creative minorities lose, for a reason we shall see, their creative power, the process of mimesis no longer works, and stung by the whips of unexplained command, the majority goes into revolt. The harmony of a walker is then replaced by the internal conflict of an invalid or schizophrenic.

*   *   *

Toynbee's inspection of the corpses scattered about the precipice of human history showed us only one climber who might conceivably be flourishing, and even here, where we have to suspend final diagnosis, the odds against survival appear to be at best sixteen to ten and possibly twenty-five to one. But theories of the inevitability of decay fail to impress Toynbee; he has no difficulty in tracing back 'cyclical' explanations to the Babylonic discovery of 'Great Years' beyond the lunar and solar cycles of our own planetary system; and theories of 'degeneracy' are unsupported by evidence. Environment, he considers, whether in the shape of 'loss of technique' or attacks from outside the society, can no more be blamed than the Nemesis of Fate held responsible by Hellenic pessimists. The technical asset of the Roman roads survived the Empire which created it, and investigations of the breakdowns of all civilizations show that so far from falling victim to external attack like the majority of primitive societies, they have all, with one or two exceptions where the evidence is incomplete, perished by their own hand. Leaving out the arrested and abortive societies, there have been seventeen suicides. Gibbon diagnosed the fall of the Roman Empire as due to 'the triumph of barbarism and religion', but only because he assumed the age of the Antonines, where he begins, to be a culmination of growth instead of the mere imposing facade of a ruin blasted by more than four centuries of war. In reality the breakdown of the Hellenic Society can be discerned at the outbreak of the Atheno-Peloponnesian War, when the Greek States, which had stood together to depose Xerxes, proceeded to fall upon one another in their moment of victory. The event is a confession of failure in creative power which reveals the nature of social breakdown as clearly as the achievement in the Nile Valley illustrates social birth.

When Athens had solved her population problem by revolutionizing production on an intensive basis for export, she brought upon herself, among the other challenges which a successful response produces, the necessity of organizing a stable international society by freely agreed limitation of City-State sovereignty. The interests of unhindered trade made this imperative. But no sooner had the need made its appearance, than the City-State institution began to acquire 'affection'. The least abandonment of sovereignty was achieved by force, whether the force was external, as when the pressure of Xerxes produced the Delian League, or applied by Athens herself in the tyranny of the Athenian Empire which issued in war with Sparta. The history of the Hellenic Society from 431 B.C. now becomes a series of intensifying wars and class struggles as the unsolved City-State problem swells into the unsolved parochial Great Power problem, and Rome and Carthage and Macedon in an ever-expanding society slaughter one another's armies on a greater scale than the Greek City-States. This tragic process, blowing up into enormity instead of progressing to solution, is only ended by a knock-out blow; Rome then rules by force a world which has doomed itself to disintegrate after the brief Indian summer which forcible unification tends to produce.

A political pattern of this kind seems to emerge from most of the civilizations that have broken down; the event itself is marked by the onset of a 'Time of Troubles' whose great length has, apparently, a limit set to it by the human capacity to suffer before resorting to desperate remedies. The Babylonic 'Time of Troubles' is compounded of the aggressiveness of Assyria and the refusal of a culturally superior Babylon to be absorbed; in China the member-States composing the Sinic Civilization devastate one another for four centuries after the first struggle for hegemony between Tsin and Ch'u; in the Sumeric Society the 'Time of Troubles' begins in the twenty-seventh century B.C., when the class-war between Urakagina of Lagash and the local priesthood is followed by the militarism of Urakagina's successor.

The final act also tends to be the same: one of the fratricides—

if any has the strength, and if not, an adventurer from outside—
emerges as conqueror and imposes by force the peace which the
member-States failed to achieve freely before their problem became
unmanageable. Then, promoted by war-weariness, the *Pax Aug-
usta, Pax Mongolica, Pax Incaica, Pax Ottomanica*, purchased at
the price of submission to a universal State, conceals for a varying
period the profound wounds, strains and deprivations inside the
body of the dying society, which expires sooner or later from an
infection that the wind of history does not fail to carry.

In the pattern after breakdown there are regular characters,
such as refugees and deserters, and mounting sequences: prophet—
drill-sergeant—terrorist; punishment—judicial murder—atrocity;
there are comparable periods of rout and rally, a regular patho-
logical intensification of problems; and in a kind of ominous political counterpart, the powers on the periphery of the dying society
grow into giants overshadowing the original contestants in the
centre. The distinctive 'style' which came with growth was the
result of different challenges differently responded to, but when
a challenge remains unanswered, it continues to demand a solution
which at the same time becomes increasingly difficult; it presses
'with a merciless uniformity' on its victims until the cramping and
distorting effects have spread into every aspect of life.

Probing the core of creative failure, where he refuses to see 'degeneracy', Toynbee accuses a fatal intractability of institutions as
being the fault which sets off the series Decline and Fall, crippling
the epigoni 'like those hideous strait-waistcoats in which, in Ancient
Egypt, well framed and healthy children were deliberately deformed
into artificial dwarfs'. New forces, emotions and aptitudes arise in
a society and demand the readjustment of institutions created to
suit earlier drives; but the adjustment is not made, or is made insuf-
ficiently, with the result that the institution is swept away by
revolution ('a retarded and proportionately violent act of mimesis'),
or becomes distorted into a social 'enormity'. Thus the drive of
democracy applied to education with the hopeful intention of making it 'available for 'the masses' (apart from its traditional background and regardless of the 'law' that learning is sterilized by diffusion), has resulted in enormities like the Yellow Press and the
cinema. Other modern enormities are parochial sovereignty and
war, geared up to take the drives of industrialism and democracy.

A psychological or moral flaw is the cause of the intractability
of institutions, and it is almost invariably because creative minorities are dogged by two temptations, yielding to either of which will
convert them into dominant minorities. They are tempted to rest
passively on their oars and admire their achievement, as Athenian
statesmen deified their City-State as 'the educator of Hellas', or

more actively, in an intoxication of victory, to rush, like Assyria, from success to suicide. The walker, turned sprinter, slips and crashes; the self-satisfied climber relaxes his grip; in religious terms, the sin of idolatry has been committed in the worship of the created thing instead of the Creator.

Short of this, the creative individual can be counted on to repeat somewhat mechanically the motions which have brought him success in the past, so that *the party that has distinguished himself in dealing with one challenge is apt to fail conspicuously in attempting to deal with the next.* Psychologically, the odds are on the dark horse, not the favourite. But in society the *ci-devant* creators are the most likely candidates for office; their past achievement, which disqualifies them for the future, tends to assure them of its control. It would be difficult, for instance, to estimate the damage done by war-winners at peace conferences.

As the pattern of decline stands out more and more clearly from the variations unravelling themselves in all corners of the screen, we become aware, in spite of warnings against precise guesses about our own condition, that something suspiciously like a 'Time of Troubles' may have set in among ourselves about four centuries ago. Certainly, war weariness has not yet brought submission to an enforced universal State; but the extent of Hitler's success is significant. Parochial warfare has now eaten into the body of the Western Society for four centuries: the fanatical religious wars beginning in the sixteenth century have become the jet-propelled nationalist wars which began with Napoleon. And if, as is now inevitable without an all-round eleventh-hour conversion to humility, a totalitarian universal State supersedes the individual members of the species, there is no doubt where Toynbee would place the original breakdown.

In 'medieval' Christendom, when the West might still be called an articulated society, the master institution was the Papacy of Hildebrand, founded to combine centralism in ecclesiastical affairs with political devolution among the member States. The parochial States themselves were recognized as man-made institutions deserving 'that conscientious but unenthusiastic performance of a minor social duty which we render, in our time, to our municipalities and county councils'. But, intoxicated by the victory of its own reforms, the Papacy demanded unrestricted sovereignty in its own field instead of a limited constitutional authority over an undivided Christian Commonwealth. The result of this disastrous authoritarianism—a parallel to Periclean Athens—was that the Pope saw the whole of his power vanish in the States that turned Protestant, and most of it in those that professedly remained Catholic. But the Pope's loss was small by comparison with our own, for the emotional attitudes, the devotion and self-abasement, whose proper field is religion, were collected by the parochial States in the form of 'patriotism'. The scene had been set for the enormities which today overwhelm us.

Clear as he is, when Toynbee records the final passages of disintegration, one has the impression of a choreographer disturbed (within the limits of his moderation) by the attempt to transcribe the climax of Walpurgisnacht. Split now by its own choice of stasis, the civilization sees the harmony of its growth-period disintegrate into splinters. Three major cracks traverse the picture: the internal proletariat secedes from the dominant minority, alienated by an emotional disaffection which includes and spreads wider than the Marxian 'exploitation'; while the external proletariat, still in the society's field of radiation, separates itself off behind a frontier from which it embarks on predatory raids. The dominant minority itself splits into active and passive variations on the attitudes which before the breakdown made creative contributions to birth and growth; the products are now hangmen and wastrels, public servants, the makers of universal States, and philosophers. A wider range of types in the internal proletariat is further complicated by the influence which begins to penetrate from alien cultures. The effect is creative among the internal proletariat whose attraction to alien sources of inspiration is increased by distaste for the institutions of the dominant minority. From the submerged cultures around them the Hellenic internal proletariat chose, in preference to the Roman State religion, Mithraism from Iran, Isis-worship from Egypt, Cybele from the remote Hittite Society, and Christianity from the Syriac Society.

Meanwhile, resorts to Archaism and Futurism, two substitutes for growth which entail impossible jumps forwards and backwards in time, fail to restore unity to a civilization which is increasingly menaced by the attacks of the external proletariat on its borders and the pressure of the internal proletariat at home. Of the polarized attitude gentleness-violence which marks the internal proletariat, it is gentleness which is most remarkable in the disaffected Hellenic 'proletariat', and violence (beginning with the revolt of the High German peasantry in the sixteenth century) which has stamped our own. Similarly the Hellenic internal proletariat, like the Egyptian in the phase of Osiris worship, finally settles on a religion which promises resurrection in a life transcending the disastrous situation on earth. Biologically in this dramatic and final act of secession from the dominant minority, the internal proletariat achieves the response by which a new 'related' civilization is born from the wreckage of the old; in religious terms it does literally gain access to eternal life. (If we can discover no counterpart of this breakaway, apart from Communism, in our own society, that may be one of the few important, if negative, grounds for belief in our future; it would suggest that in our heart of hearts there is a lurking confidence that our civilization will survive.[5])

At this point Toynbee is interrupted by the war of 1939. In his next and final volumes, begun in 1946, he moves on from individual civilizations, which have been his units of intelligible study hitherto, to consider the interaction arising from their contacts in time and space.

*   *   *

The criticism of Toynbee which is worth noticing tends to take the form of examination by a specialist of an area in *A Study of History* and an implied charge of subjective interpretation. But these are small and technical operations in the shadow of such a panorama, even when the findings are correct as far as they go. Our own rough sketches of Toynbee's personality and his account of civilizations invite us to choose the risks—they are substantial—of a head-on approach.

His style, decisively influenced by the authors who were his favourites before he left Oxford, has become a precision instrument with Greek instead of Arabic markings on it, and a cutting edge sharpened by the moral intensity of the West. The influence of Bergson can be seen in his clear-headedness in the most difficult surroundings, in the technique of metaphor, for instance, which guides us successively as climber, walker, racehorse and leaping fish through the scenery which spreads and dwindles on his Penelope's web of history. Bergson suggests, too, the method of interpretation on multiple layers, biological, religious, psychological, and the appeals to mythology. The Bible is a kind of supplementary language to Toynbee, but more deeply embedded than Greek or Latin, because in the rare spots where one suspects fatigue of taking toll, the argument is wholly encased in it. Gibbon provides some of the scale and grasp, the 'extensiveness and penetration' which he defined as his own qualities, but acts otherwise as a kind of catalyst, his cynicism being reversed to bite into self-importance and every kind of prejudice engrained by parochialism. Toynbee has, too, the exactness and disciplined sense of scholarship which were lacking in Gibbon. It would, for instance, be un-

---

[5]Originally Toynbee considered this a crucial indication. His preface to *Greek Historical Thought* (Dent, 1924), foresaw a new religion 'yet unborn, which will undoubtedly lay up a new treasure in a new heaven as our world sinks, to founder at last like its predecessors in "the abyss where all things are incommensurable"'. *A Study of History* (vol. V, 1939) can only trace two conceivable candidates, both of Islamic origin, and founded in the nineteenth century: the Bahà'iyah derivative of the Bâbi sect, and the Ahmadiyah, both of which have sent missionaries to the West.

thinkable to find him making a radical alteration in the scope of his book, as Gibbon did while writing *The Decline and Fall of the Roman Empire.*

Clothed in its own great dignity, the thought of *A Study of History* has nevertheless a strong contemporary imprint. Toynbee's sense of relativity, which has the freshness and depth of Proust or the early psycho-analysts, is no intruder in our atmosphere of popularized physics where Bergson's idealism is itself partly out of date. Again, while it needed a peculiar sensibility and wide references to link the deaths of maritime empires in Crete in 1912, the climate of opinion after two world wars has caught up with Toynbee's premonitions. His relationship with modern psychology is fundamental because of the depth at which he transfers emphasis from external accidents to internal determining influences, diagnosing connections where conservative historians pride themselves on seeing a series of unrelated happenings. Thus the psycho-analyst's credo: 'The act knows so often how to disguise itself as a passive experience', is an ideal summary of Toynbee on breakdowns; they are neuroses leading to suicide, not street accidents from fatigue ensuing on various kinds of bad luck. In terms of his own social analysis, one might note as another contemporary sign in Toynbee, his command of a dozen languages, which although rare even among scholars, is representative of the present multi-lingual stage of social development, just as his evocation of different periods at the same time and a tendency towards gigantism, are mirrored without the same impeccable taste, in the structure of our cities.

While we cannot accuse Toynbee of having influenced buildings whose foundations were laid before his birth, we should be very closely on guard against unconsciously seeing the contemporary scene through his eyes. His influence has been greater than is known, operating for the most part indirectly as an inaccessible Book of All Power where minor prophets as varied as Aldous Huxley, E. H. Carr, Lewis Mumford and Jacques Maritain, and statesmen from General Smuts to Viscount Samuel, have drawn without precisely indicating their source.

Moving closer to what is peculiar in Toynbee's contemporaneity, we are struck by the emphatic Hellenic influence which extends down to the wording of *A Study of History.* The prominence of Greece and Rome in his education has, in fact, become a gravitational pull. 'If Austerlitz was Austria's Cynosephalae,' he says in a typical comparative epigram, 'Wagram was her Pydna.' And if, when he travels, the hills behind Chinese Kowloon remind him forcibly of the Isles of Greece, it may well imply that his approach to Far Eastern history, as well as Austrian, and *a fortiori* his conjectures about the almost unknown course of, say, Andean civiliza-

is the point of precision which emerges from the charges of subjection, are influenced by his knowledge of the Hellenic world. This tivism. But we must go on, if we suspect Toynbee of applying Greek history as a pattern, to ask what is special in his own interpretation of Greek history. 'This analysis is and must be subjective,' he wrote at the end of an outline when he was thirty-one; and his pattern has itself changed slightly even in fundamentals—in his estimate of Nemesis, for instance, he has heightened the importance of guilt, but minimized the necessity of incurring it; he has redrawn details of time as well as moral emphasis, and can be found trying out different possibilities to discover how the points of resemblance between Hellenic civilization and our own can be made to throw light on our prospects.

One discusses these 'off-stage' adjustments with reluctance, not only because they may provide a sense of naive reassurance to the critics training instruments on bits and pieces, but also because Croce's scorn of the 'insinuations' of psychological criticism is at its most justifiable when applied to a work whose scholarship is threaded with a scrupulous awareness of its limitations. Nevertheless, and if only to clear the air of vague charges, let us face the possibility that we are here in the presence of an impulse more primitive even than astrology, an anxiety of the kind which drives 'British Israelites' to search the pyramids for a miraculous foreknowledge of history, and to discover—when other measuring scales have failed to extract bread from the pharaonic stone—a special 'pyramid-inch' which neatly does the trick.

Toynbee has made a life study of death. At almost any moment where we can see him—in childhood fascinated by a Victorian Race Game where lead horsemen crash at obstacles according to the throw of the dice; as he learns the classical languages whose perfection only emphasizes the fact that they are extinct; in Bergson, where more vividly than in Plato or in Heraclitus, reality is drained from the clear-cut appearance of things to be given instead of their mutability; on his travels as he watches the horizon ahead ('Have you ever seen roads die? It is a fearful and a wonderful thing to see . . .'), as he quotes A. E. Housman on the barrow covering a Ming Emperor, or reflects that the star in the night sky may already be extinct—anywhere and everywhere, in his nursery and study as vividly as in cities from Pekin to London, he sees through the splendour of the moment to the death secretly preparing within.

We have noticed already what response Toynbee makes to a sense of disorder; it is the opposite of prostration—in Siberia he pulls out a map from his pocket, at Kobe he buys a Japanese railway-guide; the call to surrender is answered by an act of mastery.

Only a profound character-trait of this sort could have made it technically possible to marshal the myriad facts of known history, and to tackle them with the superbly disciplined planning which is obvious on the first title-pages. Occasionally we even catch sight of this mechanism working so to speak in free-wheel, when for instance the events he is relating in *A Study of History* pass near the point in time or space where he himself happens to be describing them and to dispel a sense of muddled significance, he makes a footnote 'placing' his own accidental situation in relation to the major events. The order which is then achieved is really only of interest to himself. But when we find a sense of insecurity of this personal kind (and we may fairly call it personal if it is already to be found in the stable world of a Victorian childhood), confirmed in reality by the cataclysmic upheavals which have shaken our civilized world since the turn of the century, what are we to expect? Not, from what we know of him, the neurosis which incapacitates the majority of sensitive people from action or creation of any effective kind, nor, even more certainly, a 'sensible' gesture of the map, time-table variety. If a mind like Toynbee's makes any response at all, it will be on a scale inspired by the chaos around him.

We can thus see the working of Challenge and Response as the central clue to Toynbee himself; in these terms *A Study of History* becomes the gigantic response of an individual to the challenge of a disordered civilization, it is an attempt to achieve order out of disintegration. And if, excited by this revelation of Toynbee's personality as the pollarded willow, we go on to switch other of his interpretations back from the scene of history to his own mind, we shall of course not fail to apply them successfully. 'Withdrawal and Return' can be seen in the deep habit of a historian who works in cycles of research and exposition as well as in his peculiar alternation between academic and practical life. An increase in self-mastery must have been the internal development which enabled the writing of *A Study of History* to take place at all.

Ways of achieving immortality multiply and gain interest in the presence of death. The biological method of producing children, and the religious flying leap into eternal life, are both noted by Toynbee as symptomatic of civilizations in decline, just as Trotsky on a smaller scale observes that Marie Antoinette and the Tsarina 'both see rainbow dreams as they drown'—they are convinced precisely by the chasm opening under them that their surroundings have achieved a miraculous stability. But there is yet another means by which the determined individual can win a way out from disaster into permanence; more certain than the other, it is also open to fewer candidates because the qualifications are high. Inspired by the disintegrating action of the Peloponnesian War, Thucydides was only so confident of survival because he could detail with precision the amount of labour and self-discipline which went into the making of his History. These are not the type of conditions which would deter Toynbee, and if we are right in suspecting that *A Study of History* is his answer to the challenge of chaos, it would be out of character if he failed to deliver his answer on several planes at once, and not least to make it an everlasting possession in itself.[6]

The astrology column of a newspaper and the 'pyramid-inch' are means of dealing with anxiety for a million uncritical subscribers, but they neither have souls for the after-life of religion, nor have much likelihood of survival in their own right as objects of interest to a future civilization. Toynbee, on the other hand, is a candidate for both these forms of immortality, and if he suffers from a *manie de l'ordre* which intrigues, without satisfying, our taste for astrology, he will make no further concessions to it than his rival candidatures allow. For religious reasons (although he often presents them on a purely logical plane) he declines to recognize any necessity in the recurrence of historical patterns; they can be changed for the better, he insists, by a state of grace, a rebirth in humility of the kind which would characterize a communion of saints. By producing at a scarcely credible personal cost in self-discipline a guide as to how this may be done, he invites comparison, as we have noticed, 'with the prophets who saved their own souls in the act of saving their followers'. Equally as an artist and historian, Toynbee declines to be lured by a primitive need of reassurance into lowering his standards; on the contrary, to sense the temptation is by itself enough to make him raise them, so that the specialists with surveying apparatus are hard put to in their search for a chink in his armour of precise reservation. With a subtlety and caution which contrast with the rashness of the psychologists in their curative enthusiasm, he produces something more than a guide to salvation: his book is a philosophical essay as well as a work of art.

We find then that there is an exacting element in Toynbee's own most subjective tendencies which holds the rest in check. We may suspect, for instance, that he exaggerates the seduction of easy surroundings and the helpful stimulus of pressure. Was it really true that Odysseus was more nearly capsized by Circe and Calypso than

---

[6]In an autobiographical note (in *Britain Between West and East,* Contact Books, 1946) Toynbee points out that 'the works of artists and men of letters outlive the deeds of business men, soldiers and salesmen. The poets and the philosophers outrange the historians; while the prophets and the saints overtop and outlast them all.'

by the rocks thrown by Polyphemus? So Toynbee argues, and so he lays the stress, convincing us of the unexpected advantages of danger and handicap until we are tempted to revolt; but in the end, urbanely, he defeats the revolt by joining it, pointing briefly to a law of 'diminishing returns' which leaves no room, intellectually, for a charge of exaggeration, although we may feel that he has impressed our emotions more vividly with the virtues of extreme hardship.

So, too, with his diagnosis of the 'late' stages of Greek history. Was the pride of Athens exclusively responsible for breakdown? May not the process of civilization automatically store up reserves of undischarged aggression which will find an outlet sooner or later in suicide? Toynbee is far from ruling out the mounting tension of guilt and rival fears and greeds, but he sees in the idolatry of an institution the point of focus which can explain and illuminate the rest without sacrificing it. Nor does he deny, like Spengler, the validity of other interpretations; if he is a prophet, he is not the repository of final truth. He is cautious, groping his way through history with fingers which search for something almost without expecting to find it. If there are extremes in his character, they are in his scope and strength, not in a dogged pursuit of his own eccentricities. His diagnosis of recurrent patterns never ends in anything so crude as a theory that history repeats itself, although he knows there is truth in that exaggeration; his love of taking bearings never turns his love of speculations into prediction. His tabulating habits, his swift exchange of one plane for another, his gravitation towards Greece, form a system under which history becomes intelligible without suffering restriction.

It is rather as though a man finding himself unexpectedly in possession of a dozen spot-lights turned them on the scene of civilized history. We see at once that a gigantic drama is proceeding on a scale which we had not, for one reason and another, suspected of extending beyond a misty area at our feet. The number of actors, the intensity of the conflict, the depth beyond depth which spreads out among the illuminated patches, are all new to us. In spite of something austere in the atmosphere we have a sense of liberation, a feeling that hitherto our minds have been unbearably cramped. We may of course complain about the placing of the beams, about their individual colour, though we are unlikely to mistake their peculiar brilliance. Just as this scenery has looked different to other periods, so its perspective and emphasis will change again, for the spotlights, as Toynbee might say, are 'provisional'. Thrown from our epoch, they illuminate as far as we can see at the moment. What remains astonishing is that we should have produced any individual of the size and strength to perform this creative act.

TOYNBEE'S SYSTEM OF CIVILIZATIONS*

PIETER GEYL

I

To survey history as a whole, to discover trends in its movement, to seek out its meaning—Professor Toynbee is not the first to undertake the attempt. He joins the company of St. Augustine and Bossuet, Voltaire, Hegel, Marx, Buckle, Wells, Spengler; nor is he the least among them.

Six volumes now lie before us, three published in 1934, three in 1939 [*A Study of History;* Oxford University Press]; and that another three will complete the work may well turn out to be an illusion. What we have so far been given is an imposing achievement. The reading, the learning, are almost without precedent. Toynbee moves confidently in the histories of the old civilizations of Asia, the Chinese and the Indian, of Egypt, of America as well. He is thoroughly acquainted with Roman and especially with Hellenic history. Classical literature he also knows, and when I say knows, I mean he is profoundly familiar with it and is able to draw on it freely to evoke a deeper background for his arguments and his reflections. And indeed for that purpose he has a great deal more at his disposal, above all, the Bible. Toynbee lives with the Bible, and its texts lie scattered thickly over his pages. But from Goethe too, from Shakespeare and from Marvell, from Shelley, Blake, Meredith, he quotes liberally. He knows how to use for his arguments modern ethnological, sociological, philosophical, psychological concepts. At the same time he himself writes in a splendid, full and supple style, which retains command over this wealth of quotations by a constant flow of images and with an intense and untiring vividness of argument. And, what is still more important, this rich and variegated abundance serves a majestic vision. He is sensitive to the colorful world of phenomena, to life; but above all he is profoundly aware of the unity of the architectural pattern into which he fits—a remarkable mind, unusual in our every-day world of historians.

In his first volume, that is, in 1934, Professor Toynbee announced thirteen parts to be treated successively in his work. Of these, with the appearance of Volume VI, five have been dealt with; the remaining eight will, he expects, demand less space. What

*Originally a paper read for the Annual Meeting of the Utrecht Historical Society and published in its *Jaarverslag,* 1946; reprinted in *Tochten en Toernooien,* 1950; in English in *Journal of History of Ideas,* N. Y., 1948; reprinted in *The Pattern of the Past,* Boston, Beacon Press, 1949, pp. 3-72.

a plan! What especially fills one with awe is to see the author from his first volume onward referring to later parts which are to appear after an unknown number of years and of volumes. As he proceeds, there are cross-references backwards and forwards. In his mind evidently the immense structure forms a unity.

His work is intended to be a comparative study of civilizations as a basis for general conceptions about history. Civilizations are for him the real units of history, not states, which he is wont to indicate contemptuously as "parochial," or nations, whose hypertrophied self-consciousness, under the description "nationalism," he detests.

In the six thousand years of which we have knowledge, he lists twenty-one civilizations. He enumerates them, fixes their mutual relationships—in so far as they were not self-contained, which is a rare occurrence—and observes that they are all decayed or have perished, with the exception of Western civilization, that is the Latin-Christian civilization, which he represents as having sprung from the Hellenic, in its Roman phase. About the prospects of this, our own civilization, that big swallow-all, Professor Toynbee leaves us in uncertainty; he has already repeatedly touched upon the problem, but only in his twelfth part will he treat it thoroughly. Meanwhile he believes it possible, even at this stage in his investigation, to state rules; sometimes he uses the word *laws,* on other occasions he speaks of *standard patterns of development,* of *tendencies* occurring in certain circumstances.

How do civilizations *come into being?* Not by climate, soil or situation favoring the process; on the contrary, by overcoming obstacles: thus the shock is administered by which portions of mankind have passed out of the equilibrium of an existence without, or before, civilization, "from the integration of custom to the differentiation of civilization." The author proceeds to examine these adverse conditions at length under a number of headings: "hard countries," "blows," "pressures," "penalizations." "Challenge and response" is the formula in which he summarizes this movement in human history, a rhythm which makes itself felt over the entire field of human action.

Next comes the *growth* of civilizations. There is an increasing command over the environment, in the first place the physical environment; there follows a process of what Toynbee terms "etherealization," in which the physical environment loses its importance, and action shifts from outside to within. Progressive differentiation is and remains typical of the process of growth. Here too we are shown in all stages the action of challenge and response. But the author thinks it possible to be more specific: the growth of a civilization takes place through creative persons or creative minorities, whose action is conditioned by a movement of "withdrawal and return." The larger half of Volume III is taken up by illustrations of this process.

In Volume IV the phenomenon of the *breakdown* of civilization is discussed. The vast majority of civilizations known to us have after a longer or a shorter period been overtaken by this fate. The duration of growth differs greatly. It is not possible therefore to speak of a normal stretch of time from rise to breakdown, and Toynbee expressly denies that the decline is inherent in an iron law of fate such as governs the physical world. The decay proceeds from the doomed civilization itself, but it must be understood as the result of a shortcoming not decreed by any law; it is a human failure, there is no necessity about it.

The volume is mainly devoted to an analysis of the causes of breakdown. Very emphatically he rejects the view that the downfall can be ascribed to forces from the outside. He finds the causes of breakdown in the retarding force which arises from the mechanical element in the "mimesis" of the majority—that very mimesis through which the creative personality or minority can obtain a hold on them; in the "intractability of institutions," giving them a paralyzing or vitiating effect (he mentions very dissimilar instances, like those of democracy and industrialism acting upon "parochial" sovereignty, the effect of "parochialism" on churches, of religion on caste systems); in what he calls "the nemesis of creativity," the stiffening or exhaustion following upon creative action, as exemplified in the "idolization" of an achievement or of an attainment, of an institution, of a technique; under this heading he brings the intoxication of successful violence, militarism, triumph—not only in the military sense, though, for of the historical examples with which he illustrates his argument, none is elaborated at greater length than that of the papacy, which, after having been carried by Gregory VII to the height of power, was ruined by the blind self-conceit of Boniface VIII. (This, by the way, is his method throughout: a large number of particular cases, from antiquity or from modern times, from alien and distant civilizations and from our own, is always adduced to prove the theses presented.)

Breakdown is followed by *disintegration*. This process is studied in Volumes V and VI. Nowhere else in human history has Professor Toynbee found so fixed a regularity. The "creative minority" changes into a "ruling minority," the masses into a "proletariat"—a word by which Toynbee, detaching it from its now usual narrower meaning, understands a group which has no longer any real share in the civilization of its society. This is the "schism," for him the first sign of a civilization's having broken down—a schism into three parts, for besides the ruling minority there emerges "an internal and an external proletariat," which latter clashes against the frontiers of the State or the Empire of the ruling minority. The course of history proceeds by the rhythm of challenge and response; but while a growing society has always been able to find the right answer, and is therefore faced each time by a different challenge, a broken-down society can no longer really succeed; it is at best able to put off the evil day and finds itself after some time confronted again by the same problem. In the souls of men, too, the schism can be observed. Social disharmony creates a feeling of impotence, of sin; the standards of style and of behavior get out of order; ways out of the unbearable present are tried through "archaism"—back to the past, or through "futurism"—a leap into the future; or an attempt is made to detach oneself from society by means of philosophy or of religion. Toynbee here discerns the working of another form of challenge and response, "schism and palingenesis": a higher religion is founded by the proletariat segregating itself from society, although the creation is only apparently due to the majority. The external proletariat reacts through the formation of "war bands" and "heroic poetry." In any case this movement does not touch the now doomed society. Its history is governed by another variant of the rhythm, "rout and rally." The rout takes the form of ever more violent wars betwen states conscious only of their independence; this is "the Time of Troubles," another sign of a broken-down civilization. The rally materializes in a "universal state," the best creative work of which a ruling minority is capable. But the breathing-space of the *pax oecumenica* is of short duration, the universal state brings in its train only an "Indian summer," soon it is troubled again—another rout, followed by another rally, until the rout, each time worse than before, can no longer be stayed and leads to dissolution, to ruin. This is not, of course, the end of all things. A new civilization has been preparing itself, chrysalislike woven into the Universal Church, a creation of the Schismatic Proletariat, and this now unfolds itself.

As for the action of individuals in these circumstances, however brightly the creative spark may glow within them, it is doomed to failure. Professor Toynbee distinguishes four kinds of Saviors of Society—for this is the shape in which the great man now appears: by the sword, by power; by an appeal to the past or to the future —these two are the attempts to save society itself; then there are the two kinds of those who want to save man *from* society: the founders of a philosophy who, however, work only for the ruling minority, and the founders of a religion, whose empire is not of this world.

Professor Toynbee believes he has observed in history that this decline of a civilization after its breakdown follows a much more regular course than the growing process, to which no inescapable limit has been set. He has been so much struck by the uniformity with which the various "institutions" and phases — Time of Troubles, Universal State, Indian Summer, Universal Church, External War Bands and Heroic Age—spring from the body of a disintegrating civilization that he has reduced it all to a table.[1] Stronger still is the similarity of the psychological condition of men in disintegrating civilizations. The general tendency can be characterized by the word "standardization": the result of all this violent movement is therefore exactly the reverse of that in growing civilizations, where it leads to differentiation. And it develops, in rout and rally, sub-rout and sub-rally, down to catastrophe, in three and a half beats.

II

Here we have the dry bones of a system to which the author gives flesh and life. The idea inspiring him is that of Christianity. It is true that Toynbee at times recalls Spengler, and his view of history is in fact not unrelated to the *Untergang des Abendlandes*. He expressly rejects Spengler's identification of civilizations with animate beings, which are born, are young, grow older, and die; when they break down it is by their own act alone. Similarly, he speaks emphatically against Spengler's connecting civilization with race. But if he insists on the freedom of choice, on the spiritual factor unrelated to blood or to the perishable flesh, he too carries to great lengths the presentation of his civilizations as well-rounded units. Above all, during the centuries-long process of disintegration following upon breakdown, he sees them subjected to a regularity of decay hardly less rigid than Spengler's parallel with the biological process.

In any case, however much he may diverge from Spengler, his system is even more diametrically opposed to historical materialism. He may speak of laws, his mind may be stocked richly with scientific notions, from which his language is ever borrowing terms and images; in reality the sovereignty and the freedom of the spirit are his main concern, and his Bible texts are more than a mere decoration of his argument, for in them he finds his profoundest truths foreshadowed and confirmed. God become man in Christ is to him the veritable sense of history. Of the great constructors of systems, St. Augustine is most closely related to him in spirit, and Professor Toynbee himself, in the preface to his second series, written in that gloomy year 1939, brings respectful homage to the

---

[1]See footnote 21 below.

bishop who completed *De Civitate Dei* while the Vandals were besieging his episcopal town. Material advantage is nothing in Toynbee's view; it is obstacles which rouse the spirit to consciousness. Violence he detests, he is a searcher after gentleness. He meets history with ethical appreciations. The spirit, the highly gifted individual, the small group, these are the sources of creative force. Power is an illusion, if not a boomerang. As a civilization grows, it etherealizes. What exactly does he mean by this? He expresses it in morphological, in biological, in philosophical, and finally also in religious terms. No doubt all the rest for him is comprehended in the phrase belonging to the last-named category, according to which etherealization means: "a conversion of the soul from the World, the Flesh, and the Devil, to the Kingdom of Heaven."[2]

But of what use to us is his system? To what extent does it clear up our insight into history, help us in disentangling its mysteries, contain the solutions which, each in our own particularist or parochial sphere, we have so far looked for in vain? A system which is presented to us, not as springing from the author's mind or imagination of faith, but as carefully built up in the course of empirical research—for this, we are told all through the voluminous work, is its method: we are the spectators of an expedition in quest of the norms, the regularity, the laws, of the historical process, and before our eyes the traveler gathers his data, from which, so he maintains, each time assuming our assent, his conclusions impose themselves, a system thus presented ought to render to all of us these very services. But to me at least it does not do so. Splendid as the qualities of the work are, fascinating as I have found it, grateful as I shall ever remain to the author for profound remarks, striking parallels, wide prospects, and other concomitant beauties —the system seems to me useless.

My most essential criticism, the criticism which embraces all others, is connected with this claim that his whole argument is based on empirical methods, in which it seems to me the author is deceiving himself. Had he really examined history with an open mind, merely formulating the theses supplied him by the observed facts, phenomena, developments, he could never have printed that imposing announcement of the division into so many parts in the opening pages of his first volume, nor could he in his references, as early as 1934, indicate what he was going to say about various chief problems in part 9 or in part 13, in 1950 or in 1960. Not that this is the ground of my doubting the genuineness of his empirical method; that is to be found in my examination of the six volumes

---

[2]III, 192.

themselves. The learning is miraculous, the wealth of examples and parallels overwhelming. But alas! the wealth of human history is ever so much greater. On looking closely, after having rubbed his dazzled eyes, the reader will see that Toynbee does not after all serve up more than a tiny spoonful out of the great cauldron. But no! this is a misleading comparison. When you fish in a cauldron you cannot select, and to select is exactly what he is doing all the time: he selects the instances which will support his theses, or he presents them in the way that suits him, and he does so with an assurance which hardly leaves room for the suspicion, not only that one might quote innumerable others with which his theses would not bear company, but especially that those cases he does mention can be explained or described in a different way so as to disagree no less completely with his theses.

III

So to me the rules, the laws, the standard patterns, laid down by the author after he has expounded examples and arguments at length and with never-failing gusto, do not seem to possess more than a very limited validity. At times they are no more than truisms. In any case, all these formulas of regularity, these distinctions alleged to present themselves in a fixed order, and these schemes of parallel development do not seem to be of much practical use. Personally, at least, I do not know how to work with them, let alone (and this, strictly speaking, ought to be possible) to make them operate unerringly.

Take even the striking formula of challenge and response. This —or its application from the science of psychology to history— must be pronounced a find. It hits off happily a form of movement in human communal life. There is no question here of a law, there is merely an observation of a frequent occurrence. But it will deepen our insight when in coming across a case of this description, we are conscious of its belonging to one of the usual categories of life. However, Professor Toynbee cannot stop there. He thinks he can state as a general rule that the easier the environment the less is the incitement to civilization man finds in it. And indeed one can hardly imagine the Land of Cockaigne becoming the cradle of so active a thing as a civilization. But now this lover of systems begins to ask whether perhaps the stimulus to civilization becomes stronger as the environment is more arduous. He therefore applies "our now well-tried empirical method"[3] and in fact is able to adduce a number of striking instances. Art and labor had to be expended in making the valley of the Yellow River habitable, and even then it remained exposed to devastating floods; in that of the

---

[3] II, 31.

Yangtse, where the soil is equally fertile, no such terrible incon-
venience is to be feared; and yet Chinese civilization came to birth
not on the Yangtse but on the Yellow River. There is also the well-
known contrast between the fat land of Boeotia and stony Attica—
and everybody knows to which of the two Hellenic civilization
owes the greater debt. Twelve more such cases are expounded,
and later, after having shown by a number of instances how blows,
pressures and penalizations evoke similar reactions, Toynbee writes
that one might incline to the view that " 'the greater the challenge,
the greater the stimulus' is a law which knows no limits to its
validity. We have not stumbled upon any palpable limits at any
point in our empirical survey so far."[4]

To my ears this has a rather naive sound. But just as I am on
the point of arguing that fourteen cases of "hard countries," and
perhaps a few dozen of each of the other kinds of obstacles, do not
really amount to very much, and that it is hardly permissible to
speak of empiricism unless the readers can test this so-called "law"
by the hundreds or thousands of other cases they can dig up out of
history—the author surprises me by announcing with an air of
triumph that under the heading of "hard countries" he has not
even mentioned two of the most striking examples, Venice and
Holland.

> What challenge could be more extreme than the challenge pre-
> sented by the sea to Holland and to Venice? What more extreme,
> again, than the challenge presented by the Alps to Switzerland?
> And what responses could be more magnificent than those
> which Holland, Venice, and Switzerland have made? The three
> hardest pieces of country in Western Europe have stimulated
> their inhabitants to attain the highest level of social achievement
> that has yet been attained by any of the peoples of Western
> Christendom.

"Oh land wrung from the waves!" Every Dutchman has heard
innumerable times his people's sterling qualities explained from
their age-long struggle with the water. And nobody will contest
that here is one factor in the building up of our special type of
society. He who has kept hold of the thread of Toynbee's argument, however, will reflect that our author is really engaged in a
discussion of the *origins* of civilizations, and of civilizations in the
sense in which he calls them pre-eminently "fields of historical
study," those twenty-one civilizations of his. The civilization of
Holland, however, is no more than a parochial part of the great
Western civilization. Of the *originating* of a civilization in the hard
conditions of the Dutch soil there can therefore be no question.
I note in passing that Professor Toynbee repeatedly commits this

---

[4]II, 260.

error—an error against his own method. But even if we overlooked this and permitted him to adduce *national* instances, we would still have to remark that even within the Netherlands community the form peculiar to Holland (the Western seaboard province of which Toynbee is obviously thinking) cannot be regarded as original. If one looks a little more closely, one will observe that within the European and even within the Netherlands cultural area the rise of Holland was fairly late, and this no doubt as a result of these very conditions created by sea and rivers. If in the end it overcame these conditions, it was not without the assistance of the surrounding higher forms of civilization (even the Romans and their dyke-building had an important share in making the region habitable). But can even after that initial stage the continued struggle with the water be decisive in explaining the later prosperity and cultural fecundity of the country? Is it not indispensable to mention the excellence of the soil, once it had become possible to make use of it? and above all the situation, which promoted the rise of shipping and of a large international commerce? Was the case of Holland then wholly due to hard conditions after all? Is it right to isolate that factor from among the multifarious complexity of reality and to suppress the favoring factors? And, we cannot refrain from wondering, would it not be necessary to apply a similar argument to the majority of Professor Toynbee's few dozen cases?

It would carry me too far if I attempted this.[5] It is well-known that demonstrating an error demands more time than committing it. Let me merely make this general remark, that each of the instances discussed by Professor Toynbee of "blows" which had an invigorating effect is necessarily related by him in an extremely simplified form. But in the presentation of history simplification means, if not falsification, at least emphasizing one particular side of a matter which in reality had an infinite number of facets. Every historical fact—he himself mentions the objection he knows very well will be raised against his method—is unique and therefore incomparable with other historical facts. His reply is that the facts,

---

[5] I draw attention to what in II, 108, is said about the respective positions of France, Germany and England at the moment when that volume was written (1931). Perhaps it is unfair to pick on that passage, because the fifteen years which have since elapsed supply us with so convenient a standard of criticism; here is at least proof how little guarantee of objectivity there is in Toynbee's so-called empirical method.—Take II, 70, where the New Englanders' success in the struggle for the North American continent with their Spanish, Dutch, French and Southern rivals is said to throw light on the question of the different degrees of hardness in the physical environment of human existence and their stimulating effect. As if the assistance given or not given by the various mother countries had not been really decisive, not to speak of various other factors! But there would be no end if one went on to discuss particular cases.

in some respects unique, and in so far incomparable, belong in other respects to a class and are in so far comparable. There is truth in this—else no general ideas about history could ever be formulated—, but isolating the comparable elements is ticklish work. In a certain sense no historical fact is detachable from its circumstances, and by eliminating the latter violence is done to history. There is hardly an incident or a phenomenon quoted by Toynbee to illustrate a particular thesis which does not give rise to qualifications in the reader's mind—if the reader is conversant with the matter! Most of the time our author is writing about Greek or Arabic or Hittite or Cretan or Japanese history, where one— where I at least—find it more difficult to check him.

Professor Toynbee himself, however, feels that he cannot raise the intensity of his "challenges" indefinitely. It is in fact very simple, one does not need to conduct a learned, allegedly empirical, historical investigation. If I give you a blow on the head it is very likely that your energy will be strongly roused and that you will strike back with vigor; but the blow may prove so powerful that you will not have anything to reply, that (to put it in the style of Toynbee) the source of your energy will dry up for ever. In the world of communities it is likely enough that things will pass off in a similar fashion. So we see Professor Toynbee soon meditating "an over-riding law to the effect that 'the most stimulating challenge is to be found in a mean between a deficiency of severity and an excess of it,' " after which we get another 130 pages or more— under a chapter heading "The Golden Mean"—with instances of succumbing under pressure all too heavy or blows all too hard. One cannot refrain from the liveliest admiration for the rich variety of his knowledge, for the ease with which, after having sounded the causes of the downfall of Irish civilization, he does the same for the Icelandic, only to proceed with unflagging vivacity to Arabic history; until at long last he ventures to conclude: "There are challenges of a salutary severity that stimulate the human subject of the ordeal to a creative response; but there are also challenges of an overwhelming severity to which the human subject succumbs." My observation with regard to the blow on your head has a less impressive sound, but does not convey precisely the same meaning? Yet our author is not yet satisfied. He repeats the phrase coined at the outset of his argument, "a mean between a deficiency of severity and an excess of it," and this time introduces it with the magic words: "In scientific terminology. . . ."

So here we have a "law," scientifically established, or at least scientifically formulated. But what next? When we try to apply it, we shall first of all discover that in every given historical situation it refers to only one element, one out of many, one which, when we are concerned with historical presentation, cannot be abstracted from the others. Moreover, is it not essential to define what is too much and what too little, to stipulate where the golden mean lies? As to that, the "law" has nothing to say. That has to be defined anew each time of observation.

IV

Before Professor Toynbee sets out in his third volume to treat the problem of the growth of civilizations, he disposes of the arrested civilizations known to history. These constitute a heterogeneous group: the Polynesians, the Eskimos, the Nomads, the Osmanlis and the Spartans. The general explanation is that in these cases the challenge was so serious—a challenge of nature in the first three, of the need of keeping large subject populations under control in the latter two—as to impose a system of defense which through its demands or its artificiality used up all energies; an equilibrium was thus brought about, from which there was no getting away. One is struck by the immense ingenuity. The circumstances are in each of the five cases related not only vividly, but with a subtle sense of distinctions. Yet all this hardly makes it convincing. The heterogeneousness alone—Eskimos and Turks! —raises doubts in the mind. As far as the Eskimos are concerned, the explanation adduced is certainly plausible. But in the case of the Turks? That slave court, that peculiar method of fighting and governing by means of a special class, and slaves at that! and kidnapped boys of alien origin!—here is indeed a system we can well imagine did not allow of cultural development. But why should it arrest the civilization indefinitely? Why was it not possible to get away from it, or, when it was got rid of, why did not something better take its place? In the case of the Eskimos, struggling with the unchanging conditions of the Polar sea, this immutability is not surprising, but in the other case it is, and so a formula intended to cover both cases does not help much. Let us take another example of our own. Take the German Order in the Baltic lands. Here too we have a most artificial institution, built for fighting and for ruling. Yet here the populations were Christianized and Germanized, and with the dissolution of the Knightly Order merged into the great German civilization.

The usefulness of these general explanations, of this tabularizing, is not very apparent. Within the subdivisions the similarity is not only vague, but at times forced, and we feel that it is just the differences which matter.

Extremely dubious also, it seems to me, is the withdrawal-and-return theory, with which the remainder of this volume is taken up. This is the movement by which personalities and minorities prepare themselves for their creative task in a growing civilization. Even at first glance we wonder what the author will be able to make of the twenty-six or twenty-seven personalities he has selected as examples—men of all times and of all lands, princes and statesmen, saints, historians. What, we ask, can be the connecting element between Peter the Great and Émile Ollivier (and was the latter a great personality?), between St. Paul, Machiavelli, the Buddha and Dante? A more careful reading only strengthens the impression. This chapter is hardly an example of valid method. In some cases Professor Toynbee gives complete life histories, full of particulars which have nothing to do with the point at issue; in others he is very brief. The difference in treatment seems wholly arbitrary. But even the point all his heroes have in common, that they withdrew and after a while returned, is governed by arbitrariness. The withdrawal of one was compulsory, of another voluntary. Peter the Great set out to travel in order to learn and came back in order to put into practice his newly acquired knowledge and to rule; Émile Ollivier had to expatriate himself after 1870, remained outside politics for the rest of his life, never was able to free his mind from the tragedy of the Second Empire, and in his old age, having long before returned to France, wrote a book in many volumes about it. Professor Toynbee also mentions Kant and in a few lines describes the philosopher living quietly at Koenigsberg while his thought radiated over the world. But how precisely did he "return"? In this way one can include anybody to whom one takes a fancy. Not that it would not be easy to add more typical cases to the list: there is William the Silent (1567-72), Napoleon (Egypt), Luther (the Wartburg), Guido Gezelle, the Flemish poet (the exile at Bruges and at Courtrai)—but why continue the search? It cannot on the other hand be maintained—nor does Professor Toynbee try—that in all great lives there occurs such a period of interruption. I should not know how to include either Raphael or Vondel in the list, nor most of the great princely rulers: neither Louis XIV nor Saint Louis, neither Philip the Good nor Charles V. Is it that in these cases the rule is suspended by the peculiar conditions attached to hereditary leadership? But De Witt, too, never paused to take breath, and when he withdrew it was not to return. Nor did Shakespeare: the one was murdered, the other spent his last years peacefully as a landed gentleman. What law can we discern in all this?

Things do not improve when minorities are discussed. Professor Toynbee first mentions some penalized minorities, to observe how they acquire particular strength in their retirement and arm for their return to play important parts. Thus for instance the English Nonconformists, who after having their share in the commotions of the middle of the seventeenth century withdrew—rather, were excluded from everything!—withdrew into the world of business to return omnipotent and to become the authors of the Industrial Revolution. No doubt, there is something in this. In Dutch history, too, the Baptists towards the close of the Republican period, during which they had been kept out of the government, were among the greatest capitalists. One is at first inclined to point to the Dutch Catholics as forming an objection to the theory. Here you have a group who had also been compelled to throw themselves into non-political activities, but who even after their emancipation were not able to play more than a fairly modest part in economic life. One reflects, however, that the ever-growing power of the Catholics in present-day political life in Holland might well be connected with their exclusion in the past, for that is what taught them to prize their cohesion and organization. But other doubts are already assailing the reader's mind. Is not that peculiarity inherent in the spirit of Catholicism? Of modern Catholicism at least, and one thinks of Trent: is not this militancy of modern Catholicism the response to the challenge of the Reformation? The Toynbee terminology comes to mind very readily. But it never gets one very far. The differences will not be denied. Here comparable developments go faster, there more slowly, here they are stronger, there weaker, or they take this direction and elsewhere another direction. And the exceptions! Professor Toynbee mentions the English Nonconformists. Why does he not mention the English Catholics? These, when they "returned" after their long exclusion, were certainly not "omnipotent"!

But Professor Toynbee now attempts to bring certain decisive developments in Hellenic and in Western history within the scope of this same motive. In his view—and he is not the first to make the observation—there is a similarity between Athens, which made herself "the education of Hellas," and Italy, which filled the same part with respect to Western Europe. When he pictures Athens withdrawing from the eighth to the sixth century B.C., and Italy from the thirteenth to the fifteenth century, and argues that in each case this minority in its retirement devoted the energies released by relinquishing its share in foreign entanglements to the task of solving the problem facing the whole of its society (that is, of Hellas and of Western Europe respectively) by an original solution of its own, the construction strikes me as hopelessly far-fetched. And indeed the whole of Western European history (to confine myself to that) has to be bent askew so as to allow the thesis to be carried through. The thesis is, that in Italy there was developed the modern State, albeit on the city plan only, which became for Western Europe the model in its struggle to free itself from feudalism. True, there were city-states on this side of the Alps, in Germany, in Flanders: as early as the middle of the fourteenth century "the feudal darkness of the Western world was thickly sown with constellations of city-states."[6] In fact Professor Toynbee here sees the same motive in action: "a creative minority extricated itself from the general political life of the Western Society by building city walls and learning to live a new life of its own behind them." Italy, however, was a decisive factor, and this we are to view as the return of Italy. Is it not evident that a development proper to Western Europe herself was at least as important, and that Italy, moreover, did not so much return as was sought out in her seclusion?

But the train of thought is continued, this time with Holland, Switzerland, and more particularly England as the protagonists. In the new chapter of European history opened in the sixteenth century the problem was: how can the entire Western world take over, albeit on the scale of kingdom-states, this new Italian and Flemish way of life? "This challenge was taken up in Switzerland, Holland, and England, and it received eventually an English answer."[7] We are here given, it must be said, a very peculiar and personal and certainly most incomplete view of European history in the post-mediaeval period, and that it should be necessary to begin this way in order to bring in the withdrawal-and-return motive hardly inspires confidence. And how is it introduced into the picture this time? Holland behind her dykes, Switzerland in her Alps, England behind the Channel, were able to stand aside and thus to prepare their contribution. In the cases of Holland and of Switzerland, our author continues, the safeguards proved in the long run ineffective. (I state in passing, without laboring the point, that in the case of Holland at least, at a time when Amsterdam was the great international banking center, Dutch merchant fleets covered all the seas, Dutch diplomacy was active and Dutch intellectual life giving and taking incessantly, there was not the slightest question of seclusion; while neither of the two countries can justly be described as a very striking instance of a free state which had at the same time solved the problem of modern state organization!)

But now we are left with England alone. That the peculiar English form of government, which in the nineteenth century was to exercise so wide an influence, owes something of its development to England's relatively safe situation, is a current and indeed altogether acceptable view. But there are of course a good many more factors to be taken into account, and the picture of a creative minority in quiet and retirement devoting itself to that problem

[6] III, 346.
[7] III, 351.

strikes one as somewhat overdrawn. Professor Toynbee, however, is still not satisfied and starts systematizing in a really dizzy fashion.

It is true, he argues, that it was against their own inclination that the English were released from their entanglement in the affairs of the continent. (He places the event between 1429, when the death of Henry V and the intervention of Jeanne d'Arc brought about a turn in the Hundred Years War,[8] and in 1558, when Bloody Mary lost Calais.) But subsequently they came to realize that this had been "a blessing in disguise" and fought as hard to save themselves from new entanglements as they had once done to keep them: see their resistance to the successive attempts of Philip II, of Louis XIV, and of Napoleon to fit England into a continental European empire. (An untenable simplification of at least Louis XIV's intentions; but let this pass.)

Might it not be said with equal justice that the English in that second series of wars, besides being moved by the most natural of all instincts, that of self-preservation, were still striving, though in another way, after power outside their island? Were not the true isolationists in England—and there were such, in the sixteenth, in the seventeenth and in the eighteenth centuries—intent on keeping out of those wars? And was the loss of positions on the continent really recognized as a blessing in disguise? Yes, in so far as the view gradually gained ground that dominion over part of France was an illusion. Yet Cromwell got hold of Dunkirk, and a generation or more afterwards England seized Gibraltar, which she was never to let go. Malta, moreover, may not be situated on the continent, but the clue to England's possession of that island is hardly to be found in her anxiety to live in seclusion.

Professor Toynbee goes on imperturbably building up his system. These periods of relative isolation (which in England, according to him, began with the loss of Calais, with the accession of Elizabeth) generally fall into two phases. "The first, or originative phase is a youthful age of poetry and romance and emotional upheaval and intellectual ferment; the second, or constructive phase is a comparatively sedate and 'grown-up' age of prose and matter-of-fact and common sense and systematization." For Italy he exemplifies the two phases in Dante and Boccaccio respectively (although Dante was certainly not lacking in systematizing capacity and his high poetry is as far removed from youthful emotion or romanticism as from common sense and matter-of-factness!). In Athens he discerns the dividing point in the disaster of 404 B.C.

---

[8]III, 366. According to G. M. Trevelyan as well, *History of England,* these two events "saved the British Constitution." A curious way of putting it: in those times the *British* constitution still lay hidden in the womb of the future.

(when, it seems to me, the time to speak of isolation was long past). In England, finally, the first phase runs from Elizabeth down to the Restoration of 1660, and the second from then on to about 1860 or 1870.

One imagines that the characterization of the two phases was primarily inspired by English cultural history (not that Shakespeare or Milton, the latter expressly mentioned by Professor Toynbee, can really be lumped together in the description "youthful romanticism"). The constructive phase of England's creative isolation, at any rate, to let Professor Toynbee put it in his own words, has

> to its credit such solid achievements as the foundation of the Royal Society and 'the Glorious Revolution of 1688' and the peopling of the North American Continent with an English-speaking population and *The History of the Decline and Fall of the Roman Empire* and the invention of the steam-engine and the passage of the Reform Bill of 1832 and the establishment of the Indian Empire and *The Origin of Species* (which was published in 1859) and the invention of the British Commonwealth of self-governing nations (an invention which dates from the creation of the Dominion of Canada in 1867).

What is one to say of such a passage in this brilliant work? Does England really owe all these heterogeneous achievements to her isolation? England, Professor Toynbee writes, was dragged back into continental European entanglements by the war of 1914. I have already remarked that the wars against Philip II, against Louis XIV, against Napoleon, were just as much evidence of England's uninterrupted community with the rest of Europe. The whole of this suggestion of an isolation lasting from 1558 to 1914, or at least to 1870, is completely untenable. The Glorious Revolution is indeed a fine example of the great deeds which England was able to achieve through her seclusion! Have William the Third and his Dutchmen been forgotten? Professor Toynbee seems here to have strayed into an extreme insularity such as Macaulay could not have improved upon: one would have thought this had become impossible since Ranke. And now take cultural life. How deeply imbued with Italian influences were Shakespeare and his contemporaries! How strong were the spiritual ties connecting the Puritans, and Milton, with the Reformed confessions on the continent! Was not French influence a dominating force after 1660? and, inversely, how directly did English influence make itself felt on French, and, generally speaking, on Continental thought in the eighteenth century! Toynbee mentions Gibbon; but can Gibbon be imagined without French "philosophy"? Read Hammond's *Gladstone and the Irish Nation,* and you will see how intensely a great mid-nineteenth-century Englishman took part in European intellectual life.

One cannot help asking, furthermore, whether it really was only in the second half of the nineteenth century, or even in the twentieth, on England's "return," to use Professor Toynbee's expression, that England's contribution to Western civilization, allegedly prepared in isolation during that lengthy period, reached the rest of the world. I have hinted already how very far from true this was for the eighteenth century; but no less great and no less fruitful was the "Anglomania" in the first half of the nineteenth century. Yet another question presents itself, whether other nations, which had not withdrawn themselves, which throughout that period were in the thick of European entanglements (to follow for a moment this unacceptable thesis of England's aloofness), whether in particular France, did not by any chance make a creative contribution? The question is absurd. But all these pages of Toynbee's are fantastic.

V

We come to Volume IV, which deals with the breakdown of civilization. Professor Toynbee begins with an attempt to prove that these breakdowns are not in general brought about by external forces. On looking closely we soon discover that the author does some violence to the facts to make them fit this thesis. We have only to look at his list of sixteen defunct civilizations (sixteen out of the twenty-one, to which are to be added five arrested and four abortive ones) to think at once that it will be difficult in several cases to escape the verdict: death by external violence.

Leaving aside the old Arabic and Hittite civilizations (about which more in a moment), this suspicion arises in connection with the old American civilizations, that of the Incas, and the Mexican and Yucatan (or Mayan); also with the Turkish (not the only, but certainly the most striking, case of arrested civilizations long ago broken down and now decayed) and with the Scandinavian and old Irish (broken down before birth and now dead). Professor Toynbee admits that the ruin of the Inca civilization is often quoted as an example of ruin through external interference. He proceeds to argue, however, that the destruction by the Spaniards of the *empire* of the Incas is not the same thing as the destruction of their civilization. That empire was nothing but a "universal state," that is, according to his own system, a late incident in the disintegration of a civilization which had already broken down. After that "Indian summer" winter had to come. With the additional help of an interpretation of the oracle of archaeological finds Professor Toynbee concludes that the civilization of the Andes had received its self-inflicted death blow, before ever the Spaniards came.[9]

As far as the two Central American civilizations are concerned, these found themselves in an earlier stage of the fatal downward course; they were still in their Time of Troubles, the universal state was only just coming into sight; but here too the irresistible process of decay through internal shortcomings of the civilizations themselves had already started.

It will be observed that Professor Toynbee introduces into his argument his own theoretical construction as an established datum. This method is open to grave objection. It will not carry along the reader who has preserved his independence towards the system. But even greater are the liberties the author allows himself with respect to the arrested and the abortive civilizations. What does it matter, he says of the first, whether it was the thrust of an alien hand that caused their final collapse? Had they been left to themselves, their ruin simply as a result of exhaustion would have been merely a question of time. That is, if one assumes their arrested equilibrium to be in fact so fatally unshakable as Professor Toynbee has been trying to make out! As for the latter category:

> that in each of the four cases the intractable challenge has been delivered by some human neighbor or rival or adversary. Yet this does not entitle us to pronounce that the abortive civilizations have been deprived of their prospect of life by an external act of violence. The truth may be that these miscarriages have been due to some inherent weakness in the embryos, and that the pre-natal shocks by which the miscarriages have been precipitated have simply brought this inherent weakness out.[10]

After such subtle and speculative reasoning the author thinks himself justified in leaving the cases of arrested and abortive civilizations aside and concludes (concerning the American three as well he now no longer admits any doubt) that of the ruined civilizations only the Hittite and the Arabic appear to have met their end as the result of alien interference; and even here in the end he expresses some doubt.

I have retraced this argument, not only because it is a daring piece of special pleading, well fitted to put us on our guard against the entire work, but also in order to introduce the question: why is Professor Toynbee so anxious that civilizations should come to an end not through external violence but as the result of their own shortcomings? Obviously because the whole of his outlook postulates this view. The idea that the spirit should succumb to

---

[9]IV, 105.
[10]IV, 114.

violence is distasteful, it is to him a lowering of the grandiose drama of history.

Of course the scene of history lies thickly sown with cases of brute force triumphing over right, over delicate humanity, over innocence. In Professor Toynbee's six tomes one can indeed find a good many such discussed, especially when in Volume III he wants to illustrate the possibility of a "challenge" being too strong. But these cases are only nations or states, subsections of the large units which in his view are really the exponents of civilization. Although detesting the militarist, the conqueror, whose activities he considers to be one of the factors helping to wreck a civilization (that is, the conqueror's own; a little chapter of Volume IV is entitled "The Suicidalness of Militarism"), and letting no opportunity pass to bring out the transitory nature of military success and the retribution by which it is closely followed—he sacrifices national communities with equanimity.[11]

After this the fourth volume, as might be expected, deals with the internal causes leading to the breakdown of civilizations. The subdivision of these is extremely ingenious. No doubt the results of the ingenuity at times seem farfetched, but here as everywhere one comes across very striking ideas and extraordinarily fine pages. A most interesting view of the nineteenth century, for instance, is given in a discussion of the illusions and miscalculations of Cobden, who was firmly convinced that democracy and industrialism would secure peace.[12]

One of the weaknesses through which a civilization can go to its ruin is according to Toynbee "the nemesis of creativity," the loss of flexibility, the exhaustion, the self-conceit, frequently following upon a creative effort. No doubt this is a fruitful idea, yet again it cannot bear the far-stretched systematization to which the author subjects it. I could demonstrate this by a number of points. I confine myself to one.

In the same section where he deals with cases of extreme nationalism—that is, in his view, the allowing oneself to be hypnotized by the achievements of a previous generation—Toynbee devotes a lengthy argument to the history of the Italian *risorgimento* in order to bring out the fact that this resuscitation of a people which had in past centuries played so glorious a part was in reality confined to a region which had no share in that earlier achievement. Venice especially, he wants to show, was still too much under the spell of the memory of its glorious past to co-operate effectively in the movement which was to make Italy free and one; but the

---

[11]How unmethodical is his treatment of national as distinct from "civilization" phenomena will be discussed later.

[12]IV, 131 f.

same is true, according to him, of all the ancient city-states which had in the old days stood at the head of Western civilization, of Milan, Florence, Genoa. So it came about that a new country took the lead, Savoy-Piedmont, which had once as an old feudal territory let itself be passed by the astonishing social and cultural development of these now nerveless towns, but which for that very reason was at this juncture able to show such freshness and such energy.

This belongs to a class of explanations often loosely offered by historians: explanations which, when gone into a little more carefully, take so much for granted about the secret workings of the communal life of mankind as to stand in need themselves of elaboate elucidation. In the ordinary course, however, they are not gone into carefully, nor as a rule has the author himself so much as thought of the problems he fails to discuss. Of the same sort is the favorite remark, when an obscure phenomenon presents itself, that it springs from the *nature* of a particular people, this being itself an entity incapable of exact observation or definition. This kind of explanation merely begs the question. The interesting thing about Professor Toynbee is that not only has he carefully systematized a number of such theories, but has attempted with subtle historical arguments to demonstrate them. We have, however, already come across several instances of the attempt collapsing completely at the touch of independent criticism.

It makes admirable reading, this paragraph.[13] One follows the author with the excitement with which one watches an incredibly supple and audacious tightrope-walker. One feels inclined to exclaim: "C'est magnifique, mais ce n'est pas l'histoire." The grace, the daring with which the facts are handled are astonishing, the capacity of coining striking phrases uncommon. What a knowledge, what a wealth of general cultural backgrounds, how splendid the characterization of the new, non-Italian-Renaissance, feudal society of Savoy-Piedmont! But at the same time what the author leaves unsaid is at least as important and essential as what he mentions, and by its means one can reveal his thesis in its incompleteness, arbitrariness and untenability.

I cannot touch upon all the points I might query. There is a fascinating description of the deadness which had overtaken eighteenth-century Venice; but the explanation that all energy had been used up in the senseless attempt, inspired by faith in tradition, to keep alive a Mediterranean empire against the Turkish attacks, and that the lightheartedness and frivolity of Venetian life were nothing but the psychological counterpart to that grim effort, seems

---

[13]IV, 278-289.

to me one-sided. Was there really a large percentage of the Venetian aristocracy that bled in the Turkish wars? Should not the author have said at least a word about the concentration of all power in the hands of a tiny group from amongst that aristocracy? For it can hardly be doubted that this left a mark on the minds of the rest, just as the weaknesses of the eighteenth-century French nobility are in part to be explained by the setting up of an administrative apparatus in which they had no share. And when Professor Toynbee contrasts the bright colors of an English flag flying from a ship in a Canaletto painting with the muffled tones of the setting formed by the harbor of Venice, should he not have recalled the discovery of the sea route round the Cape of Good Hope and of America, and the displacement of trade from the Mediterranean to the Atlantic Ocean?

How is it—to confine myself to the chief point in Professor Toynbee's argument—that it was precisely Savoy-Piedmont which proved itself capable of that great political feat, the unification of Italy? He examines only the events of 1848-49. In that crisis Milan and Venice, both of which rose against Austrian rule, exhibited the greatest heroism, Savoy-Piedmont's military performance against Austria was on the contrary far from distinguished. "Yet this Piedmontese disgrace proved more fruitful for Italy than those Milanese and Venetian glories"; ten years and seventeen years later the work of liberation was performed (in conjunction with the French, it is true) by the Piedmontese army, while Milan and Venice remained passive.

> The explanation is that the Venetian and Milanese exploits in 1848 were virtually foredoomed to failure, however magnificent they might be in their intrinsic worth, because the spiritual driving force behind them was still that idolization of their own dead selves, as historic mediaeval city-states, which had been defeating the finest efforts of Italian heroism and Italian statesmanship since the time of Machiavelli.[14]

"The explanation is. . . ." Apart from other considerations so simplistic a view rouses in the historian an instinctive distrust, which is not lessened by the apodictical delivery. The nineteenth century Venetians," Professor Toynbee continues,

> who responded to Manin's call in 1848 were fighting for Venice alone, and not for Piedmont or Milan or even for Padua; they were striving to restore an obsolete Venetian Republic and not to create a new Italian national state; and for this reason their enterprise was a forlorn hope, whereas Piedmont could survive a more shameful disaster because the nineteenth-century Pied-

---

[14]IV, 287.

montese were not fast bound in the misery and iron of an unforgettable historic past.

It should be noticed that our author no longer makes any mention of Milan. And indeed in Milan the rebels had formed a "provisional government" which set itself no other object but fusion with Piedmont on the one side and with Venice on the other. In Milan at least it appears to have been possible to get away from the fascination of the historic past, and the freedom of spiritual movement which Professor Toynbee observes in the new land of Piedmont was not so unique as he wants to make us believe.

But when even the Venice revolt is examined more closely, it will appear how lacking in the complexity of life is his presentation of the facts. Manin had proclaimed the Republic at Venice; but he had done so before the rising of Milan and the advance of Carlo Alberto of Savoy-Piedmont were known there; the Piedmontese consul himself had given his approval to the decision.[15] Nor did Manin ever conceal his opinion that the unity of Italy must be the final goal. It is true that Manin resisted the pressure which was soon put on him from Piedmont, and even from Milan, to let Venice be merged into the Piedmontese kingdom without delay. It goes without saying that he was afterwards severely blamed for this by Italian historians who, after the bad habit of historians, used the event as the measure of all things; but if one looks at the circumstances of the moment, there is something to be said for his attitude. In any case it is incorrect to put forward a historically conditioned particularism as his only motive, or even to assert that he could not do otherwise because the Venetians would not have followed him. The Italian idea lived in Venice. But at the same time there were feelings of suspicion with respect to Carlo Alberto, feelings which were shared by Manin himself; his ability to live up to his promises was doubted. Especially that proud slogan *L'Italia farà da se,* behind which in reality there lurked the King's fear for the French revolution, was objected to in Venice. Manin and his friends realized that nothing could be achieved without France. And as a matter of fact in the end the great aim was only achieved with France. Could not the question why Italy's liberation failed to emerge from the heroic initiative of Milan and Venice in 1848, be answered thus: *The explanation is* that feudal Piedmont under a reactionary King was striving not so much after Italian unity as after the expansion of Piedmont, and in particular that this king rejected the help of revolutionary France? The statement would surely be no more one-sided than the solution presented to us by Professor Toynbee, his imagination

---

[15]G. M. Trevelyan, *Manin and the Venetian Republic of* 1848, 139.

afire with that striking idea of "the nemesis of creativity." For although our author of course imagines he is proceeding empirically here also, of true empiricism, of an objective observation of the facts, whatever the conclusions they may suggest this passage again is hardly an example.

There are still so many data which have been neglected! Savoy-Piedmont was able to play its great part, even after the failure of 1848-49, because it was independent and moreover was by its situation in a better position than any other Italian region to co-operate with France. These simple facts might at least have been mentioned before the Middle Ages were called in to explain the failures or the passivity of Milan and Venice. Piedmont was certainly not the strongest spiritual radiating center of the new Italian sentiment. Alfieri, who dreamt of Italy in an earlier generation, was a Piedmontese, but "dépiémontisé";[16] Massimo d'Azeglio, one of the great intellectual as well as political leaders of the *risorigmento,* also came from Piedmont, but he was married in Milan, where he lived for many years; without the Milanese atmosphere he would not have been the man he became. Silvio Pellico and Leopardi were Milanese. Garibaldi was a native of Nice, which belonged to Piedmont, but it was as a sailor and outside Piedmont that he became acquainted with the Italian idea. Mazzini came from Genoa, and Genoa was one of those towns with a great past, which had in fact offered embittered opposition to annexation to Piedmont in 1815. Mazzini, the prophet of the unitary Italian Republic, had his following scattered over the whole central and northern portions of the peninsula, but in monarchical Piedmont it was perhaps weakest. The older *Carbonari* were merged with his new organization *La giovine Italia*: those pioneers of Italian unity again had certainly not been most numerous in Piedmont. But all this is passed by in silence by Professor Toynbee, which is, it must be admitted, the most convenient method when one wants to subject history to a system.

I shall make one more remark—out of many which present themselves—and this because I can here invoke Professor Toynbee himself. In those years 1848-49 there happened another sensational event, the rising in Rome, the proclamation of the Republic there, and the resistance led by Mazzini and Garibaldi against the French army besieging the town. In Volume II Professor Toynbee assures us that Rome's heroic perseverance, even though it ended in defeat, made the profoundest impression on the national imagination.[17] He there mentions the incident merely to argue that it supplied the decisive consideration for the choice, later on, of

---

[16]Henri Hauvette, *Littérature Italienne* (1914), 383.
[17]II, 400-1.

Rome as capital of the new Italy—in itself a disputable view: was
it not the fact of Rome appearing on the strength of her ancient
glory predestined for that position which had inspired Mazzini and
Garibaldi to plant their banner there? But however that may be,
in his second volume Professor Toynbee gives to Rome's behavior in the crisis of 1848-49 an emphasis which makes it all the
more remarkable that, two volumes later, intent only on bringing
out the providential part played by the new land of Piedmont, he
has not a word to say about it.

VI

Volumes V and VI are concerned with the process of disintegration, that fatal downgrade course to which a broken-down civilization is irretrievably committed. I shall not continue subjecting
passages to detailed criticism: the examples already tested will
have to suffice. I shall rather try to survey the system itself and
discuss one or two chief points.

Professor Toynbee himself furnishes his readers with announce-
ments and repetitions or summaries, and it is thus easy to survey
the system. It all appears to fit together closely and precisely. But
when we try to apply it to the multiform world of reality we fare
like little Alice at the croquet game in Wonderland. The mallet
turns out to be a flamingo, which twists its long neck the moment
we want to strike; the ball is a hedgehog, which unrolls itself and
runs off; while for hoops there are doubled-up soldiers, who rise to
their full height and get together for a chat just when you are aiming in their direction.

"In a growing civilization, as we have seen," Professor Toyn-
been writes in his sixth volume,[18]

> a creative personality comes into action by taking the lead in
> making a successful response to some challenge. . . . In a disin-
> tegrating civilization Challenge and Response is still the mould
> of action in which the mystery of creation takes place, but . . .
> [while] in a growing civilization the creator is called upon to
> play the part of a conqueror who replies to a challenge with a
> victorious response, in a disintegrating society the same creator
> is called upon to play the part of a savior who comes to the
> rescue of a society that has failed to respond because the chal-
> lenge has worsted a minority that has ceased to be creative and
> has sunk to be merely dominant. . . . A growing society is taking
> the offensive . . . [and wants its leader] to capture fresh ground
> for its advance, whereas a disintegrating society is trying to
> stand on the defensive and therefore requires its leader to play

---

[18]VI, 177.

the more thankless . . . part of a savior who will show it how
to hold its ground in a rearguard action.

"As we have seen." Is that indeed what we have seen, and are
we in the two latest volumes seeing the rest? As for me, no! Undoubtedly, I have been shown leading or creative personalities in
one and the other function; I had indeed seen the like before. But
how do I know that the difference is caused by the triumphant creator acting in a growing society and the hopelessly struggling one
in a society in distintegration? I have not been convinced of the
essential difference between the phases of civilization, and still
less have I been convinced that a period of growth is by a breakdown irretrievably cut off, so that the stricken civilization, with its
"members," the creative minds included, must from then on have
got on to the fatal slope which will carry it to its ruin in three
beats and a half and in an unknown number of centuries—irretrievably, with this qualification however, which can hardly be
considered a mercy, that it may stay somewhere suspended between
life and death in a state of petrifaction.[19] To me, even after the
fourth volume of Professor Toynbee, this great event of the breakdown, which is supposed to lead to the fatal process, remains a
mystery and after his third and fifth and sixth volumes the conceptions of growth and of disintegration retain so much that is fluid,
vague and uncertain that I find it difficult to use them for the subdivision of history, especially in conformity with his rigid system.
I can sympathize more with the modesty of Huizinga, who, in comparing successive centuries of civilization, came to the conclusion
that the conception of "a rising civilization" will escape us as soon
as we attempt to apply it: "the height of a civilization cannot be
measured." I know very well that these are no more than very
simple remarks occurring in an unpretentious essay[20] and that
they are very far from exhausting the subject. But when placed
beside Professor Toynbee's omniscient positiveness, they seem to
me instinct with profound wisdom.

It is noteworthy that our author himself, after having written
two heavy volumes about disintegration, and after having in every
imaginable way subdivided and analyzed and even tabulated[21] the

---

[19]V, 2; 22.

[20]"*Geschonden Wereld,*" published posthumously in 1945. Huizinga is
here arguing against the believers in a continuous progress of our own
civilization, a group to which Professor Toynbee does not of course belong.
But his remarks are relevant also against Toynbee's pretention to indicate
(as he attempts to do in Volume VI) the exact *rhythm* of all civilizations.

[21]These tables—four in all—are to be found among the appendices to
Volume VI, p 327 ff. The way in which Western civilization is there dealt
with might give rise to an extensive critical discussion. I shall do no more
than make a few remarks on the first table. The first thing that strikes one
is that Western civilization is there unquestioningly drafted into a table

phenomenon, cannot tell us whether we are experiencing it at this moment. In order to explain that uncertainty he regales us with a wealth of metaphor, yet it remains curious. At first glance one should think that the two phases of growth and of disintegration, as sketched by the author himself, present a contrast like that between day and night, which cannot remain hidden from the observation of contemporaries. The creative personalities in a growing society triumphantly find the right answer, and the new challenge to which this gives rise with its once more triumphant response can be compared to the taking possession of fresh territory. There you have growth; while on the other hand in a distintegrating society the leaders are doomed to a veritable sisyphean labor. At best a respite can be gained, but after every apparent victory there follows a worse setback. And we, who may have been living in that wretched condition for the last four centuries (for that is the possibility suggested by Professor Toynbee)—should we not know it?

There is an indication here that the author is less rigid and doctrinaire in the application than in the exposition of his system. The instances in which this appears can be brought up against him to show him in contradiction with himself. They can also be placed to his credit. In any case the fact remains that innumerable remarks and illustrations scattered over the six volumes do not agree too well with the strict lines of the system, but at the same time contribute not a little to the color and the fascination of the work. Especially when our Western civilization is under discussion can this be observed.

He seeks, for instance, to establish the existence in our Western society of a proletariat (in his sense of the word) and of a dominating minority, and of other equivalents of phenomena belonging typically to the disintegration process in civilizations which he indicates have run their course to final dissolution. There are, to mention only a few points, the loss of style, the aping of alien and barbaric forms of art, the tendencies to archaism and futurism. I have no room to follow his disquisitions on all these points. I will only say that they are frequently stimulating to the highest degree,

---

particularizing the disintegration process. It is surprising, and not in agreement with remarks made elsewhere in the book, to see the Time of Troubles fixed for the Western half between 1378 and 1797 and for the Eastern half between 1128 and 1528. Two universal states are indicated, the Napoleonic empire and the Danubian monarchy. When in connection therewith one sees a *pax oecumenica* assigned to the years 1797-1814 and 1528-1918 respectively, one is inclined to ask if words have the same meaning for Professor Toynbee as they have for the rest of us.—Of the other tables I shall only say that they too seem to show to excess the author's gift of observing parallels and of building constructions on them.

but that as frequently they leave one completely unsatisfied. Wide prospects seem to be opened by his discussion of the danger threatening our civilization from the sudden assimilation of large areas with other cultural traditions, with all the consequences of "standardization" and leveling.[22] On the other hand the discussion of the twin tendencies of archaism and futurism strikes me as disappointing, meagre, and so incomplete as to become lopsided. To bring National Socialism and Fascism under the heading "archaism" is to belittle the historical significance of these evil doctrines overmuch. And is it possible to overlook the fact that both archaism and futurism can be considered disintegration phenomena only in excess, that both are among the indispensable forms of life of any civilization, of a growing civilization as well, that they need each other and are often found together?

But there is one point to which I want especially to draw attention. In the theoretical development of his system Professor Toynbee poses a dilemma: a civilization is either in growth or it is in disintegration. When, therefore, one sees him noting so many grave symptoms in our Western history, one is surprised at his leaving open the question as to the stage in which we find ourselves. But he also mentions phenomena as occurring in our modern history which *per definitionem* belong to the period of growth. It is sufficient to recall the (in certain respects somewhat fantastic) description of England as a creative minority living in retirement and of the great achievements resulting therefrom. I do not see how to solve these contradictions. But I am quite willing to rejoice that Professor Toynbee does not in practice keep growth and disintegration so strictly separate as might be expected from his program. Could we but lay aside his system, with its precise subdivisions and sequences, we could find in his analyses and parallels, in his interpretations and even in his terminology, so much to stimulate thought and to activate the imagination!

But of course the system, the doctrine, belongs to the essence of the work, and we cannot after all do without it if we want to follow Toynbee in his reflections upon our own civilization. We shall have to wait for the twelfth part before we see his diagnosis and his prognosis concerning it fully expounded, but in the meantime he has repeatedly touched upon the subject. The element of uniformity in the rhythm of the disintegration process, he says,[23] looking back on his own examination of the histories of the most widely varied civilizations, "is apparently so definite and so constant that, on the strength of its regularity, we have almost ventured to cast

---

[22]V, 89; 153.
[23]VI, 321.

the horoscope of one civilization that is still alive and on the move." Even more suggestive is the passage in which he toys with the possibility—for here again he refrains from speaking positively —of Western civilization having broken down as long ago as the wars of religion of the sixteenth century. The minds of some readers instinctively revolt against the idea of our possibly being caught up in a disintegration fatally proceeding to ruin or petrifaction. So Toynbee's disintegration theory has been misread, and by some of his most fervent admirers who were fain to think that even in case we are already broken-down he still leaves us the hope of finding "the right answer."[24] But this is not so. For Professor Toynbee everything turns upon the question: has the breakdown actually taken place, or not?

At first glance one is inclined to ask: how is it possible to single out the sixteenth-century wars of religion as having such fatal significance? Indeed to me the suggestion that our Time of Troubles began with them seems unacceptable. There really had been no lack of wars in the preceding centuries, not even of socially destructive wars: the crusade against the Albigensians, the Hundred Years' War, to mention only these.

But for Professor Toynbee the evil thing about the wars of religion is their being wars of *religion*. He is struck not only by the rending asunder of Christendom, but by the atrocious paradox that from the highest good, from the belief in the one God, there was distilled that suicidal poison of intolerance. (Of course, without leaving the plane of his argument, one might remind him of the fact, with which he is certainly familiar, that even this was far from being a new development, although undoubtedly so violent an explosion of religious hatred had never before ranged the Christian nations in opposing camps.) Suspecting that it was these events that marked the beginning of our Time of Troubles, our Christian philosopher finds confirmation in the fact that the appeasement he observes in the third quarter of the seventeenth century proceeded, not from the only true motive, the religious—not from the recognition of all religions as a search for the one spiritual aim—but from an even more cynical temper than that which in the fourth century had underlain the religious toleration policy of the Roman Empire, from weariness and indifference, from *raison d'état*. When Professor Toynbee describes the principle of *cuius regio eius religio* as "a monstrously cynical principle,"[25] he knows exactly what he means—even though the question may well be asked whether justice is done to the age by a judgment based so wholly on later

24Professor Romein in *De Nieuwe Stem* (1946), 44.
25For this and preceding utterances cf. IV, 221, 225, 228.

considerations. The expulsion of the Huguenots from France long after the termination of the Wars of Religion was a particularly barbaric application of this same principle; but even the milder forms of the Caesaropapism which was now in the ascendant, of that domination of the lower over the higher, have, so the argument continues, weakened the foundations of our civilization. The barbaric, the despotic aspects were not the worst, or rather from them sprang, as a fatal consequence, a new factor leading straight to the abyss, namely, scepticism, contempt for religion.

"In our time," he writes in an Annex to Volume V,

> this repudiation of a spiritual principle which is no doubt exposed, in human hearts, to the danger of being poisoned or perverted, but which is none the less the breadth of human life, has been carried to such lengths in all parts of a Westernized 'Great Society' that it is beginning at last to be recognized for what it is. It is being recognized, that is to say, as the supreme danger to the spiritual health and even to the material existence of the Western body social—a deadlier danger, by far, than any of our hotly canvassed and loudly advertised political and economic maladies.

Here we have, I think, the hard core of Professor Toynbee's view of history. In this spirit it is no doubt possible—although really I am now anticipating that twelfth part which we may not receive from his hands for a number of years—to construct a downward line with the sixteenth-century religious wars as a point of departure.

Must that line infallibly lead to the final catastrophe? According to the system, undoubtedly. I merely remind you of the cases of the three ancient American civilizations which were apparently in disintegration and whose ruin was therefore, according to Professor Toynbee, so wholly a question of time that he will not admit the forcible interference of the Spaniards as proof that a civilization can be destroyed by an external power. And yet . . . now that our own civilization is involved, he too seems to shrink back from the iron consistency of his fatalistic construction. On this point as well the published volumes contain several indications as to what he is likely to say about the problem in his promised fuller treatment. There is in particular a passage in Volume V, whose splendid eloquence comes straight from the heart.[26]

His starting-point is "the miracle" of the conversion of the Negro slaves in America to their masters' ancestral religion. Here, he says,

> we can see the familiar schism between the Proletariat and the Dominant Minority being healed in our West-

---

[26]V, 193-4.

ern body social by a Christianity which our dominant minority has been trying to repudiate. . . . The eighteenth century
Methodist preachers who sowed that seed . . . were at the same
time converting . . . the neglected slum-dwellers in . . . Wales
and Northern England. . . . In our post-war generation [the
writer is of course referring to the generation of the *First* World
War], in which the lately brilliant prospects of a neo-pagan
dominant minority have been rapidly growing dim, the sap of
life is visibly flowing once again through all the branches of our
Western Christendom; and this spectacle suggests that perhaps,
after all, the next chapter in our Western history may not follow
the lines of the final chapter in the history of Hellenism. Instead
of seeing some new church spring from the ploughed-up soil
of an internal proletariat in order to serve as the executor and
residuary legatee of a civilization that has broken down and
gone into disintegration, we may yet live to see a civilization
which has tried and failed to stand alone, being saved, in spite
of itself, from a fatal fall by being caught in the arms of an
ancestral church which it has vainly striven to push away and
keep at arm's length. . . . Is such a spiritual re-birth possible?
If we put Nicodemus' question, we may take his instructor's
answer." The reference is to John, III: "Marvel not that I have
said unto thee, ye must be born again.—The wind bloweth
where it listeth, and thou hearest the sound thereof, but canst
not tell whence it cometh and whither it goeth: so is every one
that is born of the Spirit."

What is the meaning of this? It means that Professor Toynbee
in his heart believes that our civilization has fallen a prey to the
disintegration process; but in spite of the inexorable sentence which
therefore according to his system holds sway over us, he leaves us
one possibility yet: the grace of a conversion, or of a return, to
faith.

VII

Professor Toynbee does not address himself to fellow-believers
only. Occasionally he alludes to the "neo-pagan" intellectuals of
the modern world in a tone of mild sarcasm, at times a little less
mild, although not unmixed with pity. But in at least one passage
he invites them into the circle of men of good will as rightful claim-
ants to a share in the Western cultural inheritance. His *method* at
any rate is not intended to be that of the religious prophet. Utterances from which it appears that he expects salvation from faith
only, drop from him out of the fullness of his heart, but as it were
in passing. His method he presents as empirical.

Now the last question I want to examine is—what has this method to give us for the better understanding of the history and the
inextricably related present-day problem of our own Western civili-

zation? That Toynbee's system is to me unacceptable I have
already stated clearly enough. But his work contains more than
the system. Does his method, which undeniably yields striking
results every now and again, promise an important contribution to
that subject which concerns us all so closely?

It is perhaps unfair to the author if, in conclusion, and after so
much criticism, I confine myself to expounding two objections to
his method in this particular connection. Let me at least remark
with some emphasis that, in spite of all that may be urged against
it, the work here too is immensely stimulating, and that the volume
in which his views on our own troubles and prospects will at last
be systematically set forth promises to be profoundly interesting.
But on two points I shall advance a formulation of my doubts.

If Professor Toynbee has not so far given a set analysis of this
particular subject, in his own opinion the comparison with the
other civilizations whose course he *has* investigated is already of
the greatest importance for the right understanding of what we are
living through ourselves. In a certain sense this is a thesis no one
will contest. An insight into any historical process trains the mind
for the grasping of other processes. But Professor Toynbee's idea
is that it is permissible to conclude from analogies, and to this
view, which underlies the whole of his work, I shall now, at this
late stage, without absolutely rejecting it, attach a label, "Handle
with caution."

I am not going to attempt an examination of the problem in its
full extent and its first principles. I shall only point out that, generally speaking, parallels in history, however indispensable and
frequently instructive, are never wholly satisfactory, because each
phenomenon is embedded in its own circumstances, never to be
repeated, from which it cannot be completely detached. This warning must be especially taken to heart by anyone setting out to compare this civilization of ours with other and older civilizations.
The circumstances have in many ways undergone so profound a
change that we seem to be living in another world from the ancient
Egyptians, or the ancient Chinese, or Iranians, or whatever peoples provide Professor Toynbee with his rules and laws, in another
world also from that of the Hellenized Romans, whose decline and
fall have obviously strongly influenced his mind in the construction
of his system.

I realize perfectly that *he* will be little accessible to this consideration. His view of history is preeminently a spiritual one. I am
far from being a believer in historical materialism, but for all that
I do not think that material changes can, in this argument, be
simply ignored. Book-printing; telegraph, telephone, radio; incredibly increased speed of transport; productive capacity im-

mensely heightened; unfortunately also powers of destruction raised to an unheard-of degree—all this has created conditions which have not left the processes of spiritual life uninfluenced and on which the possibilities of development and degeneration, the tendencies and powers of resistance of our present-day society are to such an extent dependent that it must be a particularly ticklish undertaking to draw its horoscope, as Professor Toynbee puts it, from the experiences of earlier ages.

The other point is concerned with one particular shortcoming which I seem to discern in Professor Toynbee's disquisitions on our civilization, his attitude towards the national varieties within the wider unit of Western civilization. I have already remarked upon the unruffled serenity with which, while insisting so strongly on the impotence of external violence with respect to his "civilizations," he accepts the cases without number in which violence has triumphed over national communities. National independence inspires him with distrust, national ambitions he rejects. He does not really do justice to the historical reality of national life, of national desire for self-preservation or even for expansion.

A striking instance is to be found in his treatment of the downfall of the Boer Republics in 1902. In his view the statesmen of the British Empire were driven to make use of their overwhelming military superiority because the national ambitions of the two backward independent miniature states made their preservation inconsistent with any other solution; and indeed, at the cost of a small local war, it proved possible subsequently to pursue a constructive policy within the Empire, which gave satisfaction to Dutch nationalism. A surprisingly idyllic presentation of the episode! Surprising especially as coming from the same Professor Toynbee who is so much governed by the idiosyncrasy of the apostle of gentleness that he attaches the name of "hangman" to the conqueror as representative of a dominant minority—and this with Caesar for an example![27]

The fact is that this particular idiosyncrasy of his is here overruled by that of the hater of nationalism. It is under that heading, or in his terminology under the heading of "the idolization of an ephemeral self," one of the mental attitudes leading to the breakdown of civilizations, that the South African case is cited.[28] The writer's opinion, by the way, that it presents a contrast with that of Ireland, where the nationalists go on fostering their hatred of England, and with that of Servia, which caused the dissolution of the Austro-Hungarian monarchy, is an error. The cult of super-

---

[27]V, 138.
[28]IV, 295.

annuated grievances and the raising of particular rights to the level
of the absolute, which are characteristic of a wronged nationalism,
certainly belong to the dreariest and most dangerous phenomena
of the modern age; Professor Toynbee sketches them in the cases
with which he is acquainted with the insight born of loathing. But
when he asserts that South Africa has now become a peaceable
multi-national state, after the pattern of Switzerland, and that this
proves a new country to possess a greater psychological plasticity
as compared with the petrifaction in its obsessions characteristic of
old Europe, this only shows, as do other passages also, that
he is not informed about the Afrikander national movement.
These mistakes spring from, or at least are not unconnected with,
this same inability to appreciate nationalism; perhaps it is wiser
to avoid that ambiguous word in -ism and to say that Professor
Toynbee here shows in small things the same lack of understanding
for the reality of the national factor in history.

This constitutes one of the serious shortcomings of the entire
work. If the destructiveness of nationalism when driven to extremes by oppression or even by fancied wrongs is an undeniable
fact, it still cannot be overlooked—although Professor Toynbee
does overlook it—that in the cultural construction of our Western
world national foundations are of essential importance. This does
not in the least amount to throwing doubts on the reality of the
greater civilization of which the European nations, to use Professor Toynbee's word, are "members." But we are faced by a
problem here which is not to be solved by a one-sided negation.
In the very first of Professor Toynbee's volumes he placed himself
in an untenable position. It is all to the good that the writers of
national histories should be reminded that their subject does not
form a self-contained whole, that it has to take its place, and this
without any well-marked delimitation, in a greater whole. It is all
to the good to make an attempt to survey the greatest whole of
all, so that the sense of the dependence of the parts may not only
be strengthened but may take shape. When, however, Professor
Toynbee considers himself so far superior to the distinction between "parochial states" as to ridicule professorial colleagues who
set the diplomatic relations between two of these ephemeral units
as thesis subjects, he exaggerates not a little. And when he poses
the civilization, in the sense of one of the twenty-one, as the
smallest "intelligible field of historical study," he is putting forward an impossible, an impracticable demand.

I have pointed out that he himself every now and again, when
speaking not only of our own Western Civilization but also for instance of the Hellenic, cites phenomena which are particularist or
national. This is of course quite inevitable. But since he has done

nothing but belittle the national factor instead of accurately defining its relationship to the larger whole, he is all the time coming into conflict with his own impossibly universalist system. Wherever possible he adduces examples of "parochial" phenomena as illustrations of the tendencies of a civilization in its entirety. This is certainly a great convenience to him in his arguments: it becomes easy in this way to prove anything. Our Western Civilization in particular offers a rich variety of choice. It is only once or twice that he so much as mentions the problem, and not many of his readers will go along with him when he extends an observation made in the case of one people without further ado to cover all.

The case in question is that of National Socialism in Germany.[29] "Germany's troubles in the present generation can be ascribed, without dispute, to the contemporary *Zeitgeist* of the Western Society of which Germany herself is a fraction." The "without dispute" does not make the statement any more convincing. The thesis I accept unhesitatingly: but the conclusion seems to me unjustified. Why? Because, apart from the cohesion of the large civilization area, there is the variety of national traditions, of national history. These it is that settle the question whether tendencies which will no doubt be present in several countries, without however constituting the whole of the *Zeitgeist*, will in one particular country gain the ascendancy or not. His unwillingness to recognize this fact, by which nevertheless in practice his argument is repeatedly ruled, his failure to make up his mind about this, one of the chief problems of the Western civilization area, strikes me as a serious weakness.

Considering this, taking it together with the doubtful applicability of his comparisons—doubtful especially in this particular case—I can, after all the other indications as to the necessity of caution, have little confidence any longer that Professor Toynbee, when later on he undertakes a set examination of our civilization and its prospects, will prove able to enlighten our perplexities; or should I not rather say that we need not let ourselves be frightened by his darkness? We need not accept his view that the whole of modern history from the sixteenth century on has been nothing but a downward course, following the path of rout and rally. We need not let ourselves be shaken in our confidence that the future lies open before us, that in the midst of misery and confusion such as have so frequently occurred in history, we still dispose of forces no less valuable than those by which earlier generations have managed to struggle through their troubles.

---

[29] VI, 57, footnote.

TOYNBEE'S A STUDY OF HISTORY*

G. J. RENIER

A philosophy of history which has made a profound impression upon English-speaking readers is that of Arnold J. Toynbee, Research Professor of International History in the University of London. It has been presented to the world in six large volumes under the title of *A Study of History*. It began to appear in 1934, and has had several editions and impressions. More volumes are announced. The work bears palpable evidence of its author's profound erudition, of his immense knowledge of the past and of the present. It contains many proofs of his knowledge of the world. It is varied, rich, always readable. To me it had, when I first became acquainted with it, the attraction of impish humour and a joyful iconoclasm. Its description of the operations of a Board of Studies in History at an English University,[1] its reflections upon the mentality of English historians,[2] make it difficult for me to be entirely outspoken about its lovable author. Yet I consider the work to be based upon misleading arguments, intellectually dangerous, and totally false as a picture of the function of historical studies. It is the supreme embodiment of what I call "left-wing deviationism," the confusion between history and the philosophy of history.

As an illustration of the way in which this work has conquered a place, not only in the minds, but in the hearts of some, I refer the reader to Mr. Tangye Lean's "A Study of Toynbee," in the periodical *Horizon* for January 1947. This article is the manifesto of a cult. Now, Mr. Tangye Lean has, obviously, read a *Study of History,* and he believes that he has understood it. Many of the greatest admirers of the work have only browsed in it. It is immense. Unless one buys it one cannot keep it by one long enough to work one's way through it. As far as English historians are concerned, their admiration has been conditioned by the lengthy and numerous footnotes and the erudite apparatus served with the main dish. Every literature has been put under contribution. The author's omniscience frightened the scholar-tacticians who thought twice before attacking. It is a striking fact that the first really critical reviews of the system of Mr. Toynbee appeared when a less forbidding abridgment of the work was published in 1947.[3] This

---

*G. J. Renier, *History*: *Its Purpose and Method*, Beacon Press, Boston, 1950, pp. 215-219.

[1] Vol. I, pp. 163-4.

[2] E. g., pp. 455-6.

[3] *A Study of History*, abridgment by Somervell, D. C., 1947.

73

did not enjoy the immunity commanded by the *editio maior*. The barbed wire of annotation had been levelled, and word went round that the citadel was not impregnable.[4]

With that loyalty to Mandarin standards which characterizes him, Toynbee prints a letter from Dr. Edwyn Bevan explaining in a few words why Toynbee's whole scheme is wrong: ". . . While your attention and interest is directed mainly to the common characteristics, it is the uniqueness that impresses me. . . . The 'Hellenic Civilization' I see . . . as the unique beginning of something new in the history of Mankind. Never before that culture can we see a civilization of the same rationalist character . . ."[5] The publication, without comment, of this striking criticism is symptomatic of Toynbee. Even though he does not always make it clear what it is he believes, he is unwavering in his belief. He is an absolutist. "So far, we have simply found that in the foreground of historical thought there is a shimmer of relativity," he writes, "and it is not impossible that the ascertainment of this fact may prove to be the first step towards ascertaining the presence of some constant and absolute object of historical thought in the background."[6] He pities those who have not been vouchsafed the revelation, treats them kindly, and has no desire to muzzle them.

I am not competent to criticize Toynbee's philosophy of history. But I may be allowed to mention two facts which make me suspicious about his method and conclusions. The first is that wherever he deals with the history of the Low Countries he remains superficial and approximative, when he is not actually ill-informed. The other is Toynbee's use of myths and metaphors, not merely for the purpose of assisting thought, but as the basis for subsequent reasoning and classification. Faust, Job,—"let us open our ears to the language and mythology,"[7]—Yin and Yang, Hippolytus and Phaedra, Hoder and Balder. Play with mythology leads us nowhere beyond mythology. It provides us with hypotheses—and what is there that does not?—but never with proofs. "For here we see the same 'great refusal' that the creators of the Egyptiac Civilization made in the age of the Pyramid-Builders, and *that Zeus would have made at the dawn of Hellenic history if he had not been saved*

---

[4]See Collingwood's severe criticism of the book, written before the publication of the *editio minor*, from his own specific point of view, in *The Idea of History*, pp. 159-65. Collingwood attacks Toynbee for failing "to see that the historian is an integral element in the process of history itself, reviving in himself the experiences of which he achieves historical knowledge," in other words, for not being a Croce-ite.

[5]Vol. V, pp. 6-7. See the whole letter.

[6]Vol. I, p. 16.

[7]I, p. 271.

from it, in spite of himself, by Prometheus."[8] There never was a Zeus! What Zeus said or intended is not evidence. On the few pages that follow the statement I have just quoted, I underline the words "mythology, allegory, Epic, poet, poem, feeling, anthropomorphically, allegorical imagery, allegory, hypothetical, a hypothesis which has to be taken on faith, parallel, the primordial images of Mythology, intuitive form of apprehending and expressing universal truths."[9] Why not just one single fact? And when there is an argument, it is too often formal and verbal: "A field of action—and, a fortiori, an intersection of a number of fields of action. The source of action is other than the field of action ex hypothesi. And—to apply this truism to the case in point—the source of social action cannot be the society, but can only be each or some or one of the individuals whose fields of action constitute a society on the ground where they coincide."[10] A metaphoric argument like this, or an enumeration of myths—neither leads us to truth nor to knowledge.

As I said, I have no intention of discussing Professor Toynbee's doctrines. This has been done, adequately, and finally, by my compatriot Geyl.[11] My universal eclecticism leaves room for the message of Toynbee, if there be a message in his work. I condemn his condemnation of the treatment of problems of nationhood by historians because it is illiberal, and because any theory that attempts to expel from the ranks of historians men who have honestly attempted to carry out their social task is of necessity distorted and partial. I dislike Toynbee's method, because it dwells in the sphere of myth and allegory, outside rationality, and because the intense loyalties he inspires are equally innocent of rationality. The mentality of the Dutch theorist Romein, who manages to proclaim himself an adherent of the doctrines of Toynbee while remaining a believing Marxist, is typical in my opinion, of the mentality that comes under the spell of A Study of History.

One aspect of Toynbeeism puzzles me. Toynbee's writing is magnificent. His style is Greece and the Bible and France, and the tongues of many peoples, with the quintessence extracted from them in a liberation from the tryranny of the Logos which leaves him in possession of the rhythm of all language. It is the style of a man whose soul is straight. This book cannot be a mystification. What is it, then? Though there is no deception of others, there is in it

---

[8]III, p. 255. (My italics.)

[9]III, pp. 256-9.

[10]III, p. 230.

[11]See Geyl, P., "Toynbee's System of Civilizations," in Journal of the History of Ideas, Vol. IX, No. 1.

the nearest approach to self-deception. Sometimes we dream that we understand at last the mystery of life, that we have solved the riddle of human relationships. We awake, and say: "This is great, I must preserve it!" In the morning we remember the formula. It is inane. Toynbee had a vision. He dreamt that he could formulate the human universe. His mistake is that he remained faithful to the hypnological revelation and worked it out in millions of words. He should have sighed: *"mirum somniavi somnium!"* and written a poem about his experience. Preferably in Greek.

HERR SPENGLER AND MR. TOYNBEE*

H. MICHELL

I

The reader who, with indomitable pertinacity, has read right through Herr Spengler's *Decline of the West* and the six volumes of Mr. Toynbee's *Study of History*,[1] may be forgiven if, at the end of his course, he confesses to being a trifle breathless, a little spent with the effort of concentration and, at least in the case of Spengler's great work, somewhat bewildered and confused. The fault, no doubt, lies in the reader who has attempted too much in too short a time. Both authors should be read in leisurely fashion; months not weeks, perhaps even years should be devoted to each, and prolonged meditation bestowed upon both. They are immensely stimulating and deeply interesting. Both authors are profoundly erudite, and let it be said at once without offence, prostratingly prolix. The two must be read in juxtaposition. While it is too much to say that Toynbee cannot be understood unless Spengler's book has already been mastered, it is true to say that Spengler is an almost indispensable prerequisite to Toynbee, the latter's debt to the former being duly noted.

Both authors are concerned with the birth and death of civilizations; or we may say with their emergence and disappearance. Herr Spengler's thesis is fundamentally a simple one. Cultures and civilizations—the distinction that he makes between the two may be disregarded—follow the life pattern of living organisms. They are born, come to maturity, decline in senescence, and eventually die. Mr. Toynbee quite justifiably rejects this and prefers to talk of challenge and response. To any society there comes a challenge,[2] be it from nature or from other societies, and on its response to that challenge depends its future course. If it rises to the occasion then it will advance to greater heights; if it fails to do so it will remain inert or even retrogress. When one challenge has been successfully responded to, another will come and an emergency faced once more. The question is, how often will a people, a civilization, have the inner strength, the *élan vital* in Bergson's phrase,[3]

Transactions of the Royal Society of Canada, Volume XLII, Series III, June, 1949, Section Two, pp. 103-113.
[1]Oswald Spengler, *Decline of the West*, trans. by C. F. Atkinson, 2 vols. in 1 (New York: Knopf, 1932), *Der Untergang des Abendlandes: Umrisse einer Morphologie der Weltgeschichte* (zweite Auflage, München, 1923). Arnold J. Toynbee, *A Study of History* (Oxford, 1934).
[2]Toynbee, *Study*, III, 371.
[3]*Ibid.*, I, 249.

to confront one challenge after another? To use Mr. Toynbee's well-known and admirable simile of the climbers up a cliff, how far can they climb before their powers are spent and they either fall and are dashed to pieces, or sink exhausted upon some convenient and seductively inviting ledge, to fall into the sleep that leaves them irresponsive to further challenge and eventually leads to death? Careful reflection will reveal that the method of approach of both authors to the problem is in the last analysis the same. For birth read challenge; for growth read response; and for both read death whether it come from the failure of the powers of the senile or inability to respond to renewed challenges.

The key to the philosophy of history which underlies the work of both authors is to be found in what Mr. Toynbee calls "the nemesis of creativity."[4] This he defines as "the idolisation of an ephemeral self." A civilisation reaches a pinnacle of achievement beyond which it can go no further. It has expended its creative energy, it has shot its bolt. It is filled with satisfaction at what it has accomplished. It has reached an evolutionary *cul-de-sac,* and since it can no longer advance it must recede. In Herr Spengler's phrase, after the crescendo must follow the decrescendo. The pages of history are crowded with examples of this fate, this doom that has overcome the proud peoples of the past. The nemesis that follows upon the idolisation of an ephemeral institution awaits the kings, parliaments, ruling classes, and priesthoods that have so often, as they vainly imagine, established themselves in impregnable power. The Athens of Pericles dwindles to the Athens of St. Paul. The glory of the city states of Greece fades before the imperialism of the great kingdoms that engulf them, and the appeals of Demosthenes to oppose the Macedonian fall upon deaf ears. Caesar shrinks to a ridiculous puppet, a contemptible Romulus Augustulus, and is swept away like other rubbish. The great empires of the past lie prostrate in the dust, like the image of the great king Ozymandias, a mockery and derision.

The nemesis of creativity awaits the art and learning that have adorned the cultures of the past. The glories of the Periclean age, the masterpieces of art and sculpture, drama and architecture, cannot be continued. Achievement reaches a climax, an apogee, and after that there cannot be anything but a decline into mediocrity, a shabby second-best, decay and inevitable extinction. Who should write deathless dramas after Aeschylus, Sophocles, and Euripides had delivered their souls? The last worth-while joke was cracked by Aristophanes, and comedy declines to the amusing mimes of Herodes. All through the long history of mankind we see this

---

[4]*Ibid.,* **IV,** 245 ff.

efflorescence and decay, this systole and diastole of the divine afflatus. Who should paint wonderful pictures after the great masters of the Renaissance? Who should build great cathedrals after Chartes? And who should write great plays after Shakespeare? The glories of the Elizabethan stage degenerate into the vulgarities of the Restoration dramatists. The matchless prose of Bacon and Milton petrifies into the dull pedantry of Samuel Johnson. The poetry of Shelley and Keats dies with them, and their successors are Mrs. Hemans and Mr. Martin Tupper.

With the Preacher of Ecclesiastes, Spengler and Toynbee cry: "The thing that hath been is that which shall be; and that which is done is that which shall be done, and there is no new thing under the sun." Do we vaunt ourselves on our achievements today? Do we in our foolish presumption dream that our culture, our art, our invention and genius will endure forever? With an overwhelming wealth of detail the analogies of history are presented to us, and we have not the wit nor understanding to grasp the lesson that they tell us. We are in the last stage of a declining era, and the fate of past ages, the doom that has overtaken the empires of antiquity and the civilisations that have preceded us, is fast approaching, is indeed already here. The fate that follows upon the vaunted glories of poor mortals is overtaking us. How shall we escape the doom of Κόρος, ὕβρις, ἄτη?[5] Κόρος means surfeit: we are surfeited by the wonders we have created, we are spoiled by success. We are afflicted and tormented by ὕβρις, a loss of mental and moral balance. We boast of our achievements and are vainglorious in our deeds. We strut and posture, gloat and play the fool in our insufferable self-satisfaction. Like Jeshurun we wax fat and kick. The fate of ἄτη, the blind, headstrong, ungovernable impulse that sweeps an unbalanced soul into attempting the impossible, awaits us, and destruction is our end. The nemesis of our own creativity is close upon us. We have reared a gigantic structure of achievement; but its foundations are on quicksand. We have created the atomic bomb and it will blow its creators to pieces.

What hope is there for the world as it is today? Mr. Toynbee has none. Our civilisation is doomed, and in his despair he turns from his own peoples, the nations of the Western world who have brought mankind to its present desperate state.

> If mankind is going to run amok with atom bombs, I personally should look to the Negrito Pygmies of Central Africa to salvage some fraction of the present heritage of mankind . . . [since they] are said by our anthropologist to have an unex-

---

[5]*Ibid.*, IV, 258.

pectedly pure and lofty conception of the nature of God and God's relation to man.[6]

Spengler, mainly we may suppose because he wrote before the Second World War and the discovery of the atomic bomb, does not take a catastrophic view of history. The world, and more particularly Western civilisation, is not necessarily headed for a smash-up, but rather a progressive and, as time passes, an accelerated decline, a slipping down the slope from the high attainments of the past. "Of great painting or great music there can no longer be for western peoples any question," he says. "Their architectural possibilities have been exhausted these hundred years."[7] Not only does he see no future for art, music, and architecture, but he is even more despairing of science and mathematics. "It is enough for us, that the day of the great mathematician is past. Our tasks today are those of preserving, rounding off, refining, selecting in place of big dynamic creation, the same clever detail work which characterised the Alexandrian mathematics of late Hellenism."[8] And again he says:

> Our great century has been the nineteenth. Savants of the calibre of Gauss, Humboldt and Helmholtz were already no more by 1900. In physics as in chemistry, in biology as in mathematics, the great masters are dead, and we are now experiencing a great decrescendo of brilliant gleaners, who arrange, collect and finish off, like the Alexandrian scholars of the Roman age. Everything that does not belong to the matter-of-fact side of life—to politics, technics or economics—exhibits the common symptom . . . After Lysippus no great sculpture, no artist as man-of-destiny, appears, and after the Impressionists no painter, and after Wagner no musician. The age of Caesarism needed neither art nor philosophy. To Eratosthenes and Archimedes, true creators, succeeded Posidonius and Pliny, collectors of taste, and finally Galen and Ptolemy, mere copyists. And, just as oil painting and instrumental music ran through their possibilities in a few centuries, so also dynamics, which began to bud about 1600, is today in the grip of decay.[9]

It might be objected that these quotations from Toynbee and Spengler are not perfectly fair to either author. It is easy enough, it may be said, to tear isolated passages from any author and hold them up to criticism, or even ridicule. It is the fate of even the very best at times to be caught off balance, to make unguarded and, if the truth be told, unwise statements which later reflection will seek to modify or tone down or even repudiate as unsound. We may

---

6 A. J. Toynbee, *Civilization on Trial* (New York: Oxford, 1948), p. 162.
7Spengler, *Decline*, I, 40; *Untergang*, I, 55.
8*Decline*, I, 90; *Untergang*, I, 123.
9*Decline*, I, 424; *Untergang*, I, 552.

imagine that Mr. Toynbee's reference to the hope of civilisation resting upon some presently "backward" people might well belong in this category. It might also, with less justice, be said in excuse of Spengler that he was writing before the amazing advances in mathematics and dynamics of the past few years burst upon the world. That would be fair enough, if we did not find in his work an unwillingness, a repugnance to realise what was going on around him. His statement that the day of the great mathematician is past is extraordinary. He published his first edition in 1917, and a revised version in 1923. Einstein published his first work in 1905; by 1912 his restricted theory of relativity was generally accepted; in 1915 his generalized theory was published.[10] For Spengler to say that by 1900 the great masters were dead is obviously untrue and, not to put too fine a point upon it, is equally obviously, considerable nonsense. The real fact seems to be that by 1900 Spengler's mind was shut to new perceptions. Gauss, Helmholtz, and Humboldt were for him the great masters after whom nothing worth doing was possible. But his book was not the work of an old and tired man to whom much might be forgiven. He was 34 in 1914, when he tells us that the first draft of his work was completed.

Spengler in the preface to his revised edition of 1923 defends himself on the score of pessimism raised by many of his critics.

> Of course the cry of pessimism was raised at once by those who live eternally in yesterday, and greet every idea that is intended for the pathfinder of tomorrow only. But I have not written for people who imagine that delving for the springs of action is the same as action itself [welche das Grübeln über das Wesen de Tat für eine Tat halten]. Those who make definitions do not know destiny. [Wer definiert der kennt das Schicksal nicht]. It is the hard reality of living that is the essential, not the concept of life that the ostrich philosophy of idealism propounds. Those who refuse to be bluffed by enunciations will not regard this as pessimism [wer sich nichts von Begriffen vormachen lässt] and the rest do not matter.[11]

This is an extraordinary passage and the more it is carefully considered, the more puzzling does it become. Who, more than the writer, was "delving for the springs of action"? And who was more involved than Spengler himself in making definitions? Who are those who "refuse to be bluffed by enunciations"? It is all a little difficult to understand. The truth is self-evident and no mere de-

---

[10]Spengler was either unaware of or chose to ignore Einstein. But he does refer to Minkowski, Niels Bohr, and Rutherford. *Decline*, I, 124, 384, 426; *Untergang*, I, 163, 497, 553.

[11]*Decline*, I, xiv; *Untergang*, I, ix.

nial, no tortuous argument can lift from both Spengler and Toynbee the accusation that they are defeatist. If their books are not
fundamentally pessimistic, what are they?

The pessimism of Mr. Toynbee would appear to arise from a
different cause. We may hope we are not doing him an injustice,
but apparently it comes from the over-sophistication of the intellectual, from a failure, if the expression may be allowed, to "take
things easy," to which the academic mind is peculiarily prone.
There are lots of things in our present-day life which he does not
like, which irritate and disturb him. The meretricious banalities,
the vulgar blatancy of much of our modern life distress and worry
him and there is no health in us. We are also often annoyed and
vexed; but, if we are wise, we do not let them trouble us overmuch.
Nor should we over-estimate their importance, nor think that they
betoken a rottenness at the core, a canker of degeneracy, that will
develop into the malignant disease that will bring our modern
civilisation to ruin. It really is not as bad as all that.

To take one instance, that of music. Mr. Toynbee is distressed,
and excusably so, at the prevalence of what he calls the music of
the African negro of Benin and Dahomey, at jazz and boogie-
woogie and jive, or whatever foolish names are applied to the
hideous cacophonies that assault our ears. He calls its impact on
us "swift and deeply demoralising."[12] We like it as little as he
does; but we may well ask if it is demoralising? Is it really any
more than extremely silly and, if we consider it carefully, any
worse than the crudities of former generations? Mr. Toynbee is
using a very strong word when he says it is demoralising. It is
heartening to be told by the manufacturers of gramophone records
that when some dance band has taken a beautiful melody of a
classical musician and "jazzed it up," degraded and vulgarised it,
there is an instant demand for the original. People today in millions are listening to and are deeply moved by the music of the
masters. Great music has left the confines of the concert hall, the
exclusive and expensive preserve of the consciously cultured, and
come into the homes of the people. After all, if we do not care
to listen to crooning, a mere touch, the movement of an eighth of
an inch of the dial on our radio, and we can listen to the greatest
symphony orchestras in the world.

II

If we examine the method of treating history of both authors, we
shall find that one fundamental error lies in setting dates when

---

[12]*Study*, V, 481.

such and such a civilisation "broke down." The most glaring instance, apart from Spengler's obsession that our modern civilisation reached its culmination in the nineteenth century and is now in decline and obsolescence, is when Mr. Toynbee insists upon setting the date of the "breakdown" of Hellenic culture at the impossibly early date of 431 B.C., at the outburst of the Peloponnesian war, that "beginning of great evils for Hellas." To him that little space of half a century saw the culmination of Greek genius: all that came after was second-best, a decline into mediocrity. This has troubled many, probably most, readers, and Mr. Somervell, the compiler of the admirable abridged version, does his best with it.[13] He tries persuasively, and with considerable ingenuity, to explain Toynbee's use of the term "breakdown" as meaning no more than a severe illness, such as may assail anyone and from which he may, if his constitution be strong enough, in time recover. This is special pleading and the reader remains unconvinced. Undoubtedly that is not the meaning that Mr. Toynbee wishes to convey. To him breakdown denotes an ill from which there is no recovery, an irremediable disaster for which there is no repair, no hope of improvement.

It has become a perfect obsession with Mr. Toynbee and leads him into indefensible positions. To give another instance, and this a surprising one,[14] the builders of the Parthenon had brought its form of architecture to perfection. There was nothing left to be done with it, and the architects of Justinian in Constantinople nine hundred years later triumphantly dealt with the very difficult problem of crowning a cruciform building with a circular dome and produced the masterpiece of a Haghia Sophia. They had deliberately abandoned, Mr. Toynbee says, the traditional Hellenic style in favour of a "new-fangled" one. They were architects of a society which was by this time in articulo mortis and had declined to so low a degree that "it was no longer possible within its traditional framework to perform any fresh act of creation in any field of activity. The old style had become distasteful to them through its association with a dead and and rotting past." At this point the reader is sorely tempted to accuse Mr. Toynbee of mere perversity. The architects of the Parthenon, to take it as an archetype, had exhausted the possibilities of that very simple and beautiful style of archetrave on column. Were all builders ever after never to experiment with any other form, never to try anything "new-fangled"? And were their efforts to express themselves in hitherto untried forms to be a sign that they had turned in disgust from

---

[13]*Study of History,* abridged by D. C. Somervell, 1 vol. (New York: Oxford, 1946), p. 273n.
[14]*Study,* IV, 54 ff.

the contemplation of a dead and rotting past? Of course not, and
Mr. Toynbee might well protest that we are putting words into his
mouth that he would instantly repudiate. But we have quoted exactly what he says and he must not complain if we draw our own
inferences. In sober fact Mr. Toynbee is so obsessed with the
glories of the Periclean age that what comes after it, in Spengler's
phrase, is nothing but "a mighty decrescendo."

There is an amusing passage in Mr. Toynbee's *Study of History*[15]
in which he recounts his shock at seeing the turf of the football
ground at Sheffield being kept green for the coming season and
great rows of bleachers set up for the multitude of spectators. In
America he was even more deeply scandalised at floodlit gymnasia
designed to manufacture football players by night and day. Another structure was roofed over so that practice could be carried
on whatever the weather, with beds on the side for the exhausted
and wounded. He was told that the young men looked forward
to playing in a match with much the same grim apprehension as
their fathers on going into action. "It was the industrial system,"
he says, "celebrating a triumph over its vanquished antidote sport
by masquerading in its guise." We need not attempt the unwel-
come task of defending some aspects of sport in our universities
which are widely deplored. But we may protest against the finick-
ing petulance of what John Buchan called "the brittle intellectual"
in finding his feelings lacerated by an English football ground or an
American gymnasium. In both instances the care bestowed upon
the externals is an effort to improve the game, to fit the players
more perfectly for their part, so that English soccer or American
football should be better played and another step made towards
perfection. No doubt Mr. Toynbee would disapprove of the grass
being cut and rolled in the courts at Wimbledon so that better ten-
nis should be played there and the perfection of human effort in
that very beautiful game brought nearer to attainment.

Would Mr. Toynbee be perfectly at home and happy in a Greek
palaestra? We may wonder if he would approve of the elaborate efforts expended on turning out champions, and he would deeply
disapprove we are sure of the brand of football played in Sparta.
There is no fundamental difference, *mutatis mutandis,* between a
Greek palaestra and a modern gymnasium, except that the modern
counterpart is larger and the exigencies of climate demand that it be
roofed. They strove in ancient Hellas, as we do today, to attain
perfection as human powers may attain to, because to aim at perfection, however far we may fall short of it, is to strive after the
godlike and sublime. Our runners are lowering records steadily.

---

[15]*Ibid.,* **IV,** 242.

What if they are? we may ask. What significance is there that the record for the 100 yards has been lowered a fifth of a second? Only that another human achievement has been attained, another step taken toward the perfect athlete. We may deplore, if we are so inclined, the worship of sport today and the adulation of the athlete. But Pindar wrote odes to Olympic winners.

Characteristically, Mr. Toynbee is distressed at what he regards as the fruits of modern education. That some use badly the fruits of our education is unfortunately true; but for the vast majority it brings a liberation of the spirit, an enlargement of the soul. Is the crown, the highest achievement of our schools to be conferring on our people the ability to read the comics and gloat over the scandals of the tabloids? One of Mr. Toynbee's outbursts is against the so-called "popular" journalism of our time.[16] He bewails "the inevitable impoverishment in the intellectual results of education when the process is reduced to its elements and is divorced from its traditional and cultural background in order to make it available for the 'masses'. . . . It has cheated our educationists when they have cast their bread upon the waters, of their expectation of finding it after many days." He notes that universal compulsory education was introduced in 1870, and the yellow press was invented twenty years later, at the exact moment when the children exposed to its influence were ready to find in it the excitement that their unfortunate training had given them, the faculty to feed upon and make the fortunes of Newnes, Harmsworth, and Hearst, the entrepreneurs who have debauched the masses.

Does Mr. Toynbee really mean to say that all that modern education has done is to degrade the children who are exposed to it? The answer, of course, is that in actual fact he does nothing of the sort. He knows better really but he has allowed his impatience, his fastidiousness, to run away with him, and lead him to write what, we may hope, on calmer reflection he might later repudiate or, at least, tone down. Again we want to exclaim: "Take it easy, Mr. Toynbee. It isn't as bad as that. Those same despised 'masses' have not done too badly with the education they have had. Indeed they have done amazingly well with it."

III

It may be objected that what we have been saying is not of fundamental importance, it does not go to the root of the matter. We have found fault with the attitude of mind in which Mr. Toynbee approaches his theme, and have picked a few very little holes in

---

[16]*Ibid.,* IV, 193 f.

Herr Spengler's book. The great central theme remains—the birth and death of civilisations.

Great civilisations, they say, have perished in the past and so will ours. Indeed we are already far gone with decay and our nemesis is upon us. They have very little hope of a reprieve, a respite from our troubles. It would be truer to say they have no hope at all. Why should we in our presumption dare to think that the fate of those who have gone before will be spared to us? Are we wiser than our forefathers, more far-sighted than the statesmen of the past? There seems little in us to warrant so arrogant a presumption. If the genius of man leads him to no better end than the atomic bomb wherewith he may blow himself to bits, we may doubt if our vaunted civilisation is worth very much. It may be so corrupt that it is not worth saving. If the ruins of Hiroshima are to be our monument, what is left for us but the great and terrible day of the Lord, when he shall stretch forth upon the earth the line of confusion and the stones of emptiness? Shall we curse God and die?

Mr. Toynbee has little hope for our modern civilisation. So little indeed that he looks to some pygmies of the central African jungle as a possible future race that will bring the world back to a consciousness of the presence of God. Herr Spengler has nothing to offer but the poor comfort of what he calls "second religiousness" (Zweite Religiostät),[17] "the enticement of the half-educated into a renewed interest in religion" through all kinds of spiritual excitements, esoteric cults, "revivalism," Ku-Klux-Klanism. These in turn, he says, give way "to a new resigned piety sprung from tortured conscience and spiritual hunger."

"Miserable comforters are ye all" cried out poor Job, struggling against the deluge of words that his garrulous friends poured out upon his unhappy head. There is an amusing incident in the life of Adam Smith recounted by John Rae. "I recollect when I was lamenting to the Doctor the misfortunes of the American war and exclaimed 'If we go on at this rate, the nation must be ruined,' he answered, 'Be assured, my young friend, that there is a great deal of ruin in a nation.'" There is a great deal of ruin abroad today; but we need not despair. And above all we must not lapse into that overwhelming boredom, that *taedium vitae* that afflicts the hopeless.

It is not true that history repeats itself. It seems to; but actually it does not, if we delve deeply enough into the forces that shape the destinies of peoples and civilisations. That is what Mr. H. A. L.

---

[17]*Decline*, II, 310; *Untergang*, II, 382.

Fisher meant when in the preface to his *History of Europe* he said
he could find no rhythm or predetermined pattern:

> I can see only one emergence following upon another, as wave
> follows upon wave, only one great fact with respect to which,
> since it is unique, there can be no generalizations, only one safe
> rule for the historian, that he should recognize in the develop-
> ment of human destinies the play of the contingent and the un-
> foreseen.

The analogies of history are never more than half true; often they
are false and the superficial resemblances are deceptive. Do we
really learn from all these

> Old, unhappy far-off things
> And battles long ago?

Or if we do, what is it that we actually do learn? If our study of
history schools us but in cynicism, then it were better that we make
a bonfire of our books.

> The world is weary of the past
> Oh, might it die, or rest at last.

It was freely predicted after the First World War that another
would prove too much for civilisation and the world would collapse
in bankruptcy and ruin. The second has come and gone with all
its frightfulness and destruction, horrors and desolation; but our
civilisation is still a going concern. We are pulling through, hardly
and painfully though it may be. There is no breakdown, and the
forces at work in repairing the damage are very great and potent.
John Stuart Mill was right when he said that war only destroyed
quickly where nature did it more slowly:

> There is nothing at all wonderful in the matter. What the en-
> emy have destroyed, would have been destroyed in a little time
> by the inhabitants themselves; the wealth which they so rapidly
> reproduce would have needed to be reproduced and would
> have been reproduced in any case, and probably in as short a
> time.[18]

Here is no nemesis of creativity, no surrender to pessimism. What
the world needs is a great deal more of the sanity of Mill and a
great deal less of Mr. Toynbee.

But what of the wounds inflicted upon the soul? Are they healed
so easily and quickly? We may not doubt that they are in the
infinite compassion of God. But not in a spirit of resigned piety, a
futile "second religiousness," for that is no healing at all. We are

---

[18]*Principles of Political Economy*, 1.5.7. The whole passage is worthy of
careful perusal. It is Mill at his best, and Mill was, and still is, very good.

not called upon to betake ourselves to heroics, to strike attitudes and defy the lightning. But it is entirely necessary for us to keep our heads and not allow ourselves to be blown away in a gale of funk. It is very easy to give way; in fact it is easier to get in a panic than to face our troubles and difficulties, and a philosophy of pessimism will not help us at all. The issue is as simple as that. This is no easy optimism, no "God's in his heaven, all's right with the world" stuff, but a calm and resolute need for courage in a time of distress. But we shall find no comfort, no inspiration, no incentive to high endeavour in the work of Herr Spengler and Mr. Toynbee.

Then said Christian, You make me afraid, but whither shall I fly to be safe? If I go back to mine own country, that is prepared for Fire and Brimstone; and I shall certainly perish there. If I can get to the Coelestial City, I am sure to be safe here. I must venture: To go back is nothing but death; to go forward is fear of death and life everlasting beyond it, I will yet go forward. So Mistrust and Timorous ran down the Hill and Christian went on his way.

DR. TOYNBEE'S STUDY OF HISTORY

A REVIEW*[1]

SIR ERNEST BARKER

Exegit monumentum—Dr. Toynbee has finished a monument. He has built a work which is a pyramid of piled learning, and a pyramid with a plan. Three volumes appeared in 1934: three others were published in 1939: the last four are now given to the world, after an interval of fifteen years; but an eleventh volume (containing maps and a gazetteer), and a twelfth volume of second thoughts or 'reconsiderations', are still to come. The only parallel of which I can think, in my lifetime, is Sir William Holdsworth's massive *History of English Law;* but there are many more pages in this *Study of History* than there are in that work, and there is a wider sweep of vision, alike in time and in space. I reviewed volumes IV-VI in 1939, during an August spent in a Northumbrian farmhouse, with the clouds of war hovering above me as I wrote: I am happy to be reviewing these last four volumes with a mind more quietly at ease, under a quieter if still clouded sky.

The first six volumes of *A Study of History,* as they stood in 1939, contained a study of 'civilizations' (to the number of twenty-one or twenty-three) as so many units of history based not on race or language, but on religious or secular culture. These civilizations —divided into three 'generations', according to their appearance in time—were studied particularly and individually, apart from their relations and contacts; but they were also studied in general terms of their genesis, growth, breakdown, and disintegration, and some general 'laws' were suggested, more especially in regard to the phenomena and the results of disintegration. In the final four volumes of his work, now published in 1954, Dr. Toynbee begins by examining the relations and contacts between his score of civilizations. He argues that disintegrating civilizations show a split or schism, resulting in three characteristic social products—a 'dominant minority' which tends to create some form of universal empire; an 'internal proletariat' which, in his view, finds consolation in the

International Affairs, vol. 31, 1955, pp. 5-16.

[1]*A Study of History, Volumes* VII, VIII, IX, X. By Arnold J. Toynbee. 1954. (London: Oxford University Press for the Royal Institute of International Affairs. Vol. VII. *Universal States. Universal Churches.* xxxii+ 772 pp. Vol. VIII. *Heroic Ages. Contacts Between Civilizations in Space.* x+735 pp. Vol. IX. *Contacts Between Civilizations in Time. Law and Freedom in History. The Prospects of the Western Civilization.* viii+759 pp. Vol. X. *The Inspirations of Historians. A Note on Chronology.* viii+422 pp.)

development of a higher religion tending to embody itself in a universal church; and an 'external proletariat', composed of 'barbarians' on the frontier, waging heroic warfare against the empire that is their neighbour. Volume VII and the early part of volume VIII accordingly deal with the three themes of universal empires, universal churches, and heroic ages. It is the theme of universal churches and higher religions that particularly fascinates the writer; and the reader discovers that Dr. Toynbee's views, in the years which have elapsed since 1939, have moved to a deeper and higher estimate of the role of religion in history, which leads him to regard the development of a form of society based on the religious motive as the goal and purpose ultimately served by the life of civilizations.

Turning still more specifically to the relations between civilizations, Dr. Toynbee next examines, in the later part of volume VIII and the early part of volume IX, the general issue of 'encounters' between different civilizations. Here he is first concerned with encounters between contemporaries, which come into contact with one another in the dimension of space; and in this connexion he deals particularly with the contacts between modern Western civilization and other contemporary civilizations—in Russia, in the body of Orthodox Christendom, in the Hindu and Islamic Worlds, and among the Jews. (The study of this last contact—that of the Modern West and the Jews—leads to a notable disquisition on the problem of Zionism.) After dealing with these contacts in space, he embarks on the different but connected theme of contacts in time, or in other words, the theme of encounters between a modern civilization and some earlier civilization—as, for instance, the encounter between our modern Western civilization and the civilization of ancient Greece. This issues in a discussion of 'renaissances' in history, which he regards as a species of 'necromancy' or magical exhumation, and against which he accordingly directs his argument, celebrating 'the blessedness of immunity from renaissances'.

These are the two main subjects of the four volumes under review—the subject of the universal empires, the universal churches, and the heroic ages, which are the accompaniments of disintegrating civilizations; and the subject of the contacts or encounters of different civilizations, both in space and in time. Three other subjects—treated at less length, but with no less penetration—are handled in the latter part of volume IX and the first part of volume X. The first of these subjects is the general problem of historical causation; or, in other words, the place of 'law', or 'laws', as compared with that of personality and contingency, in the development of human affairs; or, in still other words (which are Dr. Toynbee's own words), 'law and freedom in history'. The second subject, which is likely to be of particular interest to most of the readers of these volumes, is the prospects of Western civilzation. (In dealing with this crucial subject Dr. Toynbee has some notable pages in considerations of modern military strategy, and on the growth and decay of the martial spirit among the various races of the world—for with all his passion for peace he has a lively interest in the problems and practice of war, as he shows not only in these pages, but also in his previous treatment of the character and development of the 'heroic ages' of mankind.) Finally, and as his third subject, Dr. Toynbee proceeds to examine 'the inspirations of historians', that is to say the impulses which have led historians (and himself among them) to investigate the relations between the multitudinous facts of history, at once with a feeling for the 'poetry' in those facts and in quest of a meaning behind them. 'Finally'—and yet not finally: for there are two last sections in his tenth and last volume which have still to be noticed. One of them, which is really in the nature of a preface turned into a postscript, is some thirty pages of acknowledgements and thanks (modelled on the first book of the *Meditations* of Marcus Aurelius), in which he records the impulses which he has himself received from people and books, and from monuments and travels, during the course of his life. (These thirty pages are in the nature of an intimate—almost too intimate— mental autobiography: they serve to explain how the author went on his way, and to what goal he eventually came). The second of these two last sections is an index, compiled by Mrs. Toynbee, of nearly two hundred pages, in double columns, which is an indispensable and admirable aid to the reader of the volumes. It is a 'reasoned' index, with well marshalled headings and sub-headings; and it too is a 'monument'. Without it, the reader might be lost and bewildered; with it, he can find his way through the vast territory which he has to explore.

From this brief and inadequate summary of the contents of these four volumes we may now turn to the author. He shows—especially in volume X and more especially in the part of that volume which is entitled 'acknowledgement and thanks'—an almost boy-like candour and a lively frankness of interest in the spiritual Odyssey of his life. He tells his readers how he was impressed, even in his perambulator, by the Albert Memorial: he records his reading, travels, emotions, and experiences: he takes his readers into his confidence, and pours out his heart as he writes, now in a Latin poem and now in Greek elegiacs. Horace said of Lucilius that 'he trusted secrets to his books as if they were his faithful friends'. One may say of Dr. Toynbee that he does the like—not altogether in egotism, and certainly not in vanity, but rather in modest candour and from a desire to be perfectly frank. The reader is profoundly interested as he watches the author's mind at work and is shown its intimate processes. Here is a mind of insatiable curiosity, eager imagination, and tenacious memory; full of remembered learning, and furnished with a treasury of stored notes; ranging from China to Mexico in space, and from Sumer and Akkad to the middle of the twentieth century in time; fertile in suggestions, which germinate and grow in his mind almost as you watch; passionate for understanding, and carried by that passion into a ready formulation of 'laws' and great generalizations. It is the other side of these great gifts that Dr. Toynbee's judgement is not equal to his knowledge: indeed it hardly could be—his knowledge is so great. Moved by a *parti pris,* or stung by the splendour of a sudden thought, or inspired by some glimpse of a curious analogy, he is carried recurrently off his feet, and swept into long disquisitions. In a word, he has not discounted *himself* enough. He is not sufficiently impersonal; failing to look steadily at the object, he fails to be objective. The result is a subjective view of 6,000 years of history.

One notable feature of his thought, and of his general approach to history, may be briefly and imperfectly indicated by the word 'classicism'. Trained in the classics at Winchester, and a product (as indeed is also his reviewer) of the Oxford classical course in the history and thought of Ancient Greece and Rome, he carries the abiding traces of that ancient discipline. It was the intention of those who planned the Oxford classical course that the study of the ancient past should be pursued in connexion with the present: that ancient history, if 'considered ancient', should be regarded none the less as congruous with the present, and as throwing light on its problems. Dr. Toynbee has, in his fashion, been faithful to that intention. His education in the classics (and particularly in the Greek classics) has done much to inspire his view of history, his interpretation of its rhythm, and his very style. Polybius would seem to have been his particular inspiration (and perhaps, behind Polybius, the general Stoic theory of cycles of history): he has the same idea of 'cyclical recurrence' (*anacyclosis*), or what Cicero, following Polybius, calls the *mirabiles circuitus* of history. Indeed he renders his thanks fully and frankly to his classical upbringing (or, as he calls it, 'the traditional Late Mediaeval Italian system of education in the Greek and Latin classics'); and again and again he draws analogies from Hellenic and Hellenistic history (particularly the latter) for the elucidation of modern history. But these analogies are sometimes fanciful; and in any case he is a critic as well as a disciple—and even more a critic than a disciple—of things Greek. He dislikes renaissances, as has already been noticed (they are acts of 'necromancy'); he dislikes Palladian imitations of the classical architecture of Greece: he regards Greece, after all, as a ghost—perhaps best left in limbo.

A sad feature of Dr. Toynbee's classicism is its effect on his style. Whatever he may have derived from his study of the thought and history of the Greek past, he has drawn too much from his reading of Greek and Latin literature and from his early training in Greek and Latin composition. He confesses in two of his footnotes that as a result of his 'fifteenth-century Italian education' he was led to express his deeper feelings in Greek or Latin verse rather than in the English vernacular, and that he had 'acquired and retained . . . an articulateness in Greek and Latin of which he was destitute in his . . . mother tongue'. Certainly his English style, in these last four volumes, is plus-quam Ciceronian in the prolonged rotundity of its voluminous periods. He writes English almost as if it were a foreign language, in long periodic sentences, with one relative clause piled on, or dovetailed into, another. What is more sad is that he also writes on a high and strained note, with a wealth of curious adjectives (often of condemnation), and with the liberal use of a peculiar technical terminology which falls away into slogans and sometimes even into slang (especially American slang). Add recurrent quotations from the classics (and especially from Lucretius) and a great use of Biblical phrases (so frequent as to pall and even to jar); and the result is a remarkable amalgam. The reader cannot but wish that the style were simpler and the sentences shorter: that adjectives were fewer, less high-pitched, and less far-fetched: that there were more Attic restraint, and less Asiatic luxuriance. The reviewer found himself tempted, again and again, to break up and re-write the long rolling cryptic sentences: in particular he found himself anxious to banish the too frequent use of what he was taught at school to call the 'ornate alias', and to substitute, for instance, the words 'St Paul' for 'the Tarsian Jewish apostle of Christianity *in partibus infidelium*'.

Enough has been said of the author's personality, of his classicism, and of his style. It is time to turn to his argument, which is the thing that really matters. It is indeed a voluminous argument. Here are three volumes, each of some 750 crowded pages, and a fourth of some 400; and every page is crowded with an abundance of footnotes. In 1939 Dr. Toynbee estimated that his first six volumes contained rather more than two-thirds of the whole work. They have turned out, in the issue, to be more than a half—so much has been packed into the last four volumes, which are so closely printed in their crowded pages that they dazzle and bewilder old eyes 'Nothing in excess', said the Greeks; but Dr. Toynbee runs into a *copia cogitationum* which is matched and even exceeded by a *copia verborum*. He pours whole books into his text and indulges in long quotations; he adds, in long footnotes and numerous annexes all the digressions and ancillary reflections which have occurred to his fertile mind. He is a Titan of learning, but does he not defeat himself by overloading his shoulders? There was a quarrel once in Alexandria, about the third century B.C. (if the reviewer's memory is correct), between the votaries of the long 'cyclic poem' and the disciples of brevity, led by Callimachus, who held the doctrine that 'great books are great evils'. There is much to be said for Callimachus (it is remarkable, to cite one instance, how much wisdom and insight Spinoza, could pack into the seventy pages of his *Tractatus Politicus*); but there is also much to be said for great books when the theme is great, as Dr. Toynbee's theme certainly is. In any case he has achieved a great book, in conception as well as in size. In the preface to his fourth volume he spoke of St. Augustine's *City of God* as his inspiration; but he has also followed, no doubt unconsciously, the example of Vincent of Beauvais, the encyclopaedist of the Middle Ages, who produced in the part of his *Speculum Majus* which is called the *Speculum Historiale* a history of the world in 3,794 chapters. Like Vincent his is an encyclopaedist, though—unlike Vincent, who was largely concerned with chronicling miracles—he is also a philosopher, with something of the sweep of St. Augustine, and with St. Augustine's passion for rising from the *civitas terrena* (the merely 'parochial' State) up to the city of God. Indeed Dr. Toynbee's sweep of Knowledge—through time and space, and through all manner of institutions and every aspect of human affairs—is almost incredible. He seems equally at home in the *Respublica Christiana* of the Middle Ages and in contemporary problems of politico-military world-strategy and fighting on the Afghan frontier.

Mens agitat molem: a philosophy informs the body of his great learning; but it is, on the whole, a personal and individual philosophy. Many of our great historians have shared some general view of life with the age in which they wrote. Gibbon expressed the eighteenth-century spirit of enlightenment: Grote was a Radical, and Macaulay a Whig, of the nineteenth century. Dr. Toynbee gives expression to an assemblage of points of view (*praejudicia* or 'advance judgements') which are peculiar to a sensitive mind, and the fruit of its personal experiences, rather than the outcome of a 'time-spirit' shared by his age. He is anti-State and (so far as organized religions are concerned) anti-Church: he is for a world-order and a universal religion of all who are earnest 'seekers' for truth. True, he is not alone in those feelings: there are other votaries of a political world-order, and others who sigh for a single oecumenical religion: but he is unique in the intensity of his feelings. He combines a passion for impartiality (which leads him, in reaction against Western bias, to exalt the East) with a passion for universalism which makes him the enemy of nationalism and its 'parochi-

al' States, and turns him into the apostle of a 'Catholicism' transcending not only Catholicism, but also the whole of Christianity,
and issuing in an amalgam of all 'the higher religions'. His desire
is for the whole: he is like Shelley: he wants one 'white radiance',
rather than 'the many-coloured dome' which is the actual home of
man.

With the passion of unity there naturally goes a zest for schema-
tization: a zest for seeing history and the whole past in abstract general terms; a zest, if the phrase may be used, for 'botanizing' history
—for classifying in *genera* and *species* all its multitudinous data.
I am inclined to call this zest by the name of 'Linnaeanism'. Dr.
Toynbee imposes patterns on history, and gives the patterns names,
much as Linnaeus classified and named plants. But this raises the
question whether history is really like botany. I am no botanist,
but I imagine that plants have a general uniformity (so many
stamens, or pistils, or whatever it may be—I speak in ignorance),
and that they can be classified accordingly in terms which all men
accept. History is something different. It is infinitely multiform.
As I see the matter, Dr. Toynbee *imposes* patterns on history,
which I, for one, am far from accepting; and the result is that his
data are patterned and classified data—data patterned and classified
on his own individual system. They are not primary and objective
facts (so many stamens, so many pistils, and so on); they are
secondary and subjective constructions. In a word, he has collected
a set of 'advance judgements', dignified and elevated into historic
genera and *species* and brought under a series of 'laws' of history.
But this is really a subjective interpretation of history. It is 'Linnaeanism' made the servant of a pervasive subjectivity. Dr. Toynbee speaks of Spengler as 'a pontifical-minded man of genius'. Has
he not himself some tendency towards the pontifical? These 'civilizations', for instance, to the number of twenty-one or twenty-three
—what are they? I find them nebulous. Dr. Toynbee speaks of
them as significant—as meaning something more than races or
languages or States. To me they are mental constructions; and I
note that he can say, in words that are almost an admission of
subjectivity, that 'the image of a civilization presumably makes a
still more potent appeal to the Subconscious Psyche than the image
of any of the parochial States'. That leads me to the reflection that
a 'parochial State' may not 'appeal to the Subconscious Psyche', but
it is certainly a fact which starts to the eye and has a meaning for
the understanding.

Let us turn from 'civilizations', regarded as the great data of
history, to the 'laws' which they are supposed to obey. Dr. Toynbee enunciates many 'laws' of the growth and disintegration of
civilizations, and suggests an immanent purpose (or *telos*) to which

the laws are moving. Moved by a deep sense of these laws, he attacks the 'antinomianism' of historians, such as H. A. L. Fisher, who fail, or rather refuse, to trace the motion of historic laws. I confess that to me incalculable influence of personality, and the even more incalculable influence of contingency, are writ large in history, whatever 'laws' there may also be. But I must also confess that I go so far with Dr. Toynbee as to seek to find an unfolding purpose in history. I part company with him, however, when I report my own finding of such a purpose, which is almost the opposite of his. I believe in the national State (and, for that matter, in the national Church), and I do not believe, as he does, that history went wrong when Frederic II of Hohenstaufen started the movement towards the 'parochial' type of State (which, by the way, I very much doubt if Frederic II did). At the end of the matter—when I see how much teleologies can differ—I become shy of any teleology. There is a German saying that *Weltgeschichte ist Weltgericht*. World-history, in its course and sweep, may indeed be a sort of world-judgement; but is any one of us world-historian enough to be justified in condemning the course of the history of the Western world during the seven centuries since the reign of the Emperor Frederic II? Must one really believe that there was 'a lamentable victory of parochialism over oecumenicalism in Western life' about the middle of the Middle Ages?

All in all there is something of a cloudy impersonality, mixed with an ingenious and fertile play of subjectivity, in Dr. Toynbee's view of history. He sees Brocken-spectres of superhuman dimensions ('civilizations', 'laws', 'dominant minorities', 'internal proletariats', 'Herodianisms', and 'Zealotisms') walking along the ridges of history. May it not be better to see men like ourselves, rather than these great spectres: to watch them climbing: to observe and study their various initiatives, and to trace the routes they attempt? Of course there is something more than men, and something beyond individual personalities, in the making of history. Groups too matter, and matter profoundly. But groups too are flesh and blood: they are groups of actual persons, engaged in actual personal relations. They must be studied in their human individuality, and in definite and visible terms—terms of territory, terms of nationality, terms of their state-systems, terms of their religious organizations. We live on earth, and not in cloudland; and we must study ourselves as we live on earth, in terms of our earthly institutions. It does not help the reader to a just view of history when he finds man's institutions decried as 'veritable slums'. Sophocles saw further and deeper when he wrote of 'city-dwelling ways' as one of the great inventions of that astonishing creature, man.

Admiration is mixed with criticism in the reviewer's mind as he reads these last volumes of *A Study of History*. The admiration is warm, and the greater of the two: the criticism makes him almost ashamed (who is he to criticize a work so remarkable, and, as the French say, of so 'long a breath'?), but it must in honesty be reported. Dr. Toynbee's general views are his own: they will not be altered by anything that the reviewer can say: they may be left to the test of time and the general judgement of historians. But I wonder whether Dr. Toynbee could not alter his style, and abbreviate his periods: I wonder whether he could not chasten his metaphors (which he is too apt to confuse with arguments) and prune and revise his many analogies[2]: I wonder, in particular, if he could not key down the pitch of his adjectives and modulate his thunders. (He sometimes reminds the reader of Cicero prosecuting Verres or Demosthenes denouncing Aeschines: he has a similar high-pitched rhetoric which suggests a set composition to be written in a given style.) Lastly, and more especially, I wonder whether Dr. Toynbee could not condescend more on particulars. Has he studied the evidence enough (the actual documents and the State-papers) before sitting in judgement on contemporary policies—such as, for instance, the policy of Great Britain in Palestine? Does he not fly too readily to theories about the past, without fully weighing the evidence? He speaks, for instance, in several contexts, of an Egyptian national reaction against the Ptolemies. I believe that the evidence of papyri shows that Greeks and Egyptians both felt the yoke of Ptolemaic bureaucracy, and that any movement of rebellion was a common movement of all the oppressed, both Greek and Egyptian, with no national bias. He regards the great church of Santa Sophia as due to Syriac (or Armenian) inspiration, and suggests that the change of architectural style which culminates in the reign of Justinian is due to a conscious and deliberate act producing a striking acceleration of the rate of change. A simpler explanation is the progressive development of the use of concrete in Roman building from the time of Nero onwards, which affected at once internal layout and external elevation.

But Dr. Toynbee has the qualities of his defects; and they are qualities of the first order. He has, first of all, a sweep of vision and a width of view which covers the whole of the course of ancient history down to the reign of Justinian. To the fruits of his Oxford training in that history he has since added an abundant study of

---

[2]The Seleucid Empire, for instance, is treated as analogous to the Russia of Peter the Great—and to several other things: The Holy Roman Empire as analogous to the Parthian; the Carthaginian dominions to the Spanish Empire in South America; Lenin's Communist party to the Sultan's slave-household; and so the list grows.

every aspect of classical antiquity, legal, military, institutional, economic, and whatever else there may be; and those early fruits and that later study have been the basis, in large measure, of his 'laws', his many analogies, and his recurrent generalizations. But his knowledge of ancient history is only part of his equipment. He is also armed with a knowledge of Oriental history, whether it be that of the ancient Hittites and Assyrians, or the general history of the Muslim world, or the long centuries of Chinese history, and we have still to mention, as we must presently, the range and sweep of his study of contemporary history—the contemporary history of the whole of the inhabited world. But before we turn to that theme it is permissible—indeed it is more than permissible; it is a bounden duty—to pay a tribute of deep admiration to the range of Dr. Toynbee's knowledge of the history of the past. It is perhaps at its best in his study(which comes in volume VII, under the head of 'Universal Empires') of the working of imperial institutions— roads, colonies, provinces, and capital cities; languages, laws, and calendars; armies and methods of civil administration. Here is a comparative study of institutions, widely based and deeply suggestive. No less admirable, in volume VIII, is the study of heroic ages (in which universal empires are at grips with the barbarians on their frontier), and the study, by which it is followed, of the contacts of modern Western Civilization with other contemporary civilizations. Here Dr. Toynbee is dealing with facts rather than with theories (though theories will 'come breaking in'); and the less he theorizes—or in other words the more he 'historizes'—the more the reader is in his debt.

There is another range of dimension to be added to this account of the general sweep of his mind. This is the range or dimension of contemporary history. Dr. Toynbee is, in a sense, ambidextrous. He carries and wields both the history of the past (studied and taught in his Oxford days, and never forgotten since) and also the history of the present (which has been his subject during the thirty years of his connexion with Chatham House): with one hand he elucidates the history of the Greco-Roman past, with the other he describes the present of the twentieth century, and with both he draws the two (the Past and the Present) into contact, analogy, and connexion under common laws. He has something of ambivalence as well as ambidexterity. He is enamoured of the present, but he denounces it (it is a home of parochial States and petrified churches); he loves the past and he hates it (for if you seek to exhume it, by magic of 'necromancy', it turns upon you and rends you). For myself, I could wish that he loved the past with a more undivided love—especially the English past. I could wish that he had mastered English history (including the history of parliament and that of the common law) as he has mastered Hellenistic and Oriental history. He would think more highly of the State and its institutions if he had studied the genesis and growth of English parliamentary institutions and the English common law, and had come to see the service they have rendered to freedom of choice and liberty of thought. As it is, he is content to regard all this as 'merely a local exception to the general course of political development in Western Christendom'. In the index the entry 'England' occupies only half a column, and 'Great Britain' only two columns: 'Egypt' has six.

It is impossible—or at any rate it is beyond the power of the present writer—to review these four volumes adequately. They are so abundantly full, even to over-flowing. A scholar of wide range would have noticed Dr. Toynbee's use of the psychological theories of Dr. Jung, whom he calls his 'navigator psychopompus' in the work of submarine sounding of the Unconscious Psyche. That—and much else—must be left aside; and the argument must now turn, in conclusion, to some general observations on his views about the nature and future of the State, the nature and function of the Church (or Churches), and the general prospects which lie before our Western Civilization. The State—at any rate in its present form based on the idea of the territorial nation—has little attraction for Dr. Toynbee. 'In the hierarchy of human institutions' (which, as we have seen, are in one context described as 'veritable slums'), 'the place of States in general must be a relatively low one.' Anti-State, he is also anti-national: 'modern Western nationalism is an archaistic throwback to a rustic parochial past . . . stamped as an untenable anachronism'. He is also anti-neighbourhood, as well as anti-State and anti-national: he does not love that bond of peace that comes from love of the natal soil and the quiet sense of neighbourliness: it is to him a tragedy that 'the physical accident of geographical propinquity', which is all that he sees, should be made a principle of political association instead of 'spiritual affinity'; and the tragedy is made all the worse, in his view, when the new spirit of democracy, impinging on 'territorial sovereignty embodied in parochial States', gives the geographical principle a 'fanatical intensity'. For the East, at any rate, the territorial nation-State—though it may conceivably be meat for the West—is in his view pure poison. Better the 'millet' system of the old Ottoman Empire —a system of socio-religious groups, each forming a non-territorial community, and all living inside some sort of State which is not a national State. 'The antiquated patch-work of ghetto-like nation States' has no future: 'the institutional future seems likely to lie . . . with the Syriac institution of the millet'. . . . One can only wonder. But meanwhile, whatever the future may be, this general *praejudi-*

cium gives a curious slant to Dr. Toynbee's view of the pasr. The past, the past of the last 700 years since the fatal emergence of the Emperor Frederic II, becomes an 'aberration'; and first the Reformation, and then the spread of Democracy, accentuates the aberration. . . . I can only marvel.

If Dr. Toynbee is repelled by the State, in its modern form, he is attracted by the Church—at any rate in the form of a comprehensive 'higher religion' which seems to transcend all churches. This higher religion is the great *telos* to which the movement of civilizations tends; and here, in his estimate of the role of religion in history, Dr. Toynbee confesses, as has already been noted, that he has changed his outlook during the last fifteen years. He has a deep feeling for monasticism (though he makes St. Benedict, and the Benedictine motto *laborare est orare,* the parents of the weary round of modern industrialism): he has an admiration for churches as vehicles of social justice and as 'a higher species of society'. Yet he does not belong to any church: he is a 'seeker' for something above churches—something which blends, 'transcends them all'. Sometimes he seems to the reviewer a Hebrew prophet, ingeminating woe, but promising beyond the woe the coming of the rainbow, or, as he calls it 'the bow in the cloud', in the shape of a new Joachimite reign of the Spirit. Sometimes he seems like a Catholic of the Middle Ages, but a Catholic without acceptance of the *fides Catholica* or the *ecclesia Catholica.* (A professing Catholic might say, 'I fear this Greek, even when he brings me gifts'.) Sometimes, again, with his feeling for the Mahayana form of Buddhism, he seems a Christian Buddhist—who is neither Christian nor Buddhist. The reader who wishes to get to the heart of Dr. Toynbee's feelings will do well to read the Litany, half Latin and half English, which is the real conclusion of his work (volume X, pp. 143-4). It will set him thinking—and wondering.

There is only space for a very brief mention of Dr. Toynbee's review of the prospects of Western civilization. His prophecy is mournful, but his analysis searching. In his view the progress of technology has dethroned the middle classes and antiquated the system of balance of power; it has given the future into the hands of the industrial masses and delivered man's fate to the keeping of the two sole surviving giants of power, the USA and the USSR. He analyses the logistics of power, at this crisis of fate, in a striking strategic survey of the general deployment of forces; but his trust is in the spirit, and not in power. The consolation he looks for is a change of heart, and the learning of men, through suffering, to put their trust and to find their stay in some higher religion of the future—a world-church which is the complement and the crown of a world secular order. Here the reviewer can do no more than follow dimly Dr. Toynbee's flight into the far clouds, and then—turning his own eyes back to the familiar earth—muse on the final impressions which remain stamped in his mind.

Reading Dr. Toynbee's four volumes, during these last four weeks, I have felt that I was not walking in the familiar chambers of a House of Time that I knew: I was treading the 'vasty halls' of a system of categories which, to me, were the fabric of a vision. I must confess that I prefer the House of Time in which I have lived since I began to study history, nearly seventy years ago. I accept the past, in gratitude, and I believe that it has made for righteousness in the course of its long movement. I do not believe that history went wrong, from the reign of Frederic II onwards, with the appearance of 'parochial and ephemeral' national States copying old parochial and ephemeral city-States. I confess, indeed, that both the ancient city-State and the modern nation-State have suffered from the defect of seeking to be 'close' societies: and I want instead, an 'open' society. But my open society is still a national society—a generous and inclusive national society, with arms wide open for free churches and free societies living comfortably in its shelter. I would liberalize, and not transcend, the modern national State: I would not fly from it to the arms of an 'open' world-society, which might be a close society of uniform stagnation. The salt virtues of life are variety and versatility (*poikilia* and *eutrapelia*) —the virtues that Pericles celebrated and Plato held to be vices. My desire is for the many-coloured energetic play of a plurality of open national States. That, of course, is not enough. I want—we all want—a sense of 'humanity' as well as a sense of 'nationality'—or, in Dr. Toynbee's words, the 'oecumenical' as well as the 'parochial'. Let us have both, without sacrificing either on the altar of the other. A true universal society has room for particulars; indeed it cannot exist without them. A true universal society of humanity will have room for self-governing national units, each with its own way of life: otherwise it will be simply a bracket, with nothing enclosed in the bracket.

To accept the past, with all its units and all its particulars, is not to abandon the universal. The need for the universal was deep in the heart of Alexander of Macedon, twenty-three centuries ago, when he made concord (which he called *homonoia*) his watchword: it was deep in the mind of Zeno of Cyprus, when he preached the brotherhood of man in the city of Zeus. The past is deep enough, and broad enough, to nerve us for the future. We need its strength and stay. To me, at any rate, the whole travail of the world hitherto—its bank and capital of accumulated reason and insight, expressed in the institutions which it has built—is an abiding comfort. Man needs the great coral-reefs slowly raised in time for his

foundation—the national State, with its supporting body of law
and its sustaining sentiment of loyalty to the rules of law: the
organized church (even the organized national church, and indeed
not least that form of church), with its great supporting body of
scriptures, creed, and discipline which have kept it firm through
the ages, and with its sustaining sentiment of faith in the body of its
tradition.

In a word, being old myself, I accept the wisdom of the ages—
only hoping and praying that the best of that wisdom (for it is not
all equally wise) may prevail more and more, and that men may
choose more and more clearly the best of the fruits of time.

STUDY OF TOYNBEE

A PERSONAL VIEW OF HISTORY*

Early in the Palaeolithic Age one of the first philosophers, who had been badly frightened by a bear, began to meditate on the question of human mortality.

"It is true (he said) that all the men I have known or heard about have died at a relatively early age, some by accident, some killed by bears, and some for no apparent cause. But this is no reason to suppose that there is any inherent necessity in death. On the contrary, we know that men are free, with the aid of the spirits, to choose the sort of life they wish. The roots of death must lie far deeper.

"Now we observe," he continued, "that all men up to date have been vain and quarrelsome, perhaps not continuously, but certainly at some point in their lives. This angers the spirits. Sooner or later, they kill us, either by sending bears or by allowing the evil thoughts to ferment inside us until they boil up in fits and fevers, by which we are no less certainly destroyed. Evil and selfish thoughts are the cause of death; there can be no doubt about it.

"And what of my own case? It is true that I too have been vain and quarrelsome at times, and only last week I carelessly killed by brother in a fit of temper. But I am usually kind to my children and I have invented a new kind of hand-axe. Above all, when I think of my guardian spirit, I have a warm sense of personal assurance. It may be that if I succeed in controlling my temper I shall go on living indefinitely. Perhaps I should even be kind to bears."

It is not recorded whether our philosopher was eventually slain by a bear or whether he lived to a robust old age, but it is certain that he is no longer among the living.

* * *

Dr. Toynbee can scarcely be described as a simple-minded savage. His vast learning, his unflagging industry, the graces of his literary style, his moderation and urbanity, all these must command our admiration and respect. And yet when we seek to discover the bare bones of his theory beneath the rich, ample and variegated flesh of his *Study of History* (the concluding four volumes of which have now been published) we find reasoning not

---

The Times Literary Supplement, No. 2751, 22 October 1954, pp. 665-666. All reviews in *The Times Literary Supplement* are anonymous.

unlike our primitive philosopher's. He has taken Spengler's thesis that there is a regular pattern of growth and decay in the history of civilizations and, rejecting Spengler's organic analogy, recast his pattern in moral terms.

Civilizations, Dr. Toynbee says, are destroyed not by any organic necessity but by their own sinfulness. Men are *a priori* free, after all, under God to create the sort of society they please. Early in the growth-phase of a civilization, the men of which it is composed turn away from God and begin to worship themselves or their petty parochial States. They begin to fight among themselves and this is a sin, an act of *hubris*. Once they have experienced this moral breakdown their nemesis is certain. One war leads to another in a bitter crescendo; irreligion spreads, and though towards the end one State prevails over all the rest and establishes universal peace, it is too late. Society is rotten to the core; it is already disintegrating. Its life may indeed be "unnaturally prolonged" for some hundred or even thousands of years, but its doom is nevertheless inevitable. There is only one ray of light in all this. Out of their sufferings during the death-throes of a civilization the oppressed "internal proletariat" bring forth a new religion, which serves eventually as the "chrysalis" of a new civilization.

This central thesis is reinforced by a vast hodge-podge of subsidiary theories, arguments and explanations, which are by no means always mutually compatible. There is some geopolitics, some economic determinism, some Jungian and some Toynbeean psychology; there are analogies drawn from mechanics, electromagnetics and everyday life; there are even some organic analogies. Most prominent perhaps are the moral antitheses derived from mythology, poetry and in a few important instances, like "challenge and response" or "rout-rally-rout," from the ethics of the playing field, itself, of course, a schoolboy version of late Victorian muscular Christianity.

*   *   *

Such a diversity of explanations might not be unsuitable to a disconnected series of impressionistic essays, where they could be valued for their suggestiveness rather than their validity. But in a work that purports to be systematic, comprehensive and empirical the effect on the reader can only be one of bewilderment. He finds himself plunged into a tropical jungle or a *bal masqué,* where the beauty of the forms is only equalled by their elusiveness.

This wealth of theory is paralleled by an almost equal poverty of subject matter. For Dr. Toynbee, history is still primarily political and military history. And even here it is not so much the forms of political and military life which concern him as the drab sequence of rulers, dynasties and States and the melancholy tale of the horrors by which *peripeteia* is accompanied. Even the spread of culture and religion are described in military terms. Such pre-occupation with violence might seem puzzling in so pronounced a pacifist and humanitarian if Freud had not taught us the meaning of ambivalence. Where, one might ask, except for a few passing references, are the arts and sciences? Where is philosophy and technology? Where the slow growth of trade and industry, of civil order and domestic peace? Are not these the very stuff and tex-ture of civilization? We need scarcely wonder that, on so limited a view, history should seem to Dr. Toynbee, as to Gibbon, "little more than the register of the crimes, follies and misfortunes of Mankind."

When we attempt to evaluate Dr. Toynbee's central thesis and to test its empirical validity, we find that we have set ourselves an impossible task. None of his major concepts is sufficiently well defined to permit us to judge when it applies and when it does not. His rather inadequate definition of a civilization as "an intelligible field of historical study" is tacitly abandoned in the first few pages of the first volume. He himself is unable to judge whether the Egyptian "Old Kingdom" was in a stage of growth or disintegra-tion. Nor in the most crucial instance, where the available infor-mation is overwhelming, is he able to determine whether our own, the western civilization, has yet experienced a "breakdown" or experienced it during the wars of religion some 400 years ago. If a father cannot control his own children, should a stranger interfere?

*   *   *

If we turn to examine particular instances where Dr. Toynbee tries to prove one of his points, we find that he gives a few ex-amples drawn from history and that often other and quite contrary examples are readily available. Frequently his point is made at the price of a radical distortion of the facts. Even the non-specialist must find it inappropriate to call the T'ang Dynasty a "vampire-state" or Mohamed a "conspicuously unsuccessful prophet." Can the whole of western painting from Giotto to Cézanne be dismissed as a "resuscitated Hellenic naturalism?" (An instructive example of how these distortions come about is given in one of the ap-pendices to Volume VII where letters from the late B. H. Sumner and Prince Dimitri Obolensky are reprinted, in which they point out that, as a matter of fact, the concept of Moscow as "the Third Rome" never had much currency in Russia outside ecclesiastical circles. In his reply, Dr. Toynbee insists that, nevertheless, the fall of Byzantium must have firmly implanted this belief in Russian souls, citing as his only evidence a fact—if it is a fact—drawn not from Russian but from Byzantine and Jewish history.)

It would be unwise to insist too much on these faults. Although it has never received a thorough and objective empirical study, there certainly seems to be some evidence for Dr. Toynbee's (and Spengler's) thesis that there is a regular pattern of development of civilizations. If we take the sequence: "growth of a set of small states," "Time of Troubles," "universal state" as our criterion, examples can be found in the early histories of China and India, in Babylonia, Middle America and Peru, in classical antiquity and (only partially exemplified) in the recent history of the west. If the coordinate growth and development of culture is used as the key, Egypt may be included as well but not, so far as one can see, any of the rest of Dr. Toynbee's twenty-one (or twenty-three) civilizations.

*   *   *

There does not appear, however, to be any evidence for Dr. Toynbee's principal contention that civilizations die because men have lost their faith and taken up arms against one another. Even the evidence as he presents it would lead one to accept the opposite (and psychologically far more probable) contention, which has been upheld by Spengler, Polybius and a host of others, that civilizations die not of war but of peace and inanition. Does not their death, even according to Dr. Toynbee's marshalling of the facts, occur some centuries *after* the establishment of a universal State which brings with it an "oecumenical peace"? Yet the truth is probably that civilizations die neither of peace nor of war; they do not die at all. Dr. Toynbee has not, it seems, done away with every vestige of the organic analogy. Civilizations, after all, are neither organisms nor fields of inquiry nor schools of immorality. They are simply ways of life, sets of beliefs and values which find expression in the various forms and products of social life. And we may suppose that when they are fully developed, they do not die; they simply persist until superseded by another and more attractive way of life. Aside from the misleading example of Rome, the histories of the seven non-western civilizations we have mentioned on the whole bear out this supposition. It is far too early for the west to despair.

And what of the contention that universal States give birth to universal religions which in turn give birth to new civilizations? In three out of his four cases Dr. Toynbee proves his point by conveniently dividing what would normally be regarded as the "life span" of one civilization (the Chinese, the Indian, or the Muslim) in half. The earlier half can serve as the "mother" civilization and the later half as the "daughter." His fourth example, that of Ancient Rome, is more difficult. Most probably we should look on the spread of Christianity as part of a concurrent spread of ideas, styles and even population from the Middle East—this is, as part of the rise of a new civilization. But this argument is far too complex and technical to go into here. It is true, of course, that the spread of a universal religion in several instances takes place soon after the establishment of a universal State, but should we not look on them both as products of a single urge towards a synthesis and uniformity?

Perhaps the fundamental objection here is that, for the student of history, religion can neither be the progenitor nor, *pace* Gibbon, the destroyer of civilizations. It is merely a part or aspect of civilization, one of those systems of practice and belief which go to make up a way of life. It cannot be isolated from its social and cultural context and turned into a primary agent. In holding this, we need not deny that religion satisfies some fundamental human need. We may even hold that the varieties of religious practice all serve to bring men into touch with ultimate metaphysical reality. Dr. Toynbee himself maintains, in a striking metaphor, that the various religions are but differing veils through which we perceive the one Light of God. Yet in an empirical study we must look on these veils as phenomena occurring in a particular time and place.

* * *

If Dr. Toynbee's theories seem to have little basis in fact, they are no less questionable on moral and theological grounds. The classic instance of "moral breakdown" for Dr. Toynbee is the Atheno-Peloponnesian War which eventually brought about the fall of the Roman Empire. Surely, in theology as well as in natural philosophy, a cause must be proximate as well as adequate to its effect. It would have been cold comfort for a Romanized Briton about to be submerged by the barbarian hordes to be told that he was paying for the sins of the Athenian mob nearly 1,000 years earlier. One of the first lessons of history, as of life, must be that Divine justice is not done in *this* world. The wicked flourish, and it rains on the just and unjust alike. The great religions have been wise in providing for rewards and punishments in another place.

Yet the problem of evil has more subtleties and complexities than any simple system of rewards and punishments can resolve. Sometimes, the sin of *hubris* and every failure to act the opposite sin of "resting on one's oars." The only virtuous action is self-sacrifice. Christ, Socrates and Lycurgus died that others might live; the bodhisattvas, like Plato's philosopher, have chosen to return to the cave. And so civilizations must die that new civilizations may be born. There is a profound intuition here of a broad moral and psychological truth to which empirical facts are almost irrelevant. Does not every creative act involve both violence and suffering? Must we not *payer de nos personnes,* if not harm others, in everything we do? Do we not see everywhere, in animal life and in plant life, as much as in human life, perhaps even also in the inanimate world of physics a constant dissolution and transcendence? It is this interpretation of the meaning of the Cross which may well be Dr. Toynbee's most lasting contribution to our moral understanding.

In investigating the forms of human history, however, theological and moral considerations must be as firmly put aside as in the study of physics or biology. The philosopher of history who studies the behaviour of men in other centuries and other lands is pecularily prone to being misled by his personal prejudices or those of his own cultural *milieu.* It is perhaps for this reason that we are still in the palaeolithic Age of the science of human affairs. Yet this is no cause for despair. The small but definite progress which has been made in anthropology, in sociology and in psychology in the last hundred years should give us hope. And in spite of Spengler's Teutonic extravagance, his intuition, which he derived from Hegel, Herder and perhaps ultimately Vico, that all historical events can be seen as the expression of differing cultural *ethoi* may yet provide the elusive key to our confusion. A morphology of cultural and social forms and a general theory of culture-change may serve to reduce many of the puzzling phenomena to order.

* * *

The last four volumes add little to Dr. Toynbee's central theory. "Universal States," we learn, are doomed from the start, but their administrative arrangements serve to facilitate the spread of universal religions. "Heroic Ages" are evil, yet they did help to bring forth civilizations of "the second generation." "Contacts between Civilizations in Space" provide occasions for *hubris.* "Contacts in Time," more usually known as Renaissances, are mere necromancy; the raising of a ghost of the past solves nothing. In another section there are some pertinent criticisms of the antinomianism of modern historians; nevertheless, Dr. Toynbee feels, the laws of history may be transcended in the "Law of God which is perfect Freedom," thus turning a moral insight into an epistemological principle which makes all reasoning impossible.

It is in the section on "Universal Churches" in Volume VII that Dr. Toynbee's theories show the most surprising new development. Civilizations, as we learnt before, in dying give birth to new "universal" religions. But the West is actually, not metaphorically, universal; its extension is world-wide. Out of its death-throes, therefore, there is likely to be born a truly universal religion which will also be a "higher form of society." The four higher religions—Christianity, Hinduism, Buddhism and Islam—will be united, without losing their diversity, in a choral harmony in which Christianity will carry the tune. War and class-conflict will disappear; the State will be separate from, yet subordinate to, the Church. All men will turn to God and the Communion of Saints will become a reality on earth as well as in Heaven.

The mask of the "post-Modern Western student of History" has been dropped in these passages; it seems that we have been dealing all along with the prophet of a new apocalypse, the evangelist of a syncretic higher "higher religion." One might suppose that the evidence of history, as well as the teachings of the more enduring religions, would have led Dr. Toynbee to conclude that the Kingdom of Heaven is not yet, and not indeed until the end of time. A thousand prophets have proclaimed a thousand apocalypses and not one has seen his dream come true. But a prophet, of course, is not concerned with evidence; he is carried along by his own burning zeal, unaware that he is merely expressing his personal aspirations and those of his country and epoch. Dr. Toynbee's religion is no less time-bound; it is pacifist, humanitarian and eclectic—Liberalism reinforced by a personal version of mystical Christianity. For all that he professes to reject the Enlightenment, our new prophet is none the less its child and its disciple.

* * *

Perhaps we have been unfair to Dr. Toynbee's work in treating it as a study of history. We should have thought of it as the record of one soul's pilgrimage—a kind of *Umana Commedia*. At times, indeed, we might have been exploring one of those eclectic and yet intensely private systems of symbols, of which the Theosophists, the Jungians, and Mr. Robert Graves have provided the most recent examples. How else indeed should we take a sentence like this:

> In the field of encounters in the Time-dimension an Antaean rebound that wins from Necromancy an anticipatory communion with the Future has its antithesis in an Atlantean stance in which a Necromancer who has yielded to the legendary Epimethean impulse of Lot's wife is petrified by the hypnotic state of a resuscitated corpse's Medusan countenance into the rigidity of a pillar of salt pinned down by the incubus of the Past.

And what of those loving recitations of exotic names? "Nish, Uskub and Prizren." "The Saka Haumavarga and the Saka Tigrakhauda." "Kin and Sung and Tangut; Qara Qitay and Khwar-izm; Naiman and Karayit." Are not these magic charms with which to fend off the assaults of the ungodly?

Our *pelegrinus Wiccamicus,* as he calls himself, has perambu-lated all the high ways and byways of space and time. Finding them filled with a beautiful, fascinating, yet deadly violence, he has clung all the more firmly to the feet of the Crucifix. Against the day of Pentecost, he preserves the virtues of his childhood: the modesty, the tolerance, the industry, the soft answer not unmixed with manliness. If we cannot share, we cannot fail to admire the purity and steadfastness of his faith. The wise, serene and kindly face which gazes at us from the back covers of these volumes sug-gests that it is better to be a displaced Victorian than a disillusioned child of the times. In a moving passage which close the ninth volume Dr. Toynbee prays that he may follow Saint Francis and like him receive the stigmata. What can one say to this? Words fail.

And yet . . . and yet . . . to the *homme moyen pécheur* such con-cern for spiritual perfection must always seem a bit Pharisaical. Can it be right to refuse to soil one's hand in the market-place and on the battlefield? Did not Christ bring a sword and Krishna in-struct his votary to fight? Surely a saint would not be indifferent to the patient efforts of countless generations to improve their material welfare and express their hopes and fears? Is not the de-nunciation of evil also an act of *hubris? "Asperges me hyssopo,"* is Dr. Toynbee's closing cry, *"et mundabor,"* to which both the scientist and the mystic must reply: *Omnia munda mundis.*

Future philosophers of history will find in the many volumes of Dr. Toynbee's vast work much curious information, some sug-gestive hypotheses and a rich hoard of colourful metaphors. Most of all, we may suppose, they will judge it as a deeply felt personal vision of the historical process, a vision which expresses the despair of a liberal who has seen the liberal dream turn to ashes as well as the hope of a liberal who has turned again to God.

HISTORICAL CONSEQUENCES AND HAPPY FAMILIES*

LAWRENCE STONE

With this further nine pounds weight of closely printed text, Dr. Toynbee's great work is virtually complete, apart from a volume of maps and gazetteer that is still to come. Properly, these four latest volumes should be reviewed by a metaphysician, within whose field so much of their subject matter falls. But since Dr. Toynbee has always claimed to be an historian—and an empirical historian at that—he must be taken at his word and judged accordingly.

The very varied reactions that have greeted the earlier volumes are likely to be still more strongly reinforced by the new material. By the public at large his book is already regarded as the supreme historical achievement of the twentieth century: a compendium of all the significant facts about the life of man throughout the world for the last 6,000 years, a revelation of the natural laws in obedience to which civilisations rise and fall, and a work of prophecy by which may be unlocked the secrets of the future.

In violent contrast to this popular impression is the careless indifference or active hostility with which Dr. Toynbee's work is— and will probably continue to be—regarded by his professional colleagues. In one of the volumes under review, these historians— 'Late Modern Western Antinomians'—are roundly castigated as a set of fuddled obscurantists and are compared, unflatteringly, with the ducks on the Round Pond in Kensington Gardens. It is none the less worth considering the reasons for their attitude.

In the first place the questions Dr. Toynbee asks are largely irrelevant to their concept of the proper study of history, which consists in studying the past for its own sake, in attempting to understand and differentiate, to arrange and classify, the discoverable facts about the nature of a given society in a given period. They are convinced that the differences between civilisations are more significant than the likenesses, and that standardised causal patterns cannot logically be deduced from the facts of history. The fundamental objection to Dr. Toynbee's theorising is well summed up by Sir Llewelyn Woodward: 'We know so many facts which lend themselves to arrangements in patterns that we can make any number of such patterns; but we do not know enough to judge between these patterns, or to be sure that we are doing more than pick out chance or superficial resemblances.' Such an attitude of

*The Spectator, (London), 29 October 1954, pp. 526-528.

sceptical humility is uncharitably dismissed by Dr. Toynbee as 'a camouflage of the three deadly sins of Satantic pride, undutiful negligence, and culpable sloth.'

What repels the opponents of Dr. Toynbee is not that he professes to have discovered the secret of the rise and fall of all civilisations. Nor is it even that he claims to be able to arrange societies 'in a serial order to ascending value,' meting out rewards and punishments like a divine schoolmaster, a silver cup to Primitive Christianity, consolation prizes to the churches, and six with the cane to contemporary western agnostic and materialist civilisation. The offence is that all this purports to be the logical conclusions of a dispassionate, scientific study of the events of history. It is this inability to distinguish unverifiable presuppositions and subjective value-judgments from empirical deductions from the facts, that makes Dr. Toynbee's work so suspect to the academic historian or philosopher.

Nor does the methodology inspire confidence. Stupendous, indeed unique, as is the range of Dr. Toynbee's learning, nearly every specialist bears witness that, so far as his own limited field of knowledge is concerned, guesses are elevated into certainties and conclusions drawn from incomplete or partially selected evidence. Dr. Toynbee has struggled heroically against modern fragmentation of knowledge, failing to realise that such fragmentation is as inevitable a corollary to increased information as the division of labour to increased production. Everyone is vaguely aware what revolutions in our knowledge of ancient civilisations have been achieved by archaeology in the last thirty-five years. It is disquieting therefore to observe how little of his information Dr. Toynbee appears to have drawn from material published much later than 1920. It is evident that little attempt has been made to sift through the mass of excavation reports in which so much of the new discoveries is embedded. It may be objected that over so vast a field such a task is impossible for one man to achieve. Precisely! That is just what the historians hold against Dr. Toynbee. They argue that 6,000 pages of arbitrarily selected facts torn out of their contexts, of speculative possibilities dressed up as certainties, are of little help in advancing the frontiers of knowledge or increasing the range of understanding.

For all its mass and weight, the scholarly apparatus that accompanies the argument is not much more reassuring. As a result, the flaunting of the gift of tongues, the gratuitous use of classical and oriental terms where plain English would serve, the pedantic footnotes with their autobiographical minutiae, and the battery of 'Annexes,' seem designed more to dazzle the ignorant than to enlighten the learned. Finally it is hard to detect in Dr. Toynbee's turgid and prolix pages those qualities of style and expression that give the writings of a Raleigh or a Macaulay an imperishable place in our literature.

Much of these new volumes is taken up with the now familiar games of Historical Consequences and Happy Families, played with the same twenty-one-card pack of Civilisations. Agile as a gibbon, Dr. Toynbee skips rapidly from branch to branch of the historical tree, shaking down its mysterious fruit and arranging them in predetermined patterns. It is a struggle sometimes, but he usually manages to squeeze them in. Much of European history is fitted neatly into place as a 'Time of Troubles (c. AD 1378-1797)' followed by a *'Pax Oecumenica* (AD 1797-1814),' established by 'Marchmen (from France).' If this is how familiar events are made to fit their Procrustean bed, what horrible mutilations have been inflicted, one wonders, upon the more recondite stories of Sumer and Babylon, Inca and Minos? As for those items that just can't be made to fit, they are quietly tossed into the huge garbage heap of discarded facts—pigswill for old Dry-as-Dust, who will be content to spend a lifetime trying to digest a mouthful or two.

The first of these volumes is concerned with the inevitable manifestations of civilisations in decay: Heroic Ages, universal states and universal churches. For in the deterministic language of biology a Civilisation still has 'its natural term of life.' But Dr. Toynbee has now completely changed his mind about the role of religion. Instead of being one of the features of a collapsing civilisation, a higher religion now becomes the sole true objective of history, the unique end to which God is leading Man. So Dr. Toynbee stands his previous edifice on its head. In the new perspective 'civilisations . . . have ceased to constitute intelligible fields of study for us and have forfeited their historical significance except in so far as they minister to the progress of Religion.' To Dr. Toynbee, History is now 'a vision of God's creation on the move, from God its source to God its Goal.' His publishers, conscious of the difficulties raised by this new interpretation, have explained on the dustcover that certain crucial sections of these volumes 'cannot be approached without looking beyond the bounds of life on the Earth.' We are here a long way from the scientific, analytical, historian which Dr. Toynbee set out to be.

Ruminations on our present state and our future prospects take up most of the other volumes. Were it not that he finds it hard to believe that God would allow the worst to happen, Dr. Toynbee does not appear to think that the outlook is very hopeful. He speculates at length on the possibility of a reconciliation of Religion and Science and a unification of the four higher religions, but his conclusions are not entirely clear to this reviewer. He ends with a section on the Inspirations of Historians. Readers seeking the fundamental differences in character, method, and objectives between Dr. Toynbee and his academic colleagues, should compare these egocentric musings with the modest, lucid, rational, but moving declaration of faith in his profession by the great French historian Marc Bloch (recently published in translation in this country).

What, then, has Dr. Toynbee achieved in these ten massive volumes? His most important and enduring legacy, both to historians and to the general public, will unquestionably be his success in dragging them out of their parochial European background and letting them view world history in a more detached perspective. The achievement is all the more remarkable because Dr. Toynbee is himself so deeply affected by much that is best in our western civilisation: he is to the root of his being a classicist, a humanitarian, and—in a very individual way—a Christian.

Secondly he has provided, for those who like such toys, another of those speculative frameworks into which to fit the processes of historical change. He is undoubtedly assured of immortality, along with Marx and Spengler, as one of the leading philosophers of history. But to some of his academic colleagues, it is one of the tragedies of our time that for over thirty years the prodigious gifts with which Dr. Toynbee is unquestionably endowed—unquenchable curiosity, phenomenal memory, tireless industry, and vivid imagination—should have been devoted to the futile pursuit of this Will-o'-the wisp.

MUCH LEARNING . . .*

A. J. P. TAYLOR

Twenty years ago Professor Toynbee published the first three volumes of his Study of History. In these he discussed how civilisations originated and traced the process of their growth. Five years later there followed three more volumes, in which he described the breakdown and disintegrations of civilisations. Now, after a long interruption, he has completed his plan. First, he winds up the historical part of his work by examining in more detail certain institutions which in his view accompany the disintegration of civilisation—universal states, universal churches, and heroic barbarians beyond the pale; and he discusses the contacts that have taken place between different civilisations both in space and time. Finally, abandoning the role of historian for the more congenial one of prophet and moral teacher, he asserts the validity of historical laws and speculates on the prospects for western civilisation.

It is late in the day to debate the merits of the "Toynbee method." The general public has given one answer; the professional historians another. The first six volumes have broken all records as best-sellers; they rank second only to whisky as a dollar-earner. The scepticism of historians seems of small account in comparison. Yet a professional scholar would be false to his conscience and his calling if he did not raise his voice in dissent, however ineffectual, and if he did not declare that this is not history as he understands it. Professor Toynbee's method is not that of scholarship, but of the lucky dip, with emphasis on the luck. His book bears the same relation to history that Burton's *Anatomy of Melancholy* does to a modern work of psychology; and it is less entertaining. The events of the past can be made to prove anything if they are arranged in a suitable pattern; and Professor Toynbee has succeeded in forcing them into a scheme that was in his head from the beginning. Though he claimed to be making a comparative study of twenty-one different civilisations, his scheme was, in fact, a generalisation from the history of the Ancient World. First came independent states, warring against each other in a Time of Troubles; then the Universal State of the Roman empire; and finally, in consequence, breakdown and disintegration. If other civilisations failed to fit into this pattern, they were dismissed as

*The New Statesman and Nation, (London), 16 October 1954, pp. 479-80.

abortive, ossified, or achieving a wrong-headed *tour de force*. Yet the generalisation applied only to one part of the Roman world. The Roman empire survived at Constantinople. Therefore a break-down had to be discovered here also; and the Byzantine empire had to be described not as a continuation, but as a new civilisation.

Professor Toynbee is endlessly fertile in discovering historical "laws" and in seeing to it that they operate. As he explains, a historian should not fumble with his keys when he encounters a new lock; he should add a new key to his ring. But from this moment the key is ostentatiously displayed as a universal solver of puzzles. For instance, Professor Toynbee discovers the "law" that North America was not to be united under a single political author-ity; then History steps in and operates the law for him.

> During the War of A. D. 1812-14, no less than during the War of A. D. 1775-83, History kept a watchful eye open to make sure that the United States of North America should not surrepti-tiously put Canada into her pocket.

And again:

> the eventually frustrated nisus towards unity was favoured by physiological forces which were as potent as they were obvious, whereas the ultimately victorious inclination towards partition was History's "dark horse" in the field.

Does this spate of words explain anything or make the historical development of North America clearer? On the contrary, it blud-geons the reader into insensibility so that he is ready to accept anything for the sake of stemming the torrent. In the earlier vol-umes the analogies and asides had a fascination in themselves; and the best parts were those which Mr. Somervell cut out in his systematised abridgement. Now adjectives are piled on with all the ruthlessness which the Egyptians used when building the pyramids. Capitals, quotations, biblical references follow one another in a remorseless drumming.

Not only is the method remote from historical scholarship. The book is not designed to serve a historical purpose. Professor Toynbee may insist—repeatedly, of course— that he is interested in the historian's question: "How did this come out of that?" In fact, his peepshow of history is so much preliminary to answering quite a different question: "What will come out of the present this?" In his earlier volumes he was already hinting at the answer. The Time of Troubles in the Ancient World ended in a Universal State (the capitals follow Professor Toynbee's practice). There-fore our Time of Troubles, which apparently began—for no par-ticular reason—in A.D. 1552, will also end in a Universal State. Stagnation will produce disintegration, and all that remains will be a Universal Church, springing not from the Dominant Minority, but from the proletariat. Professor Toynbee did not altogether like this answer; and he therefore suggested that the Roman Catholic Church, being no human institution but the one divine revelation of God, would save us from future upsets after all.

This answer, too, he no longer favours. He still forsees the Universal State, imposed upon mankind by the atom-bomb. With a shortsightedness curious in a far-ranging historian, he insists that, since there are now only two Great Powers in the world, there will never be more; and that one of them will destroy the other, if they do not merge by agreement. The Universal State will provide men with peace and, according to Professor Toynbee's new-found enthusiasm for economics, with prosperity. But what will men do with their Leisure in this "Commonwealth of Swine"? This is the question which now racks him. He answers: they will meditate upon religion. But it will no longer be Roman Catholicism or even Christianity; it will be an amalgam of every known religion. Professor Toynbee is no longer a Christian. Mr. Martin Wight conducts a prolonged debate with him in footnotes and finally wrings from him the reluctant confession: "I do not believe that Christianity or any other higher religion is an exclusive and definitive revelation of Spiritual Truth." The Roman Church, it seems, is too rigid and dogmatic; its worst fault has been its refusal to preach artificial birth-control to the peoples of the East.

The religion for our future meditations will be a mish-mash of the Virgin Mary and Mother Isis, of St. Michael and Mithras, of St. Peter and Muhammad, of St. Augustine and Jalal-ad-Din Mawlana. The great thing is that it should be religion. Professor Toynbee finds the guideline of History "in a progressive increase in the provision of spiritual opportunities for human souls in transit through This World." He has "an intuition" that

> the 'universal churches' embodying the 'higher religions' were not merely the latest type of human society that had made its appearance up to date but were also an apter vehicle than either civilization or primitive societies for helping human beings to make their pilgrim's progress towards the goal of human endeavours.

The echo from Bunyan is not accidental. These monstrous volumes with their parade of learning are a repudiation of Rationalism. The worst sin is to believe that Man made himself. Gibbon and Frazer are numbered among the damned. Faith, or to put it more bluntly, Superstition, is the only thing that will save us from the Wrath to Come. Professor Toynbee is emphatically not among those who hold that it is better to doubt in Hell than to believe in Heaven. With his taste for quotations, he might reflect that Fear is a bad counsellor, and even perhaps a bad historian.

THE PROSPECTS OF THE WESTERN WORLD*

Geoffrey Barraclough

'In this book', wrote Spengler in *The Decline of the West,* 'is attempted for the first time the venture of following the still untravelled stages in the destiny of a Culture, and specifically of the only Culture . . . which is actually in the phase of fulfilment'—the culture and civilisation of the West.

For all Dr. Toynbee's distrust of Spengler's methods and conclusions, these words of his predecessor accurately describe the ultimate object he set himself, some thirty years ago, when he began his *Study of History.* It was, he tells us, 'an attempt to take bearings in the uncharted seas of a post-Modern chapter of Western history'; and because, for Toynbee, history is action, this object was never lost to view, however far from 'post-Modern' times he ranged. The identification and analysis of all known civilisations, their genesis and growth, their breakdown and disintegration, in the six volumes which appeared in 1939, was essentially a preliminary task; it was undertaken (and here the difference from Spengler is marked) not for its own sake, but to establish 'laws' (if 'laws' there were) and parallels, in the light of which to evaluate the prospects of the West. Could the comparative study of civilisations—thirty in number (according to Toynbee's count), if all abortive and arrested civilisations were taken into reckoning —cast light on the course our own was taking, as it waltzed erratically through the twentieth century? For of twenty-one civilisations which had run full course twenty were dead or *in articulo mortis.* What could we learn of the expectations of the twenty-first from the fate of the other 'representatives of its species'?

The question was, in any case, urgent enough for us, 'the children of a post-Christian world', in the 'Time of Troubles' of our 'post-Modern age of Western history'; and there is no shame in confessing, now that the immense feat of concluding the *Study of History* has been accomplished, that our first concern is to see what answer Dr. Toynbee gives to it. What, then, in his view, are 'the prospects of the Western civilisation'? What, in the perspective of 5,000 years, does he make of its 'expectations of life' half-way through the twentieth century.

Beyond all doubt, Dr. Toynbee finds, Western civilisation today exhibits 'authentic symptoms of breakdown and disintegration'.

The Listener, (London), 14 October 1954, p. 639.

He analyses 'Western Society's progressive economic defeat since the Industrial Revolution', traces the eclipse of the middle-classes, the growth of 'cultural proletarianisation', the 'spiritual wilderness' in which we live. Physical science, 'a series of socially and morally subversive intellectual discoveries', has 'armed a perpetually reborn Original Sin with a weapon potent enough to enable a sinful Mankind to annihilate itself'. On the one hand, Western civilisation is 'in imminent danger of destroying itself by failing to stop making war'; on the other hand, it is 'in hardly less imminent danger of stultifying itself by seeking asylum from War and Class-Conflict in Circe's pig-sty'—that is to say, in the rigid confinement of a universal state. A 'world-government', Dr. Toynbee believes, is 'eventually inevitable'; yet the history of other civilisations demonstrates that 'this barbarous remedy for a desperate malady' was able neither 'to save the sick civilisation's life' nor 'to rid a war-stricken world of war in perpetuity'. If 'Mankind is to find a happy issue out of an impending affliction', the only thing that can save it is 'a change of heart', a 'fresh religious revolution'. But since 'there is no hope in returning to a traditional faith after it has once been abandoned', the answer is not a mere revival of 'Christian orthodoxy'. Rather, it seems, Dr. Toynbee looks forward to some new syncretism, a fusion of Muslim and Christian, Buddhist and Hindu, for our salvation. In this way, he believes, it is 'conceivable that a re-transfer of energy from Economics to Religion' may 'ultimately come to a self-stultified Western *Homo Economicus'* rescue'; at all events 'this happy spiritual prospect' is 'at least a possibility' in which 'a dispirited generation of Western men and women' may 'catch a beckoning gleam of kindly light.'

'A beckoning gleam of kindly light'? It seems unlikely. As Dr. Toynbee himself insists, Christianity and the other 'universal churches' rose by absorbing 'energy transmitted by a disintegrating civilisation', which they transmitted to 'another civilisation that had germinated in the transmissionary church's womb'. Does this betoken the 'rescue' of Western *'Homo Economicus'*, or does it not rather indicate that he will be trodden underfoot as a stepping-stone to higher things? When Dr. Toynbee writes that the 'first chapter of Western history might perhaps repeat itself', what can this mean except that Western civilisation will be superseded, as Western civilisation itself superseded Rome? Is this what Dr. Toynbee wishes to suggest, in the Delphic utterance terminating his oracular vision of 'The Straits Ahead', when he writes of 'the knowledge that comes only through suffering' and the 'sacrifice . . . accepted by the Lord'? I suspect it is, for elsewhere he states, with breath-taking oblivion to the enormous genocide involved, 'that the breakdown of a civilisation is not a catastrophe if it is the

overture to a church's birth'. Churches, he protests, do not exist
simply in order to keep civilisations alive (whoever supposes that
they do?); but civilisations, it appears, exist simply to produce
churches. 'Except in so far as they minister to the progress of
Religion', they 'have forfeited their historical significance'!

Such statements reveal with startling clarity the extent to which
Dr. Toynbee has lost interest in civilisation as such. All that now
matters to him is 'Man's mysterious spiritual ascent on the wings
of material catastrophe'. And that, no doubt, is why, when at
length he comes to them, his reflections on 'the prospects of the
Western civilisation' are so lacking in inspiration. For it is obvious that the picture of contemporary Western society summarised
above is a hotch-potch of the platitudes of current social and
political analysis, combined with wishful thinking and dubious
speculations; there is nothing of the philosophic depth of emancipation from the transient preoccupations of the current hour,
which we await of an historian who views contemporary civilisation in the perspective of 5,000 years.

The reason, quite simply, is that Dr. Toynbee is no longer
interested in bringing to bear on the problem of civilisation the
perspective of 5,000 years; his eye is fixed instead on the dim and
distant prospect of a 'higher species of society', of which civilisation is at best the unwilling foster-mother. Consequently he is
astonishingly indifferent to the accuracy and consistency in detail,
without which the comparative study of civilisations is likely to
prove the worst of delusions. On one page, for example, he asserts that Hitler performed the same service 'for some future
architect of a *Pax Oecumenica*' as Caesar (102-44 B.C.) for
Augustus; on another, that 'the two dates A.D. 1914 and 431 B.C.
were philosophically contemporaneous'. Which statement (if
either) are we to believe? But what, above all else, is the value of
findings which accept without blenching a discrepancy of almost
four centuries? If we are to hope to chart, by comparative methods, the prospects of the Western world in the mid-twentieth century, the first necessity is to pin-prick with all possible accuracy
its position on the comparative time-chart of civilisations.

This, precisely this, is the historian's professional function;
but Dr. Toynbee denounces 'the professional Scribes and Pharisees' of the historical world, accusing them of 'hybris' and 'antinomianism' because they deny the 'practicability' of comparative
history and the cogency of his arguments, on the ground that
twenty-one civilisations are an inadequate number 'for testing hypotheses by the empirical method of trial and error'. But the
effective criticism is different. What makes his views and findings
so difficult to test, and so elusive, is his inconsistency and his arbi-

trary use of historical evidence. He prides himself on his 'empirical method'; but, as Geyl and others have pointed out, this is 'mere make belief'. His assertion, for example, of the inevitability of a single 'world-government' is certainly not deduction from observation; for comparative history would indicate, if anything, a long-term coexistence of Russia and America similar to that of Rome and Persia. His parallel between Hitler and Caesar is at first glance apt; but if we pause to consider that it implies the succession of a German Augustus, we may well wonder whether the revelvant parallel is not with Hannibal.

If we pause to consider. . . . But Dr. Toynbee, in his haste to point a moral to a sickly world before it is too late, has neither time nor patience for minutiae such as these. The factual basis of history is for him simply raw material which must be brought—the classical example is his manipulation of the history of Islam and of Ancient Egypt—somehow or another into conformity with his theorems. He lacks, in short, the historian's characteristic piety towards the past; and if he replies (as well he might) that respect for the past is not enough, and that the historian's first duty is to the present, the answer is, quite simply, that he can perform no useful service to the present—and is likely only to mislead and mystify—unless his history is scrupulous and consistent. If, for example, Dr. Toynbee's interpretation of Russian history is arbitrary and unacceptable—and that, I believe, is the verdict of every competent authority on eastern Europe in this country—what, considering the central part which Russia plays in world affairs today, is the validity of his assessment of the 'prospects' of contemporary civilisation?

Certainly the questions which Dr. Toynbee asks will continue to stimulate and engross, because they spring from the heart of the present and reflect preoccupations to which none of us can be oblivious; but his answers are unlikely to satisfy, because they are in the end mere intuitions which lack—by comparison even with Spengler—the fire and compulsion of inner necessity. No one would deny the abundance of stimulating ideas and formulations, which is a mark of his writings; but the stimulus is to criticism and contradiction, not to acceptance. And 'a twentieth-century Westernizing World' will make its own history, for good or ill, not to the pattern of Dr. Toynbee's hopes and fears and admonitions, but in accordance with its own genius and folly—and God's abiding irony.

TESTING THE TOYNBEE SYSTEM*

Hugh Trevor-Roper

Can we prophesy the future from the past? Professor Toynbee, it is well known, thinks that we can. His vast historical system, the labour of twenty years, is now complete. Comparing "civilisation" with "civilisation" across vast tracts of space and time, he tells us our position and our prospects, and they are grim. Since the sixteenth century (he says) our civilisation has been in a prolonged and convulsive decline: now the penultimate stage of conquest and fossilisation in a universal state is upon us; "the West," as we know it, is finished. The cause of it all (he says) is Sin, the only hope Repentance: we must all creep back under the skirts of a revived medieval Church. For Churches (he says) do not exist for societies, societies exist for them. And all this is just not a personal fit of the dumps; it is not even a tentative conclusion: it is (he says) scientific truth.

Such erudition, bowled at us in ten successive volumes, may easily knock us poor skittles off balance. Professor Toynbee's authority is great: we are crushed by the weight of ancient Assyria and dimly known Mexico. So is his egotism: the calm self-congratulations which pervades his last volume is almost sublime. And indeed, why not? Has he not been "vouchsafed" certain singular experiences which raise him above the level of other historians? Six times, he tells us, he has been "rapt into a momentary communion" with long-past events, and on the seventh occasion he even "found himself" (for like Caesar he writes in the third person)

> in communion not only with this or that episode in history but with all that had been, and was, and was to come. In that instant he was directly aware of the passage of History gently flowing through him like a mighty current, and of his own life welling like a wave in the flow of this vast tide.

After this, we feel, what he says must go. He compares himself with the Prophet Ezekiel; and certainly, at times, he is just as unintelligible.

Nevertheless, let us not lose our heads. It is not to his authority, however powerful, that Professor Toynbee demands our assent, but to his reason. His method, he never ceases to insist, is "empirical." This means that we may test his theories without pre-

---

*The Sunday Times, (London), 17 October, 1954.

suming to share his revelations, just as if he were an ordinary historian, like Gibbon or Macaulay. We must test them where we can—for no man can follow him everywhere; but that is enough. If his method proves sound there, we will trust him everywhere; if not, we must reject it, regardless of his revelations. That is what "empiricism" means.

Now in fact, when we apply this test, we get some rude shocks. Not only are Professor Toynbee's basic assumptions often questionable, and his application of them often arbitrary, but his technical method turns out to be not "empirical" at all. The theories are not deduced from the facts, nor tested by them: the facts are selected, sometimes adjusted, to illustrate the theories, which themselves rest effortlessly on air. Some astonishing instances of this in a fundamental part of the early volumes have been given by the distinguished Dutch historian, Professor Geyl. The new volumes are no better.

Take, for instance, the chapter on "Laws of Nature in Civilisations." Here Professor Toynbee states that "declining" civilisations go through regular cycles of war and peace. Each cycle contains, in this order, "premonitory wars," a "general war," a "breathing space," "supplementary wars," and a "general peace": then the cycle begins again. This is all set out, for three such civilisations, in impressive tabular form. But looking closer at the European table, I am less impressed. Why, for instance, are Philip II's operations in the Netherlands, and the accompanying desultory sea-war, described as "general war" while the Thirty Years' War, which involved all Europe, and Hitler's War, which involved the world, are only "supplementary wars"?

The answer seems to be, to fit the theory. And why, if the Balkan campaigns of 1913 and the Italian occupation of Tripoli in 1911 are worth mentioning, do we see no mention of the Balkan campaign of 1878 and the French occupation of Tunis in 1881? The answer seems to be that the first set of campaigns is needed to illustrate a period of "premonitory wars," the second, since they fall in a period earmarked for "general peace," must be suppressed —just as a whole series of French, Spanish, Portuguese, Swedish, Polish, English, Scottish, Irish, Dutch and Danish wars have to be suppressed to provide a "general peace" in the 1650s.

To question small deceptions in a great work seems ungrateful; but is is necessary. A vast mathematical system is useless if it is based on incorrect multiplication-tables, and Professor Toynbee's work claims to be a complete system. In fact, wherever we look, it is the same. Theories are stated—often interesting and suggestive theories; then facts are selected to illustrate them (for there is no theory which some chosen facts cannot illustrate); then the magician waves his wand, our minds are dazed with a mass of learned detail, and we are told that the theories are "empirically" proved by the facts and we can now go on to the next stage in the argument. But in truth this is neither empiricism nor proof, nor even argument: it is a game anyone can play, a confusion of logic with speculation.

Of course, Professor Toynbee is free to speculate. If he chooses to suppose that Western civilisation was flourishing in the time of the Papal Schism, the Hundred Years' War and the Black Death, that the Renaissance was the beginning of our downfall, and that our last four centuries have been "the paroxysms of a deadly seizure" only interrupted by a weary lull of "Disillusionment, Apprehension and Cynicism" (i.e., the age of Newton, Bach, Gibbon and Voltaire)—well, let him suppose it. These are interesting views, and from this richly stored mind he can illustrate them with interesting observations. If he did that, we would dip into his work as into the table-talk of a historically minded if rather cranky sage—a latter-day Carlyle. Unfortunately he does not do this. Conjuring with his twenty-one "civilisations," and helping out his conjuring-tricks with imperfect light, distracting noises and a certain amount of intellectual hanky-panky, he pretends that he has proved what he has merely stated. This seems to me, in so learned a man, a terrible perversion of history.

THE END OF A GREAT WORK*

W. H. WALSH

With the publication to-day of the remaining eight parts of his *Study of History* Professor Toynbee completes a monumental work on which he has been engaged since 1927. In the course of ten substantial volumes he has carried out an elaborate survey of the twenty-one civilizations identified in his introduction, has sought to establish the existence of certain recurrent phenomena in their rise and development, and the presence of clearly marked rhythms in their breakdown and decline, and has discoursed on many related topics, including the prospects of western civilization and the meaning of history as a whole. It is scarcely surprising that the main ideas of the book, with its wide sweep, great learning and topical relevance, have already won the attention of a considerable public.

Nevertheless, the book has been, and promises to remain, an object of controversy as well as of admiration. Its reception by professional historians has been mixed. Many scholars have been inclined to look with suspicion at the very idea of such a study of history as Mr. Toynbee has undertaken.

How should *A Study of History* be classified? Mr. Toynbee describes himself throughout the work as an historian or, more pedantically, as a "post-modern western historian." He emphasizes from the first his desire to correct, or counter-balance, a tendency towards specialization and parochialism among modern western historians. And he contrasts himself sharply with Spengler, to whose work his own has obvious resemblances, as an "English empiricist" as against a "German transcendentalist" and "philosopher-hierophant." The common reader, and the common historian too for that matter, may well conclude that Mr. Toynbee is professing to show how history, or at any rate a very important kind of history, should be written, and that he is making of it something far more generally attractive than the bulk of his professional colleagues.

Mr. Toynbee's own conception of the nature of his enterprise can perhaps be brought out best by reference to a revealing passage in his final volume. Here he speaks of Gibbon and indicates what he takes to be the deficiencies of the *Decline and Fall*. Among these are: (*i*) Gibbon's mistaken belief that the decline and fall

---

The Times (London), 14 October, 1954, p. 9.

of the Roman Empire could be treated in isolation from that of the
Graeco-Roman civilization as a whole, a process which began as
far back as the Peloponnesian War, and (*ii*) his wholly secular
approach to his subject, which, to speak roughly, led him to neglect the divine element in human affairs. Mr. Toynbee seems to
be suggesting that he should himself be thought of as a latter-day
Gibbon, a Gibbon purged of the shallow rationalism of the
eighteenth century, who had taken not merely the decline of the
Roman Eimpire but the rises and falls of civilizations as such for
his province. Instead of dealing with a particular problem which
concerned a specific set of events, he would on this account be
occupied with a general problem which had presented itself repeatedly since men attained the civilized state.

On this two comments may be made. First, if it is true that Mr.
Toynbee has tried to generalize Gibbon's inquiry, he has failed to
notice that in so doing he has ceased to be an historian, except incidentally. This point is, indeed, very obvious. A comparative study
of the rises and falls of civilizations as such is not the same as a
history of any particular civilization, nor can it be a substitute for
a collection of such histories; for it is possible only when histories
of particular civilizations first exist. And the point of view of one
who undertakes a comparative study of civilizations is different
from, though not for that reason incompatible with that of the
historian proper: while the former looks for general patterns and
laws, the latter concentrates, entirely correctly, on the connexions
between individual events.

There should be no quarrel between Mr. Toynbee and his historical colleagues over this point, provided only that both recognize
that his true predecessor here is not Gibbon but Auguste Comte.
His comparative study of the rises and falls of civilizations should
be taken as a contribution, not to history, but to "Social Dynamics."

Secondly, the criticism of Gibbon's attitude to religion mentioned above is far from merely incidental. It is not just being
said that Gibbon had an inadequate appreciation of what religion
means to some or most human beings. The charge is rather that he
failed in his job as an historian because he did not see in history,
to use words of the author's from another context, "a vision . . .
of God revealing Himself in action to souls . . . sincerely seeking
Him." By "ruling the supra-mundane dimension of Reality out
of his reckoning, he was unconsciously precluding himself from
finding the treasure hid in his field." By contrast, Mr. Toynbee
himself proposes to present history as, in the end, a theodicy—a
justification of "the ways of God to men"—and it is with this
aspect of it that he is increasingly preoccupied in his concluding

volumes. Yet it is surely clear that in this he has travelled far, not only from his own original project for a comparative study of civilizations, but also from what any normal historian would recognize as history proper.

The truth is that when Mr. Toynbee discusses questions about the meaning and point of the historical process as a whole he writes not as an historian or even a sociologist, but as a metaphysical philosopher. If in his early volumes he is in effect a successor of Comte, his models here are such writers as Vico, Herder and Hegel. Not that he explicitly follows any of these: neither Vico (with whom his affinities are striking) nor Herder appears in his pages, and Hegel is mentioned only incidentally. Yet Mr. Toynbee's work differs from theirs only in the enormous range of the facts it surveys and, perhaps, in the more explicitly Christian twist the author gives to his interpretation.

Mr. Toynbee himself would doubtless regard the first as well as the second difference as crucial, arguing that the very full information at his command enables him to present a reading of history incomparably better based than that of any of his predecessors. That the range of his historical knowledge is enormous and his use of it acute could certainly not be denied. The question is, however, whether any amount of *historical* knowledge can serve as an adequate ground of such deductions about the *meaning* of history as are here drawn. It is hard to acquit Mr. Toynbee of philosophical naivety on this point, as reference to a particular instance may show.

In the section on universal Churches in vol. VII Mr. Toynbee discusses the relations of civilizations and the higher religions. He had shown in his first volume how Churches sometimes act as a link between "apparented" and "affiliated" civilizations, thus enabling the torch of civilization to be carried on. Now he points out that such a link is not found in all cases, and concludes that it cannot be the *raison d'être* of the higher religions to provide for the continuance of civilization. The "roles" must therefore be "reversed," and civilizations be thought of as existing "in order to provide an opportunity for fully-fledged higher religions to come to birth." This is a result which has unflattering consequences for our own largely secular civilization ("one of the 'vain repetitions' of the heathen"), for four higher religions already exist and we show no sign of producing another.

Mr. Toynbee writes as if all this could be deduced from the study of history itself. Unfortunately he does not ask what justification there is for talking of *the* role or *raison d'être* or function of the institutions he discusses, or for assuming that one must exist "for the sake of" another. Nor does he note that his argument would not convince a reader who did not accept his value premise that "religion is the true end of man."

To point this out is not, of course, to refute Mr. Toynbee's philosophy of history, much less to deny value and interest to his remarkable work as a whole. It is only to suggest that his empiricism, like that of some others, is less simple than it seems. In calling himself an empiricist Mr. Toynbee seems to be implying that he is approaching history without preconceptions—a claim that could certainly not be sustained. Whether we find his reading of history convincing or the reverse seems ultimately to depend on whether we share his preconceptions or not.

TOYNBEE'S STUDY OF HISTORY

THE PLACE OF CIVILIZATIONS IN HISTORY*

CHRISTOPHER DAWSON

Now that Dr. Toynbee's *Study of History* has been completed by the publication of the last four volumes (making ten in all), it is possible for us to take a comprehensive view of the whole work and to form some opinion on its significance and value. But this is not an easy task. One cannot lightly pass judgement on a work of 6,000 pages which has been written with so much erudition and conviction. Nor can one get much help from the judgement of others working in the same field, for they hardly exist, at least in this country.

What strikes one at first sight is the fact that the work on the one hand has been a great popular success, especially in the United States, and that, on the other, it has been judged unsympathetically, and often harshly, by the professional historians, especially in this country [England]. This is perhaps not suprising, since, hitherto, civilizations have not been regarded as proper subjects for historical study. History has concerned itself with nations and empires, with States and institutions; while the study of civilization has been left to philosophers and sociologists.

This system answered well enough in the past, when the historians were concerned almost entirely with the States of the European world which all shared the same tradition of civilization, and when the study of the oriental world was treated as a part of colonial history. But today this is no longer possible. Modern history has to take account of the conflicts and contacts between civilizations, as much as, or even more than, of those between the European nations. The ordinary man of today wants to know something about these great world societies which have now become the protagonists in the historical drama and the ordinary history book does very little to help him. That is the obvious justification of Dr. Toynbee's study and one of the main reasons for its wide popularity. For whether we agree or disagree with his conclusions we must, I think, admit that the study of history ought to include the study of civilizations, and that a history which confines itself to the study of the States and peoples of Western Europe and America is both partial and incomplete.

If Dr. Toynbee had undertaken a comparative study of the existing civilizations of the East and the West and their antecedents, he

International Affairs, vol. 31, 1955, pp. 149-158.

would have been performing a very valuable service. Actually, however, he has done much more than this. He has attempted a study of all the civilizations that ever existed, in order to discover the laws that determine their rise and fall, and the prospects of civilization in the future. Now this is just what Oswald Spengler attempted to do more than thirty years ago and, in spite of the pronounced difference between the temperament and the philosophy of the two writers, Toynbee's theory, in its original form, bears considerable resemblances to Spengler's morphology of culture. Both writers agree in their denial of the unity of civilization, and both regard civilizations as autonomous entities which are sharply distinguished from one another and from the world of primitive societies out of which they presumably arose. But while Toynbee regards his twenty-one civilizations as units of the same species which are philosophically equivalent and contemporaneous, he does not go so far as Spengler, who treats his cultures as organisms in the full biological sense, so that 'the history of a culture is the exact counterpart of the history of an individual human being or of an animal or of a tree or of a flower'.

One cannot but be impressed by the unflinching logic with which Spengler worked out his theory or by the verve and style with which he expounded it. Yet the whole brilliant construction is vitiated by an obvious fallacy. If cultures are completely self-contained microcosms, each with its own art and religion and philosophy and science which are unique and incommunicable, how can the historian ever get outside his own culture and see the whole process from outside? Thus Spengler's philosophy of history is self-refuting. He shows how the individual can never, under any circumstances, transcend the limits of the culture to which he belongs, and at the same time he breaks his own law by a titanic attempt to look at all the cultures of the world from outside and to discover the universal law which governs their rise and fall and the whole evolution of their life cycles.

Toynbee recognizes the absurdity of this philosophical *tour de force;* and though he does the same thing in a different way, he never attempts to deny the existence of elements that are common to all the civilizations, or the fact that science and ethics transcend the limitations of the individual civilization. But in that case it is difficult to see how the twenty-one civilizations can be regarded as in any sense equivalent, since it is obvious that they do not all stand on the same level with regard to their scientific achievement or their ethical development. Granted that every civilization is an intelligible field of study which deserves to be studied for its own sake as a whole and not merely on account of the contributions it may have made to some other civilization, this does not make all civilizations philosophically equivalent, any more than the fact that we study States as autonomous political entities need imply that they are all equal to one another in political and social development.

Thus in reading Dr. Toynbee's early volumes, I was always perplexed by the difficulty of reconciling the moral absolutism of his judgements with the cultural relativism of his theory. But this difficulty, at least, has now been solved by the publication of his four concluding volumes. For in the first of these new volumes, in the parts which are devoted to the subject of Universal States and Universal Churches, he introduces the new principle which marks a fundamental modification of his earlier views and involves the transformation of his *Study of History* from a relativist phenomenonology of equivalent cultures, after the fashion of Spengler, into a unitary philosophy of history comparable to that of the idealist philosophers of the nineteenth century.

This change, which was already foreshadowed in the fifth volume, marks the abandonment of his original theory of the philosophical equivalence of the civilizations and the introduction of a qualitative principle embodied in the Higher Religions which are as representative of a higher species of society, and which stand in the same relation to the civilizations as the latter to the primitive societies. Thus, Toynbee's theory of history ceases to be cyclical, like Spengler's, and becomes a progressive series of four world stages ascending from primitive societies, through the primary and secondary civilizations to the higher religions in which history finds its ultimate goal. In his own words the study of history reaches

> a point at which the civilizations in their turn, like the parochial states of the Modern Western World at the outset of our investigation, have ceased to constitute intelligible fields of study for us, and have forfeited their historical significance except in so far as they minister to the progress of Religion. (VII, 449)

This is a revolutionary change, and to appreciate its full significance we must study the more elaborate table of civilizations and religions arrayed in serial order in Table 7 to Volume VII which shows the way in which Dr. Toynbee's new theory transforms his original scheme of twenty-one independent equivalent culture cycles. It is arranged in six stages:

1. The Primitive Societies, which are legion.

2. The Primary Civilizations, which are now seven instead of five owing to the addition of the newly discovered archaic civilizations of the Indus Valley and Northern China.

3. The eight Secondary Civilizations, which are derived from the primary ones through their dominant minorities, or through

the external proletariats; these are the Hellenic, the Syriac, the Hittite, the Babylonic, the Indic, and the Sinic (or classical Chinese) in the Old World, and the Yucatic and Mexic in the New.

4. The Higher Religions, which are apparently twelve in number, ranging from Christianity and Islam to the worship of Isis and Osiris.

5. The eight Tertiary Civilizations, of which our own is one, and which also include two other Christian civilizations (Russian and Eastern Orthodox), two Muslim ones (Iranic and Arabic), two in the Far East, and one in India.

6. Finally there are the Secondary Higher Religions, which developed out of the Tertiary Civilizations and include about a dozen later oriental religious movements, like Sikhism, the Brahmo Samaj, Bahaiism, and so forth.

This elaborate classification of civilizations and religions is extremely complex and requires considerable study before we can understand it in detail. But this at least is clear, it means that the cyclical movements by which the civilizations rise and fall are not the whole of history. They are subordinated to a higher principle of spiritual universality represented by the world religions. Thus history becomes once more progressive and purposive—a process of spiritual evolution such as Hegel and the other nineteenth-century idealist philosophers of history had conceived.

Now this view is much nearer to the ordinary man's idea of history than the Spenglerian relativist theory. For though we may have abandoned the thoroughgoing optimism of the nineteenth-century doctrine of progress, we still find it hard to abandon a belief in the unity of history and in the existence of some common standard by which the achievements and failures of the different civilizations can be judged. And the same, I think, is true of the historians, for though they have lost Lord Acton's sublime vision of a universal history of all countries which enlightens the mind and illuminates the soul, they nevertheless still believe in the unity of history and are almost unanimous in their rejection of a thoroughgoing historical relativism in the style of Herr Spengler.

Nevertheless, I do not think that either the man in the street or the professional historian is likely to accept Dr. Toynbee's philosophy of history in its final form. It is too abstruse and learned for the former, and too speculative and ideological for the latter. Few historians will be prepared to accept the system of classification by which he arrives at his total of twenty-three civilizations. It seems arbitrary to create three distinct civilizations out of the three or four successive phases of Chinese culture and the same may be said of his three Christian civilizations—the Western, the Eastern Orthodox, and the Russian Orthodox. If all these are to be classified as distinct civilizations, why should the civilization of Korea be identified with that of Japan, or the very distinctive culture of Tibet or of Burma and Siam be denied any separate place in the list? One would have imagined that Russia was closer to Europe, and Muslim Persia to Muslim Syria than Tibet or Burma were to India.

Most of all, however, the historian is likely to object to Dr. Toynbee's view of the supersession of the Tertiary Civilizations by the Higher Religions. According to this theory, civilization has fulfilled its purpose during its secondary phase by the production of the Higher Religions. By doing so, civilization, he says, had exhausted its mandate and had been replaced by a new and a higher form of society—the Universal Churches. Thus the Tertiary Civilizations have no historical function: they are superfluous repetitions of an earlier historical phase and have no intrinsic value for the historian. As he explains (II, 448) the historical process consists of four phases and four phases only—(1) Primitive Societies, (2) Primary Civilizations, (3) Secondary Civilizations, and (4) Higher Religions.

Now I cannot imagine any view more likely to arouse the antagonism of the average historian. For these Tertiary Civilizations are the main fields of historic research in its modern scientific form. If, as Toynbee says, these Tertiary Civilizations are 'now right out of the picture" (VII, 449), for the purposes of his study, that is enough to condemn his theory of history in the eyes of the historians.

It is certainly difficult to believe that these recent and contemporary civilizations are more devoid of historical significance than the Hittite civilization or the civilization of Yucatan. Nor is Dr. Toynbee altogether consistent in this respect, since it is to these Tertiary Civilizations—especially to the two Islamic cultures and the three Christian ones—that a very large part of his study of history is devoted; and though much of what he says of modern Western civilization is negative and critical, it is not altogether so. There is still enough left on the credit side to justify a claim to historical significance.

Certainly I would agree with Dr. Toynbee against perhaps the majority of modern historians in his central theme that civilization exists to serve religion and not religion to serve civilization. But this does not mean that civilization must wither away and be replaced by a church, in the same way as the State is supposed to wither away and be replaced by the classless society in the Marxian theory of history. So long as human life exists on earth, there must be civilizations and cultures, and the fact that a civilization accepts the truth of a world religion does not necessarily transform it into a church.

Moreover, I do not think that Dr. Toynbee's reduction of history to theology (to borrow an expression from Roger Bacon) will meet with any more favour from the theologians and the students of comparative religion, than it has done from the historians. In fact the criticisms of the theologians will follow similar lines to those of the historians. As the latter find it difficult to accept his list of civilizations, so the former will boggle at his lists of the primary and secondary religions. In the first place, it is difficult to see why he limits his category of Living Religions to four only: Chiristianity, Islam, Hinduism, and Mahayana Buddhism. There are few students of religion who would deny the right of Judaism to be reckoned as a living religion. And in the case of Buddhism, it seems arbitrary to exclude that form of Buddhism which is still the dominant religion of Ceylon and Burma and Siam and Cambodia and which actually seems far more living at the present day than the Mahayana form of the religion, which is now almost moribund in China and Korea and survives only in Japan and Tibet and Nepal.

And if it seems unjustifiable to reduce religion to these four examples, the theologian is likely to be even more critical of Dr. Toynbee's attempt to reduce these four to one by a process of psychological interpretation and theological syncretism. It is easy to understand that Dr. Toynbee's abandonment of the relativist principle of the philosophical equivalence of civilizations should make him look to the higher religions in order to find a principle which will unify his study. For as he writes, 'The history of Religion appears to be unitary and progressive by contrast with the multiplicity and repetitiveness of the histories of civilizations' (II, 425-6). But when he goes beyond this and seeks to prove the substantial identity of all the existing forms of higher religion, he is over-simplifying the picture and is giving way to the temptation to force the evidence in order to make it fit in with his theories.

For if there were difficulties in his original thesis of the philosophical equivalence of civilizations, the objections to the theological equivalence of the higher religions are even more serious. In the study of civilizations, the historian is dealing with a field which is subject to temporal and spatial limitations and can be judged by historical criteria. But when it comes to the world religions, he is in a world which, of its nature, transcends the sphere of history and is not amenable to empirical study. These religions must be studied theologically, if at all, and when we survey the world religions from the theological point of view, we see that they are neither identical nor convergent, but represent at least two alternative and contradictory solutions to the religious problem.

On the one hand, the religions of the Far East—Hinduism and Mahayana Buddhism—adapt themselves well enough to Dr. Toynbee's ideal of religious syncretism, but they do so by denying the significance of history and creating a dream world of cosmological and mythological fantasy in which aeons and universes succeed one another in dazzling confusion and where the unity of God and the historical personality of Buddha are lost in a cloud of mythological figures: Buddhas and Bodhisattvas, gods and saktis, demigods and spirits. On the other hand, the three higher religions of the West—Judaism, Christianity, and Muhammedanism— have followed quite a different path. Their very existence is bound up with the historic reality of their founders, and with the establishment of a unique relation between God and His people.

Thus any syncretism between religions of these two different types would inevitably mean the abdication of the monotheistic religions and their absorption by the pantheistic or polytheistic ones. Such a process is not inconceivable, but we have no historical reason to suppose that it is possible and no theological reason for supposing it to be desirable or right. Hitherto the main trend of history has been in the opposite direction and the exclusive monotheistic religions have been steadily extending their sphere of influence at the expense of their more accommodating rivals. It is true that Toynbee's Secondary Higher Religions are mostly of the sycretistic type; but, with the exception of Sikhism, they have failed to establish themselves, and the success of Sikhism and military and political rather than purely religious.

Hence it seems that the principle of the theological equivalence of the higher religions finds no more justification in the study of history than the philosophical equivalence of civilizations has done. With regard to the latter, Dr. Toynbee has now come to accept the qualitative differentiation of culture according to their degree of subordination to higher spiritual ends; and in spite of his scepticism regarding the spiritual *raison d'être* of Western civilization, he admits the startling fact that this is now the only extant representative of the species which is not in process of disintegration. Though it is by no means certain that our civilization possesses either the strength or the wisdom to create a peaceful world order, it is difficult to see how its work can ever be altogether undone, except by the destruction of civilization itself.

Now as Western civilization has been the effective agent of world unity on the material, technological, and economic planes, so Christianity has worked for nearly 2,000 years towards the spiritual unification of humanity in the Kingdom of God. If Christianity fails, we have no reason to suppose that it will be replaced by an oriental syncretism like Mahayana Buddhism or by a Christian Gnosticism. Its only effective rival is a secular counter-religion like Communism, which would mean the destruction of all the higher religions.

It is true that the political awakening of Asia and the resurgence of oriental nationalism has been accompanied by an understandable reaction against Western missionary activities, but this is not due to any considerable revival of the higher religions of the Far East, least of all of Mahayana Buddhism. It is a political phenomenon which is inseparable from the reaction against Western imperialism and colonialism. On the level of the higher culture, the advance of Western ideas has been far more rapid during the last twenty or thirty years than at any time in the past. And while this does not mean any extension of the Western religions, it does involve the progressive decline of the ancient religious cultures of the East, as Mr. Nirad Chaudahuri has pointed out so strikingly in his book *The Autobiography of an Unknown Indian* (1951), which every historian who is interested in these questions ought to read.

Perhaps I have said too much on this question. But apart from its intrinsic interest and importance, it represents the climax of Dr. Toynbee's work, the whole of which must now be read in the light of its conclusion. But, personally, I cannot help feeling that this conclusion is premature. Dr. Toynbee has been guided in his immense task by two parallel motives; first by the Hellenic philosophic quest for a theoria—a synoptic vision of the whole course of human civilization, and secondly by the Hebraic prophetic mission to justify the ways of God to man and to find a religious solution to the riddle of history and the problems of modern civilization. Both these motives are so deeply rooted in the tradition of Western civilization that we can none of us ignore their force. But there is always a danger that the philosopher will be tempted to simplify the irrational multiplicity and idiosyncrasy of the world of history and that the prophet will attempt to anticipate the mystery of divine judgement, like the friend of Job—that symbol of humanity agonizing in the toils of history.

Practically every philosophy of history that has ever been elaborated errs in one or other of these ways, and frequently in both of them. The fact is that a comparative study of civilizations has only recently become possible, and even today, in spite of the progressive extension of our field of vision by archaeology and prehistory and oriental studies, our knowledge is still fragmentary, uneven, and partial. This is no reason for discouragement. During the very years when Dr. Toynbee has been writing the present volumes, a whole series of discoveries has thrown new light on the most important of all historical problems, the origins of higher civilization in the Near East, the beginnings of agriculture and the domestication of animals, and the rise of the village community and finally of the city. But until these discoveries have been completed and co-ordinated, it is impossible for us to write with assurance about the genesis of civilization and of the features which first differentiated civilization from primitive society.

And it is here precisely that the theorists of civilization are most unsatisfactory. Since their attention is concentrated on the higher civilizations in their highest manifestations, they tend to ignore or undervalue everything that lies outside or below or before them, so that they exaggerate the gulf that divides civilization from primitive culture. Thus Spengler writes: 'A civilization is born at the moment when, out of the psychic conditions of a perpetually raw Humanity, a mighty soul awakes and extricates itself: a form out of the formless, a bounded transitory existence out of the boundless and the persistent'.[1] In the same way Dr. Toynbee tends to make an absolute distinction between civilization and primitive societies, being also equivalent, and spread out indeterminately over the hundreds of thousands of years during which the human race has existed. They are even anterior to humanity, since, according to Dr. Toynbee, 'the existence of primitive society is a condition which the evolution of Man out of Sub-Man presupposes' (I, 173; cp., VII, 420-1 and note).

But this seems a sheer misuse of terms. Certainly the societies of the ape men must have been primitive, as primitive as can be. But they are not societies in the same sense as the human societies of the prehistoric world or of the non-civilized world today. All these belong to the same world of history as the higher civilizations. They possess language and culture and religion and art. And they differ from one another as much as or more than they differ from the civilizations. There is no excuse for lumping them altogether at the bottom of the scale and grouping the civilizations all together at the top. They do not form a sort of amorphous mass of raw humanity such as Spengler imagines. The higher forms of neolithic culture, for example, stood midway, between the culture of the hunters and the food gatherers and that of the early civilizations; and the lowest form of primitive culture that we know at first hand, such as that of the Australians or that of the Bushmen, is infinitely removed from the highest forms of sub-human society.

Thus when we come to the study of the civilizations we cannot afford to disregard the existence of the neighboring and related

---

[1] O. Spengler, *Der Unterganges Abendlandes* (Munich 1923), vol. 1, p. 153.

peoples of lower culture. We are likely to learn more about the nature of Mexican culture by a comparison with the Pueblo culture of the South Western United States, than by a comparison with another 'secondary' civilization of the Old World, like that of the Hittites or the Greeks. By relegating these neighbouring cultures to the status of 'external proletariats'. Toynbee deprives them of much of their real significance and devalues their contribution to culture.

The fact is that a civilization of any but the most simple and archaic kind is a far more complex phenomenon than the philosophers of history have realized. No doubt it is always based on a particular original process of cultural creativity which is the work of a particular people. But at the same time it always tends to become a super-culture—an extended area of social communication which dominates and absorbs other less advanced or less powerful cultures and united them in an 'oecumene', and international and intercultural society; and it is this extension of the area of communication that is the essential characteristic of civilization as distinguished from lower forms of culture.

The higher civilizations usually represent a fusion of at least two independent traditions of culture, and while one of these is dominant and possibly more advanced, it is not enough to dismiss the subculture as an internal proletariat, as Dr. Toynbee does, since the word 'proletariat' denotes a class within a society and not a culture of sub-culture within a civilization. Hence I do not believe it possible to study the high civilizations satisfactorily until we have succeeded in analysing their different cultural components. In other words, the essential basis of the study of history must be, not just a comparative study of the higher civilizations, but a study of their constituent cultures, and here we must follow, not the grand synoptic method of the philosophers of history, but the more laborious and meticulous scientific technique of the social anthropologists. It may be objected that this is not possible unless we possess authentic first hand investigations similar to those of the modern ethnologist. But the prehistorian has adopted the anthropological method, not unfruitfully, in his study of the cultures of the remote past, and the same thing can be done by the historian who possesses far richer sources of information.

Contemporary anthropologists, like Professor Evans-Pritchard, have accepted the principle of the essentially historical character of social anthropology, and in the same way it seems reasonable that the historians should begin to pay more attention to the methods and the contribution of social anthropology. Now in his recent volumes, Dr. Toynbee does expressly recognize the essential relation between the two disciplines and goes out of his way to reject many of the distinctions commonly made between civilizations and primitive societies (IX, 188-9 and note).

But this only makes his neglect of the lower types of culture more incomprehensible. The only criteria of differentiation that he admits are quantitative ones—the civilizations are much fewer and larger than the primitive cultures, so that 'the two species stand to one another like elephants and rabbits' (V. I, p. 148). But after all it is not just size and scarcity that distinguish the elephant from the rabbit, and if elephants were simply gigantic rabbits, there would be no excuse for creating a new science of super-rabbits as distinct from the ordinary article. Moreover, even this quantitative difference becomes less marked if, as I have suggested, a civilization is a community or concatenation of cultures. We know in the case of our own Western civilization how large a degree of cultural individuality and multiformity can coexist within a single civilization, so that we can talk of French and German cultures as distinct entities without denying their participation in a common civilization. In studying the civilizations of the past we are apt to neglect these internal differences, because we are viewing them through a telescope and not through a microscope. My fundamental criticism of Toynbee's great work is that it is too telescopic and that a true science of human cultures must be based on a more microscopic technic of anthropological and historical research.

Nevertheless, a telescopic survey of the whole field of study also has its value, especially when it is carried out by a scholar of immense learning and universal interests like Dr. Toynbee. And I do not think that any historian or social anthropologist can read his work without gaining new insights into the nature of the problem of the relations between civilizations.

THE NAPOLEON OF NOTTING HILL*

Lewis Mumford

The long river of history, whose course Arnold Toynbee has been surveying and plotting during most of his conscious life, has with the last four volumes finally reached its destination. But as with a river, the word "destination" is a misleading one. For a river is a flowing body that begins in a hundred trickles and runnels and springs high up in the mountains, often passes through the most interesting tracts of land midway on its route; drops its heaviest stones where the currents begin to slacken; overflows its banks and leaves beneficent layers of fertile soil under violent seasonal changes; and finally meanders through its lower valley, twisting and turning, changing its direction so often that the traveller hardly knows which way his boat is pointing; and at the end loses itself in a thousand different channels of its silt-laden delta before the muddy waters eventually mingle with the blue sea. For those interested in the ways of rivers, any part of that journey may serve as a destination; while he who circles above the mouth of the river, waiting for a final revelation, courts heavy disappointment: the river loses itself at last in the eternal ocean.

Only those who have patiently tried to grapple with Toynbee's ten volumes will understand how well this characterizes both the subject matter and the treatment. It reveals, too, the special virtues of this monumental survey, and reduces some of its apparent weaknesses, the dawdling in inlets padded with water-lilies, the capturing of side-streams, the sinuous backward movements, into the necessary characteristics of a mighty river—no young torrent carving through a straight gorge, but a great, cumulative, widening stream of water that has already planed down a whole mountain mass, and in reaching physiographic maturity has lost the capacity for swift movement.

Even the small part of human history that is visible to historians is one of the most complex and mysterious of all the phenomena presented to man; and the glory of Toynbee's work—a glory that no criticism, however radical, can diminish—is that his is perhaps the first mind that has done something like justice to its complexity and mystery. Though he has had his precursors, from Augustine to Ibn Khaldun onward, he has earned, more effectively than any rival, the right to be called the Master, if not the Father, of Universal History.

---

*New Republic, vol. 131, 8 November 1954, pp. 15-18.

Because these ten volumes rest on a lifetime of study, they demand almost another lifetime for the reader to understand them and assimilate them. For those who seek quick conclusions, this is a trial of patience; and there are times, I confess, when even the most strenuous student finds himself like a swimmer caught in a tangle of weeds, almost frantic to extricate himself from the details that make it impossible for him to move forward, or even to raise his head high enough to get a glimpse of shore. Partly because of this fact, partly because Toynbee's method, which utilizes myth and drama and breaks with many of the idola of supposedly scientific and objective thought, there is a tendency in certain scholarly quarters to dismiss this great work on grounds that are more shaky than the methods they criticize. But the merit of Toynbee's work lies precisely in those fields where he challenges current preconceptions, methods, goals; and even when, after accepting that challenge, one comes to different conclusions than Toynbee's, as I frankly do, one must be grateful to him for posing such significant questions, for they lead one to explore territory that had hitherto not even been marked as "unknown" on the historian's and the sociologist's maps.

How shall one approach these final four volumes? In a sense, though they existed in the original plan of Toynbee's work in their present sequence, they are anti-climactic. Part of their material, on Renaissances and Encounters fills up blank spaces left in his first three volumes on the growth and integration of civilizations, and logically they seem out of order here; part of them, Volume Seven, in fact, is an amplification and in part a restatement of the role of a universal religion in bringing the cycle of defeat and disintegration to a close. Perhaps the best way to begin this review is to start with Volume Ten; for this volume, besides containing an index of almost two hundred pages, holds this historian's own disarming Confession of Faith and his acknowledgements to his many mentors. This biographic portion brings one close to the personal sources of *A Study of History*—though it remains teasingly silent at the point where one might most eagerly seek revelation: the spiritual encounters that opened his eyes so fully to the part played by religion in human development. Aware of poignant temporal parallels between himself and the author of *The City of God,* composing his interpretation of history in a similar period of disintegration, Toynbee has yet to follow Augustine by writing his Confessions.

In Volume Ten we follow Arnold Toynbee's personal development as historian. Toynbee grew up in the heart of London, at No. 12 Upper Westbourne Terrace: one of those modest Victorian quarters of London that still retained, along with occasional

Georgian details, some of the spaciousness of eighteenth century planning. This district is known as Notting Hill; and lover's of Chesterton's brilliant fantasy, *The Napoleon of Notting Hill*, will recall that its hero, Adam Wayne, revolted by the drab bureaucratic mediocrity of London, mad with visions of medieval pomp and pageantry, led a movement to return to the more parochial world of the Middle Ages.

Toynbee's mind moved in just the opposite direction of that of Adam Wayne. Equally inspired by history, and equally committed to Christianity—for Toynbee history is a vision of "God revealing himself in action to souls that were sincerely seeking him"—Toynbee moves on to the stage of universal history and focusses his drama on mankind. For his early awakening to history, and along with that to literature, Toynbee acknowledges his debt to his mother, who, apparently sensing his readiness, put into his hands contemporary researches on ancient civilizations, along with Milton and Browning.

Like many minds who go far in their fields, he had an early sense of his vocation. That sense was nurtured by relatives who had lived through the great episodes of nineteenth century English history, in far parts of the Empire; and it was further stimulated by all the treasures of distant lands and cultures so easily accessible, across Kensington Gardens, at the India Museum and the Victoria and Albert, to say nothing of more distant collections in that great metropolis.

No contemporary of ours has made such ample use of the resources of a great city as Toynbee has; and if his study of history is in some sense an image of an ancient river, it is also, in its vastness, its complexity, its impenetrability, and its magnificent profusion and confusion an image of that great overgrown megalopolis, stifled by its very success. If the age of the megalopolis is coming to an end, as some of us venture to prophesy, then Toynbee's vast work may stand for good and bad as its final symbol and image: its etherialization, to use Toynbee's term.

I shall not follow Toynbee's preparation in all the details he copiously spreads before us: enough to say that it was supplemented by his old-fashioned Oxford education—still "late medieval Italian," as he demurely notes—with a discipline in the Latin and Greek classics so thorough that in moments of emotion he writes verse in one of those languages rather than in English. What would seem affectation in another writer, his failure to translate ancient languages into English when quoting them, may well be second nature with him. This education accounts for both Toynbee's patience and thoroughness, and his "English" sense of obedience to the empirical fact; for though his categories of thought tend to exclude or cramp historic data that do not easily fit them, he usually gives free enough play to the data to provide his reader with the necessary correction, and sometimes generously enlists the aid of other critical minds to correct his own bias. Exhaustive in some places, his scholarship nevertheless often has curious lapses in others; as in his failure to give even passing mention to the work of important precursors like Stuart-Glennie and Henry Adams.

Toynbee's formal education has been topped throughout his life by wide travel, which brought him on a psychically crucial journal to the Near East before 1914; and that in turn was rounded off by active responsibilities in the Foreign Office in both World Wars: one of the indispensable experiences of that part of history which may be interpreted as "past politics." These facts help to explain Toynbee's felicities as a writer, his vivid, sometimes too overladen imagery, his warm humanism, which draws freely on the resources of both ancient and modern literature; perhaps also his strain of active Christian piety, bequest of the early Tractarian movement at Oxford, so different from the rather arid hedonism-cum-science that characterized the Cambridge of his slightly older contemporary, John Maynard Keynes.

One thing more must be noted: a memory so capacious that it holds together and relates a larger tract of history than anyone before has attempted to embrace, much less interpret. Toynbee's memory, indeed, comes so close to producing "total recall"—as one discovers in his acknowledgments—that it has sometimes doubtless been almost as much of a handicap in writing this study as a help. In the end he was saved from the "perils of omni-science," which he himself recognizes, by his simple discovery that

> . . . Life is action. A life which does not go into action is a failure, and this is just as true of a prophet's, a poet's, or a scholar's life as it is true of the life of a man of action in the conventionally limited popular usage of the term.

That combination, that completeness, gives substance and impact to *A Study of History,* and this compensates in no small degree for what seem to me a fundamental weakness in its sociology and its philosophy.

This *Study of History,* then, is at bottom a great act: an assertion, against the materialism and nihilism of our time, of the dignity of human life and the importance of history itself—though, for Toynbee as for Reinhold Niebuhr, there is no resolution of the ultimate problems of history except in "An Other World." The last four volumes add nothing essential to that conclusion. Toynbee had already reached it in Volume Six.

The first notes for the topics and the contents of this history, Toynbee observes in the preface to the final volumes, were made on the Orient Express, en route from Constantinople to England, in September, 1921; the first three volumes were published in 1934; the second three in 1939; and, after the hiatus of the Second World War, he finished his writing of the last four volumes, in 1952. (There will also be, he promises, an historical atlas and gazetteer, and a final critical volume of Reconsiderations.) This work is therefore contemporary with the period of disintegration that followed the sudden explosion of the First World War: that winter period of Faustian civilization, predicted by Spengler, in which the hard men of fact would seize power and turn society into a mere engine for multiplying that power. This transformation of democracy into war dictatorship, of Communism into Fascism, of imperialism into colonial nationalism, of war into genocide, all took place during this period. Though Toynbee, unlike Spengler, does not throw his own weight on the side of doom, his pessimism is even more profound; for his doctrine of religious salvation deprives him of even Spengler's lyric joy in the opening phases of a civilization's development. On the whole, Toynbee is more conscious of the degrading forces than the upbuilding ones, more concerned with the final response to disintegration, religious detachment and transfiguration, than with forces that delay it or avoid it by resuming development on an "earthly" plane: more concerned with the modes of salvation through a "universal church" than with maturation, growth and transcendence.

As a result, his inquiry, which began hopefully in the field of history, This World (to use Toynbee's capitals, along with his Christian terminology) ends in the field of theology, The Other World. The final outcome of Toynbee's exhaustive and erudite analysis is a re-affirmation of the position of his predecessor, Augustine, in *The City of God*: the way out is "the way into An Other World, out of the range of the City of Destruction." This is the answer that he reaches by eliminating, one by one (to his own satisfaction) all the other possibilities. The only way in which the conclusion he frames in Volume Seven differs from that he had reached in 1939, is that, instead of regarding Christianity as the sole source of true salvation, radically different, through the fact that Jesus was indeed God incarnate, from that offered by other high religions, he now accords an almost equal degree of efficacy to the other great revelations. Toynbee thus overcomes each "Universal" Church's parochialism by what is, from the standpoint of Christian orthodoxy, an heretical admission, though he makes it in much the same spirit as Mahomet admitted the claims of Judaism and Christianity.

To make anything like a close critical analysis of Toynbee's conspectus of history is beyond the province of the present review. There are indeed few scholars, even historians, who are capable of even coming to grips with him in his own province, for he has widened the range of his subject beyond the reach of current scholarship: so that perhaps only those who have first been his students will prove capable of correcting him at every point in detail. Fortunately, one may say something about the impressions left by his work as a whole. On the positive side, I would point out that no book that deals with human affairs has been more free from the blatant parochialisms of our age and our civilization: the obsessions of nationalism, the exaltation of Hellenic and later European civilization at the expense of nineteen other significant societies, our excessive pride in material conquests and mechanical productivity, our naïve submission to the one-eyed methodology of the physical sciences and "objective" scholarship; the bias of narrow specialism and egocentricity, the notion that our age is the climax of human existence and that its ephemeral values are eternal ones.

As far as mortals may, Toynbee approaches his theme with clean hands and a pure heart, and as one who has not lifted up his soul unto vanity: witness his judgment on the consistently brutal ways of the English-speaking peoples in dealing with native populations. Furthermore, this is one of the few works of modern scholarship, not expressly devoted to theology, that does justice to the immense part played by religion in the development of human society: a correction of the rationalist illusion which regards religion as a primitive aberration and incidentally a confirmation of Benjamin Kidd's unfashionable insight more than half a century ago.

But if Toynbee, in the very conception of his great work, broke free from many of the idola of modern civilization, he did not, unfortunately, escape an older set of idola. In particular, he succumbed to that naive dualism which is almost engrained in the grammatical structure and vocabulary of our Western languages, with its flat distinctions between matter and spirit, dynamic and static, form and process. This original dualism—Platonic, Christian, or Cartesian—helped produce the partial order of rationalism and the partial objectivity of science, which fails to take account of its own subjective biases: likewise, it fostered the one-sided materialism of modern industry—for what is that but a mirror image, in reverse, of an equally one-sided spiritualism, which Christian theology has presented as ultimate reality? The fact is that Toynbee's dualistic metaphysics and theology run like a deep fissure through his whole argument and weaken even the soundest parts of it. Matter and Spirit, External and Inner, Macrocosm and Microcosm, Society and the Individual Soul—these oppositions and antinomies are treated by him as if they in fact were exclusive and separate. But surely all sound thought, not least that of our own age, is an attempt to bring together, as diverse aspects of a dynamic, holistic, unified process, forces that the mind, through the very separateness and fixation of its categories, tends falsely to hold apart as self-sufficient entities.

This radical flaw in Toynbee's metaphysics makes it impossible to do justice to formative and purposive acts that are at work at every level of life, giving meaning to material circumstances and giving visible shape and form to what, a moment before, was an invisible idea or dream; so that even minor and menial tasks attain dignity just to the extent that they serve the whole process. "Nor soul helps body more," to quote one of Toynbee's favorite poets, Browning, "than body soul."

For Toynbee, meaning and value and form come into their own only when the hampering body has been minimized or left behind: cut off from their sources in life, they exist for him in a final act of transfiguration that brings man close to God. Since this final act, as Toynbee sees it, does not become generally possible till life in this world is shattered and desperate, every formative and creative moment in civilization—or of personal existence —serves not as a partial revelation of the Ultimate but just the opposite—nothing less than a postponement of man's final happiness, since that happiness becomes possible only when man renounces the hope of any earthly felicity.

Toynbee's conclusion is orthodox Augustinian doctrine; and it brings him very close to Reinhold Niebuhr's position in our own day; but it lacks the robust sense of health that one finds in the dualism of Thomas Aquinas, for the reason that Aquinas, like Aristotle before him, was essentially both a better sociologist and a more hopeful contemplator of life's natural circumstances and possible goods.

My conclusion is that the problems that Toynbee set himself to answer in *A Study of History* cannot be answered in terms of the metaphysical and sociological framework that he has used. For this reason, these problems seem to him insoluble "In This World" and he is therefore driven to seek an Other Worldly exit, forced upon him by his original presuppositions. This is not to say that Toynbee's pessimistic conclusions about the inherent impossibility of achieving a satisfactory life on earth may not, in our own time, be pragmatically justified, just as Spengler's views actually were, repulsive though they seemed to most of us when he put them forth. Modern man, believing only in the omnipotence and omniscience of science, now has the power to bring about the most incredible prediction of the Apocalypse: the actual End of the World, in a final sheet of flame. Because of our failure to anticipate this fact and take precautions against it—because rare minds like Toynbee's have come on the scene perhaps too late to overcome the inertia of automatic thinking—we may in fact find no way out in "This World." If by a miracle we temporarily escape this sinister destiny, we shall not overcome the fate that threatens us, and deliver ourselves from the treadmill of repetitive Civilizations and equally repetitive Universal Churches, until we acquire a more adequate and comprehensive philosophy than Western Culture as a whole has yet been guided by. That philosophy does not emerge from *A Study of History*. Toynbee's historical breadth in posing the problem of human life and destiny has been nullified, despite his good intentions, by his philosophic narrowness in seeking the answer.

Yet if our world civilization survives its threatened ordeals, *A Study of History* will stand out as a landmark, perhaps even a turning point.

FACT AND FICTION IN TOYNBEE'S STUDY OF HISTORY*

Rushton Coulborn

Among the many criticisms which have been made of the work of Arnold Toynbee[1] none, so far as I know, has yet sought to disentangle his major contributions to historical scholarship from the other matter in which he embeds them. This essay is an attempt to begin that task. The value of Toynbee's contributions is considerable—greater, in my opinion, than other scholars, especially other historians, have usually been prepared to grant. Toynbee is among the great historians. His discernment is profound; it is true much more often than not, and, less often, it is quite novel.

What makes Toynbee difficult for his fellow scholars is, of course, his religious convictions and his practice of subordinating his scholarship to them. In the newly published volumes of *A Study of History*[2] Toynbee is much franker about this than he has formerly been. He now says explicitly that his great work is a theodicy: history is "a vision . . . of God revealing Himself in action to souls that were sincerely seeking Him" (X, 2). It must be said at once that the attempt to write history in this light and at the same time to follow the strictly empirical procedure of the modern schools is not easy. Hence the somewhat pathetic questions Toynbee is still asking when he reaches the end of his intellectual pilgrimage:

> If Necessity is queen of the last act of the play, can Freedom have ever reigned at any stage? If sinners are powerless to elude their punishment, was it ever in their power to avoid committing the sin for which this punishment is the nemesis? And, if the sin has been as inevitable as the punishment is inexorable, how can the doom which the pitiless mills grind out be identified with Justice? (X, 124).

There has undoubtedly been a struggle between Toynbee the scholar and Toynbee the believer. That the believer must still ask questions of this sort at the end of ten volumes of study suggests that the scholar has fought a good fight—hence that we may place some confidence in him. Not that the believer has been vanquished; he has, on the contrary, been a tough antagonist who

---

*The substance of this paper was read before the Georgia Philosophical Society on 7 May, 1955, printed in *Ethics*, LXVI (1956).

[1] Professor Kenneth W. Thompson has made a thorough study in these pages of Toynbee's method and of his relation to other scholars, and has given an account of his prepossessions; *Ethics*, LXV (1955), 287-303.

[2] VII-X (London, 1954).

has imposed formidable distortion upon the work of the scholar. But the figure is too simple: the believer and the scholar are closely united in Toynbee, and it may well be that it is the believer we have to thank for much of the insight. In the last analysis, Toynbee's work witnesses to the limitations, the ephemeral character even, of the rules of the schools, for he penetrates usefully into all kinds of corners the prudent scholar avoids, and, if his bias produces error, there are occasions when it seems a better guide than strict academic virtue! At any rate, it is our business to see him steadily, to straighten out his distortions of fact, and so to rescue his major historical doctrine from the condemnation of academic hacks which threatens it.

* * *

Toynbee's doctrine begins quite without distortions. A series of civilized societies, he thinks, arose in the Old World in the fifth and fourth millennia B. C. and in the New World at a much later time. The "Egyptiac" and "Sumeric" Civilizations (the Sumeric in Mesopotamia), the Indus Culture in India, and the Shang Culture in China, and the so-called "Andean Civilization" in Peru, all arose in the valleys of rivers running through desert or steppe land. The process of genesis of the civilizations Toynbee describes as one of "Challenge and Response," and in these five cases the challenge was of desiccation in the desert or steppe areas through which the rivers ran, of flood, swamp, and rank vegetation in the valleys to which the human population was driven by the desiccation outside the valleys. Small primitive societies, unable to survive in the desert, were driven into the valleys. To survive in the valleys they were forced to combine together into great societies in order to grapple cooperatively with the tasks of draining swamp, confining the floods and saving the life-giving waters, and extirpating the wild vegetation which constantly threatened their agriculture. They responded successfully to the challenge and so produced for the first time those large-scale societies which we customarily call civilized.[3]

In the case of "Minoan Civilization" in the islands of Crete and the Cyclades, the physiographic challenge was different: it was

---

[3]Thompson complains that Toynbee never defines his concept of civilization "by more than a few illustrations" (*Ethics*, LXV, 299). I feel that Toynbee's looseness is right in principle. There are many conflicting uses of the term, and, rather than a formal definition, I find it practical to offer a historical one, namely that civilized societies are those societies, of magnitude far greater than earlier, primitive societies and surviving primitive societies, which arose by reason of special climatic conditions at the end of the Quaternary Ice Age (see text below) and all those societies which have been derived from them. This kind of definition suits Toynbee's use, and could be said to be implied in it.

the problem of survival in the islands where sheer space was very short. In the case of the "Mayan Civilization," which arose at the base of the Yucatan Peninsula in Central America, the challenge was the density of the tropical forest.

I wholeheartedly support Toynbee in principle in the establishment of these bold, imaginative hypotheses. If more historians had his constructive imagination and his intellectual courage, it would be better both for the profession and for society. The repetition of the same fundamental process in five different cases is an impressive regularity. However wide the variation even of the major details, we cannot escape the high probability that those five great events, the origins of civilization in Egypt, Mesopotamia, India, China, and Peru, each entirely independent of the others, were repetitive in their fundamental factors. And more, it is not impossible that the advance of knowledge will show that the civilization of Central America did not really originate in the tropical forest, and that it will show too that the Minoan Civilization in Crete began as a cultural province of Egypt. In such case the approach to uniformity would be greater even than Toynbee thinks. It may be observed that the desiccation in the desert areas which drove the human population into the valleys was consequent upon the world-wide climatic oscillations in which the Quaternary Ice Age came to an end. The similarity of the several great events is thus made the more probable by the unity of their cause.

Civilization first arose, then, in six or seven distinct and separate occasions in various parts of Africa, Asia, and America. These were, in Toynbee's term, the "Primary Civilizations." After varying lengths of time, generally of the order of two thousand years, these original societies went into decline and disintegration. In their disintegrated condition, however, they provided new challenges to mankind whose responses produced the "Secondary Civilizations," of which there were eight since Sumeric Civilization gave place to two, not merely one. The secondary civilizations lasted less long than the primary, usually some centuries over a thousand years, and then they in turn declined and disintegrated and were succeeded by the "Tertiary Civilizations." There were eight tertiary civilizations, but they were derived from only four of the secondary civilizations, the other four being without issue. Of the eight tertiary civilizations five exist today, the other three having come to grief in various ways. One of those existing today is, of course, our own "Western Christian Civilization." In addition to these are to be noticed four "abortive civilizations," one secondary, three tertiary; the meaning of the term is sufficiently clear.

What causes the decline and disintegration of civilized societies?

According to Toynbee, decline begins with "breakdown," and breakdown is usually, not quite always, due to internecine warfare within the society, that is to say, war between separate sovereign nations or else civil war. The wars which lead to breakdown occur during the "Time of Troubles," usually rather later than half way through the development of a civilized society, for what Toynbee calls breakdown is only the very beginning of the end. Decline begins after breakdown and then continues for several centuries before revival sets in. The political form of a society before its breakdown is variable from case to case, but the best characteristic political achievements of the society—such as parliamentary government in the case of our own society—are reached, naturally, before the breakdown occurs. The same is to be said of intellectual and of aesthetic achievements. Most societies reach political unification for the first time at the conclusion of the wars of the Time of Troubles. Where those wars are wars between nations, as they usually are, the end comes when one nation conquers the relics of all the other nations. The empire the victor nation establishes Toynbee calls a "Universal State," and, in his view, every universal state is a decadent institution in whose time the whole culture, political, intellectual, and aesthetic, is running downhill.

There are criticisms to be made of Toynbee at this point. His equating of the international wars in different civilized societies and his perception of their great importance are admirable examples of his historical insight, but I think his view that the wars cause breakdown is probably an over-simplification, possibly a radical error. We can see plainly enough that a society is put to a serious strain by the wars, but we do not know of any causal connection between them and the decline of the society. The rise and fall of civilized societies and their culture is an all-pervading phenomenon which is reminiscent of many other oscillatory movements in nature, and it seems to me that it is much less likely that the wars are crucial and necessary links in the chain of cause than they are important concomitants, symptoms perhaps, of a process we are unable to discern in its ultimate character.

For Toynbee, history is, of course, entirely a moral matter. The breakdown of a civilized society he therefore sees as "suicide" —it matters little whether he intends the word literally or figuratively. Before breakdown the society is led by a "creative minority," but, once the universal state is formed, the minority ceases to create, and becomes merely a "dominant minority." And Toynbee insists to the point of dogmatism upon the non-creative character of the leading people in a broken-down society. Perhaps he is, so to speak, not quite a free agent in this unfortunate matter of creativity. He takes it, together with the essential principle of his central thesis about the place of religion in history, from Henri Bergson. And Bergson's conception of creativity is a very special one: creativity for him is the outward and visible sign of the gyrations of the *élan vital* in and out and round about the souls of men.

But it is, I am afraid, unwise to take that brilliant philosopher too literally when he is performing rather as a poet. I do not believe that the leaders of society are creative at one time and uncreative at another. They may be less creative, or less frequently creative, during the decline of a civilized society than during its growth, though I very much doubt this; the Roman Empire in its decline was ruled by some extraordinarily able men who were, surely, highly creative. There is, again, the question where in society creativity is located. The *dominant* minority must presumably consist of people in high places—government, the top of the professions, etc. What about the creative minority which is supposed to precede the dominant minority before decline sets in, then: is that minority similarly placed? I do not believe it for an instant. Of course, Toynbee may not intend this. If not, however, does he contend that creativity in more humble places ceases as decline sets in? It is hardly necessary to adduce evidence to show that creativity is a subtle and ubiquitous quality; this is known to anybody who has the least acquaintance with the arts and crafts, and it must be true of all, or almost all, human doings. Toynbee, on the contrary, contends that the creative minority leads and the rest follow by mechanical mimesis. This is a hideous perversion. Creativity and imitation, leading and following, can be sharply divided from each other, I suspect, only in doctrinal formulae; in natural fact they are subtly and intimately related. Toynbee's *führerprinzip* is a crude and an over-simple one. It is dangerous, and we must beware of it.

The question remains whether there really is a relation between creativity and the rise and fall of civilizations. Very possibly there is. The movement of the arts, in which creativity is evident and inescapable, suggests this, for they rise exuberantly when a civilization is in vigorous growth, and they wither conspicuously when a civilization declines. But the relation between the two phenomena is highly mysterious, and we know little about it. My guess is that the causal process at work is not a simple upward one from creativity in the various activities of the society to produce the total effect of civilization. It is credibly maintained by modern cultural anthropologists, and was effectively shown too by Durkheim, that the causes of events in society are social. Even if this is an oversimplification, it is, I think, correct in requiring that the predominating causal process is one on the social level,

that what happens in and to the individual happens subordinately
to the overall process of the civilization. Not that this is a
smooth, mechanical operation; there is nothing mechanical about
it, *pace* Toynbee. Conflict is rife in it, as it is in all nature. Hence
the great, creative, struggling, failing Roman Emperors. Hence
Aristarchos of Samos, who perceived that the earth went round
the sun, but was rejected by the scholarship of his day. Some of
this is, no doubt, compatible with Toynbee's doctrine, and at least
it is he who has directed attention to the relation of creativity
with the movement of civilization. But I reject him when he categorically divides creators from imitators and an age of creative
leadership from an age of dead domination.

The rise of civilized societies is achieved through mediation of
religion: this is the central proposition in Toynbee's interpretation
of history.[4] On the whole, I think it is probably true although
there is at least one difficult case. This is the case of Greece. It
is hard to believe that the Olympian deities were an inspiration to
their worshippers comparable with the inspiration supplied by
Islam or Buddhism. But in fact we know very little of Greek
religion in its earliest form, and so it is impossible to judge the
question. Thus the Greek case cannot be taken to upset the high
probability given by all the better known cases.

The better known cases do not include those of the primary
civilized societies, whose origins, if not wholly unknown, are in the
main only a matter for informed speculation. To these cases
Toynbee does not seek to apply his central proposition, remaining
silent in the manner of the orthodox historian in the absence of
evidence. Hence, it is in every case the revival of a civilized
society, or the rise of a new society out of the ruins of an old one,
which he explains through religion. The involvement of the old
society in the rise of the new one thus becomes important, and
rightly so, for the change from decline to revival is a long process,
covering centuries, and the two things are so intimately involved
that, once again, we may doubt that, in seeing them as two, we
really see very far into the nature of the process. After breakdown,
then, there is, according to Toynbee, a "schism in the body social";
the society comes to comprise three conflicting interests, the
"dominant minority," the "internal proletariat," and the "external
proletariat." The internal proletariat is simply the masses and all

---

[4]Perhaps it should be said that this was the apparent central proposition
before the publication of Volumes VII-X of *A Study of History*, but that
those volumes shift the center of attention to the formation of universal
churches; cf. Thompson, *Ethics*, LXV, (1953), 295-296, and see text below.
But the shift concerns chiefly Toynbee himself. His historian colleagues will,
I venture to think, remain more interested in religion as mediating the rise
of civilizations.

others but the ruling class within the society. The external proletariat is the barbarians beyond the frontiers of the society, open
frontiers—*a limen*—before the breakdown, closed frontiers—*a
limes*—afterwards. This classification is made specifically in the
light of religious change, as that change subsequently develops.
It would scarcely seem to mean very much otherwise. Indeed, for
most purposes the external proletariat can hardly be said to belong
to the society at all.

It is Toynbee's view that these three classes respectively create
three different kinds of religion as an old civilization declines and
a new one arises. That there are three kinds of religion, or, more
correctly, three elements in religion, as it is re-created in a declining civilized society, I believe to be true and important. It is a
novelty added by Toynbee to the general doctrine (held by others
besides himself) that the rise of civilization is mediated by religion.
That the three elements proceed from the three sources Toynbee
gives I believe to be inaccurate, and that every actual religion is
from one particular source to the exclusion, or largely to the exclusion, of others I believe to be a gross error.

It is true that one element in religion is created by the external
proletariat, the barbarians, and true even that there have been
religions drawn from this source rather largely and almost to the
exclusion of other sources. But it is not true that every religion
created by barbarians has been of the same kind, namely a religion
with a pantheon of deities reflecting their human creators and the
war-band organization which often (not always) constitutes the
form of the barbarian society.

To say that there is an element in religion created by the dominant minority is a sort of half-truth. The element of truth in it is
that some religions which mediate the revival of civilized societies
consist rather largely of re-creations of the old religion of the
society before it went into decline. But other elements are by
no means excluded from these re-creations; indeed new elements
and new syntheses are usually conspicuous in them. Whether
these re-creations should be ascribed to the dominant minority is
highly doubtful. I cannot think of a case in which the champions
of the re-created religion included all elements in the old leadership of the society. As a matter of fact, the champions—who can
usually be properly described as the leading creators of the new
synthesis—were almost always priests, but they were not always
the same priests as those of the earlier religion; if they were the
same, or in part the same, they usually were not allied with other
elements in the old ruling class; and, the creative function of
priests is by no means confined to religions deriving largely from
the old religion of the society in question. Almost all religions,

if not introduced and formed by priests, soon find their way into priestly hands.

Finally, there are, according to Toynbee, the "higher religions" created by the internal proletariat, or at least "adapted," or "adopted" by the internal proletariat. These two latter terms are an afterthought on Toynbee's part, added in a table at the end of Volume VII of the *Study* (Table IV, facing p. 772). The addition seems to betray a certain doubt in Toynbee's own mind of the accuracy of the term "created" as applied to the function of the internal proletariat. Certainly, creativity as narrowly conceived by Toynbee and Bergson could by no means be attributed to the proletariat. If, however, we forget the Bergsonian-Toynbeean heresy about creativity, it may be said that the proletariat participates in the creation of religion as it does in much else, namely by adopting and making its own the religion it is offered. But this, like the function of priests in the creation of religion, gives no distinction: all religions are created for the masses. No religion is of any importance until it is brought down to the mental level of the masses and propagated among them. Its acceptance by the masses is a vital part of the mode in which new religion rescues a society from decline and sets its revival in process; new religion inspires new hope, and, even if the hope is directed towards a future existence after death, it appears to take effect, in some way we do not clearly understand, in the real existence in this world.

Where, then, is the third source of new religion if it is not where Toynbee says it is, in the internal proletariat? It is in alien civilized societies. The propensity of a failing civilized society to "catch" religion from a neighboring civilized society, indeed often from two or more neighboring civilized societies is conspicuous. It is, in fact, increasingly conspicuous the later the date taken, — and this for the simple reason that, in later times, as the size and number of civilized societies have grown and they have covered more and more of the earth's surface, — they have inevitably come into closer and closer contact with one another and so have the more readily borrowed from one another.

What, then, is a "higher religion" if it is not a religion "created, adapted or adopted" by an internal proletariat. It is, I am afraid, a chimaera invented by Toynbee in the interests of his theodicy. We need not rush to the opposite extreme and say that all civilized religions are equal—whatever that might mean—but we must recognize that all of them are in fact mixtures: they are, as I have said elsewhere,[5] "conglomerate myth." It is, therefore, unsafe

---

[5]The Concept of the 'Conglomerate Myth,' *Proceedings of the Tenth International Congress of Philosophy,* ed. Beth, Pos, and Hollak, I (Amsterdam, 1949), 74-81.

to argue that some civilized religions are "higher religions" and others are not, and, when that difference of degree is converted into a distinction of type, as it is by Toynbee, it becomes a categorical error.

Toynbee builds upon this error. All the effective higher religions he finds at the transition from the secondary to the tertiary civilizations. Rudiments and trivial cases of higher religions have occurred at other times, but have not mediated the revival of civilizations. A higher religion becomes the basis for a vehicle called a "universal church" which serves as a "chrysalis" for the new civilization. This is the process of "apparentation and affiliation": the old civilization is "apparented" to the new, and the new "affiliated" to the old. The concept is used to show continuity combined with a change or a break. In the other two modes of derivation that particular kind of relationship does not occur.

In the earliest volumes of *A Study of History,* which appeared twenty-two years ago, the "universal church" served only as a chrysalis for bringing forth a new civilization (I, 55-63, 130-146, and *passim*). In Volume V, one of the three which appeared in 1939, Toynbee asks whether the universal church is a species of human society distinct from the species civilization (p. 23). Now in Volume VII, one of the four which appeared in 1954, he answers the question in the affirmative, saying that it is not the aim— the deity's aim, presumably—that universal churches should merely serve as chrysales for new civilizations, but that at some time in the future it may be hoped that they, or a single one of them, will supersede civilizations as the form of human society (pp. 393-525). The derivation of the tertiary civilizations through universal churches was thus not in itself a good thing, and therefore something better is to be expected in the future. The somewhat trivial higher religions which have appeared in tertiary societies cannot be expected to lead to anything much, but perhaps the contact of Christianity and the Mahayana, which Toynbee likes best of the extant higher religions, will lead to a great future for man (pp. 426-428, 438-442, and *passim*).

We are offered a scheme of history, then, which begins with the rise of the primary civilized societies, moves through relatively unimportant religious change to the secondary civilized societies, then to universal churches, at that point lapses back to civilization, producing the tertiary civilized societies, but may be expected to lead on to higher things. This is Toynbee's theodicy. His faith is that higher things are to follow, and that, whatever they are to be, they will justify the ways of God to man.

* * *

This scheme of history is too neat to be true. It is an approximation to objective fact, but it gets a subjective twist in the direction of Toynbee's wishful thinking, his wish that God shall be found to deal justly and amiably with man. Really, nature is much more of a jerry-builder than Toynbee's God. The cultural ascent of man is a formidable edifice, but its regularity is marred by a number of untidy improvisations, as if nature had not had the wit to follow its own plan. It cannot be said that Toynbee is unaware of this; he knows that there are some queer shapes in parts of the edifice. He allows for them, but insists on the three tiers of civilization and the layer of universal churches. His erroneous distinctions between the three kinds of religion get worked into the general structure he sets up, as also do some of his other notions, in particular his notion about creativity. All of these produce errors, but there are other errors for which I can find no reason in Toynbee's prepossessions; they are just plain blunders.

The rest of this essay is an attempt to straighten out the distortions Toynbee has made in the history of China, India, Egypt, and Mesopotamia, the four main civilized societies of the Old World. A few remarks are added about other societies, and certain religions receive special treatment after the main structure of the four societies has been considerd. If much of the argument consists of dogmatic statements, this is because it simply is not possible, within the compass of a readable article, to explain reasons fully.

There is certainly a *tendency* for regular ups and downs of civilization to occur in the history of each society. Each tends to pass through various phases with an empire, Toynbee's "universal state," as the political frame of the last phase of every up and down cycle,[6] the rise of new religions during the decline of every cycle, and mediation of the rise of the next cycle by a religion. But this regular process is only of a rough, general character, permitting much variation in detail from case to case. Many departures even from this rough regularity occur, often in the regions where two or more civilizations overlap upon each other, for all of them have expanded vastly, and none has been without contact with others. Where the regions of overlap have been large, it has been easy to make errors in identifying particular societies and tracing their process of rise and fall. Toynbee and his predecessors have all made such errors and other errors besides. It remains true, I believe, that the rise and fall process is the most important single regularity in history, and that a critical

---

[6]The word is used without any mechanistic connotation. As used here, it may be considered as a convenient synonym for "rise, culmination, and decline." It has no further meaning.

grasp and application of it are the chief need of serious historical scholarship today.

These cycles of civilization are easily discernible in the history of China and India, and Toynbee has identified the three correctly in the case of China: the transition between the first and second occurred as the "Shang Culture" came to an end in the few centuries before 1000 B.C. and perhaps a century or two afterwards.[7] The second transition occurred during the later days of the Han Dynasties and thereafter for a couple of centuries or so. Toynbee also spotted the first transition in the history of India correctly, namely at the decline of the "Indus Culture" and the rise of Vedic Hinduism in the latter part of the second millennium B.C. The second transition, however, he put at the latter end of and after the Gupta Dynasty, that is to say about the fifth to perhaps the eight or ninth century A.D. This, I am quite sure, is the wrong period. The correct period of the transition is between the Maurya and Gupta Empires, from about the second century B.C. to about the fourth A.D. The main religious change occurred in that period, beginning earlier, and the chronology of the change is shown clearly in the emergence of new art forms, the sculpture of images of the deities, and the building of temples for their worship.[8]

Toynbee's error in this last case does not seem to result from any of his peculiar doctrines. In the case of Egypt it is one of his doctrines which leads him astray; he maintains that the entire history of Egypt is comprised within a single cycle of civilization. In fact, two cycles are plainly traceable. The transition between them occurred in what Egyptologists call the "First Intermediate Period" between the "Old Kingdom" and the "Middle Kingdom," in the latter part of the third millennium B.C. There was then the usual clear decline in the arts and in politics and a decline in thought too, though this last is less clear in the record. There follows, plainly enough, a reconstruction of religion, a revival of the arts through a period of primitivism,[9] and a great political revival. This transition is so clear in the standard accounts of Egyptian history that Toynbee is forced to consider it and indeed

---

[7]Some Sinologists might say that there was not yet a high civilization in the Hsia-Shang era, but that is disproved, I think, by the political development and by the careful tracing of the development of certain art forms by Karlgren (*Bulletin of the Museum of Far Eastern Antiquities,* VIII [1936], 9-154; IX [1937], 9-117; XIII [1941], 1-4).

[8]A. K. Coomeraswamy, *History of Indian and Indonesian Art* (New York, Leipzig, and London, 1927), pp. 15'-49. This book was available when Toynbee wrote.

[9]The general transition can be found in any account of Egyptian history, but the aesthetic change is particularly well and shortly treated in E. Drioton and J. Vandier, *Les peuples de l'Orient méditerranéan*: II, *L'Egypte* (Paris, 1938), 222-224.

to reconsider it at length in one of his latest volumes.[10] But he finally rejects it and returns to his first decision about the problem, that Egypt had had only a single civilization. His reason for this is a purely doctrinaire one, so far as I can discern. It is that the ruling minority of the Old Kingdom was creative: it created the pyramids; hence it could not have been a merely dominant minority, and so the Old Kingdom could not have been a universal state. The great importance Toynbee attaches to the idea of creativity which he took from Bergson is evident here—but I have already said what I think about that!

The twisting of his own theory Toynbee has to do to accommodate this over-literal idea of creativity is painful. He has first to explain the occurrence of the Old Kingdom: if it was not a universal state—of which it has all the earmarks—what was it? A "precocious political unification," answers Toynbee in one of the lamest passage in the *Study* (I, 136). But it is difficult to cram the long course of Egyptian history into the life of a normal civilization. Therefore, Toynbee decides that there had almost occurred a break—a transition from one cycle to another—between the Middle Kingdom and the "New Kingdom" or "Empire," that is to say, in the Hyksos period from the eighteenth to the sixteenth century B.C. The break was prevented by an "unnatural 'union sacrée: between the nascent religion of the internal proletariat of the Egyptiac Society and the moribund religion of the dominant minority" (I, 144), and from this resulted the prolongation of the life of the civilization as a "dead trunk artificially re-erected" for some two millennia.[11] The facts are that the recreation of Egyptian religion was complete by the time of the Twelfth Dynasty, immediately after the First Intermediate Period; that the popularizing which then occurred,[12] so far from being unnatural, was a perfectly normal process; and that the normal sequel followed, namely a new cycle of the civilization.

With the civilization of Mesopotamia Toynbee begins well and ends badly. He finds the correct transition between the first and

---

[10]His first consideration of the matter is in I, 136-146, and his final reconsideration in IX, 682-692, the latter one of his special Annexes.

[11]I, 139. The two millennia are from the sixteenth century B. C., when the Hyksos were expelled, to the fifth century A. D.

[12]Toynbee followed Breasted in seeing the rise of the worship of Osiris as the popularizing process; this is Toynbee's "nascent religion of the internal proletariat." Today the process is seen more broadly, the advance of the god Amon also being an important part of it. Cf. J. H. Breasted, *The Development of Religion and Thought in Ancient Egypt* (New York and London, 1912), pp. 142-164, 257-311, and *idem, The Dawn of Conscience* (New York and London, 1934) pp. 105 *ff.* with J. A. Wilson, *The Burden of Egypt* (Chicago, 1951), pp. 112-124 and H. Frankfort, *Ancient Egyptian Religion* (New York, 1948), pp. 102-105.

second cycles from somewhere about the nineteenth to the thirteenth century B.C., the end of the Third Dynasty of Ur to the
later days of the Kassite Dynasties. He then says that two distinct civilizations, "Babylonic" and "Hittite," descended from
that of the first cycle, the "Sumeric." There is no ground for
cavilling at this distinction, for it merely emphasizes local differences as against general likeness.[13] It is another matter when
Toynbee declares that in Syria-Palestine and Iran, on the two sides
of Mesopotamia, quite a different civilization arose. This was the
"Syriac Civilization," which was descended, he says, from Minoan
Civilization,[14] so far as it was descended from any earlier civilization (I, 79-82, 101-103). In fact, the only substantial relation
to Minoan Civilization is confined to coastal Palestine where the
Philistines, who really were of that civilization, settled. But their
Minoan culture was lost within a century or a little more after
their settlement.[15].

The only considerable argument Toynbee produces for associ-
ating Iran with Syria-Palestine in the same civilization is that
Jahwism, the religion of the Hebrews, and "Zoroastrianism," the
religion of the Medes and Persians of Iran, are similar. He omits
to notice that Phoenicia and inland regions of Syria had no religion
at all like either Jahwism or Zoroastrianism. The fact about this is
that Jahwism and Mazdaism—a better term than Zoroastrianism[16]—approximated to one another in the time of the Achaemenian Empire; there is no evidence that they did so earlier.[17]

The Achaemenian Empire, formed in the sixth century B.C.,
was, according to Toynbee, the universal state of the Syriac Civili-

---

[13]But it would be more consistent if Toynbee were to do this for India
and China too. He does indeed distinguish between "Far Eastern Civilization, Main Body, the third cycle in China and contiguous continental areas,
and "Far Eastern Civilization in Japan." But consistency would require subdivisions in "Sinic Civilization" (the second cycle in China), "Indic" (the
second cycle in India), and "Hindu" (the third cycle in India and beyond).

[14]The civilization of Crete, the Cyclades, and the Peloponnese; see p. 3
above.

[15]See H. R. Hall, *The Ancient History of the Near East*, 5th ed. (London,
1920), pp. 418-419.

[16]Even though the modern Parsees use Zoroaster's name, the cult really
owes little to Zoroaster and we do not know at all well what particulars it
does owe to him.

[17]Toynbee, surprisingly, says it is "recognized on all hands" that the religions of Iran and Israel had been developing on converging lines and diverg-
ing from all other contemporary religions for four centuries before the empire. I may cite in reply an authority Toynbee often relies on, Eduard
Meyer, who says, on the contrary, that the convergence occurred under the
empire and because of the existence of the empire, and that it included all
the contemporary religions (*Geschichte des Altertums*, 4th ed., Stuttgart,
1944, IV-1, 157-164). This passage was available (in an earlier edition)
when Toynbee wrote; in fact, he quoted part of it in another connection (VI,
29-33).

zation. It swallowed up the feeble remains of the Babylonic Civilization, the Hittite having disappeared several centuries earlier. Actually, the Achaemenian Empire was, I think, the universal state of the Babylonic Civilization—more inclusively, of the second cycle of Mesopotamian Civilization. There is not really any serious problem about this, although perhaps today we understand a little better than when Toynbee was writing the early volumes of the Study that the culture of the Medes and Persians, politically, aesthetically, and intellectually, was Mesopotamian. They were late-comers and they had their local cultural peculiarities, it is true. But in those things they were no different from the peoples of Ch'in and of Ch'u in the second cycle in China, or those of Magadha in the second cycle in India, and nobody has ever tried to argue that Ch'in or Ch'u had a civilization fundamentally different from that of the rest of China, or Magadha one fundamentally different from the rest of India.

Toynbee's real difficulty about Iran is that he has not seen that Mazdaism was the religion which mediated the transition from the second to the third cycle of Mesopotamian civilization. For this he is not to blame; we have only recently begun to get the facts about that religion straight.[18] He has also failed to see the derivation of Hebrew religion. For that there is certainly less excuse since the Egyptian and Mesopotamian elements in the Bible are well known. Even so, the relation of Hebrew to Egyptian monotheism was misunderstood—willfully misunderstood by some stiff-necked and pig-headed theologians, I think—when Toynbee was writing, and the facts about it are still being resisted by some specialists today.[19]

---

[18]The best authority is, in my opinion, H. S. Nyberg, trans. from the Swedish H. H. Schaeder, *Die Religionen des alten Iran* (Leipzig, 1938), though his view of Zoroaster's dates is hard to accept. For the rise of the new cycle and Mazdaism's part in it, A. Christensen, *L'Iran sous les Sassanides* (Copenhagen, 1944) is a useful complement to Nyberg. E. Benveniste, *Les Mages dans l'ancien Iran* (Paris, 1938) and F. W. König, *Alteste Geschichte der Meder und Perser* (Leipzig, 1934) are also useful, the former for later, the latter for earlier periods. It is unlikely that Mazdaism had any great power under the Achaemenids. It was formed by the Magi into a very powerful church in the late days of the Achaemenian Empire, under the Seleucids and under the Arsacids (ruling house of the Parthians) and it promoted with complete success, much as the Latin Christian Church did, the revival of its society in a new cycle of civilization.

[19]Not by W. F. Albright, whose short account of it, at both the Egyptian and the Hebrew ends (*From the Stone Age to Christianity*, Baltimore, 1946, first pub. 1940, pp. 165-170, 205-207), is the best I know. Frankfort has some illuminating remarks on Egyptian monotheism in *Ancient Egyptian Religion* (pp. 22-25). John A. Wilson, the latest authority to express himself about it, also contributes to the clarification of the movement of Egyptian religion, but he exerts himself to strengthen the old argument about the profound difference between Egyptian and Hebrew monotheism (*The Burden*

Indeed, the place of Syria-Palestine in history presents a serious problem. The whole territory was penetrated both by Egyptian and by Mesopotamian culture, but at different times and in different ways in different parts of it. Syria, including Phoenicia,[20] was drawn pretty well into Mesopotamian civilization during the second cycle, but Hebrew Palestine developed its own distinctive civilization which, so far as I can judge at the moment, was forcibly incorporated by the Assyrians in Mesopotamia, and never had free development again. Toynbee may be quite right in attributing the Hebrew *diaspora* to the suppression of Hebrew civilization.

Not knowing the function of Mazdaism in Mesopotamian civilization, Toynbee misses altogether the character of the Parthian-Sassanian period in Mesopotamia, Iran, and further afield. He set up his "Syriac Civilization" and brought it to its universal state, the Achaemenian Empire; when, therefore, that empire fell before the Macedonian Greeks, Toynbee thought that the Graeco-Roman (his "Hellenic") civilization, by that intrusion, interrupted the course of development of "Syriac Civilization" for a protracted period. The period was indeed protracted for a thousand years until the occurrence of another historic event which would not fit nicely into Toynbee's doctrine. This was the shifting of the Islamic Caliphate from Damascus to Baghdad in the eighth century A.D. Toynbee declares that this event, which united Syria-Palestine once more with Mesopotamia-Iran, was the restoration of the universal state of "Syriac Civilization," and that the break-up of the Abbasid Caliphate of Baghdad and the invasion of the territory by Turks and Mongols were the decline and dissolution of the "Syriac Civilization," which was then succeeded by two new civilizations, the "Iranic" in eastern Islam and the "Arabic" in western Islam (I, 72-78).

This leaves me gasping, and I shall therefore comment only that, in the last analysis, all doctrine is answerable to common

---

of Egypt, pp. 209-229, 314-317)). What he and some others of the Chicago school (e. g., Irwin in Frankfort *et al., The Intellectual Adventure of Ancient Man,* Chicago, 1946, pp. 224-225) do not seem to understand is that the religion of a society at the apex of a cycle of its civilization is something philosophic, intellectual, not very emotional, whereas that of a society in the early rise of its civilization is likely to be emotional to the point of fanaticism. The different temper of Hebrew and Egyptian monotheism, as Albright has been sensible enough to see, is no evidence against the connectedness.

[20]There were Minoan-Mycenean incursions into Phoenicia, but they were much lesser affairs than the Philistine conquest in the south. See, e. g., C. F. A. Schaeffer, Ugaritica, III (Paris, 1939), *ad fin.* and Z. S. Harris in *Annual Report of the Smithsonian Institution* (1937), p. 481, for Ugarit; H. Ingholt *in American Journal of Archaeology,* XLVI (1942), 472 for Hama.

sense! Islamic civilization, when it arises, is obviously something new. Its rise was mediated by Islam as a religion, of which there will be something to say below in the discussion of religions. This civilization intruded upon Syria-Palestine-Egypt-North Africa and ousted or absorbed Byzantine civilization and the remnants of earlier civilizations there. It intruded upon Mesopotamia and Iran and there absorbed Mesopotamian civilization, which had possibly been weakened, though it had certainly not been forced into suspension, by the much earlier Greek intrusion.[21] The Parsees saved themselves from Islam, but they are a feeble survival compared with the Jews. Islamic civilization does not follow the usual course of rise and fall of civilizations, and it is a grave error to try to force the facts into the regular mould. Islamic civilization is one of those irregularities that nature is prone to perpetrate to the discomfiture of those who think their formulae inviolable.

Our examination of Toynbee's treatment of the Mesopotamian and Egyptian civilizations is now complete. It may be added that Egypt proper, in its later history, was drawn first under Mesopotamian political control, then more effectively into Graeco-Roman and then Byzantine civilization, finally still more effectively into Islamic civilization. But there remained a tail-end of Egyptian civilization in Nubia and Ethiopia which revived in a third cycle, beginning probably as early as the ninth century B.C.

Toynbee's treatment of the development of Western Christian civilization is, I believe, quite sound, but his treatment of Byzantium and Russia is another lamentable distortion of the facts to fit a formula; Byzantium-Russia is in reality another of nature's irregularities. Toynbee's "obortive Scandinavian," "abortive Far Western Christian," and some others of his abortive civilizations are possibly authentic, but they are not very significant. Every time a civilization goes into decline there are numbers of abortive revivals which get swept up into the successful ones, and Toynbee should have found far more of these than he did if he wished to be consistent.

Now, as to religion—the mixed sources of some actual religions as against Toynbee's contention that each religion has a single origin. Toynbee says that the "Sinic Civilization", which arose in China in a period before and after 100 B.C., was derived from its predecessor, the Shang Culture, by mediation of the religion

---

[21]Consider on this subject the opinions of E. Herzfeld, *Archaeological History of Iran* (London, 1935), pp. 46-49, 69-75. But these opinions should be compared with those of C. M. Olmstead, quoted by A. T. Olmstead, *History of the Persian Empire* (Chicago, 1938), pp. 117-118, 178-182, 277-280, 352-353, those of G. M. A. Richter, *Hesperia* Supplement, VII (1949), 295-298, etc.

of the Shang external proletariat. Since Toynbee wrote, the archaeological evidence has destroyed this idea decisively.[22] Ancestor
worship was a large part of Shang religion, and it continued to be
a large part of Sinic religion. What is more, most of the rest of
the cult was not greatly changed, though we know this less surely.
What we do know is that the barbarians, who conquered the society and set up its new political system, brought their own heaven
deity, or their own name for the heaven deity, with them. The
barbarians were the Chou, their heaven deity was called T'ien,
and that deity was amalgamated with the Shang heaven deity,
Shang Ti.[23] In short, the new religion was a compound of the
old and of what the barbarians brought in. I should describe that
as quite a usual development.

At the corresponding juncture in India, when the "Indic Civilization" was derived from the Indus Culture, the external proletariat again imposed its religion, in Toynbee's opinion. He is in a
stronger position in this case, for this external proletariat was the
Vedic Aryans, and we know for certain that a part of the new
religion was theirs. But some scholars, for example D. D. Kosam-
bi,[24] hold strongly that the Brahmans, the priesthood of the Indic
Society, were not of Aryan origin, but instead survived from the
times of the Indus Culture, and this was in fact suggested thirty
years ago by Pargiter.[25] Archaeology suggests some continuities,
but more discontinuities, in religion from the Indus Culture to the
Indic Civilization.[26] There can, in fact, be no doubt that Indic
religion was a mixture, but perhaps the barbarian element in it
was larger than that in Sinic religion.

Toynbee says that the new religion in India at the next transition, the transition from Indic to "Hindu Civilization," was a
higher religion created by the internal proletariat. I readily agree
that that new religion was the equal of Christianity, the Mahayana,
and other religions Toynbee calls higher, but I really think, having
regard to his conception of creativity, that it is an impertinence
on his part to allege that the internal proletariat created it. If ever

---

[22]H. G. Creel, *The Birth of China* (New York, 1937), pp. 174-189, 330-345.

[23]*Ibid.*, p. 342.

[24]*Journal of the Bombay Branch, Royal Asiatic Society*, n.s. XXII (1946), 41; *Journal of the American Oriental Society*, LXXIII (1953), 204.

[25]F. E. Pargiter, *The Ancient Indian Historical Tradition* (London, 1922), pp. 304-307.

[26]For an argument emphasizing the discontinuities, see Sir John Marshall, *Mohenjo-daro and the Indus Civilization*, I (1931), 110-112; for evidence of some continuities, E. J. H. Mackay, *The Indus Civilization* (London, 1935), pp. 70-73, and D. Mackay, in *Annual Report of the Smithsonian Institution, 1932*, p. 437.

there was a case for that half-truth that the priests of the dominant minority created the new religion, that is it. The Brahmans came through this transition with flying colors. Their position had been attacked in the later days of the Indic Civilization, though probably not very seriously threatened. They triumphantly repulsed the attacks, and transformed the old Vedic Hinduism into what is really a vast series of allied, but quite incompatible, religions drawn from every conceivable source. It is the greatest strength of modern Hinduism that it not only tolerates, but ingests, any religion whatever, not excluding agnosticism and atheism for some Brahmans.

Christianity is not different from other religions in the multiplicity of its sources, but this is so well known that it need not long detain us. It was the survivor of many competing religions in late Roman times, and it had, by the time of its triumph, borrowed important elements from all the others, not excluding the religion of the Teutonic barbarians. Although the dominant minority was at one time opposed to Christianity, the large body of Neoplatonism Christianity incorporated was surely more a creation of the dominant minority than of any other class of persons.

Christianity, like nearly all other religions of civilized societies, arose during the decline of a civilized society and in consequence of the decline. Islam is very unusual in that it did not arise at such a time. Nor, at least from presently known evidence, can it be directly connected with the decline of any foregoing civilization. And Islam was unusual in other ways also. Toynbee says it was a higher religion, created by the internal proletariat of Syriac civilization. This is preposterous: it is obvious that the Hijaz Arabs, the originators of Islam, were not internal to any civilization; they were external. But they were a very irregular "external proletariat," for they were external at once to Mesopotamian civilization and to Byzantine civilization. Moreover, they were affected also by the surviving "fossil"—Toynbee's term—of Hebrew civilization in the form of the Jews who lived among them. Unlike many outer barbarians, they retained their tribal organizations and were not formed into war-bands. Hence they did not create for themselves a pantheon of barbarian deities whose relationships reflected the relationships of the leaders of war-bands. Instead, they created a barbarians' copy of civilized peoples' religions, the copy taking much from Judaism, something from Christianity, possibly something from Mazdaism, but retaining something also from their own primitive cult.

Thus, Islam exemplifies the mixed origin of religion. In this, as also in the main fact that it did give rise to a new civilization, Islam is like other religions of civilized societies. But the mixture was unusual in two ways at least. One was the source of an element of the mixture, not in an old, failing religion, but in Christianity, a religion flourishing in another civilization. Another way in which the mixture was unusual was that its chief element was drawn from the religion, Judaism, of a fossil of a suppressed civilization. Thus the case of Islam shows that religions of civilized societies, no less than their morphological development, can deviate sharply from the rough regularity of the majority of them.

* * *

The second half of this essay has been almost exclusively concerned with Toynbee's errors. These are large for a serious scholar. If there were in Toynbee's work nothing but errors of this order, it might merit the condemnation it has met with in some quarters. But the errors are in fact, bound up with profound insights, and the condemnations may, accordingly, be dismissed as a rather senseless noise.

Toynbee is finally to be judged as an artist. He is a great artist if rather a strange one. He is an idealist working in a medium where idealism is bound to create some error. For Toynbee's art is not one of words; or, if it is so in part, that is a part of his art in which he does not excel. His art is an art of representation, using historical knowledge as its medium. His subject is the whole career of man. Like all idealists, he draws upon the work of the realists in constructing his own technique. Like all idealists too, he subjugates the techniques of the realists to the idea which dominates him. His misfortune is that he happens to do this at a time when the realists, powerfully driven by scientists in their rear, are claiming the whole historical domain. But his misfortune is our good fortune. He reminds us, if we will, that the study of history is a larger matter than the best possible methodology.

TOYNBEE'S STUDY OF HISTORY

George Catlin

Lord Melbourne remarked, of William Wordsworth's *Excursion:* "it is amazing when you leave a book on the table, how much you know what is in it without reading it." There will be many who, until Mr. Somervell comes along, will be practicing this comfortable doctrine about Professor Toynbee's *Study*. "Toynbeeism is in the air", especially in America where, oddly, he is better known than in Britain. From the press one learns that "British historian Arnold J. Toynbee predicted to-day that there would be no third world war"; and, in recent press lists of the World's Immortals from Confucius to Darwin, for which Marx, Mohammed and Voltaire do not quite make the grade, Dr. Toynbee is found to be a runner-up.

Professor Toynbee began to write in the climate of the times when H. G. Wells was putting together his encyclopaedic, straightforward (if secularistically biased) *Outline of History*—"greater than Ranke", as Sir Ernest Barker said, in that he "knew prehistory", but ending in the despairing gospel of "mind at the end of its tether"—and eminent men were being impressed by the book of revelations of the immensely erudite and very readable Oswald Spengler. Toynbee, jotting down, as pencilled outline in a train in 1927, the sketch for his work to which he subsequently adhered, sought to produce a survey of history which not only would, with Dionysius of Halicarnassus, be "philosophy learned from examples", but would, with Spengler, yield a pattern. From this, studying the Past's lessons, we could peer into the Future's probabilities—but this in a more rational, empiric and liberal fashion than characterized Spengler. Toynbee is indeed not very kind to Spengler. The avoirdupois of his own product, exceeding even Will Durant's, is not in question. Everything is included, from Hammurabi to "my Aunt Grace". It is full of fascinating items of information. What impresses, however, is the erudition (although, as with Spengler, each specialist will have his own criticisms); and what attracts is the prophecy. Not only is Dr. Toynbee a very likable human being, a mystic and a poet when such are needed, but no one can fail to admire so determined an act of faith (comparable to that of Toynbee's model, Gibbon) that he would have a vision of the promised land of "conclusions"—although it must be no small comfort

---

Political Science Quarterly, vol. 70, 1955, pp. 107-112.

to have, supporting his arms, the Joshua and Aaron of Chatham House and of the Rockefeller Foundation. Many of us would find it would increase our own faith. Dr. Toynbee, however, is too honest and clear-sighted a man to wish us to do other than judge his fascinating work, not by the trust of the world's citizenry in *his* faith or by the massiveness of the mountains he has moved, but by the validity of the results which they have labored so long to produce.

This daedal product of labor is of peculiar interest to this reviewer who, in 1926, produced the first volume of a tetrology, still incomplete, which book was concerned to inquire what could be learned from history, which would have certainties as touching the limitations and control of future human conduct. His guides were Machiavelli, Hobbes, and, in lesser measure, Bryce and Alfred Adler. His concern was with method. And there still seems to be a strong case for basing the systematic study of politics (which is Dr. Toynbee's real concern, with his preoccupation with war, peace and social survival), precisely with Machiavelli, upon the constants in the nature of what Toynbee calls *homo terricola*. Recent British writers indeed are extraordinarily weak in their attention to fundamental method in the social sciences, in the very existence of which—there is no chair of sociology and until recently none of psychology in Oxford—most of them disbelieve anyhow. Toynbee's own references to the *Discourses* are almost nil, although there is evidence, in Volume III and elsewhere, of careful digestion. As touching method it is Schopenhauer who asserts that, for the very nature of the case, history as such cannot yield a science or "laws"—although sociology and political science can, of which, as Max Weber said, the critical unit lies in "the act". History indeed gives a gigantic framework of experience, mostly irrelevant. In criticism of Dr. Toynbee's labor of Hercules it is prudent, in order not to be carried away by the undertow of tendency in this vast field of erudition, to criticize from the basis of one's own professional studies.

If, we may say, the method is wrong, then, like the gentleman who recently got drowned while swimming the English channel by night, while the attempt is noble, meriting and receiving a cathedral obituary service, the result is one vast monument of expended human effort or, at best, a historical panorama like that of Wells. It offers no basis upon which to advise the distressed and questing masses of humanity; and could be very hurtful indeed if so regarded. If this work is to be read a century hence (and Toynbee has the charming quirk of so writing as if his reader were in A.D. 2052), this issue of method is quite basic. This warning uttered, it becomes disturbing to discover that, in his indexes to over a million words, Professor Toynbee makes no references at all to Schopenhauer, Vico, Herder or Weber. In the four last volumes there are only two references to Marx (who, however, gets indirectly a section as does, specifically, the self-defeating Crocean thesis of the unsatisfactory Collingwood), and a single reference to Comte, itself in a quotation from Collingwood. (The index is not unified: there are earlier references to Comte, but not methodological.) I would rather be sure about method than about the early Shang *mores*. On Toynbee's own admission, in the early twenties, he made a false start by beginning with a commentary on—among rather unexpected but prophetic things—the *Antigone* of Sophocles. Then he seems to have plunged in, his outline sketch made, bald-headed, only clear—and here utterly right—that the atomistic and antinomian orthodox historians were often sterile. His warfare against the pre-Linnaean beetle-collectors, the occupants of lofty chairs, is to be applauded. In this dive he was first guided by Professor F. J. Teggart, of the University of California; and he was later boosted on by Jung. It is a scandalous ingratitude that this rich University permits Teggart's *Theory* to remain (as I know by inquiries in Berkeley) out of print and unobtainable. But it is not ungrateful to say that Teggart's central preoccupation, like that of Polybius (with whose work Toynbee compares his own, (with differences of cultures—a word most difficult to define in applied studies—may not be the highway to great scientific advancements in the field. Nor is the speculative Jung perhaps the most fortunate choice, for the discovery of Newtonian or Einsteinian formulae, among the psychologists.

I find myself in entire agreement with Dr. Toynbee that social forms, be there just twenty-two "civilizations", all told, or not, depend upon human will. But, without being excessively voluntaristic and Pelagian, this argument would seem to make mincemeat of the approach, with its deterministic implication, primarily by way of gross "cultures"—with the old organic mythos, so attractive to the public, of growth, senescence, loves and hates, thrown in for good measure. I would leave cyclic theories to the Stoics and Spengler, and even forget about Vico and Comte. Men actually grow old and governments actually fall: I doubt whether cultures, even like the Welsh or Breton or Tennessee hillbilly, are entities of this precise order. The comments, on this matter of method, of the London *Times* reviewer, W. H. Walsh, of Merton College, Oxford, is worth quoting: "The question is whether any amount of historical knowledge can serve as an adequate ground of such deductions about the meaning of history as is here drawn. It is hard to acquit Mr. Toynbee of philosophical naivety on this point." Toynbee legitimately offers probabilities about human conduct. Here there are ordered patterns. But I am deeply skeptical about their connection with any neatly measured cultural time cycles. We must look elsewhere, I suggest, for the psychological clues. So far Mr. Walsh is right.

However, as touching Professor Toynbee's conclusions, in the tradition of Bossuet, it so happens that the present reviewer (here probably in a small minority) chances to be in a broad agreement with them. But I do not think they have to follow from Toynbee's elaborate premises. In detail, this reviewer is sufficient of an anarchist or proto-Marxist to agree that voluntary communities, such as churches, are *societates perfectiores* compared with the over-worshipped coercive states. Again, in so far as Toynbee inclines to what is technically called "indifferentism" (an especially Hindu view which, at its worst, means taking the lowest common denominator) in religion, he is liable to prove a more dangerous enemy to organized Christianity than Gibbon. But, in general, emphasis on the positive common values in the great historical religions will surely come, in the future. America suffers here from a mental schizophrenia between John Adams and Jefferson with Paine, which issues in secular schools and in such a mixture between economic conservatism and a "modernist", rationalist, engineering, secularist and (for Toynbee) "arid" mental outlook as to deprive her, it can be said, of leadership in Europe, where her true religion of Deweyite pragmatic democracy is (probably wrongheadedly) regarded with cynicism, not least on the basis of American sociology. Toynbee here administers good medicine. This schizophrenia permits, as joyous paradox, Baptist divines, in the name of the ascrosanctly foolish division of Church and State (Gandhi said an impossible division), to tell the American Executive that America shall not be diplomatically represented in Vatican City. So "presbyter is priest writ large." Jung, Cassirer and Toynbee, in his religious emphasis upon the importance of Divine Dramas and Cults, are probably true prophets and at least are corrective, in the field of values, of the heady secularism of the tradition of Paine and Ingersoll. The decisive field indeed in human affairs is that of a people's fundamental ideas, more determinant in revolution even than weapons of war. Howbeit such ideas must be not only of religion and cult, as Toynbee indicates, but also about population and soil-conservation and the like great realities of earth-politics, if terrifying race-war is to be avoided. The technical and the valuational ideas *both* matter; and must be wedded.

On the other hand, Toynbee's immediate prescriptions awake doubts, which this is no place to discuss. The reviewer can only demand another five years to digest a judgment. Here Toynbee yet seems to plummet from the world-historical empyrean into the coutryard of Chatham House, in wartime a collaborator of the British Foreign Office. It is odd that his vast studies seem to conclude in remarks which appear curiously to display the hallmark of the immediate *Zeitgeist,* especially in its Westminster epiphany. The great public has taken to its heart, like some formula by Herbert Spencer, the phrase "Challenge and Response". One would have supposed that widespread human funk about the hydrogen bomb (following a gross miscalculation by politicians about power balances) could be a Toynbean sign of decadence, only to be met by some "better idea" that could win the assent alike of common men in every country—such as a revulsion from tyranny and outdated Marxism to coöperation and sociological science or to religious pursuit of human fraternity. We learn that "Response" spells patience, coexistence and a missionary effort (which will be "dull") against that dynamic new Islam of which Lenin was the armed Prophet. Missionary about what? As Greece was to Rome? Marxism, Dr. Toynbee and Bevanite Mr. Driberg M.P. can both urge, is "a Christian heresy" (*vide Time*). Why not "Judaic" *à l'*Amos or even Saducee-Judaic? It says apocalyptically: "Brothers, unite: let us liquidate the running-dogs of non-Russian imperialism." (Marx himself included also the Russian variant.) Basically, one might suggest, the deepest psychology of Marxism is *not* Christian, but more nearly "capitalist", allied to the ultra-social-competitiveness and *Kampf* of now *démodé* Manchester secular capitalism and neo-Darwinism. However, against Dr. Toynbee's ten legions of volumes, we be but voices in the un-Rockefeller-watered wilderness; and discussions of these trifles of 1954-84 are merely quibbles *de minimis.* I can only protest the extreme importance, if we want practical results, of "Pure Politics" as of Pure Physics. Meanwhile, we must confess that the history of the world does indeed indicate the highly superior survival value of autocracies, such as the Egyptian and Chinese (although the wicked Venetian oligarchy did not do badly); and that the *pax Romana* was based on domination, desolation and conquest. The most probable prophecy would seem to be that the world will soon be ruled by a Kremlin-dynamized Peking, already ruling six hundred million folk. The appropriate philosophy will doubtless follow on owl-wings; and the kaleidoscopic pattern of the facts be expounded by some newer Toynbee. But that indeed human history could be *ad majorem Dei gloriam* I do not doubt.

TOYNBEE'S PHILOSOPHY OF HISTORY*

PITIRIM A. SOROKIN

I. OUTLINE AND APPRECIATION

Regardless of the subsequent criticism, Arnold J. Toynbee's *A Study in History* is one of the most significant works of our time in the field of historical synthesis. Although several volumes of it are yet to come, six published volumes display a rare combination of the thoughtfulness of a philosopher with the technical competence of a meticulous empiricist. The combination insures against the sterile scholarship of a thoughtless "fact-finder," as well as against a fantastic flight of an incompetent dilettante. Hence its significance for historians, philosophers of history, sociologists, political scientists, and for anyone who is interested in the how and why of emergence, growth, decline, and dissolution of civilizations.

Mr. Toynbee starts with a thesis that the proper field of historical study is neither a description of singularistic happenings contiguous in space or time, nor a history of the states and bodies politic or of mankind as a "unity."

> The "intelligible field of historical study" . . . are societies which have a greater extension, in both Space and Time, than national states or city-states, or any other political communities . . . Societies, not states, are "the social atoms" with which students of history have to deal [I, 45].

Combining religious charactertistic and territorial and partly political characterics, he takes "civilization" as the proper object of historical study, in which "civilization" is "a species of society" (I, 129ff.). Of such civilizations, he takes twenty-one (later twenty-six) "related and unrelated" species: the Western, two Orthodox Christian (in Russia and the Near East), the Iranic, the Arabic, the Hindu, two Far Eastern, the Hellenic, the Syriac, the Indic, the Sinic, the Minoan, the Sumeric, the Hittite, the Babylonic, the Andean, the Mexic, the Yucatec, the Mayan, the Egyptiac, plus five "arrested civilizations": Polynesian, Eskimo, Nomadic, Ottoman, and Spartan (I, 132ff.; IV, 1ff.) With these twenty-six civilizations at his disposal, Toynbee attacks, first, the problem of genesis of civilization: Why do some of the societies, like many primitive groups, become static at an early stage of their existence

*The Pattern of the Past, Beacon Press, Boston, 1949, pp. 95-126, and The Journal of Modern History, vol. XII, 1940, pp. 374-387.
1A Study of History. By Arnold J. Toynbee. 6 volumes. Oxford University Press, 1934-39.

and not emerge as civilizations, while other societies reach this level?

His answer is that the genesis of civilzation is due neither to the race factor nor to geographic environment as such, but to a specific combination of two conditions: the presence of a creative minority in a given society and of an environment which is neither too unfavorable nor too favorable. The groups which had these conditions emerged as civilizations; the groups which did not have them remained on the subcivilization level. The mechanism of the birth of civilization in these conditions is formulated as an inter- play of Challenge-and-Response. The environment of the above type incessantly challenges the society; and the society, through its creative minority, successfully responds to the challenge and solves the need. A new challenge follows, and a new response suc- cessfully ensues; and so the process goes on incessantly. In these conditions no possibility of rest exists, the society is on the move all the time, and such a move brings it, sooner or later, to the stage of civilization. Surveying the conditions in which his twenty-one civilizations were born, he finds that they emerged exactly in the above circumstances (I, 188-338; Vol. II, *passim*).

The next problem of the study is why and how, out of twenty- six civilizations, four (Far Western Christian, Far Eastern Chris- tian, Scandinavian, and Syriac) miscarried and turned out to be abortive; five (Polynesian, Eskimo, Nomadic, Spartan, and Otto- man) were arrested in their growth at an early stage; while the remaining civilizations grew "through an *elan* that carried them from challenge through response to further challenge and from differentiation through integration to differentiation again?" (III, 128).

The answer evidently depends upon the meaning of growth and its symptoms. In Toynbee's opinion the growth of civilization is not a geographic expansion of the society and is not due to it. If anything the geographic expansion of a society is positively associated with retardation and disintegration, not with the growth (III, 128ff.). Likewise, the growth of civilization does not consist in, and is not due to, technological progress and the society's increasing mastery over the physical environment: ". . . there is no correlation between progress in technique and progress in civilization" (III, 173-74). The growth of civilization consists in "a progressive and cumulative inward self-determination or self- articulation" of the civilization; in a progressive and cumulative "etherialization" of the society's values and "simplification of the civilization's apparatus and technique (III, 128ff., 182ff.). Viewed in the aspect of the intra-social and inter-individual relationship, growth is an inconstant creative "withdrawal and return" of the charismatic minority of the society in the process of the ever new challenges of the environment (III, 248). Growing civilization is a unity. Its society consists of the creative minority freely imitated and followed by the majority—the Internal Proletariat of the society and the External Proletariat of its barbarian neighbors. In such a society there is no fratricidal struggle, no hard and fast divisions. It is a solidary body. Growing civilization unfolds its dominant potentialities, which are different in different civilizations: aesthetic in the Hellenic civilization; religious in the Indic and Hindu; scientifically machinistic in the Western; and so on (III, 128-390). As a result, the process of growth represents a progressive integration and self-determination of the growing civilizations in growth. Such is the solution of the problem of growth of civilization.

The third main problem of the study is how and why civilizations break down, disintegrate, and dissolve. They evidently do so because, out of twenty-six species of civilizations, "only four have miscarried as against twenty-six that have been born alive," and "no less than sixteen out of these twenty-six are by now dead and buried" (the Egyptiac, the Andean, the Sinic, the Minoan, the Sumeric, the Mayan, the Indic, the Hittite, the Syriac, the Hellenic, the Babylonic, the Mexic, the Arabic, the Yucatec, the Spartan, and the Ottoman). Of the remaining ten civilizations living,

> the Polynesian and the Nomadic civilizations are now in their last agomies and seven out of eight others are all, in different degrees, under threat of either annihilation or assimilation by our own civilization of the West. Moreover, no less than six out of these seven civilizations . . . bear marks of having broken down and gone into disintegration (IV, 1-2).

Toynbee points out that the decline is not due to some cosmic necessity or to geographic factors or to racial degeneration or to external assaults of the enemies, which, as a rule, reinforce the growing civilization; neither is it caused by the decline of technique and technology, because "it is always the decline of civilization that is the cause and the decline of technique and consequence or symptom" (IV, 40).

The main difference between the processes of growth and of disintegration is that in the growth phase the civilization successfully responds to a series of ever new challenges, while in the disintegration stage it fails to give such a response to a given challenge. It tries to answer it again and again, but recurrently fails. In growth the challenges, as well as responses, vary all the time; in disintegration, the responses vary, but the challenge remains unanswered and unremoved. The author's verdict is that civilizations perish through suicide but not by murder (VI, 120). In Toynbee's formulation,

> the nature of the breakdowns of civilizations can be summed up in three points: a failure of creative power in the minority, an answering withdrawal of mimesis on the part of the majority, and a consequent loss of social unity in the society as a whole.

In an unfolded form this formula runs as follows:

> When in the history of any society a Creative Minority degenerates into a mere Dominant Minority which attempts to retain by force a position which it has ceased to merit, this fatal change in the character of the ruling element provokes, on the other hand, the secession of a Proletariat (the majority) which no longer spontaneously admires or freely imitates the ruling element, and which revolts against being reduced to the status of an unwilling "underdog." The Proletariat, when it asserts itself, is divided from the outset into two distinct parts. There is an Internal Proletariat" (the majority of the members) and . . . an "External Proletariat" of barbarians beyond the pale who now violently resist incorporation. And thus the breakdown of a civilization gives rise to a class war within the body social of a society which was neither divided against itself by hard-and-fast divisions nor sundered from its neighbors by unbridgeable gulfs so long as it was in growth (IV, 6).

This declining phase consists of three subphases: (a) breakdown of the civilization, (b) its disintegration, and (c) its dissolution. The breakdown and dissolution are often separated by centuries, even thousands of years, from one another. For instance, the breakdown of the Egyptiac civilization occurred in the sixteenth century B.C., and its dissolution only in the fifth century A.D. For two thousand years between breakdown and dissolution it existed in a "petrified life-in-death." In a similar "petrified" state up to the present time the Far Eastern civilization continues in China after its breakdown in the ninth century A.D. About one thousand years and eight hundred years, respectively, elapsed between these points in the history of the Sumeric and Hellenic civilizations (IV, 62ff.; V, 2ff.); and so on. Like a petrified tree trunk, such a society can linger in that stage of life-in-death for centuries, even thousands of years. Nevertheless, the destiny of most, if not of all, civilizations, seems to me to come to final dissolution sooner or later. As to the Western society, though it seems to have had all the symptoms of breakdown and disintegration, the author is noncommital. He still leaves a hope:

> We may and must pray that a reprieve which God has granted to our society once will not be refused if we ask for it again in a contrite spirit and with a broken heart" (IV, 321).

Such being the general nature of the decline of civilizations, a most detailed analysis of its uniformities, symptoms, and phases is developed in Volumes IV, V, and VI. Only a few of these uniformities can be touched on here. While in the growth period the Creative Minority gives a series of successful responses to ever new challenges, now, in the disintegration period, it fails to do so. Instead, intoxicated by victory, it begins to "rest on one's oars," to "idolize" the relative values as absolute; loses its charasmatic attraction and is not imitated and followed by the majority. Therefore, more and more it has now to use force to control the Internal and the External Proletariat. In this process it creates a "Universal State," like the Roman Empire created by the Hellenic Dominant Minority, as a means to keep itself and the civilization alive; enters into wars; becomes slave of the intractable institutions; and works its own and its civilization's ruin.

The "Internal Proletariat" now secedes from the Minority; becomes dissatisfied and disgruntled; and often creates a "Universal Church"—for instance, Christianity or Buddhism—as its own creed and institution. While the "Universal State" of the Dominant Minority is doomed, the Universal Church of the Inner Proletariat (for instance, Christianity) serves as a bridge and foundation for a new civilization, "apparented" by, and affiliated with, the old one.

The External Proletariat now organizes itself and begins to attack the declining civilization, instead of striving to be incorporated by it. In this way the Schism enters the Body and Soul of civilization. It results in an increase of strife and fratricidal wars that work in favor of the development of the ruin. The Schism in the Soul manifests itself in the profound change of the mentality and behavior of the members of the disintegrating society. It leads to an emergence of four types of personality and "Saviors": Archaist, Futurist (Saviors by Sword), Detached and Indifferent Stoic, and finally, Transfigured Religious Savior, posited in the supersensory word of God. The sense of Drift, of Sin, begins to grow; Promiscuity and Syncretism become dominant. Vulgarization and "Proletarianization" invade arts and sciences, philosophy and language, religion and ethics, manners and institutions.

But all in vain. With the exception of Transfiguration, all these efforts and "Saviors" do not stop the disintegration. At best the civilization can become "Fossilized"; and in this form, "life-in-death" can linger for centuries and even thousands of years; but its dissolution, as a rule, comes. The only fruitful way turns out to be the way of Transfiguration, the transfer of the goal and values to the supersensory Kingdom of God. It may not stop the disintegration of the given civilization, but it may serve as a seed for the emergence and development of a new affiliated civilization; and through that, it is a step forward to the eternal process of elevation of Man to Superman, of "the City of Man to City of God," as the ultimate terminal point of Man and Civilization. The volumes close with an almost apocalyptic note:

> The aim of Transfiguration is to give light to them that sit in darkness . . . it is pursued by seeking the Kingdom of God in order to bring its life . . . into action . . . The goal of Transfiguration is thus the Kingdom of God [VI, 171].

The whole human history or the total civilizational process thus turns into a Creative Theodicy; through separate civilizations and their uniform, but concretely different, rhythms, the reality unfolds its richness and leads from "under-Man" and "under-Civilization," to Man and Civilization, and finally to Superman and transfigured Ethereal Super-Civilization of the Kingdom of God.

> The work of the Spirit of the Earth, as he weaves and draws his threads on the Loom of Time, is the temporal history of Man as this manifests itself in the geneses and growths and breakdowns and disintegrations of human societies; and in all this welter of life . . . we can hear the beat of an elemental rhythm . . . of Challenge-and-Response and Withdrawal-and-Return and Rout-and-Rally and Apparentation-and-Affiliation and Schism-and-Palingenesia. This elemental rhythm is the alternating beat of Yin and Yang . . . The perpetual turning of a wheel is not a vain repetition if, at each revolution, it is carrying a vehicle that much nearer to its goal; and if "palingenesia" signifies the birth of something new . . . then the Wheel of Existence is not just a devilish device for inflicting an everlasting torment on a damned Ixion. The music that the rhythm of Yin and Yang beats out is the song of creation . . . Creation would not be creative if it did not swallow up in itself all things in Heaven and Earth, including its own antithesis [VI, 324].

Such is the general skeleton of Toynbee's philosophy of history. It is clothed by him in a rich and full-blooded body of facts, empirical verification, and a large number of subpropositions. The main theses, as well as subpropositions, are painstakingly tested by the known empirical facts of the history of the twenty-one civilizations studied. In this respect the theory of Toynbee, conceived and executed on a grand plan, is probably documented more fully than most of the existing philosophies of history. To repeat, the work as a whole is a real contribution to the field of historical synthesis.

II. CRITICISM

If we now ask how valid is the general scheme of Toynbee's theory of the rise and decline of civilizations as well as a number of his secondary propositions, the situation changes. Side by side with the unquestionable virtues, the work has very serious shortcomings. Among the unessential and superfluous defects, the following can be mentioned: First, the work is too voluminous and could have been compressed without losing anything in the clearness and completeness of its theory. A pronounced penchant of the author to quote abundantly from the Bible, mythology, poetry —to use overabundant poetic and symbolic images—is partly responsible for this insignificant defect.

Second, in spite of an astounding erudition, the author displays either an ignorance or a deliberate neglect of many important sociological works, which deal more fundamentally with the problems Toynbee is struggling with than other works quoted. Neither the names of Tarde, Durkheim, Max Weber, Pareto, nor those of practically any sociologist are mentioned. One of the consequences of such a neglect is that Toynbee has to write dozens and hundreds of pages on questions that were studied in such works more thoroughly and better than Toynbee does. For instance, mimesis or imitation is one of the cardinal points of his theory to which he devotes many pages. A reader who knows Tarde's *Laws of Imitation*, not to mention many later works, does not get from Toynbee's analysis anything new. More than that: Toynbee's theory of mimesis and of its uniformities has many mistakes which would have been avoided if he had studied some of the main works in this field. Similarly, he devotes several hundreds of pages in Volumes I and II to investigation of the influence of race and geographic environment upon societies and civilization. And yet, he does not add anything to the existing knowledge in that field. Even more, he fails to see the demonstrated weaknesses of the claims of some of the climatic and racial theories (like that of Huntington) which he accepts to a considerable extent. A concise characterization of the existing conclusions in these fields would have permitted him to outline his theory on only a few pages and to avoid several pitfalls into which he has fallen. The same criticism can be applied to several other problems. In spite of the extraordinary erudition of the author, it shows itself somewhat one-sided and inadequate.

Third, his knowledge of the history of the twenty-six civilizations he deals with is very uneven. It is excellent in the field of Hellenic (Greco-Roman) civilization, and it is much thinner in the field of other civilizations.

Fourth, his acquaintance with the extant knowledge in the field of such phenomena as art, philosophy, science, law, and some others with which he deals, seems also to be inadequate: little, if anything, is quoted in these fields, and the conclusions of the author sound superficial and dilettante.

Fifth, the same is true of several other fields in which he makes categorical statements. For instance, he contends that "the evil of War in the eighteenth century [was reduced] to a minimum which has never been approached in . . . our Western history, either before or after, up to date" (IV, 143). As a matter of fact, our systematic study of the movement of war (see my *Social and Cultural Dynamics*, Vol. III) shows that, measured either by the number of war casualties or by the size of the armies per million of population, the centuries from twelve to sixteen, inclusive, and the nineteenth century were less belligerent than the eighteenth century. He himself seems to repudiate his previous statement by saying that "the life of our Western Society has been as grievously infested by the plague of war during the last four centuries as in any earlier age" (V, 43). As a further example: he contends that "the sense of drift" as manifested in various deterministic philosophies grows with the process of disintegration in all civilizations (V, 422ff.). The factual movement of deterministic conceptions versus indeterministic is very different from what he claims it is (see my *Dynamics*, Vol. II, chap. ix). A third example: he contends that in a diffusion of radiation of a given culture the alien culture is penetrated first by the economic elements; second, by the political; and third, by the cultural. In this way a uniformity of the order of the penetration of the alien culture by specified elements of diffusing civilization is set forth (IV, 57). As a matter of fact, such uniformity does not exist. In some cases the economic elements penetrate first; in others, the cultural (see the evidences in Vol. IV of my *Dynamics*).

In the work there are many similar blunders and overstatements. However, in a work of such immense magnitude as *A Study of History* such shortcomings are inevitable. One should not carp at them. If the main conceptual scheme of the author is solid, such shortcomings can easily be discounted as superfluous.

Unfortunately, the work has two fundamental defects, which concern not the details but the heart and soul of Toynbee's philosophy of history. They concern, first, *"the civilization" taken by Toynbee as a unit of historical study; second, the conceptual scheme of genesis, growth, and decline of civilizations put at the foundation of Toynbee's philosophy of history*. Let us look at these assumptions more closely.

By "civilization" Toynbee means not a mere "field of historical study" but a united system, or the whole, whose parts are connected with one another by causal ties. Therefore, as in any causal system in his "civilization," parts must depend upon one another, upon the whole, and the whole upon its parts. He categorically states again and again:

civilizations are wholes whose parts all cohere with one another
and all affect one another reciprocally . . . It is one of the characteristics of civilizations in process of growth that all aspects
and activities of their social life are coordinated into a single
social whole, in which the economic, political, and cultural
elements are kept in a nice adjustment both with one another
by an inner harmony of the growing body social [III, 152; see
also I, 34ff., 43ff., 149ff., 153ff.].

Thus, like so-called "functional anthropologists," he assumes that
his civilizations" are a real system and not mere congeries or conglomerations of various cultural (or civilizational) phenomena
and objects adjacent in space or time but devoid of any causal or
meaningful ties (see the analysis of socio-cultural systems and
congeries in my *Social and Cultural Dynamics,* Vol. I, chap. i; an
unfolded theory of socio-cultural systems is given in Vol. IV of the
Dynamics). If civilizations are real systems, then, as is any causal
system, we should expect that when one important component
of it changes, the rest of the components change too, because if A
and B are causally connected, then the change of A is followed by
the change of B in a definite and uniform manner. Otherwise, A
and B are mere congeries but not the partners of the causal system.

Is Toynbee's assumption valid? I am afraid it is not: his *"civilizations" are not united systems but mere conglomerations of various civilizational objects and phenomena* (congeries of systems
and singular cultural traits) *united only by special adjacency but
not by causal or meaningful bonds. For this reason, they are not
real "species of society"; therefore they can hardly be treated as
unities and can hardly have any uniformities in their genesis,
growth, and decline.* These concepts cannot even be applied to the
congeries, because congeries do not and cannot grow or decline.
Like the components of a dumping place, they can only be re-
arranged, added to, or subtracted from; but we cannot talk of the
growth or decline of a "civilizational dumping place" or of any
merely spatial conglomeration of things and events. This diagnosis
of the "civilizations" is inadvertently corroborated many times by
Toynbee himself. In many places of his work he indicated that,
for instance, the technique and economic life of the civilization
often change while the rest of the civilization does not change; in
other cases the rest of the civilization changes while technique remains static; in still other cases, the technique changes in one way
while the rest of the civilization moves in the opposite direction
(IV, 40ff., *et passim*). If we have A and B where the change of
one of the variables is not followed by that of the other, or when
it does not show any uniform variation, this means A and B are
causally unrelated; therefore they are not components of the same

whole. Toynbee himself demonstrates—and demonstrates well—that two of the components of his civilization (technique and economy) are causally unrelated to the rest of the "whole." His whole —"civilization"—thus turns into a mere spatial congeries. In other places of his work he gives several cases where the religious or the artistic or the political element of his whole—civilization—each appears to be an independent variable unrelated to the rest of the alleged "whole." In this way Toynbee himself repudiates his basic assumption that his "civilizations" are "the wholes whose parts all cohere together."

In fact, it is easy to show—and show convincingly—that each of his civilizations is not a "whole" or a system at all, but a mere coexistence of an enormous number of systems and congeries existing side by side and not united either by causal or meaningful or any other ties (necessary for any real system). A mere contiguity or mere spatial adjacency does not make from "a book+ worn out shoes+ bottle of whiskey" lying side by side any unity, whole, or system. It remains a congeries. Not only is the total civilization of such enormous "culture-areas" as the Greco-Roman, or the Sinic, or of any other of his civilizations not one whole or system, but the total civilization of even the smallest possible civilizational area—that of a single individual—is but a coexistence of several and different systems and congeries unrelated with one another in any way except spatial adjacency in a biological organism. Suppose that an individual is a Roman Catholic, Republican, professor, preferring Romantic music to Classic, Scotch to rye, blondes to brunettes. Roman Catholicism does not require, causally or logically, the Republican instead of the Democratic or other party; the Republican party is not connected logically or causally with professional occupation. This is true also with the preference for Scotch to rye, or Romantic music to the Classic. We have Roman Catholics who are not Republicans, and Republicans who are not Roman Catholics, professors who are neither, and many in other occupations who are Catholics or Republicans. Some Catholics or Republicans or professors prefer Scotch to rye, some rye to Scotch, some do not drink whiskey, some prefer beer to wine, and so on. This means that the total "civilization" of the same individual is not one unified system but a conglomeration of various systems and singular "civilizational" traits united only by a spatial adjacency of the same biological organism. A biological organism, being a real system, changes biologically as a whole; but its total "civilization," being congeries, does not change in togetherness, nor can the "total civilizations" of many individuals display any uniformity in their change. (See my *Dynamics,* Vol. I, chap. i; and Vol. IV, for a systematic analysis of this problem.)

If, then, the total "civilization" of an individual is not one system, still less is one system the total civilization of a city block, or of a total city, of a nation, or of the still larger "civilized societies" of Toynbee. This means that Toynbee's "civilization" is not "species" but a kind of a "large dumping place" where coexist, side by side, an enormous number of various sociocultural systems many of which are not related to one another either causally or meaningfully: the State system, the Religious systems, the Art-Ethics-Philosophy-Science-Economic-Political-Technological and other systems and congeries "dumped together" over a vast territory and carried on by a multitude of individuals. One cannot style as species of the same genus different sets of incidental congeries: "shoe-watch-bottle-*Saturday Evening Post*" here, "trousers-comb-detective story-valve-rose-automobile" there: and still less can one expect uniformities of structure and change in genesis, growth, and decline of such different congeries. Having mistakenly taken different congeries for system, Toynbee begins to treat his civilizations as "species of society" and valiantly hunts for uniformities, in their genesis, growth, and decline. In this way he makes the fatal mistake of erecting an enormous building upon a foundation less stable than the proverbial sands.

All the subsequent defects of his theory follow from this "original sin." It is aggravated by another fatal mistake he commits, namely, by the acceptance of the old—from Florus to Spengler—conceptual scheme of "genesis-growth-decline," as a uniform pattern of change of civilizations. Such a conception is possibly the worst among all the existing schemes of change of civilizations; and it is doubly fatal for Toynbee's theory. Indeed, if his civilizations are mere congeries, for this reason only we cannot talk of the genesis, growth, and breakdown, disintegration, and dissolution of congeries. Congeries are neither born (alive or abortively) nor can they grow or disintegrate, since they never have been integrated. Generally, this popular conceptual scheme is purely analogical and represents not a theory of how sociocultural phenomena change but an evaluative theory of sociocultural progress, of how they *should* change. Therefore, Toynbee's theory is not so much a theory of civilizational change as much as an evaluative theory of civilizational progress or regress. This clearly comes out in his formulae of "growth" and "disintegration." They are evaluative formulae of progress and regress but not the formulae of change.

From these two sins follow all the factual and logical incongruities of Toynbee's philosophy of history. First, many a historian, anthropologist, and sociologist will certainly object to Toynbee's classification of civilizations as arbitrary, having no clear logical *fundamentum divisionis*. Several Christian civilizations are treated as separate and different; while a conglomeration of different (religious and other) systems are united into one civilization. Sparta is arbitrarily cut out of the rest of the Hellenic civilization, while Roman civilization is made inseparable from the Greek or Hellenic. Polynesian and Eskimo civilizations or "under-civilizations" (in one part Toynbee states that they were live-born civilizations; in another he claims that they remained at "sub-civilizational" level and have never reached the state of civilization; while all the Nomads of all the continents are united into one civilization, and so on.

Second, Toynbee's mass onslaught against civilizations in making most of them either "abortively born," "arrested," or "petrified," or "broken-down" or "disintegrating" or "dead and buried" is open to objection. According to Toynbee, out of twenty-six civilizations, only one—the Western—is still possibly alive at the present time, all the others being either dead or half-dead ("arrested," "petrified," "disintegrating"). Since, according to the assumed scheme, civilizations must have breakdowns, disintegration, and death, the author must either bury or make them "abortive," "arrested," "petrified," or at least broken down and disintegrating. Since such is the demand of the scheme and since Toynbee does not have any clear criteria as to what death or breakdown or integration or disintegration of civilization really is, he willingly takes the role of an undertaker of civilizations.

Third, courageously following his scheme, he is not deterred by the fact that some of his civilizations which, according to his scheme, ought to have been dead a long time ago, after their breakdown, lived centuries, even thousands of years, and are still alive and very much so. He disposes of the difficulty by a simple device of "petrified" civilizations. So China has been petrified for thousands of years; Egypt for some two thousands of years; so after the Peloponnesian War the Hellenic civilization was either disintegrating or petrified up to the fifth century A.D. The whole Roman history was but an incessant disintegration from the very beginning to the end; and so other civilizations. In his scheme civilizations hardly have time to live and grow; if they are born abortive—as some are—they are arrested; if they are not arrested, they have their breakdown almost immediately after they are born and then begin to disintegrate or are turned into a "petrified trunk." Of course, philosophically the birth is the beginning of death; but an empirical investigator of either the life of an organism or of civilization can and must be less philosophical and can and must study the process of life itself, before the real death, or paralysis, or incurable sickness occurs. And for most of the organisms and civilizations there is a great distance between the terminal points of birth and death.

This means that Toynbee studies little the greater part of the existence of the civilizations and drowns centuries and thousands of years of their existence, activity, and change in his penchant of an "undertaker of civilizations." By this I do not deny the facts of either disintegration or even dissolution of real cultural or civilizational systems. Such facts occur, but occur with real systems, not with congeries of civilizations; and occur not immediately after the "birth" of the system but often after their long—sometimes very long—life and change. As a matter of fact, the elements of the congeries of Toynbee's civilizations still exist, even of those which he considers dead and buried a long time ago. Quite a large number of Egyptiac or Babylonic or especially Hellenic cultural systems and cultural traits (philosophy, ethics, architecture, sculpture, literature, art, and so on) are very much alive as components of the contemporary Western or other cultures. And they are alive not as objects in a museum but as living realities in our own and other cultures.

Fourth, the foregoing explains why in Toynbee's work there is little of the analysis of the phase of the growth of the civilizations. There are only fairly indefinite statements that in that phase there is a Creative Minority successfully meeting the challenge, that there is no class war, and that everything goes well and moves and becomes more and more "etherealized." That is about all that is said of this phase. Such a characterization of the process of growth of his twenty-one civilizations is evidently fantastic in its "idyllic" and other virtues. If we have to believe it, we seemingly have to accept that in Greece before 431-403 B.C. (the breakdown of the Hellenic civilization, according to Toynbee) there were no wars, no revolutions, no class struggle, no slavery, no traditionalism, and that all these "plagues" appeared only after the Peloponnesian War. On the other hand, we expect to find that, after it, in Greece and Rome creativeness ceased, and that there was no Plato, no Aristotle, no Epicurus, no Zeno, no Polybius, no Church Fathers, no Lucretius, no scientific discovery—nothing creative. As a matter of fact, the actual situation in all these respects was very different before and after the breakdown. The indicators of war per million of the population for Greece were twenty-nine for the fifth, forty-eight for the fourth, and eighteen and three, respectively, for the third and second centuries B.C. Indicators of Internal Disturbances (revolutions) were 149, 468, 320, 259, and 36, respectively, for the centuries from the sixth to the second B.C., inclusive. This shows that the real movement of wars and revolutions in Greece was very different from what

Toynbee tells us. The same is true of Rome (see the detailed data in my *Social and Cultural Dynamics*, Vol. III). The scientific, philosophical, and religious creativeness likewise reached their peak rather in and after the fifth century than before that time (see the figures of discoveries, inventions, and philosophical systems in *Dynamics*, Vol. II, chap. iii, *et passim*). In regard to the Western civilization, as mentioned, the diagnosis of Toynbee is somewhat ambiguous. In many places he says that it already had its breakdown and is in the process of disintegration; in other places he is noncommittal. Whatever is his diagnosis, the Western civilization before the fifteenth century is regarded by him as in the phase of growth. If this is so, then, according to his scheme, no revolutions, no serious wars, no hard-and-fast class divisions existed in Europe before that century. Factually, the thirteenth and fourteenth centuries were the most revolutionary centuries up to the twentieth century in the history of Europe; likewise, serfdom and other class divisions were hard and fast, and there were many wars—small and great (see the data in Vols. II and III of my *Dynamics*). Finally the medieval Western civilization of the period of growth does not exhibit many of the traits of Toynbee's growing civilizations but displays a mass of traits which are the characteristics of Toynbee's disintegrating civilizations. The same is true of his other civilizations. This means that Toynbee's uniformities of growth and decline of the civilizations are largely fantastic and are not borne out by the facts.

Fifth, a large number of the uniformities he claims in connection with his conceptual scheme are also either fallacious or overstated—for instance, his uniformity of negative correlation between the geographic expansion of civilization and its growth; between war and growth; between progress of technique and growth. Granting a part of truth to his statements, at the same time in this categoric formulation they are certainly fallacious. If Toynbee's twenty-one civilizations did not diffuse over large areas and a multitude of persons remained just the civilization of a little Sumeric, Greek, Egyptiac, or Arabic village, they could hardly become "historical" and certainly would not come to the attention of historians and Toynbee and would not become one of his twenty-one civilizations. All his civilizations are vast complexes, spread over vast areas of territory and vast populations. They did not emerge at once in such form; but in starting with a small area they expanded (in the process of their growth) over vaster and vaster areas and populations and through that became historical. Otherwise, they would not have been noticed. If Toynbee contends, as in a few places he does, that such a diffusion over vaster areas was performed peacefully, without war, through spontaneous submission of the "barbarians" to the charm of the diffusing civilization, such a statement is again inaccurate. All his twenty-one civilizations in their period of growth (according to Toynbee's scheme) expanded not only peacefully but with force, coercion, and wars. On the other hand, many of them in the period of disintegration shrank, rather than expanded, and were more peaceful than in the periods of Toynbee's growth.

Sixth, following Spengler, whose ghost heavily weighs upon the author, Toynbee ascribes different dominant tendencies to each of his civilizations: aesthetic to the Hellenic, religious to the Indic, machinistic-technological to the Western (he does not give further such dominant penchants to each of the remaining eighteen civilizations). Such a summary characterization is again very doubtful. The Western civilization did not show its alleged dominant characteristic at all up to approximately the thirteenth century A.D.: from the sixth to the end of the twelfth century the movement of technological inventions and scientific discoveries stood at about zero in this allegedly technological civilization par excellence; and from the sixth to the thirteenth century this machinistic civilization was religious through and through, even more religious than the Indic or Hindu civilizations in many periods of their history (see the data on discoveries and technological inventions in my *Dynamics,* Vol. II, chap. iii). The supposedly aesthetic Hellenistic civilization did not show its aesthetic penchant (in Toynbee's sense) before the sixth century B.C. and displayed quite a boisterous scientific and technological *élan* in the period from 600 to 200 A.D. (see the figures, Vol. II, chap. iii, of *Dynamics*). The Arabic civilization (whose dominant trait Toynbee does not stress) displayed an enormous *élan* of scientific and technological penchant in the centuries from the eighth to the thirteenth—much more so than the Western civilization during these centuries (see the data Vol. II, chap. iii, of *Dynamics*). All this means that the Spenglerian-Toynbee ascription of some specific perennial tendency to this or that civilization, regardless of the period of its history, is misleading and inaccurate.

One can continue this criticism for a long time. A large part of the statements of Toynbee taken in his conceptual scheme are either inaccurate or invalid. However, many of these statements, properly reformulated and put in quite a different conceptual scheme of civilizational change, become valid and penetrating. For instance, most of the traits which Toynbee ascribes to the civilizations in their period of growth and partly in that of "petrification" are accurate for the phase of civilization dominated by what I call the "Ideational supersystem of culture" (not the total given culture in which it appears). Many of the characteristics of Toynbee's "disintegrating" period are typical for a phase of civilization dominated by what I call the "Sensate supersystem" (not the whole total culture or civilization). Many of the characteristics of Toynbee's stage of acute disorganization are but the characteristics of the period when a given culture passes from the domination of Ideational to Idealistic or Sensate supersystems, and vice versa. Such periods of shift happen several times in the history of this or that "total culture" or "civilization." They are, however, neither a death nor "petrification" nor "arrest" but merely a great transition from one supersystem to another. Put into this scheme, and reinterpreted, many pages and chapters of Toynbee's work become illuminating penetrating, and scientifically valid. In such a setting his conception of the creative character of human history acquires still deeper meaning. Likewise, his hesitant diagnosis of the present state of the Western civilization becomes more definite and specific: as the status of the civilization entering not the path of death but the painful road of a great transition from the over-ripe Sensate phase to a more "etherealized" or spiritualized Ideational or Idealistic phase. Translated into more accurate terms of the real socio-cultural systems and of the great rhythm of the Sensate-Idealistic-Ideational supersystems of culture, *A Study of History* is a most stimulating and illuminating work of a distinguished thinker and scholar.

THE LAST FOUR VOLUMES*

The first six volumes of Toynbee's *Study of History* were published in 1934-39. Of the new (four) volumes completing this vast work, Volume VII gives a further analysis of the nature and role of the Universal States and the Universal Churches as phases in the growth and decline of civilizations. Volume VIII deals with the Heroic Ages and the contacts of civilizations in space. Volume IX is devoted to a study of the contacts of civilizations in time, of the law and freedom in history, and of the prospects of the Western civilization. Volume X is made up of essays on eminent historians and on chronology, of acknowledgments, and index.

Since Toynbee's fully developed "philosophy of history" was given in the first six volumes, these new volumes do not add much to his theoretical framework. Their novelty consists mainly: (a) of some new details concerning the Universal States, the Universal Churches, the Heroic Ages, and the interaction of

*The Annals of the American Academy of Political and Social Sciences, Vol. 299, 1955, pp. 144-146.

civilizations in space and time; and (b) of the change of some of Toynbee's conclusions given in the first six volumes.

As to Toynbee's theory of history, it has its strong and weak points. In my previous criticism of his *Study of History* I have shown that Toynbee's framework is a variation of O. Spengler's scheme which, in its turn, is a variation of N. Danilevsky's theory of history published in 1863. All three theories make a fatal error in taking a vast dump of diverse social and cultural phenomena, not integrated together by meaningful or causal ties, for a real unified system called "Culture-Historical Type", "High Culture," or Civilization." Not being integrated unities, such dumps of cultural and social phenomena cannot either be born or grow or disintegrate and die. For this reason, many of the conclusions of these authors concerning "the birth," "the growth," "the breakdown," "the disintegration," and "decline" of civilizations are built on a foggy foundation and crumble by themselves as soon as the fatal error is perceived.

The main changes in Toynbee's views concern two points. While in the previous volumes the Universal Religions were viewed as "the bridges" between the great civilizations, in the new volumes the great civilizations are considered as the bridges between the great Religions. While before Toynbee interpreted all great civilizations as philosophically equivalent and contemporaneous, now he classifies them in chronological and evaluative order as the progressive steps for realization of the ever greater and higher religions. Since both interpretations are not so much scientific descriptions of the empirical relationship between civilizations and religions as much as the subjective evaluations of whether civilizations ought to be the means for the end-value of religions, or religions should be the means for the bigger and better civilizations, the significance of this shift in Toynbee's views lies beyond the sphere of science.

When we turn to Toynbee's empirical generalizations, many of these appear to be either platitudinal or onesided or fallacious. Thus he indefatigably repeats that "spiritual progress is subject to a 'law' proclaimed by Aeschylus" that we "learn through suffering," and that this "learning by suffering" is the only way to spiritual ennoblement of mankind. Stating so, he evidently forgets that suffering produces not only saints, but also criminals and "the worst of beasts"—human animals. He entirely overlooks the negative effects of suffering: suicide, mental and physical disease, aggressiveness, criminality, brutalization, which "suffering-frustration" generates more frequently rather than spiritual ennoblement. Instead of the much more adequate "law of polarization" in frustration, suffering, and calamity, he gives us a onesided pseudo law of the "learning through suffering" which does not stand an elementary empirical test. Another example. For corroboration of his preconceived theory that the "declining" civilizations go through the cycle of: "premonitory wars," a "general war," a "breathing space," "supplementary wars," and "general peace," he gives us five cycles of this kind for the period: 1494-1945. When, however, his data are checked by the number and duration of the wars, the size of the armies, the magnitude of war casualty for each of his cycles, several of his periods of "general peace" turn to be as belligerent as his periods of "general war," and *vice versa*. His theory of the cycles of war-peace is thus clearly contradicted by the relevant empirical data. Third example of Toynbee's empirical fallacies is given by his credulous acceptance of Jung's theory of the unconscious, by the identification of this unconscious with the divine element in man, and by Toynbee's classification of the great religions (Hinduism, Christianity, Islam, and Buddhism) as "introvert" or "extrovert." Contrary to Toynbee, the future of mankind would indeed be hopeless if its spiritual and creative progress were depending upon the unconscious biological drives and their instinctive-reflexological mechanisms given in all animal species. By definition the "unconscious" activity is automatic and fixed; it cannot think and cannot create because any thinking and creative activity are always conscious or supraconscious processes. Instead of investing his hopes for the future spiritual ennoblement of man into "the supraconscious"—which is the main source of all the great creative achievements of man—Toynbee expects the salvation from the least creative unconscious forces viewed by him as the divine element in man. As a fourth sample of Toynbee's empirical errors his diagnosis and forecasting of the future of the existing civilizations can be mentioned. According to his theory practically all civilizations, except the Western one, have been either dead for many centuries, or are in a hopeless mortal agony at the present time. This equally concerns the Hindu, the Chinese, the Russian, the Arabic, and all other "fossilized" and disintegrated civilizations. The only hope for the future of mankind lies in the Western civilization which also is a dangerous state.

If we take one by one of Toynbee's empirical generalizations, most of them will be found to be either onesided or fallacious. This is largely due to Toynbee's poor knowledge of a vast body of sociological, psychological, and anthropological studies in the fields of social and cultural mobility, migration, diffusion, and transformation; in the field of sociocultural rhythms and periodicities, social organization and disorganization, cultural integration and disintegration, and son on. Despite vast literature quoted and referred to in Toynbee's volumes, they contain almost no references to hundreds of important studies by psycho-social scientists of the problems treated by Toynbee.

When Toynbee discusses such problems as "law and freedom in history," "the truth of science and the truth of religion," he rarely touches the fundamental points of this sort of problem. He rather goes around or dodges these points and delivers to us mainly the vague generalities and unclear conclusions often backed up only by numerous quotations from the Old and the New Testaments. His footnotes in these parts show again his limited knowledge of the most important philosophical and scientific works dealing with this sort of problem.

Viewed as a whole, these volumes represent an eclectic mixture of science of history, philosophy of history, ethics and politics, theology and religion.

Side by side with these shortcomings, the *Study of History* has many strong points. It contains a multitude of remarkable insights and excellent elaborations of several basic topics of historical and social sciences. It opens the new vistas on many dark problems of these sciences. Now and then it furnishes fresh and strikingly fruitful interpretations of several historical and social processes. Even when Toynbee speaks as a prophet, religious thinker, philosopher, or moralist, his utterances deserve our full attention.

To sum up: in spite of an overabundance of misreadings of historical events and other shortcomings of Toynbee's *Study of History,* it is one of the significant works of the middle of the twentieth century in the field of historical and social science.

TOYNBEE AND THE HISTORICAL
IMAGINATION*

HANS J. MORGENTHAU

The last four volumes of Mr. Toynbee's work confront the reviewer with formidable difficulties. They are the culmination of a gigantic effort, gigantic both in quantity and quality, the like of which no other contemporary has dared to undertake. Thus it is impossible to try to assess the value of Mr. Toynbee's last volumes without raising the general question as to the intention and achievement of his work as a whole.

This inevitable expansion of the scope of the reviewer's task raises, however, a deeper difficulty still. We can do real justice to somebody else's intention and achievement only on the condition that his intention and achievement is commensurate with our own. We can judge what others have tried to do and have done only if we ourselves have tried to do, or at least have dreamt of doing, what they have done. What transcends the limits of our own intention and achievement, we can praise or condemn but cannot judge; for our inner experience has been prevented by its self-imposed limitations from creating the standards of valuation commensurate with the intentions and achievements transcending it. I can judge a poem, or a novel, or a work of history without ever having written one; for I have at least dreamt of writing one.

Who in our time has dreamt of doing what Mr. Toynbee has been trying to do? Since hardly anybody has, Mr. Toynbee's work has received scant justice. It is being praised by the multitude and those critics who write for it; for there is a great satisfaction in identifying oneself, through praise, with an undertaking which is so much bigger than anything oneself would even try to engage in. It has been damned by the specialists who, in applying their narrow standards, have found it wanting in this or that particular. Both types of critics have looked at Mr. Toynbee's work as a kind of monstrosity whose bigness either overwhelms or irritates them.

However, it ought to be possible to scale down Mr. Toynbee's work, as it were, to normal human proportions, isolating certain specific problems which it poses. These problems must fall short of the general intention of the work, but they surpass in breadth and depth any of the many technical problems of fact and interpretation the work raises. Our judgement of the contribution which Mr. Toynbee has made to the solution of these "intermediate" problems may shed some light on the general value of the work.

---

*Encounter, March, 1955.

Three such problems have come to the mind of this reviewer: historiography, philosophy of history, and religion.

Mr. Toynbee's work poses anew, by implication, the problem of historiography. If what Mr. Toynbee is doing is a valid writing of history, then most of what is going by the name of academic history is, at worst, irrelevant or, at best, mere preparation. On the other hand, if the writing of history is a science with all that the word "science" connotes in terms of the use of documentary evidence and the renunciation of judgements of value, then certainly Mr. Toynbee is not a historian. This conflict between two conceptions of history is not likely to be resolved through methodological argument; for within that argument the philosophic assumption predetermines the conclusion. Method being a means to an end, achievement is the only valid test of method. What, then, is it that we expect history to achieve?

Burckhardt has told us that it is the purpose of history "to make us not clever for one day but wise forever." History imparts its wisdom by giving a meaningful account of the life and deeds of men who came before us. This account receives its meaning from the connection which the selective and appraising mind of the historian establishes between the data of history and the perennial concerns of man.

If this be the standard by which history must be judged, then Mr. Toynbee's contribution dwarfs scientific historiography, not in this or that of its manifestations, but as a category of historic thinking. The great achievement of Mr. Toynbee as a historian lies in that very subjectivity which is the horror of scientific historiography. Mr. Toynbee has recovered the courage, which the scientific dogma had put to sleep, to ask from history questions which are meaningful for him and, through him as a man, for other men as well, and to force history to answer him. Never mind that history may have no answer to some of the questions Mr. Toynbee asks, that the facts are sometimes arranged to produce the answers expected, and that not all the "facts" are facts in the scientific sense. Mr. Toynbee has awakened the historic imagination from its dogmatic slumber; he has communicated his own wonderment about the ways of man to his readers, and through innumerable flashes of insight, suggestive reinterpretations, and fertile hypotheses he has demonstrated by his own example the worth of historiography in the classic manner.

Compare with the richness and infectious dynamics of his historic imagination the unproblematic poverty of scientific historiography! The "science" of history leaves nothing to the imagination. What cannot be proven by the document not only is not true but can have no meaning to be communicated by the historian.

To have demonstrated, not through argument but through example, the richness of philosophic historiography, however problematical in detail, as over against the self-impoverishment of "scientific" history, unproblematic in detail but a problem in its very conception of history, is the great merit of Mr. Toynbee's work. What in our time had become a mere historic recollection, Mr. Toynbee has again made a living reality: the creativeness of the historic imagination.

This historic imagination is not at the service of history, properly speaking. It is not Mr. Toynbee's purpose to give a coherent account of the historic process. His purpose is philosophic rather than historical. He searches for the laws which determine the rise and fall of civilisations.

On the face of it, such an undertaking appears to be sociological rather than philosophic. For it appears to require, not the philosophic assessment of the different civilisations from an overall world view, but rather the empirical analysis of the morphology of civilisations, proceeding from empirically verifiable similarities to ever broadening generalisations. The main categories which Mr. Toynbee employs, such as challenge and response, contacts in space and contacts in time, point to such a sociological intent. And in page after page the work reads like a gigantic collection of sociological essays and aphorisms, of illuminating similarities and analogies across the accustomed barriers of historic time, but loosely held together by the work's general plan. Still, the general plan is philosophic and could have been no other. For what Mr. Toynbee sets out to do is beyond the ken of empirical verification.

The possibility of all empirical verification resides in the shared perspective of all actual and potential observers. Astronomy as empirical science is possible because observers with the same perceptive and rational faculties look at the same object from the same planetary perspective. The deeper we move from the world of nature into the world of man as the subject and object of valuations, the more we find the objectivity of empirical science qualified by the ever narrowing limits of common perspective. For astronomy these limits are for all practical purposes irrelevant, since they coincide with the confines of the earth. In the sciences of man the rational core, common to all science, is diminished, obscured, and distorted by the inevitably partial perspective of the observer.

That impairment is minimised when both the object and the perspective of observation are identical with the confines of a particular civilisation. A parochial civilisation, looking at itself from the perspective of its own values, can achieve a high degree of empirical objectivity, given the limits of that perspective. Impairment is maximised when the perspectives of one civilisation are applied to an object lying beyond its confines. For in order to do justice to such an object, the observer would have to transcend the confines of his own civilisation and apply to that object categories which transcend the confines of any particular civilisation and, hence, are applicable to all. This, however, is an epistemological impossibility. It is this impossibility which Mr. Toynbee has endeavoured to achieve.

The examination of but a few of Mr. Toynbee's basic concepts will show that it is impossible to verify them empirically, but that they must be validated philosophically if they are to be validated at all. The very concept of civilisation lacks empirical precision, once we leave behind the two extremes of primitivity and such generalisations as Western and Eastern civilisations, and share Mr. Toynbee's concern with the major historic civilisations. At what point can we say that a civilisation is autonomous, that it is a derivative "offshoot" of another, or, that it has no autonomy of its own, being a mere variety of a dominant one? Obviously American civilisation is both distinct from, and similar to, British civilisation. An Englishman might well try to comprehend American civilisation in the terms of his own, or at best regard it as a mere "offshoot" of his own, while the American might assume its autonomy; for the Chinese observer, on the other hand, the differences between the two civilisations, obvious to both Englishman and American, might be hardly worthy of notice. From the point of view of imperial Rome, Roman civilisation was the culmination of the civilisation of Greece; for Hellenism it might very well have looked like Greek civilisation in a state of decay; and Western Christian civilisation has seen the civilisation of Greece and Rome as a mere preparation for itself. Can one speak of one Chinese civilisation as a continuum extending through the whole history of the Chinese state, or is it possible and necessary to speak of a number of civilisations following each other within the geographic and political space called China? Here again, the answer will differ according to the observer's perspective. There is no need to multiply examples in order to show that judgements about a civilisation are mere reflections of the valuations of a particular one. It is not by accident that there has been a tendency for history to be written in terms of political or geographic units rather than of civilisations; for the former lend themselves more readily to empirical verification than do the latter.

What is true of the very concept of civilisation applies also to the specific concepts referring to its alleged life cycle. What are the verifiable characteristics of the birth and death of a civilisation, when does it flower, when break down and disintegrate? Did the

Greek, Roman, and Jewish civilisations ever die or were they but transferred by political circumstances from one geographic locale to another? If we should assume that Greek civilisation actually died, did it die through the degeneration of its inner life-substance, or was it killed, as it were, by military assassination, which in view of its own inner potentialities was a mere accident? If Western civilisation should dissolve tomorrow into radio-active rubble, would it have died a "natural" death because of inner exhaustion or would it have committed suicide in an isolated act of intellectual and moral degeneracy, or would it have been killed by an atomic assassin? If Western civilisation should be spared atomic destruction and if it should move into an age of material abundance, who is to prove scientifically that such a civilisation would be inferior, or for that matter superior, to, say, the 13th or 18th or 19th centuries of Western civilisation? The answers to all these questions obviously depend upon what we mean by civilisation. To speak again of Western civilisation only, there are those who see nothing but decay from the 15th century onwards; there are others who see nothing but darkness before the 15th century and nothing but decay from the 17th century onwards. For still others, Western civilisation culminates at the turn of the 19th century, while there are those for whom all history preceding Marx is a mere prescientific preparation for the self-emancipation of man.

The concept of civilisation and of its different stages, then, which we apply to other civilisations, cannot but be a function of the valuations of one's own. The very simile of life and death has an objective, empirically verifiable meaning for biological units and is still susceptible of a high degree of empirical precision in the political sphere: a state or a party can be said to live and die. However, when we speak of the life and death of a nation as a cultural entity, we sacrifice, in a measure which will change with differing historic situations, empirical precision for a philosophic metaphor. That substitution of philosophic valuation for empirical science is bound to become total when we enter the realm of civilisation, which as a concept is a kind of synthesis of the valuations of a member of a particular civilisation. The appraisal of civilisations other than one's own is possible only through the erection of a partial world view into a philosophic system claiming universal validity. From Vico through Hegel and Comte to Marx, philosophy had the self-confidence to sit in judgement over all history and to assign to its different periods what appeared to be their rightful place. Our age has transferred its confidence from philosophy to science. Thus it must endeavour to prove scientifically what other ages have tried to demonstrate through philosophy.

This is the tragic paradox which Marx was still able to overcome by identifying philosophy and science, but before which Spengler and Toynbee could not but founder. For, unlike Marx, they have no philosophic system to fall back on which would lend their systems of valuations at least an element of rational objectivity. In this respect Mr. Toynbee is philosophically more sophisticated than Spengler. He is aware of the dilemma without being able to overcome it. Spengler, with that Hegelian consistency which takes absurd conclusions in its stride as long as they follow logically from premises, forces the history of civilisations into the biological strait-jacket and, again not unlike Hegel, finds in the apparent trends of the contemporary scene experimental proof for the pseudo-scientific premise of biological necessity.

Mr. Toynbee, with an intention as sweeping as any of the system-builders before him, has too much common sense to sacrifice the evidence of history on the altar of logical consistency. He allows for human creativity to modify, if not to stop altogether, the life cycle of all civilisations, and particularly of our own. Yet this concession to the unpredictability of history, which is a function of human freedom, faces Mr. Toynbee with still another dilemma. If a civilisation can escape its life cycle by an act of human will, if, in other words, it can refuse to die if it so wills and knows how to live for ever, what, then, is the cognitive value of the biological scheme? Is there a tendency in civilisations to die, which tendency can be reversed? Or were other civilisations bound to die while ours—faint echo of *Roma eterna*—might live for ever? Obviously, what Mr. Toynbee's concession to common sense has gained for history it has lost for philosophy.

It is a measure of Mr. Toynbee's philosophic sophistication that he not only allows human freedom to qualify, if not to disrupt, the determinism of the biological life cycle, but that he is also aware of the need for standards of evaluation which transcend the empirical sequence of biological phases. He does not, and cannot, find these standards in philosophy; for our age has lost the rational boldness and self-reliance which still allowed a Comte and a Marx to build a philosophic system which pretended to explain the laws by which history proceeds. Instead Mr. Toynbee turns to religion. By doing so, Mr. Toynbee raises three issues: the meaning of the return to religion, the value for civilisation of a return to religion, the ability of a civilisation to return to religion by an act of will.

Mr. Toynbee's claim that only religion can save Western civilisation coincides with a popular movement, especially strong in the United States, which also seeks in religion salvation from the evils and dangers of the times. Church membership is rising; prominent intellectuals are converted or return to the fold of their church; politicians justify themselves and their policies in religious terms; and the display of religious observances has begun to become standard practice for public men. Much of Mr. Toynbee's popularity in the United States can be attributed to the apparent convergence of his call for the renewal of religious faith with these popular tendencies. He is in danger of becoming a prophet of a new cult, a kind of Billy Graham of the eggheads.

This popularity is unjust to Mr. Toynbee's intent, but it illuminates the weakness of his achievement. Mr. Toynbee has no illusions about the impossibility of reviving a lost religious faith by joining or rejoining an established church. He calls not so much for a return to a particular established religion as for a revival of religious faith which might find confirmation in any established religion or a combination of elements of them. Mr. Toynbee's personal preference, if I understand him aright, seems to be a kind of intellectual and aesthetic eclecticism which open mindedly accepts and receives all that is congenial in the different historical religions.

However, this stress upon a new syncretic religion tends to obscure a distinction which is vital for the understanding of the religious problem and, in turn, has strengthened the popular misunderstanding of Mr. Toynbee's position to which we have just referred. This confusion concerns the distinction between religion and religiosity. It can well be argued—and I would support the argument—that most of the failures of the modern age and many of its accomplishments stem from one single source: the lack of religiosity. Modern man, as he sees himself, has become a self-sufficient entity who knows what he sees and can do what he wills. He has lost the awareness of his dependence upon a will and a power who are beyond his understanding and control. To warn modern man against the irreligious self-glorification, which in a sense is his self-mutilation, for it deprives human experience of mystery, tragedy and guilt, is one thing; to advocate a kind of religious eclecticism is quite another.

This distinction between religiosity and religion has a direct bearing upon the question which is central to Mr. Toynbee's concern and for the sake of which he has raised the issue of religion in the first place: What makes a civilisation live and what will enable our civilisation in particular to survive? Mr. Toynbee answers: Return to religion by reviving your religious faith. Yet this answer is open to serious doubt. The doubt arises not from metaphysical speculation but from the experience of history itself. Is there any historic evidence to show that religious ages are monopolistically or even especially productive of the values of civilisation, as commonly understood? And is there not rather overwhelming historic evidence in support of the proposition that the weakening of religious faith coincides with the flowering of civilisations, as commonly understood?

We are using the term "commonly understood" on purpose; for here the observer's subjective preference, as pointed out above, is bound to colour his judgement. If we assume that only religious civilisation is worthy of the name, it cannot be hard to demonstrate that the flowering of civilisation depends upon religious faith. Yet if we give to civilisation its common secular meaning, it can hardly be open to doubt that from Plato to Kant, from Sophocles to Dostoievsky, from Michelangelo to Rodin, the weakening of religious faith and the flowering of civilisation not only coincide in time but also are organically interconnected. It is true that these great achievements of civilisation owe their greatness to the religious experience of mystery, tragedy and guilt. Yet it must further be allowed that the achievements of material civilisation, in terms of rational control of nature and society, owe much, if not everything, to the modern denial of both religious faith and religiosity, which assumes the limitless powers of man and demonstrates them within self-chosen limits.

But even if it were true that the return to religious faith can save Western civilisation, can a civilisation recover its religious faith by an act of will? Here it is necesssary, paradoxical as it may seem, to invoke the very spirit of religion against its most learned advocate. It requires nothing but an act of will to join a church and to perform its rituals. To have religious faith demands an act of grace, for which, however, man may well prepare himself through rational instruction. Religiosity, in turn, is the fruit of experience, more particularly of suffering, transformed into intellectual and moral awareness by mind and conscience.

The clarion calling a civilisation to return to religion, *en masse* as it were, finds, and must find, its response in an eclectic idolatry, often blasphemous in man's self-identification with the deity, which popularises the trappings of religion without reviving the dormant substance of its religiosity. To restore man to the fullness of his stature and thus give his civilisation a new lease on life requires indeed the teaching of men like Mr. Toynbee. Yet their teaching must seek to illuminate a mysterious, tragic and sinful experience common to all men in terms of a religiosity likewise common to all men. Neither a teacher nor a whole civilisation can by an act of will create the symbolic and ritualistic expressions of religiosity thus restored; least of all can they create them out of the fragments of religions, whose decline has made the restoration of religiosity necessary in the first place. What religions will grow from this new religiosity man must leave to fate. He must be content to be ready, and to make others ready, to see the signs and to read them aright when they appear.

What Mr. Toynbee has been trying to do as a philosopher of history could no longer be done in an age which tries to reduce truth to science. What Mr. Toynbee has been trying to do as a herald of religious faith no man could have achieved in any age. One hundred years ago he might have been the last of the great philosophers of history. Four hundred years ago he might have been the last of the great scholastics—or mystics. Such achievements are not for this age. Yet Mr. Toynbee's Icarean effort does for our age what the great representative works of the mind have done for others. It both presents its spirit and attempts to transcend it in the search for the perennial truths by which all ages must be judged. His achievement belongs to the ages; his failure belongs to his own and, hence, is ours as well as his.

TOYNBEE'S APPROACH TO HISTORY REVIEWED*

Kenneth W. Thompson

With the publication this autumn of the last four volumes of Arnold J. Toynbee's *A Study of History,* the debate over the character and authority of his work is being resumed. Inasmuch as in the final volumes he deals more directly with the prospects of contemporary Western civilization, the canons of judgment invoked by his critics tend to relate to his success in anticipating the course of current events. Critics without reviewing his methods or grand design praise or condemn him according to his prescience in foretelling the pathways of the present. By the pragmatic test of determining whether his words on universal states or universal churches square with contemporary political or theological realities, the worth of his massive enterprise is being established.

It must be admitted that in this hasty assessment of labors that have consumed over three decades there is a touch of bitter irony. Mr. Toynbee might be excused for expecting that his work would be considered as a whole. He might have a right to ask that someone consider in more general terms his approach to the nature of history, the methods he has successively espoused in seeking to uncover its meaning, and the fundamental criticisms to which he clearly exposes himself. If we proceed now to consider these three problems in some detail, it is because for us they comprise the real issues in connection with Mr. Toynbee's history.

TOYNBEE'S PURPOSE AND HIS PREDECESSORS

A dual problem confronts anyone who proposes to discuss and evaluate historical writing. First, he must be certain of the purpose and objective which underlie the work he examines. One useful guide is the distinction between historical writing and the philosophy of history. In general, historians seek principally to report and describe past events. Philosophers of history, however, ordinarily accept an additional task. They consider the problem of why events took place as they did and attempt to fathom the meaning and formulate the principles of history. It is not always possible to draw a sharp line between these two approaches, but the standards of a historian are most unlikely to correspond at all points with those of a philosopher. Although both Thucydides and Augustine formulate principles of history, only the former has

---

Ethics, vol. LXV, no. 4, July 1955, pp. 287-303.

written narrative history. The historian is judged by the accuracy with which he portrays the past; the philosopher will be judged by the value and significance of his "world-view" for understanding and interpreting the present. There are philosophers of history who boldly set about casting horoscopes of the future. Indirectly all philosophies of history have this aim. While Mr. Toynbee repeatedly disavows any intention of historical prophecy,[1] numerous references and analogies and indeed the whole character of his major work suggest that as he proceeds he keeps an anxious eye toward the future. He applies to the facts of history an underlying philosophy and writes of a time span that approaches the universal. On this account, we must judge him not merely as a historian but as a philosopher of history.

Having identified the nature of our subject as a philosophy of history, we are faced with a second problem. Philosophy of history has three possible meanings. It may refer to the methodology of history or the metaphysics of history or the logic of history. That is, any philosophy of history may be construed as a *method* for dealing with the complexities of history or an interpretation of the *meaning* of history or a statement of the *laws* of history. This discussion will be confined to Mr. Toynbee's historical method but will indirectly, at least, throw light on his conception of the meaning and "laws" of history. Before describing his historical method, a brief survey of the ideas and the writers who together provide the foundation upon which he has built may be useful.

For Mr. Toynbee, history and the techniques for studying it are a curious blend of science and fiction. Most social studies are planned and designed either to treat a subject systematically by scrupulously precise and scientific procedures or in an opposite sense to illuminate some profound myth or spiritual truth through poetry and fable. The notion of joining these techniques and using the one to supply deficiencies in the other is so uncommon that almost no one has challenged Toynbee in terms of this fundamental dualism. Instead empiricists and social scientists have consistently challenged his mysticism[2] and humanists his scientism. It is important, therefore, to examine the relative place given to each as twin pillars supporting his method of history.

Mr. Toynbee's stress and emphasis upon the scientific method would at first seem to place him in the tradition of Buckle, Pareto,

---

[1]"While we can speculate with profit on the general shape of things to come, we can foresee the precise shadow of particular coming events only a very short way ahead." Arnold J. Toynbee, *Civilization On Trial* (New York: Oxford University Press, 1948), p. 204.

[2]The most devastating and intelligent of these attacks was by R. H. S. Crossman, "Mystic World of Arnold Toynbee," *New Republic*, CXVIII (July 14, 1947), 24-26.

and Huntington. There have been few scholars as sanguine as Buckle regarding the certainty of the creation of a science of society and human behavior. He was convinced that any human phenomenon could be isolated and studied "by observations so numerous as to eliminate the disturbances."[3] Statistics had "thrown more light on the study of human nature" than all past or present approaches.[4] No aspect of behavior need be outside this province, for:

> When we perform an action we perform it in consequence of some motive or motives . . . those motives are the results of some antecedents . . . therefore, if we are acquainted with the whole of the antecedents, and with all the laws of the movements, we could with unerring certainty predict the whole of their immediate results. . . . If, for example, I am intimately acquainted with the character of any person, I can frequently tell how he will act under some given circumstance. Should I fail in this prediction, I must ascribe my error not to the arbitrary and capricious freedom of his will, nor to any supernatural prearrangement, for of neither of these things have we the slightest proof; but I must be content to suppose either that I had been misinformed as to some of the circumstances in which he was placed, or else that I had not sufficiently studied the ordinary operations of his mind.[5]

If Pareto is less expansive regarding universal scientific laws and principles, he is equally sure that truth can be uncovered only through scientific testing and probing. The sole legitimate field of study is "the field of experience and observation strictly. We use those terms in the meanings they have in the natural sciences such as astronomy, chemistry, physiology, and so on. . . ."[6]

These are merely two examples of methodologies which in differing degrees have been founded upon principles derived from the natural sciences. The natural scientist seeks to deal with separate, discrete factors neatly defined. Then he proceeds to consider the relations between these individual units. Toynbee puts his separate, discrete civilizations through their paces in roughly the same way, for he observes:

> In methodology what I am trying to do is to apply the scientific notion of "law," "regularity" and "recurrence" to the history of human affairs and find out experimentally how far this way of looking at things will go in this field. . . . I do think that the

---

[3]Henry T. Buckle, *Introduction to the History of Civilization in England* (New York: Albert and Charles Boni, 1925), I, 90-91.
[4]*Ibid.*, p. 18.
[5]*Ibid.*, pp. 10-11.
[6]Vilfredo Pareto, *The Mind and Society* (New York: Harcourt Brace & Co., 1935), I, 33.

scientific apparatus can be applied fruitfully to human affairs to some extent, e.g., where they are considerably affected by the physical environment and where it is the subconscious part of the psyche more than the will and the intellect that is in command.[7]

An early source of inspiration for Mr. Toynbee was the comparative history of E. A. Freeman. In *A Study of History* he acknowledges that "he owes a greater debt than he can repay to the reading of Freeman's *Historical Essays* as a boy."[8] It was Freeman's contention that societies could be studied and compared as separate and distinct units. In Mr. Toynbee's system "the comparative method of studying analogies and parallels"[9] is consistently pursued. He contrasted the methods used in contemporary business with those of historical writing:

> While our Western historians are disputing the possibility of making a comparative study of historical facts, our Western men of business are all the time making their living out of a comparative study of the facts of life around them. The perfect example of such a comparative study for practical ends is the collection and analysis of the statistics on which the business transactions of insurance companies are based; and some such study, in which statistics are collected and averages taken for the purpose of making forecasts, is at the basis of almost all profitable business . . . in this adventure, at any rate, we need not hesitate to follow the lead of our latter-day masters.[10]

The course of history for Toynbee is a consequence of man's relation to his geographical environment as well as to his fellow men. The influence of geography on history is a topic for scientific or pseudo-scientific study, and here Toynbee does acknowledge his dependence upon the tradition of Ellsworth Huntington, who is referred to as "one of our most distinguished and original minded students."[11] Some statements raise doubts as to who is the pupil, who the teacher. For example, Toynbee asserts: "The cycle of the seasons governs life itself by governing our food supply."[12] Yet from Buckle to Huntington to Toynbee, there is a descending order of emphasis upon geography as the all-determinative force. What the three students have in common is a belief that to a greater or lesser degree man's destiny is shaped by the relatively permanent factors in his physical surroundings. How these can best be studied

---

[7]Letter from Mr. Toynbee to this writer dated September 22, 1949.
[8]Toynbee, *A Study of History* (London: Oxford University Press, 1934), I, 339.
[9]*Ibid.*, p. 340.
[10]*Ibid.*, pp. 180-81.
[11]*Ibid.*, p. 293.
[12]Toynbee, *Civilization on Trial*, p. 31.

is a question the historian must answer. First, Mr. Toynbee calls on scientific techniques through which correlations between a society's development and its geographical base may be established. He attempts to find out whether there are geographical factors which are common to societies with similar patterns of growth or decline.

But this attempt soon raises the issue of whether geographic factors in particular, or measurable and predictable elements in general, can ever account fully for human conduct or for the birth, growth, and death of a society. The late Morris Cohen once issued a sharp warning on this point:

> To say that anything is determined by its environment is actually to say only that in order to explain anything we must look to its relationship with other things—which amounts to an undeniable tautology. The essential fact is that the environment of every human being and the context of every human act contain human and non-human elements inextricably intertwined. Only as we realize that the events of human history include both mind and matter as polar components can we escape the grosser errors of those who would spin the world out of ideas and those who look to earth, air, fire and water to explain all human phenomena.[13]

In this vein, Mr. Toynbee has maintained that ideas and myths as well as more tangible factors are a part of the historian's equipment. Quite consciously and deliberately he uses myths as an instrument of scientific inquiry and a pointer to put reason on the right path. His geographical determinism is thus never more than half-hearted, and the scientific approach, which some have erected into a philosophy and religion, becomes for him a useful but imperfect technique about which more and more he has come to have some question:

> Have we not been guilty of applying to historical thought, which is a study of living creatures, a scientific method of thought, which has been devised for thinking about Inanimate Nature? . . . Let us shut our eyes, for the moment, to formulae of Science in order to open up our ears to the language of Mythology.[14]

Throughout the *Study* the overriding influence of Toynbee's early grounding in Anglican Christian socialism is continually in evidence. As a young man he absorbed the ideas of Maurice, Kingsley, Canon Barnett, his uncle Arnold Toynbee, and his father-

---

[13]Morris Cohen, *The Meaning of Human History* (LaSalle, Ill.: Open Court Publishing Co., 1947), p. 171.
[14]Toynbee, *A Study of History*, I, 271.

in-law Gilbert Murray, and these molded his social consciousness. But the prime source of Toynbee's individualism and mysticism stems from the influence of Bergson. His writings, by Toynbee's admission, hit him "with the force of a revelation."[15] The ideas of creative and emergent evolution permeate the whole structure of Toynbee's philosophy of history. The emphasis on impermanence, on purpose in the midst of changing values, and on mind and intuition as the twin progenitors of truth introduces a new element which eventually comes to dominate Mr. Toynbee's historiography. From this point on his work becomes at least as much a great epic thrust as a projected science of society. The *élan vital* is the spirit of God in man. An adversary in the form of the devil confronts man. These two "mythical" forces contend for the mastery and control of human destiny and become, in microcosm, rival principles and forces engaging one another within the human mind. In this struggle and drama, the final victory must be God's, but the challenge by an adversary sets in motion dynamic forces which His perfection alone would never have evoked. This is the cosmic drama which we may scrutinize, not in a laboratory, but in the minds of men and in their social relations.

The presence of this second element of legend and myth is not in itself proof that Toynbee has failed in his scientific venture. The ideal of our greatest historians has always been a reconstruction of the past which would be scientific in its methods but imaginative in insight and formulation. Moreover, it is a truism that any observer begins not with a *tabula rasa* but with a substantial fund of hypotheses and expectations. The great British historian H. A. L. Fisher observes:

> Mr. Toynbee . . . does not wholly confine himself to facts. He is fertile in large historical ideas and suggestive comparisons. . . . We do not think that his volume loses in practical value by reason of these stimulating excursions. Mr. Toynbee keeps an impartial mind.[16]

Another English scholar, G. M. Trevelyan, writes:

> Truth is the criterion of historical study but its motive is poetic. Its poetry consists in being true. There we find the synthesis of the scientific and literary views of history.[17]

To these authorities one may add another for whom scientific discipline and rigorous scholarship was of first importance. The

---

[15]Tangye Lean, "A Study of Toynbee," *Horizon*, XV (January, 1947), 24.

[16]Royal Institute of International Affairs, *Survey of International Affairs, 1924* (Oxford: Oxford University Press, 1926), pp. v-vi.

[17]G. M. Trevelyan, "History and Literature," *History* [N.S.], IX (1924), 91.

scientific historian Jacob Burckhardt places the same elements of fact and spirit at the center of his outlook on history: ". . . the task of history as a whole is to show its twin aspects, distinct yet identical, proceeding from the fact that, firstly, the spiritual, in whatever domain it is perceived, has a historical aspect under which it appears as change, as the contingent, as a passing moment which forms part of a vast whole beyond our power to divine, and that, secondly, every event has a spiritual aspect by which it partakes of immortality."[18] Nonetheless, it is one thing to ascribe to spiritual and moral factors their proper place in history; it is something else again to allow a concern for this dimension to blur and obscure one's perception of material and corporeal factors. Some have condemned "spiritual" history in general for refusing to confront the problems of that social and political stratum in which men live out their common material lives.

Mr. Toynbee has a deep familiarity with classical literature, knows the English Bible at least as well as the theologians, and has so profoundly absorbed the insights of St. John, Goethe, and Blake that he uses them as his own. But of particular importance are three additional sources which have influenced the elaboration of his system. Of course there is an obvious thinker who has prepared the way for any study dealing with the life histories of whole societies. This is Oswald Spengler. Although Toynbee's inquiry had already been launched, his reading of Spengler reassured him positively of the validity of his plan and negatively of the importance of proceeding empirically. In two respects Spengler has influenced Mr. Toynbee's methodology. First, both men attempt to establish laws of history which will apply in general to all societies. Where they differ is on the nature of these laws. For Spengler these laws are irrevocable, but Toynbee is not so certain. Both concede, however, that there is an element of inventiveness in man's conduct which makes absolute science impracticable. Spengler has observed:

> There is a vast difference between man and all other animals.
> . . . Technics in man's life is conscious, arbitrary, alterable, personal, *inventive*. It is learned and improved. Man becomes the *creator* of his tactics of living—that is his grandeur and his doom. And the inner form of this creativeness we call culture.[19]

A similar conviction, as we have noticed, induces Mr. Toynbee to abandon an exclusively scientific route in his approach and to consider civilization in human and spiritual terms. However much

---

18Jacob Burckhardt, *Force and Freedom* (New York: Pantheon Books, 1943), p. 83.
19Oswald Spengler, *Man and Technics* (New York: Alfred A. Knopf, 1932), pp. 28-31.

Mr. Toynbee may deviate from the theory of Spengler, it has left its permanent mark on his own morphology of history.

Finally, two less widely known scholars may be mentioned as probable contributors to Toynbee's system. His thesis of challenge and response is dimly foreshadowed in a little book published in 1872 under the title *The Martyrdom of Man* by Winwood Reade. What Mr. Toynbee calls the "stimulus of hard countries" would appear to be reflected in propositions such as the following: ". . . the struggle for bare life against hostile nature, first aroused the mental activity of the Egyptian priests, while the constant attacks of the desert tribes developed the marital energies of the military men."[20] In the same way, the concept of an internal and external proletariat is implicit in the final chapter of *A History of the Ancient World* by the great Russian historian Michael I. Rostovtzeff.[21] In a private interview, Mr. Toynbee confirmed his indebtedness to Rostovtzeff but added that he got the idea of challenge and response from the poet Browning.[22] He has also noted that the ideas of Turgot as reflected in the writings of Teggart early caught his imagination. Thus Toynbee has been influenced both by social scientists and humanists, and his method for dealing with history, which we shall now examine, discloses unmistakable evidence of these two mainsprings.

TOYNBEE'S HISTORICAL METHOD

It is somewhat easier to identify the forerunners of Mr. Toynbee's historical approach than to analyze systematically what his method is and does. For one thing, his approach has been different at three distinct periods in his life. These changes in emphasis and in frame of reference reveal his ability to formulate a theory, discover its flaws through trial and error, and exchange it for something he considers better. They also disclose that his conception of history as a saga of civilizations and ultimately of religion is an idea that dawned on him only gradually.

Mr. Toynbee's first publications are clearly the child of his training. His education at Winchester and Balliol coincides roughly with the first decade of this century. The symbol and key to the times was the Diamond Jubilee of Queen Victoria, and as a small boy he had stood in the processions. Englishmen then shared the feeling of having reached the summit where history itself was being terminated. This philosophy can hardly have been very convincing

---

[20]Winwood Reade, *The Martyrdom of Man* (London: Watts & Co., 1925), p. 26.

[21]Michael Rostovtzeff, *A History of the Ancient World* (Oxford: Clarendon Press, 1927), II, 351 ff.

[22]Private interview with Mr. Toynbee on December 2, 1950.

to Mr. Toynbee, for his earliest writings reflect a concern for divers peoples and nationalities in the spirit to which President Woodrow Wilson was to appeal in his creed of national self-determination. From 1914 to 1916 Toynbee's first essays and books were published.[23] In them his methodology is defined not in so many words but as reflected in the subjects he considers. Not civilizations but nations are the "intelligible units of history." He reserves for nations in general the same optimism that the Victorian era showed for Britain in particular. In our age "the national state is the most magnificent . . . social achievement in existence."[24] National culture is sacred and to oppose it is to defy God. One recognizes the inspiration of the secular religion of Wilsonian nationalism in the fervor with which Mr. Toynbee handles his subject.

Some of the same terms and metaphors which he later uses to describe the role of religion are made use of to characterize the function of nation-states. For example, he finds that "within the chrysalis" of absolute government a "common self-consciousness or Nationality"[25] is born, and democratic nationalism is becoming a healthy and strapping youngster. "From the Ottoman Empire there would emerge . . . as from a chrysalis, a Turkish nation. . . ."[26] In the same way he later finds that civilizations emerge from the "chrysalis" of great religions.

These examples of a rather naïve belief in bourgeois progress through humanitarian nationalism are of course qualified in many ways. At an early date a profound belief in some form of international authority is in evidence. Eastern Europe has problems which require a Balkan Zollverein. Culture is not inherent in any one language but is the heritage of the race. But these foreshadowings of later "universalism" are more the expressions of an idealistic philosophy of international relations than a denial of the primacy of nations as units of history. Indeed his position which regards World War I as a kind of accident which has but temporarily disturbed Europe's progress toward a warless internationalism is concrete evidence that at this stage in Mr. Toynbee's thinking idealism and nationalism are indissolubly wedded. The European national state is the norm of civilized society, and has so far re-

---

[23]Arnold J. Toynbee *et. al.*, *The Balkans*: *A History of Bulgaria, Serbia, Greece, Rumania and Turkey* (London: Oxford University Press, 1915); Arnold J. Toynbee, *Nationality and the War* (London: J. M. Dent & Sons, 1915); Arnold J. Toynbee, *The New Europe*: *Some Essays in Reconstruction* (New York: E. P. Dutton & Co., 1916).
[24]Toynbee, *Nationality and the War*, p. 481.
[25]*Ibid.*, p. 273.
[26]Toynbee and Kenneth P. Kirkwood, *Turkey* (London: Ernest Benn, 1926), pp. 4-5.

vealed a "faculty of indefinite organic growth."[27]   A premonition
that this perspective may change, however, comes in the last sentence of *Nationality and War*. If nations continue cribbed and
confined within parochial states in their struggles for existence and
survival, their fate may prove to be no different than that of the
Greek city-states. This was the type of history he wrote as a young
man of twenty-five.

This early outlook was shattered by World War I. Any bourgeois illusions about human progress could scarcely have withstood
so grim a parable of man's violence and brutality. For five years
Toynbee immersed himself in propaganda and intelligence work for
the government. His assignment was to sift and rewrite reports of
German atrocities. These lurid accounts flow incongruously from
the pen of the judicious historian. After the war he observed:
"atrocities seem to be outbreaks of bestiality normally 'suppressed'
in human beings but almost automatically stimulated under certain
conditions, and that so powerfully, if the conditions are sufficiently
acute or protracted, that the most highly civilized people are
carried away."[28]   Moreover, he registered serious misgivings concerning the nation-state as the measure of things. No known civilization but ours has grounded statehood on community of language.
This formula has occasioned bloodshed and massacre in the Near
and Middle East. It has climaxed in a totalitarian Moloch, in a
demoniac effort after uniformity.

A second impression penetrated Toynbee's consciousness during
this crisis. In the spring of 1918 as the German offensive under
Ludendorff exploded in one final thrust, a profound anxiety hung
over his thought. In 1911-12, immediately after taking his degree,
he had made a nine-months walking trip through Greece and
Crete. One impression engraved itself indelibly on his memory.
In the faint shadows of the Minoan civilization in Crete, he came
upon the deserted country house of a Venetian landowner. As
he looked at these ruins of two and a half centuries he imagined
those of Britain heaped alongside them. In 1918 he recalled this
memento mori of an extinct Venetian colony in Crete, which had
lasted four and a half centuries longer than any British colony.
The ominous prospect that the German drive might prove the
"knock-out blow" for the West found Toynbee rereading Thucydides and Lucretius, including the latter's imperishable, if melancholy, counsel on how to face death. These somber accounts of
Peloponnesian and Hannibalic doom, the fierce and brutal catas-
trophes which Toynbee himself was reading about and narrating,

---

[27]Toynbee *et. al., The Balkans*, p. 183.
[28]Toynbee, *The Western Question* (London: Constable & Co., 1922)
p. 266.

and his impending sense of the ephemeral nature of civilization swelled to an obsession following his trip to the Balkans. They were the three elements destined to be blended in an alloy of fit temper and resiliency to provide Toynbee with a new vessel of history.

The second stage or period in Mr. Toynbee's historical method began in 1922, when at the age of thirty-three he drafted on half a sheet of paper the main outlines of *A Study of History*. It was to be a work twice the size of Gibbon's great classic and on it, as we now know, Mr. Toynbee mortgaged most of his intellectual strength and vigor. During the war years forces were carrying him toward a perspective which embraced and encircled the whole historical landscape. This was made clear when in 1919 he addressed the candidates for *literae humaniores* at Oxford following his first year of postwar teaching at the University of London. The thesis of the lecture is a concise paradigm of his new theory of history. Gone is the nation-state as the primary unit of study, for ". . . the plot of civilization in a great exposition of it—like the Hellenic exposition or our own Western exposition—is surely the right goal of a humane education."[29] Western society, he asserts somewhat later, is ". . . a closer and more permanent unity Mr. Toynbee is ready with a second innovation. How are these great units to be analyzed and dissected? The answer Mr. Toynbee gives is the same as that given by Spengler, although the latter's writings were not yet known to Toynbee. The life histories of civilizations must be compiled, compared, and generalized in a "morphology" of history. It can be observed that civilizations pass through determinate states of growth and decay. For the purpose than . . . the independent states that form and dissolve within its boundaries. . . ."[30] Having substituted civilizations for nations, of describing these stages they can be considered as "biological organisms." In this limited sense one can speak precisely about the life cycles of societies as living creatures.

In the same way, Toynbee casts the life patterns of his civilizations in the form of a second metaphor, that of a drama or tragedy. He plainly expects that ". . . the great civilizations . . . may all reveal the same plot, if we analyze them rightly." It is this plot and its three "acts"—growth and development; crisis, breakdown, and rally; and final dissolution—which the universal historian must gird himself to study. The Graeco-Roman civilization is Mr.

---

[29]Toynbee, *The Tragedy of Greece: A Lecture Delivered for the Professor of Greek to Candidates for Honours in Literae Humaniores at Oxford in May* 1920 (London: Oxford University Press, 1931), p. 6.
[30]Toynbee, *The Western Question in Greece and Turkey: A Study in the Contact of Civilizations* (London: Constable & Co., 1923), p. 4.

Toynbee's model, and he develops his own thesis to account for its decline. For him, the moment of moral failure and breakdown came in 431 B.C. with the Peleponnesian War.

A third and final technique should be mentioned. After choosing civilizations as his subect and breaking down their histories into three parts or "acts" of a drama, Mr. Toynbee poses a third methodological problem concerning the relationships between these units or societies. There are issues in history that would be lost sight of if one examined merely the uniqueness or, as with Spengler, the "culture-soul" of each separate civilization. So for Toynbee the most absorbing problem in history is that of the encounters or contacts in which new civilizations are born.

The present encounter between Western civilization and the rest of the world is not something novel or unique. It is rather an outstanding instance of a recurrent historical phenomenon which can be examined in comparative terms. From the study of encounters between historic civilizations, "laws" can be deduced regarding cultural contacts. One "law" Mr. Toynbee tries out focuses on the nature of relationships in the face of resistance by an assaulted society. A civilization is ordinarily not susceptible to the total culture of a foreign society. When two civilizations collide, the culture of the more aggressive one is diffracted into its components, just as a light ray is diffracted into the spectrum by resistance from a prism. The more trivial components which will not cause too immediate and violent a disturbance of the threatened society's traditional ways of life have the best chance of penetration. Illustrative are the two successive assaults of Western civilization upon China and Japan. The Far East which in the sixteenth and seventeenth centuries had repulsed an attempt to introduce the Western way of life en bloc—including its religion—yielded in the nineteenth century to the more trivial force of technology. It was able at least to accept this while retaining the more basic qualities of its own way of life.

This diffraction of culture into its components leads to another recurrent feature of encounters between civilizations. An institution or social phenomenon that is an organic part of a total culture may, when separated from the whole in the form of a culture-ray, threaten or undermine the assaulted society. Thus the nation-state, when founded on common linguistic groups, as in Western Europe, has been less explosive. Outside this geographic area, in Eastern Europe, Southwest Asia, India, and Malaya where the linguistic map has not always provided a convenient or logical basis for the political map, the nation-state has been a disruptive force. From the Sudetanland to Eastern Bengal, nations have been established by the methods of barbarism, because the historic and traditional local patterns of social life in the areas clashed with the imperatives of national self-determination. The original setting of modern nationalism, where linguistic groups were compact and homogeneous units, has frequently been missing in non-European societies, and the idea of nationalism therefore has become an unsettling, even volcanic, force.[31]

It must be evident that Mr. Toynbee's *modus operandi* in dealing with history has undergone radical transformations since 1914-15. The most decisive change of all, however, takes place in 1939 and ushers in the third period in his historical method. At the age of fifty, Mr. Toynbee shifts the pivot of his approach from "civilizations" to "higher religions." Hitherto religion had been a means to an end, an agent responsible for the reproduction and perpetuation of civilizations. In the second batch of volumes of *A Study of History,* twice published in sets of three, an unexpected note is sounded as a distinct counterbeat to these earlier views. In Volume V he explains:

> When we examine the universal churches we shall find ourselves led to raise the question whether churches can really be comprehended in their entirety in the framework of the histories of civilizations, within which they make their first historical appearance, or whether we have not to regard them as representatives of another species of society which is at least as distinct from the species 'civilizations' as the civilizations are distinct from the primitive societies.
>
> This may prove to be one of the most momentous questions that a study of history . . . can suggest to us. . . .[32]

The change is bound up with the pattern of disintegration which is manifested in the later stages of all civilizations. The whole apparatus of disintegration with internal and external proletariats as well as religion is a key element in Mr. Toynbee's conception of the pattern of history. Our interest here, however, is restricted to the one suggestion that in a curious but perceptible fashion Mr. Toynbee has moved from "nations" to "civilizations" to "higher religions," and these shifts in historical focus have altered profoundly both his interpretation and the tools and techniques he employs. He has summarized this change and its consequences in words that leave little doubt as to this most recent perspective:

> Our present view of modern history focuses attention on the rise of our modern Western secular civilization as the latest great new event in the world. As we follow that rise, from the first

---

[31]Mr. Toynbee deals with these questions in the last four volumes of the *Study.*

[32]Toynbee, *A Study of History,* V, 23.

premonition of it in the genius of Frederick II Hohenstaufen, through the Renaissance to the eruption of democracy and science and modern scientific technique, we think of all this as being the great new event in the world which demands our attention and commands our admiration. If we can bring ourselves to think of it, instead, as one of the vain repetitions of the Gentiles—an almost meaningless repetition of something that the Greeks and Romans did before us and did supremely well— then the greatest new event in the history of mankind will be seen to be a very different one. The greatest new event will then not be the monotonous rise of yet another secular civilization out of the bosom of the Christian Church in the course of these latter centuries; it will still be the Crucifixion and its spiritual consequences.[33]

We have tried to examine Mr. Toynbee's historical method systematically by observing it at three distinct periods in his life. This is a common way of looking at the methodology of any scholar and no novelty therefore with regard to Mr. Toynbee. There is another less common way which may be worth passing notice since it is the one which our historian employs in talking about himself. In 1948, Mr. Toynbee asked himself the question, What are the chances for the survival of Western civilization? In trying to answer this question he discovered that three routes or historical methods could be followed in searching for an answer. To some extent he pursues them all in much of his writings. The hierarchy of order in which he ranges them in his reply to this question is therefore of greatest significance.

One method is the statistical approach. Some would call this the scientific method. In general Mr. Toynbee has the highest regard for the science of statistics. But he doubts its usefulness in at least two spheres. In a letter to this writer he refers to one: "When I study Sorokin's attempt to bring this last field [that is, any area where there are prospects that free will or intellect may be in command of man's behavior] under the rule of statistics, I find myself skeptical of the applicability of this method here."[34] And in his inquiry into the future of our civilization he rejects the statistical method for another reason. Natural scientists have an almost unlimited number of specimens for their experiments; a historian looking at civilizations has twenty or thirty. This sample may be adequate or it may be too small. Standing in history and perceiving only the dim shadows of the future, the historian has no way of knowing.

Another method is one designated "psychological." Mr. Toyn-

---

[33]Toynbee, *Civilization on Trial*, p. 237.
[34]Letter from Mr. Toynbee to this writer dated September 22, 1949.

bee here uses "psychological" loosely and unscientifically to refer to the appraisal and comparison of feelings of any kind. He asks what are the impressions and judgments of various leaders, past and present, about the future of civilization. He finds that some of the keenest and sharpest insights about historical problems come from the visions of prophets and poets. Goethe, the Chinese philosopher, and the Bible have earlier helped him unravel the mystery of the origin of civilizations, but on the West's future the method draws a blank. There is such confusion and contradiction in the testimony of the prophets that our future remains an open question.

Finally, Mr. Toynbee introduces the "comparative" method. If a scholar should find certain experiences recurring in a number of civilizations, he would have grounds for formulating a working hypothesis or principle based on this phenomenon. If militarism in Assyria, Rome, and in other civilizations brought certain inevitable consequences, then there is justification for looking for militarism and its consequent manifestations in Western civilization as well. In some ways this method comes closer to being a rule-of-thumb than a science. In its most elementary form it is simply an attempt to look at a historical question from as many observation posts as possible. Mr. Toynbee does this in dealing with contemporary diplomatic problems: "By taking the bearings of his contemporary object of study from various local observation-posts and then combining these several readings into a single formula, the student [of foreign policy] is able to bring the object into focus and to calculate its position and to measure its dimensions with some approach to objectivity even though the time-vista is denied to him."[35] With civilizations, he takes his bearings both in time and space. Having made certain readings, he sifts and examines these for elements of recurrence and novelty between the genus civilization and the particular representative which he is observing. The fruits of these comparisons are of little value until they are contemplated and pondered by the imaginative mind. Even then their purpose is to illuminate the understanding, rather than to provide ready-made previews, of future events. For the sanguine scientist of society, this may be craven incompetence. For someone who will settle for the rewards of greater insight and deeper understanding, the use of this method is not without value.

THE REAL ISSUES IN THE CRITICISM OF TOYNBEE'S HISTORY

Most critics would agree that Mr. Toynbee's *A Study of History* is a work of epic proportions. Several commentators have noted

---

[35]*Survey of International Affairs,* 1931 pp. 13-14.

that Toynbee, as a historian who has zealously recorded the many contrasting beats of history, has himself injected a marked counterbeat into historical writing. Since 1910, few works have exceeded the limit of one volume; in literature the short story has been threatening the novel. In contrast, both the length and the temper of *A Study of History* are exceptions to this prevailing ethos. Mr. Toynbee has consciously struck a blow in a spirit of burning conviction against the fashionable specialized and "scientific" studies which isolate tiny fragments of experience for the most intensive study.

In this sense he has attacked the scientific method. His chief foe, however, has not been the discrete use of scientific techniques but rather the idolatry of that method and the ready acceptance of the superficial philosophy of "scientism" with its easy optimism and materialism. His method, in its turn, must be evaluated and critically assessed, for the boldness of his approach makes it inevitable that certain questions and criticisms should be raised. The first person to anticipate this would be Mr. Toynbee himself, who observed at the time he was launching his major work: "In the world of scholarship, to give and take criticism is all in the day's work and, each in our day, we may criticize our predecessors without becoming guilty of presumption so long as we are able to look forward without rancour to being criticized in our turn by our successors when our day is past."[36]

All historians, including those who construct theories of universal history, have their forte or special competence. For Mr. Toynbee, his specialty is Graeco-Roman history. Its lands and people are familiar enough to make them virtually his second "homeland." But it is exactly his attachment to Hellenic history which causes his readers some uneasiness and anxiety about the pattern of world history that he has discovered. The conceptual scheme with which Toynbee has proceeded from the beginning is suspiciously well tailored to fit the decline and fall of one civilization, but it hangs rather awkwardly on the twenty some others. It is apparent from even a cursory reading that Hellenic civilization had its "Time of Troubles," "Universal State," and "Universal Church" in relentless and seemingly preordained succession. This pattern is more difficult to maintain when Mr. Toynbee discusses other civilizations. He is obliged to confess that Egyptian history comprises one kind of exception (for its universal state was revived after it had run its normal course), Arabic civilization is another exception, and other civilizations comprise still further but different exceptions.

---

[36]Toynbee, *A Study of History*, I, 48.

When a reader attempts to apply the conceptual scheme which has been derived principally from Hellenic civilization to, for example, Western civilization, this problem at once becomes dramatically clear. In a table designed to portray the stages in history of the various civilizations, the "Time of Troubles" for Western civilization is charted as having already taken place between 1378 and 1797.[37] Elsewhere in the book, Mr. Toynbee is far more cautious on this point and essentially gives the impression that although many of the symptoms of decay may be present, it is necessary to wait and see before conceding this decline. If the nature of growth and disintegration is as clearcut and distinct as elsewhere implied, then it is curious that the position of the West should remain so beclouded and uncertain for Mr. Toynbee.

Furthermore, there are flaws in Mr. Toynbee's formulation of the pattern of history which are distinct from the problem of its concrete application to contemporary civilizations. The first and most basic concept in his scheme is that of "civilization," and yet he never defines by more than a few illustrations precisely what he means by this term or how it can be distinguished from that of "society."[38] Still, as the analysis proceeds he talks about these units as if he were using them with all the precision of a zoölogist. Sometimes the species "civilization" is interchanged with the generic category of "society." Most of his definitions are literary rather than scientific, and there is the same breadth and vagueness to much of his terminology that generally characterize spiritual interpretations of history. For example, when he deals with the movement of "Withdrawal-and-Return" of creative leaders by whom growth is inspired in civilization, he leaves to the reader's discretion the precise common denominator in terms of which the experiences of thirty some individuals are meant to correspond. If Mr. Toynbee has used the experiences of Buddha, Caesar, Peter the Great, Kant, and Lenin to point up an interesting parallel, this flaw would not be particularly significant. When he uses them to establish scientific formulas and laws, then this practice may legitimately be questioned. Indeed his discussion is curiously marred by the unequal attention given to the various personalities and minorities who are responsible for civilizational growth. In some cases Mr. Toynbee presents shortened versions of the complete life histories of the creative leaders. Often many of these data, while interesting, have little to do with the point at issue. At other times he allows a paragraph or two to suffice. This difference in treatment can hardly be based upon any systematic principle. More-

---

[37]*Ibid.*, VI, 327.
[38]*Ibid.*, I, 17 ff.

over, it is difficult to appreciate the similarity he has detected between the quiet habits of the philosopher Kant, whose thoughts, to be sure, made an impact throughout the world, and the "Withdrawal-and-Return" of Peter the Great, who came back to Russia from Europe with new ideas which he personally put into practice.

This concept is no less difficult to fathom when Mr. Toynbee discusses particular creative nations. The notion that England withdrew from the continent between the sixteenth and eighteenth centuries only to return as the center of world trade and world power in the nineteenth century has more meaning as a description of the general foundations of British foreign policy than as an exact statement of historical fact. That is, British policy was based upon England's relative insularity, but this hardly constituted withdrawal. If it is farfetched to assume that a nation, even in the sixteenth century, could withdraw from concourse with others, it is hardly less extravagant to imagine that other nations which were in the thick of European power politics would be incapable of making a creative contribution. Any theory which would exclude seventeenth- and eighteenth-century France in this manner would hardly be supported by other objective observers. Yet it would be equally an error to blink the fact that the concept of "Withdrawal-and-Return" by its utter intangibility illuminates some of the shadowy corners of history which scientific studies have left untouched. It is only the overly ambitious claims which Toynbee sometimes makes for it that cause honest observers to object.

Another principle or law which is so indefinite that almost every historical episode can be molded to fit its broad outlines is that of "Challenge-and-Response." The questions that both spiritual and scientific interpretations of history have consistently asked has been, What is the true mechanism of history? Some historians have discovered this mechanism in a particular dialectic or process, and the most notable of these are the Hegelian and Marxian dialectic. Others have found the dynamic of history in economic pressures or geographical factors. Mr. Toynbee's formula is both more difficult to verify objectively and more likely to encompass most of the unfolding events of history. Between an environment which is too severe and one that is too easy there is a "golden mean" which constitutes the maximum incitement to civilization. In general, the basis for this optimum condition is a favorable climate and adequate land and natural resources.

The main objection which scientific historians would raise to this conception is that it is too simple in character. New nations and societies have achieved their positions in history not alone because of these rudimentary factors but also because the whole context of their historical experience was favorable. The American Colonies were blessed with a whole continent in which resources of un-paralleled variety and richness were available for use and exploita-tion. This privileged position, however, was only one fragment of the larger historical episode in which factors such as outside assist-ance and unexpected freedom from colonial domination were also involved. There is some question whether Mr. Toynbee's formula of "Challenge-and-Response" is at the same time sufficiently broad to encompass these various factors and concrete enough to per-mit their separate consideration. In the eyes of most modern sci-entific historians every historic event is an entity that is separate and unique and therefore so infinitely complex that an observer can evaluate it only in terms of its concreteness. Only by patient re-search and painstaking scrutiny can such an event be clearly and unerringly illuminated.

There is a final assumption behind Toynbee's writing to which modern historians would probably take exception. He sets forth the postulate that civilizations break down and decay because of elements within them that are inherently self-destructive. Yet some historians would point to the early American civilizations, particularly those of the Incas and Aztecs, as examples of civiliza-tions which have been destroyed by external forces. These ex-amples could probably be multiplied, yet it would hardly be con-sistent in a spiritual interpretation of history to concede that a people had succumbed to outside violence. So it is maintained in A Study of History that these civilizations had already experi-enced the most profound internal malaise before they were invaded and conquered by Spanish adventurers. They had succumbed to something that was destructive within themselves rather than yield-ing to destruction from without.

It is most likely that societies have been weakened by internal dissension and decay before falling prey to a more powerful foe and invader. It seems naïve to imagine, however, that history has not been sown with numerous cases of brute force triumphing over weakness and right. This has surely been true of small na-tions in history. It would be surprising indeed if the same were not true of civilizations such as the early American ones to which we have already referred. Mr. Toynbee's assumption of the trans-cendence of spiritual factors in history makes it impossible for him to accept the primacy of force and power as the cause of death for a civilization. He admits that the two Central American civili-zations had not yet attained their universal states at the time of the Spanish conquests but insists that they had for some time been within their "Time-of-Troubles."

By indirection this explanation assumes that the successful con-queror has not himself suffered this same self-inflicted blow and is therefore morally and politically superior. If pursued to its logical conclusion, this principle would mean that in all important respects a conquering invader would surpass his victim. Any list of victorious conquerors shows how fantastic this assumption is. It symbolizes the great weakness in those spiritual versions of history which too complacently identify virtue and power. It reflects the tragic paradox of our times that in Western civilization with the breakdown of common moral standards even the spiritual historian becomes a utopian of power.

The supreme dilemma which confounds students of human affairs is reflected in the dual problem with which Mr. Toynbee has grappled. In seeking to establish general principles and "laws" of history, he has chosen as his subject great civilizations. Of these he has found that over twenty are separate and discrete. These give a student of history the same kind of individual facts with which physical science has dealt. These facts are related by independent links in the same way that physical data are connected.

At the same time Mr. Toynbee has called upon this physical science analogy, he has abandoned a practice which is central to all scientific pursuits. The criticism which has been leveled most frequently against him has been that his "well-beloved empiricism" is in fact no empiricism at all. He has selected his data and has imperturbably made use of them in the building of a system. But each separate historical datum can be used in a variety of ways. Mr. Toynbee has generally used them in ways that served his purpose and may not always have cited those facts which would not support his principal theses. However valid this criticism may be for Mr. Toynbee's empiricism in particular, it is unerringly true with respect to empiricism in general. The cauldron of history is so immense and limitless that the individual historian can serve up but a tiny spoonful, and whether this can symbolize or represent the full mixture of history is always a most doubtful issue. The limits upon Mr. Toynbee's history are the limits of his subject matter. The infinite variety of history is the chief factor which creates the eternal boundaries within which any student must formulate his principles.

There is one standard in addition to that of historical method on which *A Study of History* can be judged and appraised. From point of sheer erudition and learning the work is almost matchless. It is more wide-ranging than Spengler's masterpiece, and its pages are literally teeming with brilliant passages and firefly flashes of insight. One section includes an extensive account of the history of warfare; another part describes the whole movement of colonization in North America. His accounts of the history of the Jewish people in Eastern Europe and Spain, of the Spartan form of society, and of the Ottoman slave-court are illustrations of the amplitude of historical experience to which a reader is introduced. Even if one finds that some of Mr. Toynbee's main theses are untenable, a reader would be insensitive indeed who was unable to gain new perspectives and feelings about the world from these passages. The value of Toynbee's history does not depend on the acceptance of each of its parts as if it were a Euclidean demonstration. It is so rich in historical allusions that the study of its pages has a value independent of agreement with its assumptions and conclusions.

Even as a philosopher of history, Mr. Toynbee holds up a warning sign to all historians and political scientists. He has maintained with unflagging steadfastness the proposition that history in general is unpredictable. The soundest predictions and estimates will be harassed and confounded by elements of chance and contingency. No one can say in advance what the conduct of leading participants in the historical drama will be, and few have prophesied accurately the more far-reaching events in history. Some look for the gradual elimination of this area of uncertainty through a more careful investigation of the well-springs of human behavior by the specialized social sciences. Mr. Toynbee has affirmed his confidence in future advances in our knowledge through the use of some of these techniques, particularly social psychology and statistics. It would be stretching a point, however, to imply that he shared the extravagant and cheerful expectations of some about the elimination of accident and change through the discoveries that are possible through the use of rigorous social surveys.

TOYNBEE AND CLASSICAL HISTORY

HISTORIOGRAPHY AND MYTH*

W. DEN BOER

Klio, whom Huizinga called the most uncompromising of the Muses, is also the most whimsical of Mnemosyne's daughters. Her devotees, bent on studying and surveying her movements, constantly experience—often, to be sure, without relish—the consequences of her severe judgment and her fitful character. Some of these devotees, however, set themselves a task, harder than the necessary work of investigation, which in itself is arduous enough. They endeavour to establish and analyse the laws to which, in their opinion, even the capricious Muse should, and does, adhere. Klio's whimsicality does not affect them, because they do not credit her with this attribute. To them her austerity is only apparent in the criticism of their co-devotees, whom they face with the assurance of believers, an assurance that is proof against all rational argumentation. The system they build up has a validity surpassing the bourne of time. Just as in religious experience and its dogmatic formulae myth traces all history back to a model supra-historic occurrence and to a world alien to our human world; so also to the historian who discovers and formulates laws, his system ultimately is a revelation surpassing the knowledge of the present world. Why invoke Klio's severity against these system-builders who in a way are believers? Would the blood of those punished by a harsh verdict not be the seed of their "Church"? The answer, no doubt, would be in the affirmative, if the system-builders presented their work as myth, but their mythopoeism also includes historiography. So long as historical method is employed and the believer's glossology is not completely resorted to, discussion on a historical basis is at least possible. Indeed, just as belief has its degree of initiation, and in the lower regions reason is not wholly ruled out, so historical mythopoeism is frequently linked to a respectable piece of historiography. The method followed often clearly shows the coherence between mythopoeism and historical work.

The method is based on the belief that a certain period in history may serve as an example for the whole history of humanity, and therefore has perfect validity. The preoccupation with historical facts aims at discovering or revealing myth, while inversely mankind's mythical tradition is investigated with the object of

---

*Translated by the author from the original Dutch article which appeared in *De Gids*, vol. 4, 1948, pp. 12-40.

explaining historical facts. So history is explained by myth, and myth by history.

Many system-makers attribute the Graeco-Roman history a special place in this union of myth and history, but they do not all go equally far. Those who have gone furthest hold that the future of their present civilization is effected by the rise, the prospering, and the decline in the history of Greece and Rome. In the opinion of others only the past may be brought under the Graeco-Roman "law", the future remaining a sealed book. With them the acceptance of the myth possibly is not wholehearted or they lack the sense for deduction which characterizes the former group. To this first class belongs St. Augustine who, in *De Civitate Dei,* based the world and its ultimate future on a sublime conception of Christian revelation. In the latter group we find Arnold J. Toynbee, of whose unfinished work, *A Study of History,* three volumes appeared in 1934 and another three in 1939. His views, like those of St. Augustine, are closely linked with Christianity, but with regard to the future they lack the prophetic assurance that inspired the ecclesiastical teacher. Toynbee, to be sure, has great affinity with the Bishop of Hippo, whom he often quotes with great reverence, but the 20th century Anglo-Saxon searcher proceeds far more cautiously than the undoubting theological rhetor of the 5th century. There is longing in the one and assurance in the other, the joyful prospect of a sure future as opposed to hoping against hope in the midst of doubt and fear.

Toynbee began his career as a student of classical history. His views in *A Study of History* in many respects reveal the views of his teachers, and for the right understanding of his great work it is instructive to draw a picture of the sphere in which he studied, and also to review his earliest independent published work.

Toynbee was born in 1889 and was educated during the period when the study of Greek history and civilization was dominated by the ethnological influence of Sir James Frazer, by the archaeology of Sir Arthur Evans, and by the school of religious history of which Miss Jane Harrison was a prominent advocate. It was also the period in which for the first time the great influence of Sir Gilbert Murray made itself felt; his ideals of humanity have both attracted and irritated following generations of British classicists. The work of these leaders is lavishly quoted in *A Study of History.* Gilbert Murray, moreover, was a direct adviser on the compilation of this work, practically the only one on the part dealing with Greek history, with which Toynbee is most familiar. With regard to the Hellenistic period, his principal source is W. W. Tarn, whose views on Alexander the Great he shares. As for Roman history the author quotes no authorities from his student days, but his main advisers for a description and interpretation of phenomena in the time of the Empire are M. P. Charlesworth and N. Baynes. An incredibly wide reading enables Toynbee to avail himself of literature outside the Anglo-Saxon world, but in two respects he keeps faith with his old tutors, viz., Murray's humanism and the pragmatism of the British school of religious history.

Among Toynbee's own works in the sphere of classical history one of the oldest essays is worth mentioning here. It is a study of Spartan military organization (*Journal of Hellenic Studies*, 1913), which is still being quoted, though its conclusions for the greater part have been rendered out of date. In this study, written when Toynbee was 23 years of age, he submits a series of bold hypotheses on Sparta's military organization which reveal a constructive mind. A number of data, far from sufficient upon which to base a complete picture of the course of history, is forced into a sketch acceptable only so long as these data are adhered to. It is no wonder that the sketch had to be abandoned, when the amazing discovery and interpretation of a papyrus clearly showed his starting point—in the arrangement of the data —to have been unsound.[1] Two conclusions may be drawn from this first proof of ability which, of course, the discovery of new data cannot belittle. Even from the outset Toynbee understood the art of building up a system from inadequate data. At the peak of his career he does the same with proportionately more abundant material which, however, in view of the wide field, remains inadequate. Our first conclusion, then, is negative: Toynbee constructs and . . . does it haphazardly. A second conclusion is a positive one: in his study of Sparta Toynbee already surprises his readers by some brilliant textual interpretations of Herodotus and Thucydides which have remained valuable to the present day. The philologist and historian in his great work again and again surprises us with clever interpretations of details which, even if his method should not be acceptable, fully deserve our consideration.

Toynbee not only remained true to himself, but in his evolution there are various particulars which show him to be guided by the British tradition in historiography. To begin with a fact of minor importance: in a period in which it was the obvious thing for a promising young Oxford classicist to do, he visited Greece and Rome. The impressions thus picked up have remained fresh, and after 25 years he is able to use his travelling experiences as material for his *magnum opus*. They are important and speak well for his keen powers of observation, which also take in the non-

---

[1]See Tyrtaeus, frgm. 1 (Diehl) and von Wilamowitz Moellendorff in *Sitzungsberichte* of the Berlin Academy, 1918.

obvious. He is a past master at telling a travel story, and there is thus often provided a pleasant break in the application demanded of the reader, resulting in a high degree of vividness and the appearance of a clear visual picture; for instance, the story of the deserted Venetian villa on Crete reminiscent of the past glory of the merchant's republic, and also the last phase of a civilization being compared with an Indian Summer as experienced on a motor trip through the American landscape. The ease with which travelling experiences are used as illustrations is a special gift often tastefully displayed by British writers.

This, however, is not the most striking quality which secures for Toynbee a place among the leading typically British historians. There is also the consciousness of being part of the present-day world. The British classicist, like his continental colleague, no doubt knows the seclusion of the study, but he is also well aware that he is a member of the community. The war years have given ample proof of this. Gilbert Murray, in his 75th years, was an inspiring speaker at many meetings of his fellow citizens and called for the vindication of the elementary humanity which he admired in ancient Greece and knew to be proof against all barbarism. A comparison of these refined war speeches, delivered with strong conviction and collected with other essays in *Greek Studies,* with the *Kriegsreden* by a German Greek scholar during the first world war, viz., von Wilamowitz Moellendorff, makes it clear why a Dutch classicist in making his choice looked westward. What happened in this respect in Britain during the last war—and Murray is but one example among many—had also been observed during the period 1914-18. In these years two scholars answered their country's call, viz., Alfred E. Zimmern and Arnold J. Toynbee. Both realized the importance of international relations and devoted their humanistic idealism and their great talents to the improvement of these relations. The former, author of one of the most popular works on the age of Pericles, *The Greek Commonwealth,* became a leading figure in the League of Nations' committee on educational matters and was professor of international relations in Oxford University where he was chiefly occupied with the study of political history. Arnold J. Toynbee became known as one of the leading compilers of the annual *Survey of International Affairs,* with which he has been steadily associated since 1925. The experience gained in long journeys abroad stood him in good stead, and he came into contact with politicians of many countries. His book *A Journey to China* was the outcome of these extensive trips. The admirer of Hellas and Rome left the *mare nostrum,* travelled along the Pillars of Heracles and sailed the seven seas. His outlook broadened and ancient history became part of the world's history. Rising above parochialism, frequent among classicists, he brings Greek and Roman history into relation with the whole world of civilization. There, step by step he constructs his masterly work, six volumes of which have now been published, but which must have been in the author's mind as one whole when he commenced writing.

Yet no man can escape from his past and Toynbee is no exception. In two respects he remains faithful to Ancient History. When dealing with the origin, the rise and fall, and the degeneration of his 21 civilizations, he borrows for the 20 others his first and most striking parallels from what he calls Hellenic Civilization, i.e., the period beginning with the arrival in Greece of the Dorians and terminating with the collapse of the Western Roman Empire. But he does not stop at pointing out a causal parallel. The whole course of Hellenic history clearly inspires the construction of the outline into which other civilizations are pressed. Here is a classicism not expected from an investigator intent on dealing with each of his 21 civilizations as "intelligible fields of historical study." The inconsistency resulting from this classicism causes civilizations, meticulously kept distinct by the historian—a distinction which in practical historical study cannot be maintained without straining factual history—to be classified according to one standard pattern, i.e., the Graeco-Roman pattern.

The objections, both against the division into "intelligible fields" and against this classicism have been formulated in a masterly manner, in clean cut questions by the prehistorian V. Gordon Childe:

> Is it legitimate or profitable to carve history into bits, label them 'civilizations' and then treat them as distinct and independent instances of general laws? Are the bits thus isolated really separate representatives of a species from a comparison of which an inductive description can be constructed like the anatomical chart of the human body based on a dissection of a number of distinct bodies? Are Toynbee's 'civilizations' not rather like the several limbs or organs of one such body? If so, would the specific description or general diagram of a generalized toe (to take the most favourable instance) composed only of the features common to all ten toes, be really helpful for an operation on the left big toe?[2]

The last question, in my opinion conveys too favourable a picture of the situation. The scheme is not made up from the characteristics common to all of the 21 civilizations; the history of the Graeco-Roman civilization provides the pattern for all the others.

[2] V. Gordon Childe, *History*, Cobbett Press, London 1947; Abelard-Schuman, New York, 1947, p. 63.

To use Gordon Childe's metaphor: the anatomy of one toe determines that of the nine others (assuming that one is fortunate enough only to have toes to deal with).

It is worth while to leave these objections for the present and consider Toynbee's vision of antiquity within the scope of his system. Two remarks may be made at the outset. First, the author himself frequently states that classical antiquity is his "standard of comparison"; and second, the use of this pattern stands or falls with the link between the Greek and Roman component parts. This link is developed to the extent of joining Greek and Roman history in a union in which the Greek component dominates. Therefore Toynbee does not speak of Graeco-Roman but of "Hellenic" civilization.

When the Cretan civilization had crumbled under the influence of Indo-European tribes—Toynbee refers to them as the *external proletariat*—these invaders toward the close of the 2nd millenium developed a civilization of their own. We know too little of the earlier culture of the Cretans to be able to trace its influence upon this new Hellenic civilization. It shall appear presently that Toynbee with the help of his scheme gives an opinion on this point. These invading Hellenes in the first centuries of their settlement round the Aegean, and even beyond, continually shifted their abode. We are dealing here with a challenge, a struggle of life to be won by repeated emigration and colonisation, from Greece to the coast of Asia Minor and thence back to the Mother Country and the outlying coastal regions of the Eastern and Western Mediterranean. Every challenge of territory and circumstance had to be met and was met. A striking example is Magna Graecia, Southern Italy and Sicily, where the Greek settlers, far from the mother country, met the challenge in the right manner and so brought Hellenic culture westward. Toynbee here formulates a law, viz., that new territory stimulates the development of civilization. Another law is that leisure is hostile to civilization. Comfortable environments, new or old, enervate, and vigour steeled by affliction is shattered, as in the case of Odysseus who made himself at home with Kalypso. The lotophagi in the Odyssey are a mythical and also a typical example of a people to whom challenge is unknown. Leaving the dim saga, one only needs to contrast the poor soil of Attica with that of fertile Boeotia to realise that poverty has had a beneficial, and prosperity a fateful, effect. Political rejuvenation emanates from the cities overseas, and Western legislators give to the Greek city-state its legal standing, their regenerating influence being felt in the mother country. Confining our attention to Athens we notice how the challenge of new commerical and industrial conditions was faced by Solon, even though he had to put his new wine into the old bottles of the parochial municipal institutions. Splendidly Athens finally met the challenge of the Persian wars. Here, indeed, is a growth to which the proverbial 50 years from 480-430 B.C. testify to the present day.

The year 431, however, is an ill-fated period in the course of this civilization. The Time of Troubles begins, and downfall looms. The hopeless struggle against extinction continues during the Hellenistic period and the Roman Republic, especially during the Punic wars and the social and economic unrest in the 2nd and 1st century B.C., culminating in the political struggle for power in the interior and in the occupied territories, and terminating in a period of relative calm, Augustus' "Universal State." The period of breakdown is brought to an end by the Battle of Actium in 31 B.C. Yet the breathing spell accorded a doomed civilization is of short duration. From 31 B.C. to 378 A.D. we observe the disintegration in process, although an Indian Summer like the period of the Antonines and the relative quiet under capable rulers like Diocletian and Constantine give the impression that the downward movement is halted. In reality, disaster and recovery, rout and rally, follow each other with accelerating speed and the breathing spells become shorter. Constantly hordes of a new external proletariat pound the walls of this civilization. The internal proletariat, Christendom, partly aided by the barbarians, creates a new civilization, draining the old civilization till complete disintegration has become a fact.

How is this conception, which we will for the moment not question, generalized? This is accomplished in the following manner. A civilization arises when a primitive community receives from elsewhere a certain stimulus, a challenge to rise above its present vegetative existence, and meets the challenge in the right manner. The scheme of challenge and response directs not only the birth but also the growth of civilizations. A progressive civilization itself finds the right answer to every one of a whole series of challenges. But, the time comes when the right reaction is no longer found. When this transpires, civilization collapses and finds itself in a Time of Troubles which may be of short or long duration. Finally the blunders grow to the extent of causing degeneration. Both breakdown and degeneration are caused by internal conditions, just as growth originally started internally. In these periods of downfall and degeneration the creative minority (of real exponents of culture) no longer inspires the masses by its example, but develops into a dominant minority which takes its stand beside and against the masses, and internal proletariat no longer participating in the cultural possessions of the civilization. This schism is all the more serious because side by side with both these groups is an external proletariat ready to prey on the old civilization. It is not incorporated in the whole of the culture, but being fed on the perversion of degeneration it cooperates in a fatal manner in the complete destruction of the civilization. The rhythmic duality of challenge and response makes room for a new one, rout and rally, of which the former—which is really a challenge not met—determines the level of civilization. A period of improved conditions is possible, as is shown by the Universal State, but recovery is illusory and not to be looked upon as growth. It is a temporary revival which had better be called an Indian Summer, immediately preceding the wintry season of destruction. But this destruction is not the end of all, for the schism between the trio, internal and external proletariat and dominant minority, does indeed effect the latter's destruction, but the external proletariat has a small creativeness in a heroic period, partly connected with and partly following the destruction. It produces war heroes extolled in war poems. The epic, which becomes a cultural good of the new civilization, is its product. But the internal proletariat carries the treasure of the new civilization in the vessels of its own humility. This crowd is the originator of a "higher religion" in a Universal Church and to it a new civilization owes its origin.

So the laicized apocalypse describes a sytematic course of civilization which, as is the case with all apocalyptics, can be better observed in times of collapse and degeneration than during rise and expansion. The work is also apocalyptic in that degeneration, disaster, and collapse are well nigh personified horrors as the riders War, Hunger, and Death in the Scriptural Apocalypse, recognizable by the red, black, and drab colours of their horses. No Lamb, however, opens the seal—thereby announcing the arrival of the periods of ruin: the downfall of civilization is caused and ushered in not from the outside but from the inside.

Not only the community but also the individual conforms to this pattern. In a period of expansion, creative personalities are subject to the law of withdrawal and return, which is a different reading from the law of challenge and response. In the period of degeneration all dynamics have disappeared. Man is a standard type looking for his salvation to Archaism or Futurism; or in Detachment isolates himself from the world; or, only in rare cases of transfiguration, finds the road to a Kingdom which is not of this world. Of the latter category primitive Christianity supplies Toynbee with examples in an apocalyptic comparison of martyrs with the remainder of mankind, which is weighed and found wanting. In the matter of civilizations and individuals, the mind of this phenomenal system-builder is always drawn to the vanishishing Graeco-Roman civilization and the rise of Christianity, to the Universal State and the Universal Church. It is no exaggeration to assume that the conception of an internal proletariat and a Universal Church as a source of energy for all new civilizations, which according to Toynbee history has recorded, has been inspired by the oldest history of Christianity and its relation to the Roman Empire. Here is an essential point in Toynbee's relation to classical history.

The thesis again and again submitted reads as follows: Christianity is the religion of the internal proletariat of Hellenic civilization. Discrimination or "penalization" has been the stimulus for its tremendous expansion: "the slaves and the slaves' God won" (e.g., II, 215-216; 320-321; IV, 347). Toynbee appeals here to the 19th century historians, particularly O. Seeck and E. Meyer. He differs, however, from his authorities in that he—unlike what the German schools of Mommsen and Nietzsche would have loved to do—does not look upon Christianity as the vampire of Roman civilization. On the contrary, he comes from Christian stock and upholds it. But his view on the evolution which he wishes to be Christian is time and again handicapped by the authorities to whom he refers. For the study of the history of Christianity the consequences are grave. He continues building on the 19th century historians, yet professes that the Christian gospel has meant the salvation of Rome's civilization. He therefore opposes Gibbon, who maintained that the triumph of barbarism and religion set in after the time of the Antonines; and he points out how this very new religion, in the shape of Christianity, harboured many new germs of civilization, and viewed from Hellenic civilization was merely the epilogue of collapse and not collapse itself. Yet it would be wrong to infer that Toynbee sets great store on this epilogue between two civilizations. The Christian gospel is a medley of Hellenic motives emerging from the chaos of Greek syncretism. By this one-sidedness Toynbee almost entirely eliminates Israelitic factors. At most he admits that the religion of the internal proletariat of the Hellenic civilization received "an alien spark" from Israel (V, 360-366). German scholars like R. Reitzenstein, who exclusively brings Greek factors in Christianity into prominence, here lead Toynbee astray on tracks abandoned long ago. A clever combination of the motives which play a part in the history of the Spartan social reformers Agis and Cleomenes with those from the lives of the Gracchi and with episodes from the Gospels, the blending of Greek mythological conceptions like the adventures of gods and semi-gods with the Annunciation (in both of which the Virgin's pregnancy occurs), are the most striking specimens borrowed from the storehouse of obsolete weapons of comparative religious history in its initial stage. These and other aberrations are mainly caused by Toynbee's one-sided interpretation, however essential for his system: Christianity is the religion of the internal proletariat of Hellenic civilization.

Not only Christianity but other "higher religions" including Greek religion are by a partial interpretation adapted to the system. In several places where the historian Toynbee oversteps the limits of historical work he has recourse to religious phenomena to support his historical structure.

The thesis that a civilization originates from man's response to a challenge is proved by the Bible, Goethe's *Faust*, and Euripides' *Hippolytus*. In the Old Testament Job's story is an example of the struggle between challenged Man and challenging Satan; in the New Testament the story of the Temptation in the Wilderness and the gospel of death and resurrection are parallels. Faust was challenged by Mephistopheles, and Hippolytus by Aphrodite. Man's struggle may lead to victory or downfall. In the former case the right response was found, in the latter Man was broken and perished through his inability to find the required answer. The same, so Toynbee avers, applies to civilizations. *Quod est demonstrandum!* Why should the rhythm of civilizations correspond with the fluctuations in man's inner life as seen by mythical speculation? What is left of the empiricism which is said to be the root of the system if the mythus of the individual's religious experience is secularized and is then applied to communities and their historical relations?

These questions do not worry Toynbee. He has a reply that should suffice the believer: "The event (i.e., challenge and response) can best be described in these mythological images because they are not embarrassed by the contradiction that arises when the statement is translated into logical terms" (I, 278).

After this statement one might be inclined to give up further discussion with Toynbee on this point since historical arguments on metaphysical convictions are of no avail. Yet he deserves to be followed as far as possible. If we cannot proceed on our own strength, one of Toynbee's supporters may assist us, even though he states the master's views incorrectly. I would therefore call attention to C. H. Dodd's opinion. He only deals with Toynbee's mythical proof adopted from the New Testament.[3] On the Christian myth he says: "The Christian form of the myth is the only one that even professes to have been embodied in an historical event. . . . Christianity insists that in the death of Jesus *sub Pontio*

---

[3]C. H. Dodd, *The Apostolic Preaching and its Development* (1945), in the appendix on: Eschatology and History, spec. p. 91 ff.

Pilato there occurred a unique encounter between God and the power of evil out of which a new kind of life for mankind emerged". Well then, so Dodd proceeds, with regard to every civilization Toynbee postulates an event having the same qualities of uniqueness which Christianity attributes to the advent of Christ. "This event is momentous and in the last resort so mysterious and so little to be accounted for by any immanent evolutionary factors that it cannot be adequately presented except in the mythical form of an encounter between superhuman personalities". So by vindicating the historicity of Jesus' life on earth Dodd endeavours to make the universal validity of the idea of challenge *versus* plausible for the history of civilizations. Here two questions arise: Did Dodd succeed in his attempt, and did he understand Toynbee's meaning? In my opinion the answer to both these questions is in the negative.

To Christians, so far as orthodoxy in its many shapes is concerned, the Gospel stories have both an historical and a mythical significance. Jesus lived under Augustus and Tiberius, suffered and died from Pontius Pilate, the procurator (history). His life is a pattern for the life of all his followers, who each in his turn share suffering and the cross (myth). Belief in the historical Jesus, however, is no proof for his mythical significance, which transcends time. Dodd's view is the opposite of Toynbee's. Dodd leaves out of consideration the examples of Job, Faust, and Hippolytus, and this agrees with his point of view since he cannot use them as historical figures. Toynbee, on the other hand, deals with these four characters only as figures of the myth. That the historicity of Jesus should be of any account for the demonstration of the conception of challenge and response is out of the question for him. Were it otherwise Toynbee would never have referred to "spontaneous human experience which has found a cumulative expression in mythology" (II, 73).

So Dodd's defense and elaboration have failed, yet they provide us with an opportunity to establish the fact that Toynbee's use of the myth lies outside the question whether myth is also history. The psychical tension in which the mythical hero lives is a foreshadowing and a proof of the rhythmical course of history; these tensions themselves belong to all ages and transcend time.

The same mental short-circuit, the transposition of human life to cultural evolution, marks the discussion on growth. Here, too, historical knowledge is inadequate for an explanation of the schematic procedure, Biblical and Greek myths being called in to prove part of the system to be sound. The mythical expression of growth is the figure of Prometheus, the challenged one, to whom will fall the triumph over his celestial challenger. Prometheus is the prototype of the Hellenic civilization, which, challenged by the Persians or by the poor soil equally, gains a glorious victory. Job, who after enduring a painful challenge finds greater riches in a second life, is another mythical example. Here Toynbee's allegory handles these stories in an extraordinarily offhand manner.

Prometheus, representative of a bygone period of the Titans, is not the victor over Zeus, but he joints the latter's government. As only Aeschylus' *Prometheus Bound* is left to us, it is possible to represent Prometheus as the unyielding, as both ancient and modern allegorists have done all too often. This construction, however, does not agree with the Greek idea of the myth, which does not speak about victor and vanquished but—in any case with Aeschylus to whom Toynbee refers—about a battle of the Gods in which both parties, enriched and reconciled, unite in a new harmony. That the end of Job's story is an appendix which has nothing to do with the problem involved in the story is less to the point than the entirely anthropocentric interpretation of one of the most momentous documents of Isrealitic tradition. Toynbee scorns the religious experience which considers disintegrating factors outside man as possible and certain. This doctrinaire attitude causes him to underrate the significance of the Book of Job, which pictures the everlasting tension between divine and human conduct, between causality and free will, creator and creation, God's omnipotence creating vessels both to honour and dishonour, and creatural understanding humbling itself in dust and ashes. The anthropocentric factor with Toynbee is sharply accentuated when he opposes predestination and fatalism. This, of course, is quite legitimate, but why should the mythical tradition of divine dealing with man be called in as evidence for the soundness of an anthropocentric system of civilizations. Just as the Dutch historian of the 19th century, G. Groen van Prinsterer, deals with Jewish-Christian revelation, so Toynbee deals with Biblical and Greek tradition. All human mythical thought abundantly utters . . . what? An immanent progress of history shorn of all transcendent intervention *ad maiorem gloriam* of the system built up by Toynbee.

We have here an historian whose moralistic ideas of immanent justice, which make history a succession of guilts and punishments, goodness and reward, clash with the Jewish revelation of God's dealings in history, which are beyond human standards and responsibility. The Greeks, too, although to a lesser degree than the Jewish, had a knowledge of divine intervention in the life of the individual and of the community. In both cases, of Jews and Greeks, Toynbee explains religious notions and documents in a mythical allegorical manner. Why should this be the case? Does the system stand in need of this method? Toynbee's reply to the latter question will be in the affirmative. He evidently is too deeply rooted in a tradition which opened the Bible at random in order to explain all the world's events, to abandon this method offhand. At the same time he is uprooted, too, since the belief which was at the bottom of the childish custom fails him. .

So, in his system, particularly growth and collapse are based on a moralistic interpretation of religious conceptions and writings of Jews and Greeks, a few examples of which are given here.

When in the 107th Psalm a hymn in praise of God's dealings in Israel's history the chorus is heard: "Then they cried unto the Lord in their trouble and He delivered them out of their distresses", Toynbee calls this: attributing to God by later poets the work of heroes in Israel's earliest history. And when, in the Magnificat, clearly reminiscent of this psalm, the mighty deeds of God and the redemption thereby received are attributed to God's sovereign good will in the sending of the world's Saviour, the moralist Toynbee's reaction is but a sarcastic remark on "primitive human minds" (IV, 255; V, 151; VI, 125; I, 335). With the bath water of what he considers to be fatalism he throws out the baby of religion.

When the prophet Ezekiel states that Assyria was doomed because it had lifted itself in height like a tree, Toynbee asserts that the primitive notion of "Envy of the gods", who are jealous of human bliss, is taught here (VI, 472). He rejects Ezekiel's statement on the ground that Assyria perished through militarism, i.e., by internal causes and not through an act of any power whatsoever. The possible co-existence of both internal and external causes—whether this was the case may be passed over for the moment—is not even considered. Toynbee's struggle here resembles that between Luther and Erasmus in the matter of free will. Reading both Toynbee and Erasmus we are reminded of Huizinga's profound insight into the problem of right and wrong.[4] Toynbee is the disciple of British scholars in religious history one of whom in his later years relates a youthful episode, viz., how the story of the casting out of the devils in the country of the Gadarenes and the drowning of the innocent swine—quite a loss to the owners!—so shocked him that he turned his back on the Christian faith.[5] This is a consistent attitude for one, averse to temporizing and moralizing, who sticks to the text that is before him. Toynbee does not share the other's repugnance and rejection, but he accepts Murray's dualism when he adapts the mythical tradition of Jews

---

[4] J. Huizinga, *Erasmus*, pp. 174-177.
[5] G. Murray, *Stoic, Christian, and Humanist*, p. 8. The first edition appeared in 1940.

and Greeks to his thesis that the experience of men and of communities are but the outcome of internal causes. This fully agrees with his thesis that at the beginning of all religious experience there is not the appearance of the deity—or revelation—but the discovery of man himself, particularly of an internal proletariat (V, 161).

This theory has an important bearing on Greek religion. To Toynbee the very anthropocentric element is Greece's glory; in this respect they were far ahead of the Jews. Aeschylus was the first to express the view that the cause of rise or fall lies with man himself. Yet Toynbee forgets that Aeschylus also knows of the suffering of the innocent, particularly the curse of the race. The devout poet does not deal with this side of the problem, as he does not want to increase "the idle burden of thought". He resembles the unchallenged believer who leaves the problem of contradictory tendencies in religious experiences for what they are. This unproblematical piety is influenced by personal political experience. The Persians are conquered and Aeschylus himself fought at Marathon. Did not the Persians clearly lose through their own errors and sins? Did not immanent justice reveal itself in a powerful manner? Did not evil bring its own judgment? Surely, but to the Marathon warriors this judgment also is the work of the gods. In human downfall, guilt and divine intervention go together. To Aeschylus, however, this paradoxical connection is not yet a problem guiding his considerations any more than was the case with Solon before him. This Athenian lawgiver knows that in the life of nations evil brings its own punishment, and his legislative work is based on the principle of immanent justice. Yet Solon also knows the curse of races, that the iniquity of the fathers is visited upon the children. "One pays his debt forthwith, another after some time. And if they escape and divine fate does not smite them, still retribution is sure to come, for then the innocent, their children and offspring, must pay for their deeds" (Frg. 1, 29 ff.). With Solon, as with Aeschylus a century later, this problem is a religious struggle, contrary to the second tragic poet Sophocles (in his Oedipus). The latter is the innocent man who unwittingly committed incest and patricide, and by the mere fact of having been born would bear the guilt for acts for which he was not responsible.

It may well be asked why these tragic myths deserve such extended attention. The answer is that Toynbee himself, not once but repeatedly adapts Greek tragedy for his theory. The most important material borrowed from tragedy is the conception of "peripeteia", or reversion, which he takes to be change from within. In a cultural process startling changes occur again and again. In tragedy, too, things turn out contrary to expectation. The Persian ruler loses, happy King Oedipus becomes unhappy, mighty King Pentheus, who bans the Bacchantes, is torn to pieces. The Bible is full of peripetai: of the pharisee and the publican the latter is pardoned, the former is not; the stone refused by the builders becomes the headstone of the corner; God hath chosen the weak things of the world (IV, 245 ff.). Here, in any event, the notion of election makes its appearance. Is there really a valuation and a government of things independent of immanent causes? Are Xerxes, Oedipus, and Pentheus doomed because the godhead wills it so?

The theory here seems to waver. But Toynbee recovers himself, thanks to moralism, which appears to be his most profound conviction. Indeed, there is a divine agency with regard to human lives and civilizations. The action is salvation, never damnation. Consider how Toynbee deals with the attitude toward life in times of disintegration (VI, 49-168):

> In a period of disintegration part of those who are able to guide resort to archaism and meaningless rite. The rule of the 400 in Athens, Augustus' constitution and the senate's resorted glory under the military emperors serve among others as examples. At best, the archaist is but a victim of self-deception. His attitude towards life is his own choice. This archaism may turn into detachment or philosophical isolation, an aloofness as of the later Stoa so conspicuous in the 2d century A.D.

Side by side there is an attitude which looks to the future (often built up out of past rites). Here we find the iconoclasts and Jewish messianism. There is a longing for stability, yet a break with the present. To this group of futurists belongs all cultural pessimism. We are dealing here with those who belong to an internal proletariat, whereas archaism and detachment occur in the dominant minority. Toynbee's verdict on these three groups is far from lenient: "The way of Archaism ends in self-defeat, the way of Futurism is self-transcendence, the way of Detachment is self-stultification" (VI, 149). With none of them does a power from outside come to shoulder the responsibility.

There is, however a fourth group also belonging to the internal proletariat, which progresses further and looks farther ahead than the three others. They are the "converts", who urged by love are the renovators, the builders of a new civilization. Their transfiguration is not man's handiwork. "The act of Transfiguration is a mystery because it is an act of God's presence" (VI, 161). To this divine intervention testify antiphonically the Greek poet Hesiod, to whom the Muses revealed the birth of the gods, and the angels in Bethlehem's fields when they proclaimed peace on earth.

Before this testimony of sincere faith which fills the finest pages of this mighty work it behooves us to be moderate and still. The gulf between the ardent plea for the immanent course of history and the passage quoted is caused by the inconsistency of religious experience which is heedless of all systems. This, however, impairs the basis according to which religion is a human invention. In Toynbee's work, too, the starting point does not stand against the phenomena of the early Christian tradition and those of Greek origin.

The nine Muses may together chant their hymns in celestial spheres, but Klio when alone treads early paths, hard to follow though they be. Toynbee is a mythical thinker whose mental activity goes side by side with intuitive belief. But he is also a historian and as such he makes use of a piece of history, the Graeco-Roman history, which as we saw supplies the standard pattern for all historical development. We pointed out some objections to this classicism, but the question whether the picture of the course of Graeco-Roman history is correct has up to now not been discussed. A complete answer involving all facts dealt with in these six volumes would take a whole book. A few remarks on the following important points will have to suffice.

It is a precarious task to combine the activities of a historian and a prophet. For us it is, in Toynbee's own words, sometimes rather easy to distinguish a period of growth from one of disintegration . . . *post eventum*. For who could maintain that the growth of Hellenic civilization was prior to the Peloponnesian war and that all subsequent periods of rise in the Hellenistic monarchies and in Rome were no more than a temporary recovery in an inescapable process of disintegration? In this manner all Roman history becomes an appendix of Greek history, no allowance being made for its origin and growth. Toynbee pays little attention to the old Roman republic, and this is not to be wondered at as its history is of little use to him. He starts with the Romans as converts to Hellenistic civilization and in doing so also neglects what he calls the Universal State of Augustus. If there ever was a ruler who saw in his work a revival of the old Rome, it was this Princeps. Think of Vergil outside the old Italian tradition and you rob the *Georgics* and the *Eclogues*, and even the *Aeneid*, of their very marrow. Though in the words of Horace the vanquished triumphed over the victor, the interpretation which considers the history of Italy and Latium to be bound up with Greece even before this victory is alien to historical reality. When Greek sources, Polybius and Strabo, are used in defense of the Greek nature of Roman civilization, would the modern historian in voicing their ideas not be the victim of what these Greeks had to say about Rome? Let it be clear that

I have no intention whatever of underestimating the Greek influence on Rome, but I feel bound to make a stand against a theory which with no other object than an interpretation of the development of civilizations chooses from a multitude of facts only those which make Roman history fit into the Greek pattern. The political, the economical, as well as the religious evolution of Rome are misrepresented through such an artificial construction. Not only the exigencies of the system, but also Toynbee's moralism is responsible for the elimination of Roman civilization. He is so averse to all war and conquest that whenever possible he groups the imperialistic inclinations of states in periods of breakdown and disintegration. Purposely I use the words "whenever possible", for only when the system permits it have violent actions been placed in the period of downfall. This has resulted in measuring by two standards.

Toynbee cannot apply his artificial theory to Sparta, which both before and simultaneously with Athens existed independently as a Greek city-state and exercised its influence on the Greek world. Here he found a different avenue of escape, viz., that of "arrested civilizations". Just as with the Polynesians, the Esquimaux, and the 'Osmanlis', civilization in Sparta passed through a process of germination, but before the time of flourishing it faded into decay (III, 50-79). With Sparta stagnation was caused by the self-imposed rigorous military régime which was partly necessitated by the problem of keeping a tight hand over the helots. The military state absorbed all activity and thereby prevented the development of a thoroughgoing civilization. Sparta is so much separated from Hellenic civilization that Toynbee, in adding up all civilizations, arrives at a total of 26, five arrested civilizations being added as independent units to the 21 civilizations which came to maturity (IV, 1). Yet Athenian democrats, whatever their aversion to Sparta might be, never classed this state among the barbarians. One need only look at the different treatment of Macedonia, despised by many for its barbarism, to feel convinced that Spartans are reckoned as Greeks. But in Toynbee's theory Sparta has been segregated and removed from Greek civilization as an alien body, a chopped off stump from which no twigs will sprout. So the legitimate child is disowned and the adopted child, Rome, becomes heir. All the evil that Sparta brought upon the Greek world—and I will admit there has been plenty of it—does not justify this maneuver, which finds its sole explanation in Toynbee's aversion to violence and militarism.

Toynbee is well aware that growth is also accompanied by war and violence, but war in such a period he either glosses over or he belittles the action of the mighty state in its period of expansion, as in the case of Athens whose Delian League could just as well have been placed in a period of breakdown like Rome's display of power against the mercantile republic of Rhodes. Only that what Athens did in a small way towards Samos and other islands Roman policy carried out on a much larger scale. The quantitative difference permits us to bestow a blessing upon Athens and a cure on Rome. Once this has been accomplished, the work of system-making can once more proceed according to plan.

In this manner the period from Nerva to Marcus Aurelius can only be appreciated as an Indian Summer, and this relatively speaking is permissible as, judging after the event, one may look upon Dacians and Marcomans as the first billows of the all-destroying deluge. But is it lawful to look upon the whole pagan and Christian tradition, which honoured Trajan as the best of all Roman rulers (who together with Augustus lives on in the expression *Felicior Augusto melior Traiano,* as an empty eulogy? Are all leaders to be condemned for the mere fact that their activity belongs to a period labelled "disintegration"? Here the prophet's mantle should be discarded for the historian's unobtrusive garb. If values are to be weighed—and this is the foremost mission of historical science—let it be done by honest standards, unmindful of results.

In support of my belief that he takes on the disguise of a prophet, let me draw a parallel which might please the Scripturist Toynbee. Just as preachers of penitence like Jeremiah through a theocratic conception of Jewish history hammered the world's great men by their stern judgments, so Toynbee with his harsh theory of development of civilization confronts the great men of its history with the severe verdict: you brought salvation through the sword and are therefore condemned. One condition only is decisive, viz., that the period in which the condemned leader lives is according to program labelled as a period of disintegration. For this estimation ethics, surely, also count, and in many respects success, too, has its merits. Pericles and Solon come off lightly, Caesar and Tiberius Gracchus not so well. On account of the latter's moral eminence Toynbee would fain have accorded him a more exalted place among the saviours of mankind, as witness his comparison of the reports on Tiberius' activities with the Gospel stories about Jesus as the world's Redeemer. But when ethical appreciation or admiration for success clash with the skilfully designed system, Toynbee unhesitatingly chooses the latter, and he never places a figure or a period in the "Growth" department if it ought to fit into "Disintegration". So Klio is tied, and woe to her should she playfully attempt to gambol. He who caught her and discovered her tracks, sternly returns her to her enclosure.

But we may well ask whether her keeper is actually certain that she did not escape before her on to the road which he had previously broken.

Periods of Growth do not know Saviours with the Sword, so Solon and Themistocles do not share in the negative verdict. The very opposite is the case, and so Solon's significance is represented as far more important than actual facts warrant (II, 37 ff.; IV, 200 ff.) He is said to be responsible for the "economic revolution" to which Greek civilization owes its great development. This argument, in the first place, exaggerates Athens's share. During the course of the 5th century B.C. Athens becomes Hellas' Hellas, but at the beginning of the 6th century the Athenian legislator's work has by no means a general Greek importance. In the second place, Solon's measures are overestimated when we speak of an economic revolution spreading its influence over all Hellas and laying the foundation for economic expansion. Economically Athens prior to the fall of Miletus and the Persian Wars was insignificant. If Athens' leading position in the economic field in the 5th and 4th centuries is to be explained, then the elimination of the rival cities in Asia Minor, particularly of Miletus, the profitable working of the Attic silver mines, the success in the Persian Wars of the navy financed from the output of the mines, and the formation of the Delian League, which through her naval supremacy came under the control of Athens, represent a number of factors of more weight than Solon's economic measures of more than a century earlier.

In Toynbee's system, however, Solon's legislation belongs to a period of growth, just as later on Themistocles' political and military activities do, and so both come in for praise. On the other hand, Demosthenes' appearance and the desperate struggle against Philip occur after the fatal year 431 B.C. in which the breakdown started. This disposes of the struggle against Macedon as having no prospects.

Was Athens, then, after the year 431 doomed to ruin? Toynbee answers in the affirmative (IV, 263 ff.). After that year the old driving force has disappeared and ruin is inescapable. Once a challenge is not heeded a snowball starts rolling and grows into a crushing avalanche. Toynbee, who attributes a development for good or for evil only to internal factors, here unfolds a system of determinism that leaves no hope for recovery. In a fine exposition of Athens' history up to Byzantine times this unavoidable fall is demonstrated. But again it is rather the preacher and prophet than the historian addressing us. How else could he draw a picture of the story in the Acts of the Apostles relating to St. Paul's arrival in Athens and his address on the Areopagus, containing such a horrible verdict on the citizens that the author might well be taken for the Judge on Doomsday?

Toynbee, like Jeremiah, is sure of his ground. On Mars' Hill the nemesis is revealed which rests on all creativeness. The Athenians indulge in self-glorification (the process starting exactly in 431) and so remain deaf to the message of salvation. Corinth, city of slaves, which after its sack in 146 B.C. had to learn the lesson of humility, accepts salvation, Athens haughtily rejects it. So Toynbee for matters sacred to him undauntedly constructs a relation of guilt and punishment. It finally amounts to this, that Athens, on the eve of the Peloponnesian War being unable to meet the challenge of political and military influences, was forced to reject the Christian message. This explanation is one-sided and unsound, since it does not consider the possibility that in Athens, also, Christian teaching touched a responsive chord outside the circle of those foregathering on the Areopagus, nor does it reckon with the probability that neither in Corinth was the Apostle cordially welcomed by the philosophers. It is, moreover, hard to understand why this historian, who expects the salvation of our Western civilization only from a rebirth and from divine grace, apparently excludes in advance past civilizations from these new opportunities. Those who might not have gathered this from the story of the prophet Jonah, who by all means wanted Nineveh devasted, may learn from our prophet Toynbee, whose prophetic activities have the past for their object, that sometimes the zeal of the preacher of penitence surpasses the necessary and the justifiable. This vision of history as categories of guilt and punishment is far from justified. Moralizing with regard to Graeco-Roman antiquity is, as with all historical periods, incompatible with historic insight. Athens is not in need of champions or accusers of this class.

The inconsistencies in the ethical judgment are manifest. Why the outrages of Athens against her allies, the founding of colonies of parasites and overseers in so-called allied countries, should not point to degeneration in contrast with Roman foreign policy is a question that remains unanswered. Equally mysterious is the view that the awful fate of the slaves in the silver mines should be a symptom of declining Hellenic civilization only after 431 B.C. an not during the preceding half century. Another puzzle is why exactly round the year 430 B.C. an external proletariat in the person of the Thracian king Sitalces appears on the scene, whereas all preceding threats from the North, just as unimportant, are not mentioned. Why Brasidas and Lysander, not Pericles and Cimon, figure as instruments of violence in a period of breakdown is still another riddle. The answer to all these questions lies in the exigencies of the system. 431 B.C. is the year of doom.

Toynbee's views on the great wreckers of Greek independence, Philip of Macedon and Alexander, are equally inconsistent, for if the Greek struggle at Chaeronea was a stupid reaction of the doomed against the predestined new rulers, then part of the latter's sins have been atoned for by their opponents' narrow-mindedness. Even as a Saviour with the Sword a ruler has his good points. Once this has been admitted a distinction can be made between the individual and his significance. The Macedonian kings are to be condemned as Saviours with the Sword, their means being unsound. But it is short-sightedness to call a halt there. Did not more than half a century ago D. G. Hogarth say with regard to Philip: "The attempt to acquit him by the laws of individual morality would be as futile as absurd"? (*Philip and Alexander of Macedon* (1897), p. 68). Toynbee is not likely to endorse these words, but in practice he will apply a splitting of this historical individuality, which introduces twofold scales. The Saviour with the Sword remains rejected, but his spirit is not found wanting, being measured by its value in the world's history.

This is not the devout act of a historical moralist. It rather determines the whole impressive conception of Hellenic civilization and it has a bearing on one of its predominant figures, Alexander the Great. According to the system he belongs to the leading characters of a dominant minority, but in Toynbee's work he is far more than that. He is the dreamer of a unity of mankind, for which he is said to have prayed after a mutiny in the army, and he aimed at a blending of Greeks and Barbarians so that they might become one flock under the one shepherd. This, then, made Alexander a pioneer for all who strove for unity in the Greek and in the Roman world. Not only the great of the earth but also the lower classes were gradually inspired by this ideal. "It was Alexander's spirit that moved one Roman centurion at Capernaum to make his humble appeal to Jesus to heal his servant by simply speaking the word without coming under his roof" (VI, 7). Not only this troubled master of a faithful servant, but also the centurion who sent for St. Peter at Caesarea and so led to Christian missionary work among the Barbarians, was full of Alexander. The Greeks, also, who according to the Gospel came to Jerusalem to worship in the Jewish Temple, were stirred by his spirit and probably Jesus himself had the same conception as the great ruler who strove for the unity of mankind.

So Alexander's figure wrecks the system. Whether this interpretation of Alexander is correct may be passed over, but it is clear that a leader in a period of disintegration has been able to cherish and to promote an ideal that was bound to conquer the world. Does it matter whether his violent deeds are to be condemned?

He cannot rise beyond being instrumental in the permeation of a glorious ideal.

The last mentioned inconsistency is the most convincing triumph of the abundant historical material supplied by Greece over the system Toynbee endeavoured to retain. But Alexander died and the realization of his ideals was impossible for the struggling rulers after him. So there is, after all, a judgment on a degenerated civilization which saw its saviour vanish? One is inclined to think so, but such a view is not to be found in Toynbee and we cannot hold him to what he did not say. This one occasion on which Toynbee refrains from impersonating Providence (in the past) does not, however, exempt him from reproof in all the other cases.

Not only is his treatment of Hellenic civilization inconsistent—there may sometimes be an advantage in this—but above all it is that of a moralist who can check Providence as it works in myth and in history. This check, however, is absurd for believer and unbeliever alike, for the latter because he does not believe in its agency, for the former because with complete submission he places the ultimate verdict on rise and fall, guilt and punishment, cause and effect, outside historical knowledge. As Toynbee deliberately ranges himself on the side of the believers, his views on the collapse of civilizations amounts to carrying unholy fire to the altar. One cannot with impunity forsake caged Klio to indulge in an affair with Providentia.

TOYNBEE'S TREATMENT
OF CHINESE HISTORY*

WAYNE ALTREE

Benedetto Croce tells us that "The material of history is the singular in its singularity and contingency, that which is once and then is never again, the fleeting network of a human world which drifts like clouds before the wind and is often totally changed by unimportant events." The uniqueness of historical data poses a fundamental problem for the historian. His task is to describe and interpret. But to describe adequately he must necessarily understand what he wants to describe, and he cannot understand that which he cannot truly describe. To confront this difficulty, he must have a working hypothesis of the tendency of history, a frame of reference, a conceptual scheme, by which he can cage the significance of the singular in terms of the general. To fashion a system of history revealing meaning and purpose and direction in the stream of human events has been the preoccupation of some of the greatest scholars laboring in the field.

Arnold J. Toynbee's *A Study of History* represents such an attempt. It is the ambitious task of this great work to determine the generic and uniform features implicit in the life course of the different civilizations appearing in history. On the basis of constants which he finds in his search, Toynbee has developed an elaborate morphological explanation of the origin, growth, and decline of civilizations.

His system is postulated upon a number of general assumptions. The proper object of study for the historian, believes Toynbee, are societies, not national states nor particular time periods. Societies alone are intelligible as wholes in isolation from outside phenomena. In the course of history, twenty-one different societies are discernible. They are defined by their cultural distinctiveness. Toynbee proposes to study these "civilized" species of societies as the anthropologist has hitherto studied "primitive societies." *A Study of History* constitutes a systematic comparison of all the different civilizations that have emerged in time. The purpose of this comparative study is to elucidate the general laws governing the development of civilizations and their relationships among each other. The result is a system of history which furnishes an explanation of the careers of all societies.

The value of this system in illuminating the meaning of history, if valid, is readily apparent, and its significance is heightened by the fact that Toynbee is a mature and distinguished historian.

---

*See Editor's Foreword to this volume.

.s validity, therefore, becomes a matter of importance. This paper is a brief exploration of the system insofar as it describes and interprets the history of one of the great civilizations comprehended within the general scheme; that is, the Chinese.[1] It is an attempt to ascertain the congruence between Toynbee's hypotheses and the data out of which they are derived in a particular instance. A law, or a system of laws, is valid only insofar as the data upon which it has been based is confirmed by empirical findings. If it can be shown that Toynbee's theory of the rise and decline of civilizations, insofar as it relates to China, is soundly derived from authoritatively established data, then an important argument will have been established for its validity. Should such a demonstration prove impossible, then an equally important argument will have been established for its rejection.

The paper consists of (1) a statement of Toynbee's system, (2) a description of his synthesis of Chinese history, (3) an analysis of that synthesis, and (4) a judgment of Toynbee's philosophy as an approach to the study of Chinese history.

1. TOYNBEE'S SYSTEM

The chemical process through which a primitive society is transformed into a civilization is precipitated when the human beings who make up that society encounter a great challenge which they conquer through unprecedented effort in circumstances of unusual adversity. Challenges may be the issue of different stimuli. but the most common are presented by the harshness of the physical environment. The greater the severity of the challenge, the greater the stimulus to action. Nonetheless, a challenge may attain such formidability that a point of diminishing returns is reached where the success of the response is correspondingly less. A society may die in birth, or be arrested at any stage in its development once born. A society has no inevitable life course.

Thus the growth of societies is the result of challenges encountered by a series of successful responses. The dynamic of history assumes its form in the interaction of challenge and response. But, as stated, growth does not ensue as a matter of course. Growth occurs when challenges evoke successful responses and possess sufficient momentum to overbalance into new challenges. Growth becomes the function of a recurrent, repetitive rhythm, of equilibrium, challenge, response, and fresh challenge. This rhythm is fired by a psychic factor, the élan which distinguishes the being of a maturing civilization.

Growth in a society has an inward and outward aspect. Outwardly, it manifests itself in the conquest of material challenges. Inwardly, growth shows itself in ever-mounting spiritual "self-determination." Real progress is measured by the degree to which the scene of action of Challenge and Response is transferred from the material to the spiritual level. This transfer of action from the macrocosm to the microcosm is the process of Etherialization. The conquest of material challenges is only important insofar as it releases energies to prevail over spiritual challenges. Increasingly, the crucial victories of a civilization must be won by challenges presented to itself by itself within the inner arena of its self. Consequently, the geographic expansion of a society, or the perfection of its techniques cannot be regarded as meaningful criteria of growth. Indeed, they are often testaments of its retrogression because they entail diversion of strength. Growth works itself out in a constant process of differentiation in all the interstices of a society. This process of maturation marks the civilization off from similar entities and endows it with a particular "bent" or ethos. A growing society is self-articulated and self-determined. Since it is self-determined in a period of growth, a civilization will be impervious in all critical respects to extra-mural influences.

A society is a field of action, but the springs of action are the men who compose the civilization. However, only a minority of men, the Promethean spirits, are transfigured with the "elan" which blazes into the creative action that is the seed of growth. Inspiration to creativity comes to the minority in the experience of Withdrawal and Return. The great mass of men is inert. It is led onward and upward thru the constant struggle of challenge and response, usually not willingly, by the Creative Minority. The lure that entices the mass is the creativity of the minority, and the former follows along in a sort of social drill, in a compulsive mimetic process. Thus as successive challenges are met by societies, the Creative Minority fashions the appropriate response, and the masses follow along thru Mimesis, only half-understanding and only half-willing.

The inevitability of growth has previously been denied. Breakdown may occur at any point in the upward march of a civilization. Breakdown sets in when responses no longer match challenges. Breakdown spells a loss of creativity. It marks the end of differentiation and self-determination. Its causes are spiritual, not material. They come from within not from without. The onset of breakdown, out of an inner malaise, will thus always appear before its ostensible material causes. Indeed, a civilization may enjoy material well-being and prosperity while far gone in the throes of breakdown. This Indian Summer is but an epilogue of the Golden Age. Material factors do no more than give the coup de grace to the stricken society, for stricken that society is, since breakdown augurs disintegration and final dissolution.

Breakdown may be due to mechanization of human life which is implicit in the process of Mimesis. It may come from the intractability of old institutions faced with the necessity of accommodating new social forces. Or breakdown may engulf a society whose creative minority has become infatuated with itself, betrayed by pride of past achievement, and thus inclined to use old responses, once successful, to resolve new challenges. Idolization of self, or ideas, or institutions results. Breakdowns may spring from the intoxication of victory which leads to aspiration after inordinate aims and goals. Here we have the nemesis of creativity. The ex-creators are alienated from their true mission. They become separated from life. The price is the loss of the Promethean elan which informed the process of growth.

With breakdown, a Time of Troubles emerges. A challenge presents itself, and it is not met. The same challenge repeats itself to the same end. The recurring challenge and recurring defeat is a clue to disintegration. The self-determination of a growth period, the differentiation, the unique ethos, now dwindle away. The elements of society lose their coherency. Bereft of its creativity, the minority no longer retains the allegiance of the masses. Forcible repression takes the place of charm to win mass loyalty. Alienated by this tyrannous behaviour, the masses begin to secede from the society. They form an Internal Proletariat. Peoples living on the periphery of the civilization, and hitherto peacefully residing within its orbit of cultural influence, likewise secede and form an External Proletariat. A hard and fast frontier now occupies what once was an indefinite march. The ex-Creative Minority, transformed by its behaviour, turns into a Dominant Minority. These schisms result in class warfare. Stasis, not self-determination, prevails.

In a futile effort to recover social unity, the Dominant Minority imposes a unified political regime, a Universal State, on the civilization. If this task cannot be achieved by the indigenous Dominant Minority, the result will be achieved by elements from without. An alien universal state, however, always encounters the implacable hostility of the subjugated. All Universal states are in the end abortive because they are used in an attempt to retrieve a situation that is past retrieving by such means. Nonetheless, while in existence they may present the semblance of order and good government.

The Universal State, upon its failure, runs out into an Interregnum. At this juncture, disintegration is in full course. In flight from an intolerable world, the Internal Proletariat forms a Universal Church. Art creativity is characteristic of this development. The church is usually of alien inspiration, and this alien inspiration is one instance where a society is not self-determined but derivative. While alien inspired, the church is transformed into a native product before it is fully accepted. The External Proletariat, a wholly negative force, now forms Warbands to prey upon the corpse of the dying society and begins to maraud and plunder in a Volkerwanderung. The Dominant Minority develops a philosophy as its characteristic product. With the death of growth and the prevalence of strife, standardization becomes the rule.

Social schisms have their counterpart in spiritual schisms. The ordeal of living in a time of decay may be faced with a variety of behaviour patterns. Alternative modes include a wish to return to the simple life of nature ("abandon"), or repugnance to social disorder expressed in excessive self-discipline to regain control over circumstances ("self-control"); there may be placid acceptance of defeat ("sense of drift"), or a personal acceptance of responsibility for that defeat ("sense of sin"). The sense of style, which characterizes the differentiation of a growth period, is lost in an undiscriminating cosmopolitanism. Art forms become standardized and composite. Traditional style is abandoned. Syncretism distinguishes religion and philosophy. The manners of the Dominant Minority are "proletarianized" by imitation of the vulgarities of the masses. There is a search of universal values, a search for "Oneness." Reality may also be avoided by escape into the past—"archaism"—, or by anticipation of time to come—"futurism". All these alternatives are doomed to failure, because they seek salvation on the material plane in terms of the old society. A real solution can only be found in terms of a new society built within the microcosm of the Spirit, and not the macrocosm of the outer world. The ultimate society is the Civitas Dei on earth, beyond the time dimension, beyond mundane analysis.

The process of disintegration possesses an inherent rhythm. There is no uniform progression, but an alternation of routs and rallies. The growth period is a rally; the Time of Troubles a rout; the Universal State a rally, and the dissolution of the Universal State a final rout. But each beat of the rhythm has a minor counter stroke of rally or rout interspersed within it.

The final chapter witnesses the disintegration of the Interregnum running out into dissolution. The dying civilization may die completely, it may be assimilated by a surviving society, or it may give birth to a succeeding "affiliated" society to which it becomes "apparented." The womb of the new society is the Universal Church of the the Internal Proletariat, the challenge which initiates the new society is the class warfare of the old. The creativity of the Universal Church is sufficient to vanquish that challenge, and so again the process of challenge and response is renewed. The home of the new society will displace the cradle of the moribund civilization. What was once the frontier will now become the heartland.

2. TOYNBEE'S SYNTHESIS OF CHINESE HISTORY

Into the matrix of this system, Toynbee imposes the history of the twenty-one civilizations that occupy his analysis, and he finds an ineluctable correspondence among them in shape, form, and destiny. In terms of his morphology, the story of the Chinese people assumes the following contours.[1]

The lower basin of the Yellow River is the home of the Sinic civilization. The initial challenge that evoked this civilization stemmed from the harsh physical features of terrain and climate. The adversities of the region, "a watery chaos," included jungle-covered swamps, extremes of weather, and an unnavigable river, clogged in winter with ice and often in flood. Here the early Chinese faced "an ordeal of bush and marsh," and this stimulus was the dynamic factor that impelled them upward on the road to civilization. In the South of China, no such hard fight for life was necessary. There the inhabitants, racially identical with the Northerners, remained culturally sterile. The urge to creativity, potential in both groups, was brought to fruition only under the necessitous conditions of life in the lower Yellow River basin. Thus the physical challenge was the yeast of the civilization.

The growth period of the Sinic Society comprehends, Toynbee tells us, the era described in the classic history *Shih Ching,* and this interval ends with the disastrous wars between the states of Ch'in and Ch'u. This internecine warfare precipitates the breakdown of the society, and the year 634 B.C. is used to date that development. The subsequent Time of Troubles continues to be marked by bitter conflict among the different feudal states of the civilization; but an interruption, or rally, occurs in the so-called Disarmament Conference of 546 B.C., when an attempt was made to resolve by peaceful means the basic problems of the Sinic world. Hegemony is finally achieved over the lesser states by Ch'in and Ch'u; and, under a "Grand Confederacy", a fugitive surcease from strife is enjoyed. However, the eventual disappearance of Ch'u as a great power in the year 538 B.C. destroys the precarious balance among the states; and a new battle for predominance rages over an

---

[1]Toynbee's treatment of Chinese history in terms of his system may be largely found in the following references.
   I. *Sinic Civilization*: General description, I, 88-92; Genesis, I, 318-321; II, 31-33; III, 90; Challenge and Response, II, 31-33; IV, 119; Breakdown, IV, 65-66; V, 140-147; VI, 291-295; Universal State, I, 89; II, 373; IV, 65 (and note); V, 49, 146, 548 (and note), 270-272, 464-465, 144-145, 271, 418, 549, 654-655; VI, 286, 295, 311 (and note), 37 (and note); Expansion, I, 90;

expanding area. This is the period of "Contending States" in the orthodox chronology of Chinese history, a "time of intellectual vigor and suicidal politics", in Toynbee's perspective. The outer states of the Sinic civilization now gradually grow in strength and influence, but finally Ch'in emerges triumphant.

Victorious Ch'in proceeds to impose a Universal State, which is subsequently maintained by the following Han dynasty. This attempt to reduce the maelstrom of Chinese politics to some semblance of order is an institutional embodiment of a social rally after the Time of Troubles, in Toynbee's assessment, a period in which the society is being slowly torn apart. The Universal State experiences a minor interregnum in the time of the statesman Wang Mang. Toynbee sees the later Han as a new and distinct dynasty. The zenith of the Sinic Universal State is reached in the reign of the Emperor Wu Ti, the "Indian Summer" of the civilization. This is a period of geographic expansion on a large scale to the Great Wall in the North and beyond the Yangtze in the South.

The inevitable failure of the Universal State, which comes with the downfall of the Han in 172 A.D., is the fourth debacle of the Sinic Society. Now the real Interregnum ensues. An effort to rescue the civilization from impending chaos is represented by the attempt of the "United Chin" dynasty to subject all China to its rule, but this rally is followed by an even deeper period of disorder and confusion. The internal struggles of the society at this point open the door to the marauding Eurasian nomads, who found a series of "successor states" in North China. The Warbands be-

---

II, 143; III, 143; V, 141-144, 270-271; VI, 292-293; "Indian Summer," VI, 193; Dominant Minority, V, 49, 58, 206; External Proletariat, V, 270-274, 477-478; Internal Proletariat, IV, 65; V, 140-142, 161; Rout-Rally-Relapse, V, 548 (and note); VI, 285-286, 291-295; Time of Troubles, I, 88-89; III, 143; IV, 65-66, 254; V, 140-141, 146-147, 270 415; VI, 291-295, 55-56, 58 (and note), 294-295; Interregnum, I, 88; V, 273, 477; Disintegration, IV, 3, 14, 16-17 (and note), 21-24; V, 402, 464,465, 477-478, 534-535, 549, 555-556, 557; VI, 55-69, 81-83, 111-112, 292-296.

II. *Far Eastern Civilization*: Apparentation, V, 4-5, 148, 363; Genesis, I, 90; II, 331; Home, I, 89; II, 90, 331; III, 173; General description, V, 3-9; Challenges, II, 83-84; IV, 117-118; V, 4 (note); Time Span, V, 4; Breakdown, IV, 84, 86, 93; V, 3: VI, 306; Barbarians, I, 236; III, 330; IV, 86-87; V, 308-309; VI, 307-308; Time of Troubles, VI, 84, 86; V, 3-4, 308-310; VI, 306-308; Universal State (Mongol), IV, 3, 87; V, 3, 54, 105-106, 115, 116, 308-309, 348-350; VI, 305; (Manchu), IV, 3, 87; V, 105-106, 309-310, 315, 348, 349; VI, 186, 192, 208, 327; Disintegration, III, 143-144; IV, 86-88; V, 111, 117, 410, 447, 449, 457-458, 537; VI, 3; Expansion, I, 268; III, 143-144; Indian Summer, VI, 192-193, 195; Nomads, II, 120-127; III, 143-144, 442-443; Dominant Minority, V, 457-458; External Proletariat, V, 308-310; VI, 307; Internal Proletariat, V, 107, 115-117; Rally and Relapse, VI, 305-308; Religion, V, 107, 112-114, 117, 365-366, 507 (note), 537, 539, 709; VI, 23-24, 208, 329; Contact with Western Civilization, I, 160-162, 345-346; II, 125-127; III, 188-189, 330; IV, 49-51, 56, 84, 87, 188, 420; IV, 49-51, 84, 87, 188, 420; V, 4 (and note); VI, 306.

gin to form about 300 A.D., according to Toynbee's timetable, and the Volkerwanderung of the barbarians on the frontier follows not far behind.

These incursions from outside are not the first trouble with the barbarians. Originally, as Toynbee sees it, the Sinic Society had been insulated from warring nomadic intruders by a protective cordon formed by the highland inhabitants of the present provinces of Shensi and Shansi. But the vigorous militarism of the states of Ch'in and Ch'ao had destroyed by conquest this outer barrier, and henceforth the Sinic Society was to find itself face to face with the aggressive warriors of the Asiatic hinterland. This menace, Toynbee tells us, was staved off by "Herculean" effort on the part of the Sinic states. Their defense included the establishment of an artificial frontier in the Great Wall and later by the Emperor Han Wu-ti's positive "forward policy" of preventive warfare in the steppe region. But no stability could be permanently achieved on the borders, and gradually power shifted to the encircling enemy. The first state to fall is Chin in 317 A.D., and from then on the incursions of the nomadic peoples are increasingly successful.

This constant pressure from the barbarians on the outer reaches of the society serves as a stimulus to the Sinic states located in the paths of invasion, and these states successively mature under the challenge of constant attack to a point where they have sufficient political experience and military power to dominate the interior states of the society. These dominant border states then proceed to transfer their capitals from their original home base to the strategic political center of the society in Honan. During this period, consequently, the capital of the civilization tends to oscillate, as dynasties rise and fall, between the West and the East, from Honan to the valleys of the rivers Ho and Wei.

The Volkerwanderung of the Sinic external proletariat is accompanied by the development of the "Higher Religion" of the internal proletariat, as demanded by our historian's scheme. This church assumes in time the shape of Mahayana Buddhism, an alien creed from Central Asia. The next few centuries see the gradual transformation of Buddhism into an indigenous Chinese religion. With the Triumph of Barbarism and Religion, the final chapter is written in the history of Sinic Society. The *coup de grace* has been been administered, and the Interregnum runs out into dissolution true to form. The disintegration of the society has kept time with the customary rhythm of decline. Rally in the time of the Shang and Chou dynasties; rout in the Three Kingdom Period; rally in the Chin dynasty; final rout in the victory of the barbarian successor states.

The disintegration of the society experiences the usual thought and behaviour patterns of such a time. Thus Confucian philosophy is an exhibit of "Archaism" in its respect for the past and ritualized etiquette. A "Sense of Unity" manifests itself in the Taoist search for "Oneness' in the universe, in its pursuit of the Way or the Tao. Toynbee sees the Emperor Ch'in Shih's burning of the books as a symbolic act of "Futurism"; philosophy and religion have a definite tendency toward syncretism in the Han dynasty; and standardization appears in politics and the arts. All this is as it should be.

At this stage, upon the remains of the defunct Sinic civilization rises a new "affiliated" Far Eastern Society, "apparented" to the old society by the higher church of the Sinic internal proletariat. Geographically, the new civilization displaces, in prescribed fashion, the home territory of the old. What were once the frontiers of the Sinic society now become the limits of the inner core of the Far Eastern civilization, which extends outward in all directions, but especially southward beyond the Yangtze. This physical transfer of Chinese culture to "new ground" in the South evokes a challenge which in turn is to stimulate a cultural efflorescence in the region so great as to give it in time a cultural predominance over the North.

The "Golden Age" of this new Far Eastern civilization we find described in the *Study* as the T'ang Dynasty. The breakdown of this great creative period comes, however, with the suicidal civil wars that accompany the reign of the Emperor Ming Huang. Here is the decline and fall. The Time of Troubles, the inevitable sequel, is interrupted by a temporary rally in the greatness of the Sung dynasty. Politically, technically, and artistically, this dynasty is a resurgence, but the breathing spell is brief. The reign of Hui-tsung marks the beginning of a new relapse brought on by the renewed onslaught of the Warbands of the nomads—the Khitan, the Jurchen, and finally the Mongols. The barbarian invader is rapidly Sinicized and disappears into the Chinese people. But the Mongols with their distinctive culture and alien tincture, as Toynbee puts it, remain immune to the attractions of Chinese culture, an aloofness which spells their defeat as rulers of China in the long run.

Nonetheless, the Time of Troubles is brought to an end with the establishment of a Universal State by the Mongols. This unification is thrust upon the distracted society from without because the Dominant Minority of the Far Eastern civilization lacks sufficient vitality to accomplish the task. The "Indian Summer" is the reign of Kublai Khan. In time the alien domination of the Mongols proves hateful to the Chinese, and a nativist reaction overthrows the

Yuan dynasty. However, the succeeding Ming dynasty never quite achieves the reintegration of China in a Universal State. Success in this enterprise is left to yet another alien intruder, the Manchu. The rule of the Ch'ing dynasty, however, proves more congenial to the Chinese than that of the Mongol because the new conqueror follows a calculated policy of meticulously observing Chinese custom and rebuffing any foreign influence. Thus the Ch'ing dynasty succeeds where the Mongols had failed to establish their rule. The Indian Summer of this second Universal State comes in the reigns of the masterful emperors K'ang Hsi and Ch'ien Lung. Winter sets in, as it must in time, with the thrust for power of the T'ai-p'ing rebel chieftain Hung Hsiu-ch'uan in the 19th century, prelude to an era of pervasive social disorganization.

At this point, Toynbee finds himself obliged to explain that the evolution of the Far Eastern civilization at this juncture has not followed the normal pattern of disintegration and dissolution which his research reveals in the life course of other civilizations. There has been an arrest, Toynbee argues, in the development of the Far Eastern civilization. "Petrification" rather than final dissolution has attended the breakdown of this society. In the pages of the *Study,* this abberation is found characteristic of only one other civilization, and that is the Egyptian.

Toynbee's explanation of this deviation from the usual development of civilizations is that it can be attributed to the intrusion of the Western powers into China in the 17th century. This deflection of the historical process can be seen in the effort of the Jesuit missionaries to fashion Christianity into the Universal Church of the declining society and its aftermath. This attempt comes to nothing because the Pope interferes during the famous Rites Controversy and prevents the Jesuits from translating the Christian dogma into the traditional religious and philosophic idiom of the Chinese as they sought to do, and of course such a translation is necessary to the acceptance of any alien religious faith as the true basis of a Universal Church. Thus the society remained without the Universal Church which could bear a new civilization to succeed the faltering Far Eastern society.

Toynbee's analysis of the current scene in China suffers from the fact that he made it prior to the Communist ascent to power. At the time he wrote, he regarded the prevailing anarchy in China —which has to be distinguished, he feels, from the beginning of the society's decline nine centuries ago—as an outgrowth of Western imperialistic pressure which has turned the life of the country "upside down". As he views contemporary China, he sees the country with a new march separating the nation from the world beyond. This new borderland is the maritime frontier of the sea-coast. Here is the new high pressure area of Chinese civilization. As in former times, the capital of the country shifts to Nanking, the strategic location in that high pressure area. The borderland of the Sinic society was the Northwest. The frontier of the Far Eastern society, prior to the coming of the West, was the whole northern region along the Great Wall. Consequently, the capital remained nearby in Peking, in the "key political area". Now, with the disappearance of the nomad menace, the North is no longer the pressure area that generates the political power that subjects the interior, and the focus of political power correspondingly shifts southward.

In Toynbee's assessment of the future, present prospects reflect the possibility that the Far Eastern civilization may be assimilated in the all-encompassing "Great Society" of the Western World, although it would be hasty, he says, to read the final end of the civilization in the context of present events. Perhaps the challenge posed by foreign encroachment will be met by new and creative responses that will introduce a new period of growth. The T'ai-p'ing and Boxer rebellions and the anti-foreign movement of 1924 furnish clues that blows and pressures from without may still awaken the Chinese people to renewed effort and faith in their particular destiny.

3. AN ANALYSIS OF THE SYSTEM'S RELEVANCY TO CHINESE HISTORY

Now let us inquire as to whether Toynbee's version of the development of Chinese civilization coincides with the commonly accepted data of Chinese history. An affirmative answer to this inquiry, as has been said, would be valuable support for his general system of historical analysis; a negative answer should cast doubt on its acceptability. Cursory analysis, based on data derived from sources in English readily available to Toynbee, indicates that the facts of Chinese history do not square with the theory. We try to buttress this conclusion by token examples briefly developed in the paragraphs that follow.

A. *The "Challenge" of the Yellow River Basin.* Toynbee sees the rise of civilization in the lower basin of the Yellow River as a response to the physical challenge presented by the rigors of terrain and climate, conceived as an ordeal of marsh, swamp, and flood. This picture of a formidable environment is based on material from Maspero's *La Chine Antique,* which in turn relies on the traditional account by Mencius of the subjugation of the physical hazards of North China by the Emperor Yü, whose engineering feats rendered the region fit for agriculture. With this data, Toynbee shows the North to be a "hard" country, quickening a civilization to life, in contrast to the South, which is "soft" and thus sterile. His general thesis that adversity is a spur to civilization, in terms of the challenge-and-response formula, consequently, gains credence from this example.

Unfortunately, the facts do not lend themselves to this interpretation. Modern scholarship shows the Emperor Yü to be a folk hero of a Southern legend which was adopted late by the North.[2] The physical conditions in the Yü legend, therefore, were characteristic of the South and not the North. This fact is very embarrassing to Toynbee's argument. On his own evidence, and in terms of his theory, Toynbee should have found the cradle of Chinese civilization below the Yangtze. Had he done so, Toynbee would have been in agreement with a contemporary Chinese scholar who writes, "The swampy jungle-covered Yangtze Valley of ancient China must have offered infinitely greater obstacles to early settlers than the northern steppes and Yellow River or Huang-ho."[3]

No matter what conditions prevailed in South China, Toynbee's description of the Yellow River basin is false. It was not a "hard" region; it was not a place of adversity. Present knowledge indicates that North China in ancient times was largely open grassland. There was little forestation. The soil was loessal and rich in quality. The Yellow River with its silt content was an important fertility factor. The region was well watered. It is hard to believe that there were marshes of any extent, since the loess is not sufficiently durable to resist drainage and wheeled vehicles were extensively used from earliest times.[4] It has been established that the climate was warmer than now. The oracle bones, replete with weather references, contain only one mention of snow. The growing period for vegetation was much longer than at present. Warm weather animals such as the elephant, tapir, rhinoceros, and water buffalo were prevalent.[5] Karl Wittfogel describes the climatic situation as one which "resembles conditions prevailing today in certain warmer regions along the lower Yangtze Valley."[6]

V. K. Ting explains the rise of Chinese civilization in terms quite different from those of Toynbee when he says, "It is in this continuous semi-steppe region stretching from the sea to Turkestan free from heath, forest, and marsh and favorable to agriculture and wheeled vehicle that made early settlement and continuous

---

[2]Chao-ting Chi, *Key Economic Areas* (Allen and Unwin, Ltd., 1936), p. 47 ff.

[3]*Ibid.*, p. 129.

[4]V. K. Ting, "Professor Granet's 'La Civilisation Chinoise'," *Chinese Social and Political Science Review,* Vol. 15, pp. 267-269.

[5]K. A. Wittfogel, "Meteorological Records from the Divination Inscriptions of Shang," *Geographical Review,* Vol. 30, pp. 110-133.

[6]*Ibid,* p. 176.

diffusion of culture possible."[7] Ting's description of the region is supported by Professor Latourette's statement that, "The northern plain has been, however, the friend of civilization, because, except for a few stretches marred by alkali or sand, it is very fertile. Together with a smaller plain in the valley of the Wei, a tributary of the Huang Ho, it was the scene of the development of the culture which shaped the rest of China."[8] In the same vein, C. W. Bishop goes on to say that the region was "well fitted to become the seat of a high civilization."[9]

Confronted by the above facts, it is difficult to find an adequate explanation of the rise of Chinese civilization in Toynbee's concept of the response to a physical challenge emerging from the adversity of environment. To the extent that he uses the Chinese experience to support his proposition that civilizations develop initially out of a physical challenge, his system loses in conviction.

B. *Shang and Early Chou as a Time of Growth.* As pointed out in Section III, the Sinic time of growth was the interval in Chinese history prior to 643 B.C. The distinguishing marks of such a period should be self-determination, differentiation, and increased spirituality in cultural development. A growth period is autonomous; it has an integrity of its own. To the degree that outside forces are influential, true growth declines. Real growth can only be a function of the creative elan of the society's creative minority. The period, likewise, is a time of social harmony when the minority leads, and the masses, both within and on the periphery, peacefully follow.

These prescriptions are very difficult to discern in Chinese society prior to the Eastern Chou. It was not a society autonomous and self-determined, but a civilization derivative in an important degree from outside sources.[10] It was most certainly not an indigenous product. The geographical situation of the early Chinese in North China exposed them from the earliest time to contacts with outside peoples.[11] Across the steppe on the northwest boundaries freely flowed stimuli from older western civilizations, the nomadic inhabitants often serving as intermediaries. "It seems certain," says V. K. Ting, "that the ancient civilizations of Eurasia

---

[7]Ting, *op. cit.*, p. 269.

[8]K. S. Latourette, *The Chinese: Their History and Culture* (The Macmillan Co., 1946), p. 6.

[9]C. W. Bishop, "The Rise of Civilization in China with Reference to Its Geographical Aspects," *Geographical Review,* Vol. 22, p. 617.

[10]V. K. Ting, "How China Acquired Her Civilization," in Sophia Ch'en Zen, ed., *Symposium on Chinese Culture* (China Institute of Pacific Relations, 1931), p. 11.

[11]Bishop, *op. cit.*, p. 617.

had much of their cultural capital in common."[12] The route of cultural transmission was from central Asia, then more populous than presently, through the Tarim Basin, thence to Kansu and the Yellow River Valley. Cultural impulses were carried along this route after every important development in the life of western Asia.[13]

In this outside world originated the polychrome pottery which has been found in the Yang-shao culture of early China. This Chalcolithic society inhabited the upper and middle portions of the Yellow River valley, the sections most susceptible to foreign contact. Thus China must necessarily have had intercourse with the West after the third millenium B.C. Around 2000 B.C., bronze work of a mature character appears in China without evidence of any prior Chinese development. It can be reasonably surmised that the complicated technique of bronze working came from elsewhere. Archaic art motifs are now recognized as having their origin in Scytho-Siberian designs.[14] Competent scholars believe that the art of divination, hieroglyphic writing, the calendar, and the dating system were borrowings.[15] Chinese astronomy was very early influenced by the development of the science in India. Most of the domestic animals, plants, and foods of China were importations.[16]

Any view of early Chinese society as a self-contained entity, developing solely on the basis of its own creativity, does not appear tenable. Therefore, one of the prime criteria of a growth period cannot be found in Toynbee's Golden Age of the Sinic Society. Moreover, the fact that Chinese society was neither wholly self-originated nor self-determined furnishes a much more likely clue than Toynbee's explanation as to why civilization first rose in North China, rather than in the South. Foreign cultural inspirations, and not an internal challenge, may very well have furnished the original impulse. The South, isolated from such inspiration, remained unmoved.

Other characteristics of a growth period seem to be equally lacking. It should be a time of social harmony, free from internecine struggle, and progressively evolving toward a higher spiritual life. Reality in ancient China was much different. The bulk of the population was made up of serfs who retained their old primi-

---

[12]Ting, "How China Acquired Her Civilization", p. 12.

[13]Bishop, *op. cit.*, p. 617.

[14]P. W. Yetts, "Links between Ancient China and the West," *Geographical Review,* Vol. 16, p. 614.

[15]Ting, "How China Acquired Her Civilization", p. 12.

[16]C. W. Bishop, "Early Culture Contacts between China and the West," *Geographical Review,* Vol. 23, p. 153.

tive neolithic culture completely through the period.[17] The masses were cruelly oppressed. The Shang were a warlike people.[18] Inscriptions on the oracle bones show evidence of constant fighting and preparation for war.[19] Their subjugators, the Chou, were even more distinguished for their martial spirit. The Book of Odes contains six different selections entirely devoted to war. This classic indicates that military organization was large scale and efficient. Raiding and Guerilla warfare among neighboring tribes was commonplace. The Shang state was established and maintained by force.[20] The Chou ruled by a system of military feudalism. Human sacrifice was practiced. Slavery was an accepted institution. Religion was relatively primitive.

These aspects of the early life of China are hard to reconcile with Toynbee's qualifications of a growth period. The evidence does not support his argument. It was not a time of self-determination, harmony, peace, nor the higher spiritual life. Indeed, the civilization has been described in the following strong, but authoritative terms: "It was a cruel and complicated feudal society, still crushed beneath the terrors which haunt the primitive mind, and what is more, living amid the miseries of a blood thirsty system of law—a permanent condition of private war accompanied by an unprecedented indulgence in mass murder."[21]

C. *Origin of the Time of Troubles.* The Sinic Society, as Toynbee sees it, breaks down in 634 B.C. This breakdown is precipitated by fratricidal war. Now to find a fundamental distinction between the periods before and after 634 B.C. in the prevalence of war subsequent to that date would appear to be somewhat artificial. In the sources cited in the preceding section, it has been shown that war was endemic and commonplace in earlier times. In Toynbee's Time of Troubles, conflict simply becomes more widespread and intense. It is a matter of degree, not a difference in the quality of civilization. The explanation for the intensity of strife after the seventh century is not to be found, as Toynbee would, in any loss of creative élan on the part of leadership, but in the fact that material circumstances now permitted that leadership to war in a far more fierce and extensive fashion.

Agriculture was fast becoming more productive. This development rose out of innovations, then first used, such as the employ-

---

[17]Bishop, "The Rise of Civilization in China," p. 629.
[18]L. C. Goodrich, "Antiquity to the Fall of Shang," in H. F. MacNair, ed., *China* (University of California Press, 1946), p. 51.
[19]H. G. Creel, "Soldier and Scholar in Ancient China," *Pacific Affairs,* Vol. 8, p. 339.
[20]*Ibid.,* p. 339.
[21]Rene Grousset, *China* (Knopf, 1935).

ment of iron tools, draft animals, irrigation, and manure. Larger production meant increased surpluses. Urban growth led to a market economy, and agricultural production became far more valuable. Surpluses stored in granaries, therefore, became tempting prizes for seizure through war. At the same time land became more coveted, and the nobles sought to increase their manorial holdings, most often by force. More men were available as soldiers, since the individual serf now could produce in greater quantity, and the introduction of the land tax, in place of the traditional poll tax, made the nobility less anxious to keep the peasantry tied to the soil to work out taxes. Population was growing, and the expansion of states increased the possibility of tension. The character of war was also changed by the use of large and mobile units of cavalry. The increasing role which border states played in Sinic life intensified the ruthlessness of war, since these states had developed in an atmosphere of unending frontier struggle, and they were ever ready to use war to further their interests. The construction of water control projects, such as the Cheng-Kuo canal in Ch'in, placed in the hands of certain states the economic strength to carry on protracted conflict. These considerations help explain the intensification of warfare during this historical interval. The explanation cannot be found in the changed nature of men despite Toynbee's denial that it can be found in technological developments.

D. *Role of the Dominant Minority.* The assertion that the dominant minority of the Sinic world imposed a forceful political unification upon their society, following its breakdown, to escape the disaster of dissolution is not convincing. Who imposed the hegemony of the Ch'in-Han dynasty? Certainly, it was not the feudal class of the preceding era, the only class that would be equivalent to Toynbee's dominant minority. The feudal nobility were practically extinct by 221 B.C., and the remnant that still did exist at that date fought the empire with its entire strength, because the imperial regime was completely antithetical to all the interests of the old aristocracy. "The chün-tzu of the conquered kingdoms," says one historical account, "were unanimously opposed to the Ch'in empire and the centralized state."[22] Being well aware of this hostility among the remaining old dominant minority, the founder of the empire transported the conquered aristocracy to his capital at Hsien-yang where they were obliged to live under close surveillance.[23]

---

[22]C. P. Fitzgerald, *China: A Short Cultural History* (Cresset Press, 1935), p. 139.
[23]H. T. Lei, "The Rise of the Emperor System in Ancient China," *Chinese Social and Political Science Review,* Vol, 20, p. 257.

The feudal nobility gradually declined during the Chan Kuo period. The wars of the times constantly enhanced the strength of the princes at the expense of the lords. So long as China was a congeries of small states, the nobles of each state could find security in an equilibrium between their power and that of the prince. They had a vested interest in political separatism. As a few states began increasingly to predominate, their princes grew in power and influence and the nobility were correspondingly reduced in strength. The feudal nobility was also weakened by the new economic developments that accompanied the increase in argricultural productivity. The lesser nobles through subinfeudation, were closer to the countryside and in a position to build up their land holdings more effectively. A new rival class thus begins to rise, founded on wealth. The introduction of private land ownership and the land tax also went a long way toward destroying the feudal system of land holding based on personal service. Finally, the ranks of the nobility were gradually decimated by warfare.

Consequently, in the final struggle for universal power, not the feudal nobility but a new class of military and political adventurers played the big role. The men who actually founded the Han Empire were of plebeian origin—"ignorant upstarts" from the "unlettered classes," Hu Shih calls them.[24] Thus, one of Liu Pang's chief advisers was Sang Hung-yang, son of a small shop keeper.[25]

Quite contrary to Toynbee's assertion, the Sinic dominant minority did not create the universal state of that society, for they were destroyed or dispersed. New men founded the hegemony of the Han, and that hegemony was imposed not to preserve the old order but to destroy it.

E.   *The Problem of Growth in Late Chou and Han.* In Toynbee's historical scheme, the late Chou and the Han empire are incidents in the inevitable decline of a disintegrating society. However, there are reasonable alternatives to this interpretation. The late Chou may very properly be regarded as a period of growth and expansion in the cultural evolution of China. This growth and expansion can be seen in the development of commerce, urban life, economic production, population, and great intellectual vitality. It has the marks of a highly individual and complex age. Chinese life begins to have wider horizons, and it cannot be accommodated within the narrow, parochial, conventionalized pattern of feudal culture, the inheritance from ancient China. The late Chou, so regarded, becomes a revolutionary period in which the confining

[24]Hu Shih, Religion and Philosophy," in *Symposium on Chinese Culture,* p. 38.
[25]Fitzgerald, *op. cit.,* p. 166

shell of feudalism is burst apart. The whole tendency is toward a wider integration of life and an escape from the petty barriers and exactions of the primitive feudal structure. To use Toynbee's terms, the challenge of the late Chou is feudal parochialism; the response is the movement toward cultural integration.

From the same point of view, the Han may be seen as a new and creative interval. Certainly, the Han is not, as Toynbee asserts, a period of conservative retrenchment. The Han sets a new direction for China. The late Chou broke feudalism and created the possibility of a richer culture. The challenge of the Han was to fashion out of this opportunity a new society in which the fresh impulses in Chinese life could find adequate expression. In the late Chou, the basic pattern of subsequent Chinese thought was shaped and feudalism discarded. In the Han, the basic political and social pattern of Chinese life first began to find form. The immediate sequel is a time of great prosperity, fresh ideas, advances in art, and innovation in religion. Both periods faced challenges; both periods confronted those challenges with creative responses. To say that either period is devoid of growth is to rob the term of any value.

F. *The Role of Buddhism.* Sinic society, having run out into its Interregnum, now had to experience, by Toynbee's diagnosis, the secession of its internal proletariat who proceed to form a higher religion out of Mahayana Buddhism. Here we have an additional example of the formula not jibing with the facts. Buddhism was not developed in China as a proletarian creed. At the time of its introduction into China, its was patronized almost exclusively by court circles. The masses remained unattracted.[26]

In 65 A.D. an imperial prince had become a Buddhist. In 165 A.D. an emperor was converted.[27] "By 300 A.D. it (Buddhism) was talked about by all the Chinese intellectuals as the greatest system of philosophy ever invented by the genius of man." writes Hu Shih.[28] Buddhism received its first great impetus when it was officially adopted in 453 A.D. by the Toba Wei dynasty. The Tartar invaders, who had driven the Confucian scholar class southward, began to enlist the Buddhist monks as the only literate group left capable of forming a bureaucracy. Thus it may be said that Buddhism received its earliest and crucial support from the invading barbarian who ruled the region above the Yangtze and whom Toynbee would describe as an external proletariat. During the Six Dynasties, emperors are known to have become monks.

[26]H. T. Lei, "Periodization: Chinese History and World History," *Chinese Social and Political Science Review,* Vol. 20, p. 481.
[27]Hu, *op. cit.,* p. 47.
[28]*Ibid.,* p. 47.

Liang Wu-ti abdicated and entered a monastery. The missionary activities of the imperial princess Wen-ch'eng were largely responsible for the introduction of Buddhism into Tibet. The government of the Southern Ch'i was dominated by Buddhists.

Consequently, we see that it was not the masses who brought Buddhism to China or fostered its growth after its arrival. Buddhism received its support from emperors, scholars, and men of affairs, the class that Toynbee would regard as the dominant minority. In describing the foundation of the early Ch'an school, Hu Shih says that, "It is a most significant fact that the first Chinese sect of Buddhism was one of such extreme simplicity and this sect was founded not by the common folk, but by a monk scholar of great reputation and no mean learning."[29] The first Buddhist sect with widespread popular support was Amida, and it did not flourish until the latter part of the T'and, long after the supposed birth of the Far Eastern civilization. It should likewise be remembered that at no time was Buddhism the exclusive religion of any portion of the Chinese masses, since it always divided their loyalty with Taoism and Confucianism. It never displaced the older gods or ancestor worship. Buddhism was introduced when it was, not primarily because of any deep seated religious urge on the part of the Chinese people, but because it was strongly entrenched in Central Asia at that particular time and was professed by men of deep missionary instincts. Once in China, the fact that the religion received support in high places did much to gain for it the measure of popular support which it enjoyed.[30] Consequently, to argue that the Far Eastern civilization was created out of a popular religious movement in the decline of Sinic society is somewhat simplistic.

G. *"Geographical Displacement" and the Development of South China.* A "geographic displacement" of Sinic society accompanied the birth of the Far Eastern civilization. Chinese culture spread with the new society into the hitherto undeveloped South. This transfer of civilization to new ground, says Toynbee, produced a challenge that resulted in a great Southern cultural efflorescence. Consequently, the South achieved a predominance over the North which is still retained.

Granted Southern predominance, a much more simple explanation of that fact is available than Toynbee's concept of the "challenge of new ground." For several centuries prior to the T'ang, there had been an extensive migration to the Yangtze region and

---

[29]Hu Shih, "Founding of Zen Buddhism," *Chinese Social and Political Science Review,* Vol. 15, p. 481.

[30]Latourette, *op. cit.,* p. 167.

beyond. Between the years 280 A.D. and 464 A.D., there was a
fivefold increase in Southern population.[31] The cause of this
movement was the general barbarian invasion of the North. After
the final defeat of Chin, a wholesale exodus of the wealthy and
educated class took place. Thus those who best represented Chinese civilization were driven out of the North. Serfs and barbarians
remained. Cultural poverty is the result, and constant war accentuated this condition. The South, remaining largely unaffected by
war,[32] received the "cream" of Northern culture, the product of
centuries. Thus enriched, the South experienced a rapid development. The North lagged behind. Toynbee ignores the additional
important stimuli that came to South China from beyond the seas.
Before the T'ang, China had access to the outer world through the
Tarim basin. Turkish conquest of Central Asia cut that avenue.
Now the threshold becomes the littoral below the mouth of the
Yangtze; and, just as foreign intercourse had helped to make the
North a cultural center of gravity, an ever-growing maritime trade
put the South into contact with new peoples and brought home to
that region, as the geographer Cressey phrases it, "a priceless cargo
of ideas." So endowed with wider intellectual horizons, and the
abundance of a rich sea commerce, the South develops into a key
region in later Chinese history.

H. *The Nature of the T'ang.* Toynbee apparently designates the
T'ang dynasty as the growth period of the Far Eastern civilization.
This dynasty provided China with one of the golden ages of its
history, but many of the characteristics of the empire at this time
run counter to Toynbee's particular criteria of a growth period.
The career of the dynasty amply refutes Toynbee's conviction that,
"It is one of the characteristics of civilizations in process of growth
that all aspects and activities of their social life are coordinated
into a single whole, in which the economic, political and cultural
elements are kept in nice adjustment with one another by an inner
harmony of the growing body social."

The history of T'ang China scarcely justifies this formula of a
growth period distinguished by social harmony and peace. Indeed
the history of China at this time is shot through with social disunity
and militarism, the dark undercurrent of cultural greatness. There
were, for example, critical rifts in the governing class. The great
families of the land who had supported the rise of the dynasty to
power engaged in a bitter running conflict with rival Northern

---

[31]L. Carrington Goodrich, *A Short History of the Chinese People*
(Harper and Brothers, 1943), p. 82.

[32]Wittfogel, *op. cit.,* p. 20.

families who had collaborated with the preceding Wei regime.[33] The bureaucracy was likewise riven with factional disputes,[34] and the court was often engaged in a fight with the official class in a struggle for predominance, a conflict described by Arthur Waley as the battle of the Within and the Without.[35] The lower classes were ground down by heavy taxes and high prices. The great revolution of An Lu-shan reveals the popular disaffection at the very height of the dynasty's grandeur and influence. The interval between 756 A.D. and 766 A.D. is a time of deadly struggle.

In a growth period, we are told, the peripheral peoples of a civilization are supposedly content with their lot, entirely amenable to the leadership of the creative minority as it works out the destiny of the society. This was not the happy experience of China under the T'ang rulers, for there were unceasing difficulties with the peoples beyond the borders. War followed war without end. The empire was caught up in a long struggle with the Tibetans, whose success in battle once allowed the capture of the capital at Ch'ang-an. The T'u-yu-kun in the Kokonor also rose in a rebellion of the fiercest kind. Client states on the western borders joined with the Arabs to defeat the Chinese, who were finally defeated in the Ili Valley of Sinkiang. The T'ai people of Nan Cho occupied Yunnan at one point and seized Chengtu in 850 A.D. The frontier peoples, who were neither Chinese nor yet nomads, were always in ferment,[36] and it was from this rich source of dissatisfaction that An Lu-shan drew important elements of strength for his bloody revolt that decimated over thirty million people.

The T'ang empire in its early period had a standing army of upward of one million men, raised by press-gang methods, and the emperor Li Shih-min pursued an unrelenting policy of aggressive militarism. He refused to accept the Great Wall as a boundary for his ambitions, and Chinese armies were sent far afield into Turkestan, Manchuria, Mongolia, and Korea. A similar policy by the Han Emperor Han Wu-ti is regarded by Toynbee as a sign of inevitable decay, because it was practiced in the Universal State of the Sinic society. Prosperity and superficial political unity cannot obscure the reality of the turmoil and dissension that were endemic in T'ang China.

Self-determination is the decisive sign of a Golden Age, for creativity must be self-germinated by the creative minority. The culture of the T'ang, however was anything but self-determined.

---

[33]Arthur Waley, "Social Organization in Ancient China," *The Modern Quarterly*, Vol. 2, pp. 208-214.

[34]*Ibid.*

[35]*Ibid.*

[36]*Ibid.*

Primarily, it represents a cumulation of prior tendencies and beginnings. Innovations there were during the T'ang, but many of its most important developments had their seeds in past times. The political pattern was an elaboration of a pattern begun in the Han.[37] The only great technical advance was printing which had much earlier antecedents. Original philosophic thinking was of small consequence and purely derivative in nature. Secular art was reminiscent of the Han tradition in its depiction of animals and scenes of human life.[38] It was also influenced by the Six Dynasties school.[39] Poetry, the greatest artistic achievement of the T'ang, was the finished product of a long development.[40]

Not only was T'ang culture shaped by the past, but it was powerfully moulded by contemporary foreign contacts. The T'ang was a cosmopolitan civilization. "Until modern times," asserts one historian, "there was no period in Chinese history when the country was so open to foreign influence as in the T'ang dynasty."[41] A Chinese scholar goes on to say, "There is no doubt that this westward expansion and the absorption through conquest of many western tribes were in part responsible for the brilliant renaissance of Chinese culture that took place in the T'ang period."[42] On the material plane, foreign commerce helped make possible the great wealth of the period, and this prosperity was the underpinning of the great cultural advance. Religion was syncretic in a marked fashion. The T'ang were tolerant of all religious beliefs, and Christianity, Islam, Manicheism and other creeds were practiced and gained adherents. The same tendency toward synthesis is observable in art. ". . . the T'ang aesthetic ideal showed itself ready to welcome the Greeks, Iranians, or Indian influence with which it came into contact at Turfan, or Kucha, Khotan, or Samarqand."[43]

Thus it can be seen that the T'ang fails to fit any neat formula of characterization. It had no peculiar temper or impulse in terms relevant to Toynbee's morphological scheme, but as in any other age there were discordant elements of ebb and flow in the mainstream of the life of that time. Geographically, the empire was expansive in size. It was militaristic. In many ways social life was poor in cohesion and unity. Culture was cosmopolitan and syn-

---

[37]Latourette, *op. cit.,* p. 172.
[38]*Ibid.,* p. 210.
[39]Grousset, *op. cit.,* p. 221.
[40]Richard Wilhelm, *A Short History of Chinese Civilization* (The Viking Press, 1929), p. 221.
[41]Fitzgerald, *op. cit.,* p. 321.
[42]Tsui Chi, *A Short History of Chinese Civilization* (G. P. Putnam's Sons, 1943), p. 136.
[43]Grousset, *op. cit.,* p. 207.

cretic. All in all, the T'ang resists any definition to be found among Toynbee's touchstones of a period of growth.

I. *Interpretation of Later Chinese History.* The career of the Far Eastern society after the T'ang dynasty cannot be analysed in terms of Toynbee's system since he admits that his formulations do not fit. This non-conformity, he says, can be attributed to the distortion of Chinese history by successive foreign invaders, principally the West. This explanation is somewhat incongruous, given Toynbee's reiterated argument that the development of a society is self-contained and immune from decisive outside impressions. This autonomy underlies his whole proposition that a society is the only proper and final field of historical study. Are we to assume that the Far Eastern society is not an intelligible field of study? Is it an anomaly?

At no time does Toynbee say explicitly what challenge, not met, undermined the society. It would also be interesting to know why the Yüng and Ch'ing dynasties may be regarded as universal states and not the Ming. Why was Catholicism in the 17th century an incipient higher religion but the Christian background of the T'ai P'ing rebellion only an evidence of Chinese barbarization by Western influence? Since a higher religion must be a mass movement, how can 17th century Christianity in China qualify when it attracted but a handful of converts from the upper classes?

Toynbee's generalization that nomadic invaders of the Far East society were sinicized is effectively refuted by the research of Wittfogel which shows the restricted limits within which the invaders absorbed Chinese culture.[44] Toynbee says only the Yüan remained untouched. Wittfogel reveals that the Mongols followed the same pattern of response.

Toynbee believes that any universal state imposed from without will be shortly overthrown because its alien character makes it repugnant to those it subjects. The long tenure of the Ch'ing dynasty, an alien regime, is explained away by its rapid and complete assimilation of Chinese culture. Since Wittfogel amply proves that the Manchus retained much of their foreign character, the success of the C'ing remains unexplained.

4. A GENERAL CRITICISM OF TOYNBEE'S VIEW OF HISTORY

The burden of the previous section was an attempt to determine whether there was a congruence between Toynbee's system and the data of Chinese history. Analysis indicated that the approximation was not sufficiently precise to furnish any measure of

---

[44]Wittfogel, *op. cit.,* p. 14.

support for a general system of historical laws having predictive value. This section attempts a general evaluation of Toynbee's approach to Chinese history.

A. *The Procrustean Method.* Toynbee sees Chinese history as a series of facts, parts, and instances. His job as historian is to take the data of history and to relate and classify and then to formulate laws on the basis of observed constants. His relationships and classifications are based on sharp and clear distinctions. History thus becomes a pattern of pigeon-holes, an amalgamation of separate and self-contained unities, all mutually exclusive. This method of dissection and abstraction fundamentally falsifies history by destroying its pervasive unity and integrity.

Toynbee regards Chinese society as a completely independent field of study. China has developed in isolation. Its whole being is in its own particular experience. This conception, while necessary to the rest of Toynbee's system, presents an illusory picture of China's indebtedness to the rest of the world. Chinese cultural growth, as we have previously suggested, has been a function in real measure of external contact.

Not only does Toynbee set aside Chinese society from other societies spatially, but he goes on to draw a clean distinction through Chinese civilization on the time scale. So emerge two societies, the Sinic and the Far Eastern. These two societies are separate and distinct. Such a differentiation is artificial. The cultural pattern of Toynbee's Sinic society is largely the cultural pattern of his Far Eastern society. Varying elements may have received greater emphasis in earlier periods of Chinese history and been allowed to fade in later times; but the general cultural pattern has come down through the centuries intact. Confucianism, the highly centralized state, the agrarian economy, the bureaucracy, the aristocracy founded on literary achievement, these are a few of the strands that bind ancient and modern China together in a common inheritance. The persistence of cultural elements from the pre-T'ang period completely refutes Toynbee's thesis. Far Eastern society is not "an intelligible field of study" in itself. The continuity of Chinese civilization is one of its most prominent characteristics. Its study must be approached whole to be meaningful.

Toynbee accompanies his distinction between the Sinic and Far Eastern cvilizations with a division of each particular society into a sequence of time intervals representing cultural growth or decay. The tendency of these intervals is ascertained, implicitly if not explicitly, by their degree of political stability, despite the fact that political integration in Chinese history is oftentimes no gauge of cultural vitality. The careers of the Sinic and Far Eastern civilizations are envisaged as running through a progression of birth, growth, breakdown, universal state, disintegration, and dissolution, although the Far Eastern civilization has not yet run the whole gamut. What transpires in each interval is shaped by a behaviour pattern peculiar to that particular stage.

Thus Toynbee argues that the fate of the Manchus cannot be explained in a fundamental way by contemporary affairs in China but by the fact that the regime was inescapably implicated in the stream of dissolution which had begun 900 years before in the breakup of the Far Eastern society. The history of China subsequent to the T'ang becomes a sort of rip-tide, and the destiny of the Ch'ing dynasty necessarily proceeds from a behavior pattern inevitable in a Universal State. The Manchus, thinks Toynbee, were not overcome by the West. They succumbed because they were the creatures of a society in the throes of disintegration, a society that had committed "suicide" in the year 875 A.D.

It may be agreed that the fall of the Manchus cannot be explained by events transpiring in the short interval subsequent to the Ch'ien Lung emperor, but it distorts history to regard the Manchus as the helpless victims of an inexorable course of disaster that develops out of Toynbee's scheme of birth, growth, and decline. Toynbee denies that his theory of history has any quality of inevitability, but his analysis of history shapes up into an interpretation that is shot through with the idea that the ebb and flow of history, once precipitated, is inescapable.

If any one reason accounts for the fall of the Ch'ing dynasty, it probably can be found in the mistaken policy of peasant exploitation that wrecked the economy of the country. This agrarian crisis was the issue of a basic contradiction in Chinese society that runs through the whole imperial history of China and far transcends in time Toynbee's Far Eastern civilization.[45]

The Chinese administration, requiring intricate scribal techniques, depended upon scholar bureaucrats for effectiveness. These administrators were drawn from the wealthy landlord class which alone had the leisure to acquire the necessary academic preparation. Thus the government and its officials both competed through taxes or rents to preempt the basic form of wealth in the surplus production of the land. The gentry-administrator class used its strategic position in government to evade taxation by shifting it to the peasantry. Beset by the government demanding taxes and the landlords demanding rents, the peasantry was progressively im-

---

[45]Owen and Eleanor Lattimore, *The Making of Modern China* (W. W. Norton and Company, 1944), pp. 28-29.

poverished, rebellion was a logical consequence, and a new regime would initiate this predatory system afresh.[46]

Once having seized power the Manchus did little to forestall this critical problem of exploitation of the agrarian population. As more and more wealth was diverted to private hands, the government was obliged, in its pursuit of revenue, to raise progressively the tax levy which fell almost entirely on a dwindling number of peasants who were increasingly unable to pay because of destitution and consequent dispossession from the land. During its tenure in power, the dynasty increased the tax rate twenty to thirty times. As the wealth and power of the landlords grew, the resources of the taxable small farmers declined, and the government was enfeebled by fiscal difficulties. By the middle of the nineteenth century, the country was susceptible to both rebellion and invasion, because the whole economic foundation of the state was undermined.[47]

The problem of the land tax has been considered here at some length because it represents a pointed illustration of the irrelevancy of Toynbee's basic scheme of categories in any fruitful analysis of the course of Chinese civilization. The decline and fall of the Ch'ing after the "Indian Summer" of Ch'ien Lung becomes intelligible in terms of a basic contradiction characteristic of Chinese history since the inception of the first empire but unintelligible in Toynbee's categories of Breakdown, Universal State, and Dissolution in a Far Eastern society.

Our present criticism of Toynbee's inclination toward abstraction and pigeonholing, as destructive of the continuity and interdependence of Chinese history, is further underlined by his differentiation of the Chinese social structure into discrete entities. Thus, a creative (or dominant) minority is conceptualized, plus an internal proletariat and an external proletariat. Each of these categories is completely coherent and apparently self-conscious of its particular historical function. Class behavior becomes predictable. This arrangement is too neat to suit reality.

Toynbee seems to equate the creative minority with the ruling group, but certainly there were creative elements in the Chinese population outside that confined class. The anonymous creators, for example, of much of the art in the Chinese collections of our museums testify to that fact.

Given its creative purpose, we should suppose the minority to have a consistent sense of identity and direction. Yet the Chinese

---

[46]Wang Yu Ch'uan, "The Rise of Land Tax and the Fall of Dynasties in Chinese History," *Pacific Affairs*, Vol. 9, p. 212.
[47]*Ibid.*, pp. 201-220.

ruling class was riven with internal dissension.[48] A persistent struggle for power divided the bureaucracy and court, and both were united in opposition to the commercial magnates and military leaders. Of course, this is not to deny that there was, as in any society or any class, a generalized agreement on basic fundamentals.

Toynbee would have us believe that the creativity of the minority is contemporaneously self-determined, as a resultant of a mystical process of withdrawal and return in which the masses do not participate. To conceive of the Chinese population docilely and uncomprehendingly emulating its "Promethean" elite scarcely advances our knowledge of the historical experience of the Chinese people.

Moreover, any creative historical act is the end product of a slowly maturing pattern of change. Is it not reasonable to assume that the spread of potentially creative individuals throughout Chinese history has been constant? It is difficult to understand, therefore, why creativity should effloresce at particular times save that the condition of society had evolved to a point where it was ready to experience change. Creative individuals, or minorities, do not "create" through mystic inspiration; they express that which has been formulated by their milieu, which in turn is necessarily conditioned by the mass of mankind and by the physical and material circumstances of the time.

In Toynbee's eyes Confucius is a "creative" individual, one in a company of such incongruous figures as Jesus and Machiavelli. Toynbee sees Confucious playing a great role in Chinese history in a personal capacity. As a matter of fact, very little is known of Confucius. Indeed, what is known indicates that he was a conservative individual whose thinking was derivative of the temper of his day. Toynbee confuses Confucius with Confucianism. The man probably had small part in fashioning the ideology which was to become a vast residual accretion of the thought of centuries. The Confucian myth became an important factory in Chinese history, but that myth, needless to say, was not the work of Confucius. It was the work of history. The role of Confucius, the man, is impossible to assess.

We question also the validity of Toynbee's concept of the role of "creative minorities" in Chinese history. It is impossible to deny that different groups fulfill different functions in society. There is a division of labor necessarily. But to urge that leadership, in any period, comes to men set apart by a different spiritual fiber and

---

[48]See Weber's analysis in H. H. Gerth and C. Mills, eds., *From Max Weber: Essays in Sociology* (Oxford University Press), pp. 442-443.

impulse is quite a different matter. Leadership acquires its role through a variety of circumstances in which ability, accident, and social institutions figure. The creative minorities in the growth periods defined by Toynbee in Chinese history acquire and keep their leadership through naked military prowess, a fact not consonant with the historian's description of the nature of the creative elite.

The whole concept of an external proletariat seems equally artificial as a hard and fast category. Toynbee pictures the formation of an external proletariat precisely upon the fall of the T'ang empire. However, the border peoples of China had been harassing the empire during the whole T'ang period. It would appear that they became transformed into the external proletariat of the Sinic society only at the particular juncture demanded to confirm Toynbee's morphology.

Toynbee's ultimate categories are the Macrocosm and the Microcosm. All aspects of life pertain to one sphere or the other. The Macrocosm represents the material world and is fundamentally unimportant. Chinese civilization, like any other civilization, advances only insofar as it transfers its being from the Macrocosm to the Microcosm, from the material to the spiritual sphere. This point of view is essential to Toynbee's idea that the progress of civilization is to be measured by the degree to which it realizes the City of God on earth and that any obstacle to that realization is evil, negative, and retrogressive. It is also essential to his idea that the City of God is to be attained only through the leadership of a creative minority which secures its inspiration on a supermundane plane.

This point of view would cause us, if accepted, to disregard the elementary fact that the material and non-material are so inextricably fused in Chinese civilization as to render the establishment of the priority of one over the other completely impossible. Toynbee describes the material aspect of civilization as "trivial," the cultural element as its "essence." Art, literature, and philosophy certainly make up the "cultural" tissue of civilizations, yet their material background in China is easily seen. Confucianism may serve as an example. Geography made the economic basis of Chinese life agricultural. The needs of Chinese agriculture profoundly conditioned the social pattern of the Chinese family. Out of the family system evolved the particular social system of China. It is commonly accepted that Confucianism is the philosophic outgrowth of the Chinese social system. The Chinese scholar Fung Yu-lan observes, "A great part of Confucianism is the rational justification of this social system, or its theoretical expression. Economic conditions prepared the basis of this social system, and Confucianism expressed its ethical significance."[49]   In a similar fashion, the quietism and affinity to nature of Taoism may be explained in terms of the agricultural activity of the Chinese people.   Their closeness to nature as farmers is traceable in the preoccupation of Chinese artists with landscapes, animals, and growing things.   These instances must illustrate my point that the material and non-material in Chinese civilization cannot be separated, just as they form additional evidence to support my general proposition in the foregoing section that Toynbee's methodology denies the continuity and interdependence of the Chinese historical process by its insistence on distinctions and categories that have no reality in themselves, save as abstractions that cannot be accommodated by history.

B. *Subjectivism*. Toynbee's depreciation of the material aspects of civilization and his mystical orientation deprive him of any set of objective criteria for the measurement of the progress of civilization. *A Study of History* is based on values that are subjective and unverifiable. It is not really an explanatory system of the rise and decline of civilizations but a normative system based on a very private interpretation of the course of human destiny.

Toynbee's subjectivism is revealed in many of his verdicts on Chinese events. As we have previously pointed out, he regards the political confusion of the Warring States period as the breakdown of Sinic civilization. Here he confuses change with decay and disregards how pregnant the period was with some of the most consequential developments in Chinese history. Again he distrusts the material greatness of the Han empire and describes the first imperial state as a reckless attempt to retrieve better days of a prior time. However this may be, the fact remains that out of the greatness of the Han emerged some of the intellectual and spiritual achievements of later history that catch Toynbee's admiration. And in a similar fashion, he discounts the Six Dynasties as the final dissolution of the Sinic civilization. Yet this was an age that served as the crucible out of which poured some of the preeminent aesthetic accomplishments of Chinese genius.

On the other hand Toynbee is quick to see the greatest significance in Jesuit missionary activity at Peking and in the allegiance of the T'ai P'ing to Christian principles. Both of these movements he regards as higher religions that might have wrought, save for untoward foreign intervention, new civilizations to succeed the Far Eastern society. Any realistic evaluation of the missionary activity of the Jesuits necessarily denies it any fundamental conse-

[49]Fung Yu-lan, "The Background of Chinese Philosophy," *Princeton University Bicentennial Conference Paper* (Mimeographed), p. 5.

quence. The religious element in the T'ai P'ing ideology was a highly syncretic amalgam of diverse creeds of which Christianity was but one. Elsewhere cultural syncretism is a sure sign of decay in Toynbee's scheme, but it is not such when Christianity is a constituent element. The City of God is the pole-star of civilization's evolution, but evidently it is to be the City of Toynbee's God. This ethnocentric tendency shows itself in additional small ways, such as Toynbee's description of the sinological studies of the Jesuit fathers as having an excellence that has not been "appreciably" improved on to this day, a statement wholly false.

The subjective bias of "A Study of History" leaves us disappointed in the hope expressed in the introduction of this paper that there might be found in the pages of this work an empirical frame of reference within which Chinese history might begin to assume meaning in general terms of the story of man on earth.

C. *Sources.* One last word remains to be said about Toynbee's sources. The distinguished sinologist J. J. L. Duyvendak, in the introduction to his volume, *Trends and Men in Chinese History,* apologizes for its fragmentary character by explaining that a general history of China cannot yet be written because of the inadequacy of the source material. This material's inadequacy is not in its dearth but in its plenitude. So great is its extent that it has not yet been sufficiently examined by authoritative critics to establish its validity and worth. Where the cautious Dutch savant fears to tread, Toynbee walks with a firm step, and he proceeds to give a confident account of the whole history of China. In so doing he has been obliged to depend on the historical works in European languages that were accepted as standard at his time of writing. Most of these secondary sources were written on the basis of research done in a much earlier period. In a critical study of the materials upon which western ideas about China have been based, called *Western Concepts of China and the Chinese,* Mary Gertrude Mason says, "Much of the information laid before the public in the nineteenth century was uncritical and incorrect."[50] The writing of Chinese history has just begun, and an immense variety of material must be analyzed and worked over.[51] It is not to be expected that the material will ever be sufficiently complete to make possible an exact account of Chinese history, but the quality of sources available to Toynbee furnish legitimate reason to question the final significance of his attempt to write such an account.

[50]Mary Gertrude Mason, *Western Concepts of China and the Chinese* (The Seeman Printery, N. Y., 1939), p. 27.
[51]See: Arthur W. Hummel, "What the Chinese Are Doing in Their Own History," *American Historical Review,* Vol. 34, pp. 715-724.

ARNOLD TOYNBEE'S CONCEPTION OF THE FUTURE OF ISLAM*

Gotthold Weil

The English historian, Arnold Toynbee, is widely known beyond the narrow circle of scholars and professional historians. His great work, *A Study of History,* in particular, has attracted attention among the educated of all countries. In this book (of which six volumes have so far appeared and further volumes are projected), Toynbee presents his view of the development of human civilization in the form of a cut-and-dried system; at various points (scattered throughout the various volumes, in accordance with the general arrangement of the work) he deals with Islamic civilization. It is not, however, *A Study of History* which has given occasion to this article, but Toynbee's more recent *Civilization on Trial,* published about two years ago. This book is made up of a collection of thirteen articles and lectures dealing with subjects some of which have not yet been treated in the larger work and have not yet been evaluated within the framework of his system. Among these essays mention should be made of the essay "Islam, the West and the Future," one of the few which is published here for the first time.

In his paper on the future of Islam, Toynbee presupposes a knowledge of the specific terminology he has coined in connection with his conception of history. It is necessary, therefore, to premise a few remarks on his scheme and his terminology. Toynbee regards the history of humanity as a unity and hence concludes that the history of any single nation-state cannot be understood in isolation. The smallest historical unit he believes to be capable of being studied and understood per se is the "civilization" embracing a variety of peoples and states. Every civilization owes its existence to the fact that some human "society" endeavors, by a special effort, to rise above mere primitive humanity. Attempts of this kind have been made for thousands of years. Toynbee lists more than twenty such attempts by name, most of which have by now become extinct, such as the Egyptiac, the Sumeric, the Hittite, the Minoan, the Hellenic, and the Syriac civilizations. At present no more than five still survive, to wit, the Western, the Orthodox Christian, the Islamic, the Hindu, and the Far Eastern. However, even of these survivors, four are by now in a state of disintegration, only one, the Western, being held to be still vigorous. Toynbee considers each of the five civilizations still existing to be affiliated with some other, preceding civilization; thus Western civilization

Middle Eastern Affairs, vol. 2, no. 1, January 1951, pp. 3-17.

has sprung from Hellenic society. He thinks it possible to develop a uniform morphology for all societies and civilizations by scientific means, and to find a more or less permanent scheme to fit the rise and decline of all of them. No doubt Toynbee differs fundamentally from Spengler as regards his aim, but he is at one with him in holding that various cultures pass through parallel courses of development, and that certain periods of extinct cultures may even be philosophically contemporary with other, succeeding ones. Toynbee's morphological system and his scheme of the course of civilizations are alike derived from the rise and development of Hellenic civilization.

At the core of every flourishing civilization is the "minority," possessed of the "creative power" which enables it to find the true and effective "response" to each "challenge" presented by nature or by some other society. The gift of creative power renders the minority capable of becoming and remaining the "dominant minority." As soon as its powers begin to dwindle, the "disintegration" of civilization sets in and with it the "time of troubles" from within and without. Yet the minority once more succeeds in mastering the situation and postponing the decline by founding a "universal state," uniting all societies into one political Commonwealth. The universal state of Hellenic civilization is the *Imperium Romanum*. But its days, too, are numbered. After the collapse of the universal state, the "Interregnum" sets in, linking the dying civilization to some other young and rising one. Three factors fill the interregnum with their activities, splitting the body politic into three: 1) the ruling minority which has ceased to be creative and is consequently losing its supreme command; 2) the "internal proletariat," founding a "universal church" (in this particualr case the Christian church); and 3) the "external proletariat," i.e., the barbarian peoples of the adjoining countries who, after a "migration of nations," founded several "successor states" on the territory of the former universal state. Both proletariats[1] are remote from, and foreign to, minority, constituting social elements which are *in* society but not *of* it. The church strikes root, grows, and wins adherents; it serves as a bridge between past and future. It is the "chrysalis" from which the new civilization bursts forth (in this particular case the Western-Christian civilization).

This fixed terminology—civilization, dominant minority, creative power, challenge and response, disintegration, time of troubles, uni-

---

[1]Toynbee does not use the term "proletariat" in the usual restricted sense of a definite working-class in the towns, but in the wide, general sense in which it is employed in Roman law: *Proletarii dicti sunt plebeii, qui nihil republicae exhibeant, sed tantum prolem sufficiant,* i.e., we call proletarians those citizens who render no service to their state save that of supplying it with offspring.

versal state, interregnum, internal proletariat, universal church, external proletariat, migration of nations, successor states, religion as chrysalis—and the corresponding scheme, derived from the development of Graeco-Roman civilization, are hardly applicable to that civilization itself, much less to the twenty other civilizations. Toynbee himself is aware of the fact, but he believes in the reality of what he advances as the common scheme of development of the different civilizations and of the terminology he has coined, which is the living expression of the various stages of development. Hence he always finds some argument to explain the numerous irregularities and deviations confronting him, as well as some new term.

Let us take Islamic civilization as an example. Just as he distinguishes between the Christian religion and church (which arose during the period of Hellenic civilization) on the one hand, and Christian civilization (which originated six hundred years later) on the other; so we have to distinguish between the religions of Islam, which arose during the period of Syriac civilization, and Islamic civilization, which originated six hundred years later. Islamic civilization is, therefore, a daughter of Syriac society and civilization. In its prime, kings like Solomon and Hiram stood at the head of its dominant minority, and the Achaemenian Empire was the universal state of Syriac civilization. However, that is only the first stage of its development, for in place of the disintegration and decline which, according to Toynbee's scheme, were bound to follow, there occurred an extraordinary event: the intrusion of Hellenic civilization into the Near East. This event resulted in the "reintegration and resumption" of historical development, i.e., Syriac civilization ran its course for a second time.

The intrusion of Hellenic society is a challange to Syriac civilization, to which the latter has responded several times. The wars of the Jews and the Parthians are violent reactions to Syriac civilization. Christianity, too, and more particularly the peaceful activities of Saint Paul, constitute gentle reactions to the eruption of Hellenism. However, the final response to the Hellenic challenge, according to Toynbee, was not given by the internal but by the external proletariat of Arabic society. From the start, Syriac civilization was divided into two parts: Iranic society and Arabic society. However, immediately after the victorious advance of the Arabs and their conquests, the time of troubles sets in, and for the second time a universal state is founded within Syriac civilization, to wit, the Abbassid Caliphate. In accordance with the scheme, disintegration assumes ever increasing proportions, and simultaneously a vigorous activity by the two proletariats sets in. The activity of the external proletariat finds its expression in the 10th, 11th, and 12th centuries, in the migrations of the Turkish and Mongolian peoples in Asia, and in the migrations of Arabs and Berbers in North Africa, as well as in the founding of many successor states in the territory of the Abassid Empire. The quiet and peaceful activity of the internal proletariat, on the other hand, finds its expression in the fact that the primitive teachings of Islam are being recast in Hellenic terminology, and that the structure of Islamic thought is being systematically developed.

Thanks to its tolerance, Islam exercises a power of attraction and charm which results in the adoption of Islam by all Eurasian nomads, and more particularly by the Turks, until about 1000 A.D. It is only owing to this development that Islam becomes the unifying factor within Syriac society, over which it had previously won but a superficial military victory. The cultural-religious unification was so strong and effective that, after the destruction of the universal state by the Mongols, the Islamic church remained alive, struck root and grew strong within the whole complex of the Caliphate, from Andalusia to Transoxania. Thus Islam, like Christianity, acted as a chrysalis in order to guard and protect the hidden seeds until these had gained sufficient strength to render possible the emergence of a new secular civilization: Islamic civilization, which is still in existence. Toynbee fixes the date of its birth in 1275 A.D. In Islamic as in Syriac civilization, the Iranic and Arabic societies existed and acted side by side until Iranic society, represented by the Osmanlis, overran Arabic society at the beginning of the 16th century, without assimilating it or absorbing it into its social and cultural body. Despite all the military successes of the Osmanlis, it is clear that at this very period the creative power of Islam came to a standstill. At that time Islam ceased attracting other peoples by its charm; from then on most Mongols adopt Buddhism as their religion. An even more striking proof of the decline of Islam, however, is to be found in the fact that it no longer gives birth to any great individuals; in Toynbee's view, Ibn Khaldun was the last great man in Islam to produce eternal values. Thus Islam has been in a state of decided disintegration since about 1500 A.D. But if that be the case, we must again note a deviation, for so far the universal state, which according to Toynbee's schemes should have been founded long ago, has failed to arise and embrace all Islamic societies. Hence Toynbee assumes that in Islamic civilization the Pan-Islamic movement has played the role of the universal state. That brings us to the threshold of modern times.

Before dealing with the question of what tasks Toynbee imposes on Islam for the future, we must pause for a moment in order to determine how Toynbee visualizes the development of Western civilization in generations to come.

Western civilization, which originated before 700 A.D., developed normally and quietly beside the other four existing civilizations during the first centuries of its existence; the social structure of all of them was largely identical. At bottom each of these civilizations lived in isolation from the rest. There was some contact between them, but on so restricted a scale that they did not, and could not, become a single society. There were two lines of communication leading from Britain to the Chinese Wall; one across the steppes from the Sahara to Mongolia and situated entirely within the complex of Islamic civilization, which then enjoyed the commanding position in world trade.

With the 16th century, however, there set in a vast and fundamental change in the development of Western civilization, its power steadily growing from generation to generation, and from century to century. As the result of its control of the oceans the West had turned the flank of the Islamic world peacefully without any struggle, thus shaking the foundations of its trade. By conquering North and South America, Africa, Indonesia, and the primitive zones, Western society rose to world supremacy and began to draw all other societies into the orbit of its political, economic, and technical organism. Finally, by means of its technical achievements and its mastery of the air, Western civilization penetrated to the very core of the other civilizations which regard this unwanted penetration as a challenge.

What stage of its development has Western civilization reached at the moment? asks Toynbee, and he replies: the time of troubles has by now begun, but we are still at an early stage of disintegration, since the universal state of Western civilization, embracing all societies and peoples, has not yet been erected. The English-speaking peoples represent its dominant minority, and generally speaking these have so far been in a position to give a successful response to all external challenges and to absorb the other societies into its political and economic organism, thus creating an external technical world-unity of a kind. However, Western civilization still owes a response to the internal challenge confronting it. For although it has succeeded in erecting a gigantic provisional scaffolding for the regulation of the requirements of practical life (thanks to the wealth of its technical means), it has not so far succeeded in uniting culturally and spiritually the societies housed therein and in turning them into a single large and united society. As for the spiritual values of the West, the other civilizations thus far have consented only with considerable reservations, or not at all, to mingle with it or to merge themselves in it. This is a most serious deficiency, and it is to be feared that the external and internal proletariats of Western civilization—the world proletariat—will react at this deficiency, there still being some fifteen hundred million not yet awakened peasants. Hence the West stands in need of "re-education".

To the question: "What is the reason for this internal, cultural failure of Western civilization?" Toynbee replies: The reason is that Christianity, for several centuries past, has ceased to be a creative and determining factor in Western culture; hence it is necessary to place the reeducation of the West on a religious basis. Today, according to Toynbee, only the germs of Christianity remain. In this, our present Western culture resembles the culture of early Christianity, in which there were also no more than the germs of Christianity, visible in the shape of a chrysalis guarding these spiritual values and taking care to make them come alive. But just as early Christianity assimilated the best of what it found in various Oriental religions, so today the existing "higher religions" can "contribute new elements to be grafted onto Christianity in days to come." In this way Christianity might one day become the spiritual heir of all the other higher religions and hence a power welding all societies of the world into a unity. In Toynbee's view there are at present the following higher religions: Christianity, Islam, Hinduism, and Mahayanian Buddhism. With the influence of Hinduism and Buddhism on Christianity he does not deal specifically. All the more important is his special essay on "Islam, the West and the Future," to which reference is made above. For the essay must be regarded as a characteristic illustration of how and to what degree Toynbee concedes, not only to Islam, but to the other religions as well, an effect on the West, and how he visualizes the future of other civilizations.

The attack of the West on Islam is only part of the gigantic action of the West which aims at incorporating all mankind in a single great society. The present encounter of the West with Islam, which began as long ago as the last century, is more active than all previous encounters, and the prospects of Islam, driven into a corner, are bad. For Toynbee states that "the modern West is superior to her not only in arms but also in the technique of economic life, on which military science ultimately depends, and above all in spiritual culture—the inward force which alone creates and sustains the outward manifestations of what is called civilization.'" He who is placed in such a dangerous situation has, in Toynbee's view, two alternative ways of reacting and responding to the challenge. In describing these two possibilities Toynbee uses two terms coined during the wars of the Jews against Rome when a similar situation arose, or, to use Toynbee's phrase, "in the encounter between the ancient civilizations of Greece and

Syria." The one attacked can react either as "Zealot" or as "Herodian."

The zealot is the man who refuses to take cognizance of anything new and turns in on himself in face of the unknown; he is guided by instinct only. The strongholds of the Zealots in Islam are situated in sterile and sparsely populated regions, such as those of the Senussis and the Wahhabis. Even if they do succeed in surviving there in isolation, they are no more than a "fossil" of an extinct civilization. In most cases, however, the West regards them as obstacles in its path, and then they are doomed to destruction. Thus the West has recently subdued the Islamic Zealots in the Moroccan Rif and Atlas and on the northwest frontier of India.

The second way of reacting to pressure and of responding to the challenge of the West is that of the Herodian, and in Toynbee's view, this is the more efficacious response. The Herodian tries to lay bare the secret of the attacker's superiority and to meet him on his own ground, fighting back with the same weapons and using the same tactics. He looks danger straight in the eye, and is guided by reason only. While the Zealot under pressure develops a kind of archaism, the Herodian in a like situation develops a kind of cosmopolitanism; his activity is not creative, however, but is confined to imitating the attacker. The first Herodian in the region of Islam to have gone this way with impunity was Mehmed Ali, while the Ottoman Sultan Selim III had no success with his Herodian reforms and was killed. The Herodian is carrying out a very dangerous policy indeed; his position may be likened to that of a rider swapping horses in midstream and, as likely as not, being swept off by the current in the process. Hence all the Herodian epigoni in old Turkey and in Egypt were unequal to a task which was beyond their strength. Only modern Turkey has carried through the Herodian idea with admirable consistence, filling the whole structure of its state and society with Western thought. But, asks Toynbee, has the labor and travail spent to reach this goal been really worth while? And does the erection of one more national state on the Western model really constitute an enrichment of culture? His answer is in the negative. For a success like the setting up of the Turkish republic brings blessings only to a very small minority, while the majority has no chance of becoming even passive members of the imitated civilization's ruling class; on the contrary, its task is that of swelling the ranks of its proletariat. Nor is this all. Most peoples in Islamic society do not adopt a clear-cut method like the Turks or the Wahhabis, not following the course of either Herodians or Zealots but confining themselves to giving their respective countries the outward form of independent national states on the Western pattern. These peoples run the risk of turning wholly proletarian.

Having demonstrated that the fate of the majority of Islamic society will be that of being merged in the mass of the world proletariat, Toynbee asks the question: If that be so, then in what can the influence consist which Islam as a religion and a civilization can exercise on the West in the future? His reply runs as follows: Being merged in the world proletariat must not necessarily result in cultural sterility; perhaps the very opposite is true. As we have seen, Toynbee compares our period with that of early Christianity, during which Syria was under the impact of Hellenic civilization, just as in our time Islam is exposed to the impact of Western civilization. At that time, however, (Toynbee pursues the argument), Zealots and Herodians remained sterile while the underworld of the Oriental proletariat, represented by Nazareth, showed the right way and led to redemption. Likewise, in the future, if the religion of the West should assume a new face, India and the Far East, and Islam in competition with both, could influence with their choicest ideas the spiritual shaping of the world. Toynbee even thinks he discerns certain tendencies in this direction in modern Islam and in this connection he points to the Bahai and Ahmadi movements, which might conceivably become the embryos of new "higher religions." True, he himself is compelled to admit that such assumptions, inspired as they are by imagination, are like prophecies and their realization would be possible only thousands of years hence, if ever. Thus he again turns to the present and states that there are even now important moral tasks by fulfilling which Islam might have salutary effects on the social development of the West. For two serious dangers are threatening the present relations between the cosmopolitan proletariat and the dominant element in our Western society: racial pride and alcohol. And in these very questions certain principles of Islam could have a beneficial effect. For in contrast to the intolerance of the English-speaking peoples in matters of race, Islam, because of its belief in the unity of Allah, has developed the idea of the unity of the faithful; this idea, excluding the possibility of racial consciousness, is one of its most significant achievements. If, Toynbee hopes, Islam comes to the aid of the small number of those who are fighting for peace among the races within Western society, then the issue may be decided in favor of tolerance. The same applies to the evil of alcohol which is working havoc among the primitive populations in tropical regions. Preventive measures would be unavailing so long as they come only from without and are carried out by the Western administrators foreign to the souls of natives. Here, too, Islam has an important task. For since the natural bent of Islamic man is primitive, he is made to calm the troubled minds of the natives and to fill the spiritual void in their society with new content.

These are examples of valuable influences which Islam might exert. But what will happen if the friction between the West and the other civilizations, instead of being removed by peaceful means and by the power of the spirit, should lead to an explosion? In that case Islam might accept the task of constituting the active element in a powerful revolution of the cosmopolitan underworld against its Western masters. Such a danger, however, does not now exist, in Toynbee's judgment, because Pan-Islamism is too weak and powerless. This movement was created at the time for the purpose of driving out Western civilization and of realizing the unity of all Islamic societies under the protection of a Caliph; all attempts, however, to revive the institution of the Caliphate have failed and were bound to fail. For, firstly, Islam is dispersed abroad and solidarity while it is easy to think about, is difficult to put into practice, as is shown by the case of the Sherif of Mecca who during the first World War sided with the Christians and against the Ottoman Sultan. Secondly, while Pan-Islamism is aiming at, and endeavoring to prevent the spiritual treasures of Islam from being assimilated to the spirit of the West, the actual trend of the Islamic peoples of today is precisely in the opposite direction; here the tendency is to imitate the West outwardly and to set up single Islamic national states on the pattern of modern Turkey. The ever-increasing spread of the idea of nationalism in the Near East is a clear proof of the rapid progress of assimilation and of Islam's endeavor to adapt itself to Western civilization. However, times may change and it is conceivable that the world proletariat might one day revolt against its powerful Western oppressors and seek a leader in this racial struggle, and this call might possibly revive the warlike spirit of Islam. *Absit Omen!* With this benediction Toynbee concludes his essay on Islam.

In the presentation of his scheme of development of civilizations, Toynbee reveals an extraordinary constructive power. True, there are disciples of philosophical positivism who see in this very merit a deficiency in a scholar and most particularly in a historian. They would restrict the task of scholarship to determining facts objectively; hence they regard Toynbee's observations on the development of civilizations as no more than a subjective view and a personal opinion which cannot claim the validity of a scientific statement. I cannot subscribe to so general an objection. There is no doubt whatever that the first task of scholarship is that of finding facts by research of the utmost objectivity, but we cannot by any means rest content with the isolated results of such research. Every science, including historical science, must strive to trace the general line determining the course of events and to ask about the "whence" and "whither." To these fundamental questions, however, no ready-made answer can be found in the source-material itself; rather is it the task of the scholar to unite and shape these disconnected statements of facts into a whole by his constructive power. Hence every science must somehow be subjective and somehow constructed. On the other hand, the scholar must keep within the limits set by hard facts which do not admit of any shifting or concealment. Toynbee is beyond the reproach of lightly disregarding historical sources and facts, for his knowledge, even in remote fields of research, is amazing; moreover, he pays adequate tribute to the results of other men's research. Yet at times his passion for erecting his theoretical thought-structure gets the better of his critical sense, and then the constructive artist in him triumphs, as it were, over the carefully weighing historian.

Toynbee makes extensive use of metaphors and similes in his system and his descriptions, and this habit has a certain scientific significance as well. For comparison is an important means of throwing into bolder relief the differences between the things compared and thus of giving added emphasis to their characteristic peculiarities. Toynbee possesses to a high degree the ability to draw vivid and illuminating comparisons and to give expression thereto in well-chosen key-words likely to stick in our memory and well suited, because of their clarity, to be employed as fixed terms. There arises the danger, however, of such a term—which is no more than a simile or metaphor—becoming an end in itself and of being taken for an explanation of historical phenomena, nay, of being elevated to the rank of an historical law or category to which other historical facts can be subordinated even if sometimes only by force. This is not the place for dealing with this theoretical question of historical method. One example from Toynbee's article on Islam may suffice to show up the dangers inherent in the use of comparisons if they are introduced as fixed terms: that of the pair "Zealots—Herodians."

No doubt, these terms describe the two extreme tendencies in the struggle of the attacked against their oppressors; they do not, however, cover all possibilities of dealing with this politico-cultural problem. By referring to these two reactions only and to no other possible responses to the challenge of Hellenic civilization to Syriac society, Toynbee has given a simpler and more effective form to his description, but only by sacrificing the genuine and more complex reality of events. The unbiased reader of Toynbee's essay on Islam must assume that at the time of the Syriac-Hellenic clash only the groups of the Zealots and the Herodians were active; for Toynbee does not so much as hint at the other currents and does not even mention the name of the Pharisees. True, those who have read his great book, *A Study of History,* know his view of this period and are not at a loss to explain his silence concerning the Pharisees. Since the Jews in their zealous obstinacy refused to swim with the general tide of the Hellenic civilization which had attacked them and to merge themselves in the internal Hellenic proletariat, they cannot occupy any place in Toynbee's scheme save that of "fossils" from the extinct Syriac civilization. The Pharisees, however, the initiators of this obstinancy, are incapable of being fitted into either of the two groups of his system, Zealots or Herodians. Hence for them he uses another pair of terms, coined for similar exceptions in his scheme: "Withdrawal and return." In other words, he makes the Pharisees disappear from the stage of history in 200 B.C. only to have them reappear in 100 A.D. in the person of Saint Paul who, in Toynbee's view, is the greatest and most progressive genius to have arisen in Pharisaism. Despite all this, the quiet spiritual activity of the Pharisees during these three hundred years remains a fact. Further, the fact remains that the Pharisees reacted to the impact of Hellenism in a special way, distinct from that of both Zealots and Herodians; and it is precisely owing to this original, positive mode of their reaction that Judaism has survived and has basically changed its constitution. But Toynbee ignored this in order not to transcend the framework of his scheme and his terminology. Hence, in his essay on the future of Islam, he has not done well in closing his eyes to the facts and in declining to deal with the third answer, that given by the Pharisees. This is all the more regrettable because a parallel spiritual development is conceivable in Islam as well.

It may be pardonable to make a further observation on Toynbee's personal view of the development of civilizations in the distant future. He believes that religion will be the decisive element in the development of Western civilization in the future, and I have no intention of seriously contradicting him. If this be so, however, it is strange how small a part he assigns to this factor in the future development of Islam. True, in another article, also reprinted in his book, *Civilization on Trial,* Toynbee states (in dealing with the subject "Unification of the World") that "Islam's creative gift to mankind is monotheism" and that "Islam remains, with a mighty spiritual mission still to carry out." It is all the more striking, therefore, that in his special essay on "Islam, the West and the Future," he does not make a single allusion to this supposed mission of Islam; neither does he explain how he visualizes the religious influence of Islam on Christianity and on the West in days to come. He furnishes a number of examples as to how the Islamic

Zealots and Herodians reacted to the pressure of the West, but these examples touch only on reactions of a military or economic nature, there being no mention of any religious reaction. The only religious movements to which he makes a passing reference are the sects of the Ahmadis and Bahais. The Bahais, however, do not regard themselves as members of Islamic civilization any longer and are not so regarded. In contrast to them, the Ahmadis do belong to Islamic civilization but, in the opinion of a competent critic, "the absence of any clear principle of action, or of any constructive proposals for reform, are warnings to us not to expect too much from them."[2] Toynbee's silence is conspicuous. He does not devote so much as a single word to the various attempts which have been made within Islam proper during the last hundred years to effect a revival of religion. He mentions neither Indian thinkers like Ameer Ali or Muhammad Ikbal, nor social and religious reformers like Ziya Gokalp, nor yet theologians like Muhammad Abdu and others still living who hold the view that the religion of Islam is destined to develop into the world-religion. Instead he confines himself to assigning to Islam a sort of auxiliary service in the race question and the struggle against alcohol. This means that he demands from the Islamic peoples that they forget their own inner needs resulting from the Western impact in order to assist the West in calming disturbing elements, to satisfy whom is beyond the West's own strength.

If Toynbee were dealing with Islam in our time only, his approach might conceivably be justified, for at the beginning of his essay he expressly states that there are no more creative forces in present-day Islamic society. Since, however, his thoughts are reaching out into the remote future of humanity, perhaps two or even three thousand years, it appears to me that his conception does no justice to his subject-matter. For having bestowed upon Islam the honorable title of a "higher religion," he should have allowed it the same prospects which he has granted to Christianity, a religion he holds also to be in a state of disintegration. There is, however, no question of this; the very opposite is the case. While emphatically demanding the reeducation of Western Christendom and more particularly its revival on the religious side, he does not say anything about any reeducation within Islam, nor does he talk about religious revival or reforms in its social structure. Instead, he assigns to it its final place within the "vast, cosmopolitan, ubiquitous proletariat" of Western society, consoling it with the prospect that even there it has only the chance of participating in the purification of Christianity and its sublimation.

---

[2]Laurence E. Browne, *The Prospects of Islam*, 1944, p. 84.

With that we have touched on a very weak point in Toynbee's system and description, the contradiction between the principles on which his scheme of the development of civilization is based, and his personal judgment of historical phenomena as they really are. In principle, he vouchsafes to the other higher religions (Islam, Hinduism, and Buddhism) the exalted place to which they are entitled in his scheme of the future development of the world; however, when he speaks in detail on the future of humanity and invites us to participate in his visions of the remote future, the other religions do not appear as being equal to, and competing with, Christianity. At best their task might be that of smoothing over or otherwise influencing Christianity; but in the last analysis, Christianity—perhaps in a thousand years, perhaps in two thousand—will emerge as the only higher religion of humanity.

As an historical scholar, Toynbee embraces within his wide sweep all civilizations as a unity and recognizes in them attempts, made on equal terms, to rise above mere primitive humanity by an act of creation; hence he surveys the six thousand years of their development so objectively, through a telescope, as it were. As an individual, however, he belongs, to use his own term, to the dominant minority of Western civilization. And while he admits a good many defects in this society, he is convinced of the superiority of the English-speaking peoples with every fibre of his being and hence condemns most other peoples to the role of constituting the proletariat of Western civilization. A duality of this kind appears in other cases as well. As we know from other publications of his, Toynbee has the fullest understanding and respect for the Turkish people's struggle for liberation. Not only does he think highly of its efforts, he also shares the joy in its successes. On the other hand, he is the creator of a scheme; in that scheme the Osmanlis occupy a fixed place as "arrested civilization," and Toynbee, as the defender of his scheme, regrets the setting up of an independent Turkish republic. All his sympathies notwithstanding, he arrives at the conclusion that it would have been better for Turkey to have remained within the group defined by his scheme than to create a national state on the Western model and thus become part of the large proletariat of Western civilization.

We encounter the same scheme-bound point of view in his judgment of the development of ancient and modern Judaism. He esteems Judaism and speaks with respect of its spiritual achievements, especially of those attained within the Syriac civilization, so long as it responded with creative power and by peaceful means to all challenges, and made headway through "the learning that comes through the sufferings caused by the failures of civilizations." In such learning Toynbee sees the sovereign means of progress.

Abraham and the prophets created and acted out of the sorrow caused by the disintegration of civilization around them. Among the Jewish exiles in Babylon, too, eternal values were born of suffering and sorrow. The reply, however, which Judaism has given to the challenge of Hellenic civilization was given in the reverse spirit; it was a warlike reply and a fanatical reaction. On the strength of this reply the Jews have succeeded in surviving for the last two thousand years, but they have not, in Toynbee's view, survived as a creative member of a living civilization, but as a "fossil" of the extinct Syriac society, and since that time, therefore, their activity is confined to the development of an archaism. True, Toynbee admits that it is difficult for a strange and peculiar people to exist in an alien world as the only fossil of an already extinct civilization, yet he prefers such an existence as a characteristic and original state of things. For this reason, too, he sees no progress in the activities of the "Zionist Jews" who are going the way of the New Turkey and trying to liberate the Jews from their special position as a peculiar people and to organize them in the form of a national state on the Western pattern. For by renouncing the great and tragic past, the "Zionist Jews" may conceivably secure a comfortable future for themselves, but at the same time they are threatened by the danger of being submerged in the gigantic structure of the West.

Whoever wants to offer a just criticism of Toynbee's view and system must admit that even such extreme and contradictory views as those on the Turks and the Jews are not subjective judgments in the full sense of the term, as they are often held to be by people with preconceived ideas or of interested views. They are rather logical results of his scientific analysis of history. He is so profoundly convinced of the truth and objectivity of his study of the past that he considers himself entitled to pronounce judgment in accordance with the results of his analysis and to put forward corresponding principles for future developments. Having fixed certain norms supposed to determine the rise and decline of all civilizations, and having summed up these norms in striking keywords, he looks upon every deviation from his analogistic scheme as an exception, which he condemns as being in opposition to the normal development of civilization. However, only he who believes in the absolute accuracy of Toynbee's analysis and scheme can and will accept as true his value-judgments on the events of the last decades and on the probable shape of things to come.

Those, however, who regard his terms not as norms, but as a serious attempt to unite the motley of historical events in a stable framework, often feel an abyss opening at their feet, as it were, an abyss between his scheme and a reality which cannot be bridged.

REFLECTIONS ON TOYNBEE'S A STUDY OF HISTORY: A GEOGRAPHER'S VIEW*

O. H. K. SPATE

A Study of History is in scope nothing less than a complete rationale of human societies in their developed forms which Toynbee calls civilizations; 'complete' is a large word, and obviously not even Toynbee can put the totality of civilization into six or nine volumes, but there are very few aspects indeed which do not come within his grasp, from theology to costume. Whatever view be taken of its permanent significance, *A Study* remains most important for our own day both in its own right and as a symptomatic historical document: 'this is how history looked'. To erudition on a scale rarely paralleled Toynbee adds the yet rarer gifts of style and of a massive architectonic grasp: the swing and sweep of the work compel admiration from the most antipathetic critics. Yet it is open—as work on such a scale must always be—to considerable criticism in detail. More important is its general outlook, that of liberal humanism in its later phase of not unnatural doubt, the phase in which it looks back to older and less rational (or less well rationalized) schemes of values to secure some footing in a morally anarchic world. This seems slippery ground on which to build so towering a structure.

To analyse *A Study of History* in full detail would be fascinating but pointless, since critics competent to do so would be better employed on their own syntheses. But it is of interest to examine some of the methodology and assumptions underlying the work, and in particular to examine Toynbee's handling of geographical factors, which form a not unimportant part of the argument, and on the whole perhaps the weakest. In general the writer is conscious of the acute disparity between himself and Toynbee—

> Well knowing that, a puny Jonah, I
> The great Behomoth of the Schools defy;
> Whose learning, logic, casuistry's so vast,
> He overflows the metaphysic waste,
> But yet I hope some darts of mine will stick,
> And that, like Jonah, I shall make him sick . . . .

In the field of the relations between physical environments and human cultures, however, he feels that he can meet Toynbee on not too unequal terms; and, as will be seen (whether the criticism is

Historical Studies: *Australia and New Zealand*, (University of Melbourne), vol. 5, no. 20, May 1953, pp. 324-337.

made out or not), this is of some significance in assessing, if not the validity, at least the use and interpretation of some of Toynbee's most striking concepts, notably that of Challenge-and-Response. The critical tone of this article should not be taken as a faithful reflection of the writer's total attitude to Toynbee; to draw attention to his many excellencies would be even more pointless than a page-by-page critical gloss, since those who run may read.[1]

I. THE METHODOLOGY

Toynbee's conception of what constitutes a 'civilization' is established in an introductory survey of the twenty-one societies, living and dead, which he considers as meriting the name. The ensuing discussion of the comparability of societies is a methodological vindication, by no means the only one but perhaps the most significant.

The core of the methodology is found in the section headed in the abridgement 'History, Science, and Fiction'.[2] A distinction is drawn between the legitimate 'elucidation and formulation of laws . . . where the data are too numerous to tabulate but not too numerous to survey' and 'the form of artistic creation and expression called fiction which is the only technique that can be employed or is worth employing where the data are innumerable.'[3] In the sphere of human relations, then, we have

innumerable examples of universally familar experiences. The very idea of an exhaustive recording of them is an absurdity. Any formulation of their laws would be intolerably platitudinous or intolerably crude. In such circumstances the data cannot be significantly expressed except in some notation which gives an intuition of the infinite in finite terms; and such a notation is fiction.[4]

---

[1]The first figure in references is to the pages of Somervell's abridgement, the second to the corresponding volume and pages of the original. For convenience and brevity direct quotation is from the abridgement, but in all cases the argument has been checked against the original. Tribute must be paid to the surpassing skill with which the abridgement has been made; there is of course foreshortening of the original argument, but only here and there, and never on a large scale, is there any essential difference; and that mainly verbal. On the other hand, to return to the original is to be dazzled once more by the encyclopaedic scope of Toynbee's treatment. One hardly wishes it shorter, and yet Somervell's compression suggests a certain *longueur* in Toynbee himself.

[2]43-47/I. 441-64, Annex to I. C. (iii) (e).

[3]The distinction between History, Science and Fiction is first presented as a popular view; in the original, ten pages are devoted to tracing it respectably to Aristotle and breaking down these 'popular equations', only to find that 'they do nevertheless approximate to the truth' (I.452), and are used as the basis of the discussion. The reader of Toynbee must sometimes be longsuffering.

[4]45-6/I. 452.

Yet sociology and psychology have fair claims to exist as sciences, not to be subsumed into an anthropology which deals only with primitive societies, which is the furthest concession Toynbee makes.[5] Their exponents may at times appear platitudinous and crude, but in this century to write them off, as Toynbee virtually does, is itself crudity. Moreover, rather too much is proved. Many subjects lie open to similar objections and yet are clearly susceptible of scientific treatment. The student of palaeontology, for example, meets 'innumerable examples' of 'universally familiar' cephalopods, and it would be absurd to think of cataloguing all the cephalopods which exist in museums, let alone those yet buried in the earth. Then there are, for example the permutations of mineral assemblages in igneous petrology, in which magmatic groups might be compared to the major human social groupings. It is true that within each 'species' of human reaction to circumstance the range of variation is far greater than that within each species of cephalopod; but the analogy may not be unrevealing. And are not many scientific generalizations in some degree at least statements in finite terms of infinite, or all but infinite and hence practically infinite, series? The last quoted sentence does not seem able to bear all the weight reposed on it.

A corollary is important. 'The quantity of institutional relations that are relevant to the study of primitive societies will be much greater than those relevant to the study of "civilized" societies, because the number of known primitive societies runs to over 650, and the civilizations are at most 21'.[6] 'Relevant' is of course subjective, and the statement may be doubted on the grounds that it overlooks the greater internal complexity of the civilizations with their enormous (and as it were shifting) mosaic of class, religious, economic, national, and social institutions. Their far greater range in space (individually), in time (of observable record), and in the number of individuals they include, gives room for a far greater range of permutations and combinations of personal and institutional relations than in primitive societies; it is surely the qualitative rather than the quantitative comparison which is significant and even so Toynbee's quantitative statements seem invalid. The difficulty is hardly got over by the dogmatic assertion 'the known number of "facts" of the highest order' is just the 21 and no more; 'of the highest order' rather begs the question. The implications of an earlier statement seem to be slighted: 'nearly all individual lives that are of sufficient interest and importance to make them worth recording have been lived, not in primitive societies, but in one or other of those societies in process of civilization which are

[5] 43/I. 447.
[6] 46-7/I. 445-46.

conventionally regarded as history's province'.[7] It is true that these are handed over *en masse* to biography, but one does not need to be a devotee of Carlyle's Heroes to admit that this partition is sometimes flimsy.

We may then feel that Toynbee lays himself open to two opposite objections: one, which he himself states, that it is risky to apply the scientific technique, 'the elucidation and formulation of laws', to a class of only 21 members; the other, that he underestimates the innumerability of his data in personal-institutional relations, which on his own showing are only susceptible of 'fictional' treatment. Hostile critics (but not, despite appearances, the present writer) might say that this is precisely what they get; but even were this true Toynbee is not without a tenable defence. It is true enough that 'it is hardly possible to write two consecutive lines of historical narrative without introducing fictitious personifications',[8] and beyond this all history worthy of the name must draw largely on the shaping spirit of imagination, in the etymological sense of the word. This hardly excuses, however, some of Toynbee's almost incredibly anthropomorphic personifications of societies. And the dilemma remains: either way some of the main theses of the book may prove to be precariously based.

II. Where the Method Leads

This methodological discussion ends with the assertion that *A Study of History,* is an attempt, admittedly risky, to apply the scientific technique; and certainly there is no lack of formulation and classification, of esoteric terminology and a general air of systematics. But these are the mechanics of scientific method, not its soul. The fact that Toynbee has a philosophy of history, which, for all its avowed empiricism, has at times an *a priori* aspect, has apparently been a stumbling block for some critics; but this reproach is beside the point. It is difficult to conceive of anyone being so foolish as to devote himself to so vast a synthesis without some preconceptions to start with; and however inadequate such philosophies may seem, the way forward is by trial and error, and to abandon the search is a counsel of despair. Even Toynbee's selectivity, so severely handled by Geyl,[9] might be admitted within limits; any philosophical history will almost inevitably burke some awkward facts and inflate others more convenient to the theme. As for inconsistencies, one is lucky to avoid them in an article, let alone six large volumes; and they are remarkably

---

7 44/I. 447.
8 44/I. 442-43.
9 P. Geyl, "Toynbee's System of Civilizations", *Journal of the History of Ideas,* ix (1948), pp. 93-124.

few and unimportant except for what may be termed the deliberate ones, when at the great crises of his argument Toynbee turns his back on 'science' and embraces intuition: in the discussions of the parallels between Hellenic 'Saviours' and Christ Himself,[10] of transfiguration,[11] and of the prospects of salving Western Christendom,[12] which by all Toynbeean laws broke down irretrievably generations ago. These will be regarded as beautiful but aberrant excrescences or as magnificent acts of faith, according to the reader's temper.

Toynbee's philosophy may or may not be acceptable *per se*: the real rock of offence to many (including the present writer) is the somewhat rigid schematism to which it gives rise. The sequences seem too good to be true, and at times they seem to be reached by a selective interpretation of the facts which goes rather beyond reasonable latitude. Again the formulae, Challenge-and-Response, Withdrawal-and-Return, and the like, fall too pat and become stock responses. For all the apparatus of scientific nomenclature, a larger part than the avowed method warrants is played by intuition, by brooding on myth, and by argument from analogy, surely the most dangerous of all the idols of thought. When we find Spengler's method denounced as 'to set up a metaphor and then proceed to argue from it as if it were a law based on observed phenomena',[13] our enjoyment of the epigram is tempered by a sudden vision of Satan rebuking Sin. A few examples must suffice; but before endeavouring to compile an anthology of apparent error, the writer would emphasize once more that if in some aspects *A Study of History* is a source-book for what Karl Pearson called 'a neglected branch of education—the study of fallacy in concrete examples', it is also very much more than that. Like Nature in Alfred Austin's poem, if Toynbee does indeed sin, he sins upon a larger scale because he is himself more large.

To begin with, the rich fund of illustration by anecdote and allusion has its own dangers, and at times its use seems almost disingenuous. Disputable points slip in as a lawyer slips in a prejudicial rumour: 'according to the legend' such-and-such 'is reported'—but then used as if it were undoubted fact, for example the destruction of the Alexandrian library.[14] This looks perilously like hedging, wanting the weight of the instance without openly affirming it. Arbitrary lay figures are set up and knocked down

[10]VI. 376-599, *ad fin.*
[11]526-30/VI. 149-68.
[12]554/VI. 312-21.
[13]248/IV. 11-13.
[14]518/VI. 111-12.

again, having been gratuitously provided with an aim suited to the argument but hardly proven.

We have repeated interpretations, often brilliant in themselves, which simply do not follow from nor bear out the sweeping idealist dogmas with which they are linked. Such is the discussion of technics and civilization,[15] which is not exactly in a vacuum but yet seems loose from its moorings. As a minor illustration we may note that, while the main idea of the discussion of Palaeolithic cultures[16] is just, the facts as presented are woolly or worse: the 'immense psychic revolution' of the supersession of Neanderthal man *was* in fact attended by very notable advances in technique, and we need not, indeed cannot, 'on the technological classification confound the sensitive artists' of the Aurignacian cave-pictures with the 'Missing Link', as Toynbee does.

There is, too, what appears to be a remarkable confusion between an idealist view of the springs of social action and the anthropomorphic praise or blame of societies *en bloc*. 'The source of action' in a society 'is never the society itself, but always an individual.'[17] Yet the arrested civilizations of Nomads and Eskimos have failed through 'the idolatrous worship of a technique. . . . Their single-track lives have condemned them to a retrogression towards an animalism which is the negation of human versatility.'[18] The imputation of free choice is really rather monstrous; these peoples find themselves in such and such an environment, in which by much effort they maintain remarkable cultures, and Toynbee himself of course pays a tribute to the great original achievement of planting and maintaining a human society in such environments at all. Yet, being there, how else can one live in a semi-desert but by shepherding, on the edge of the Greenland ice-cap but by hunting and fishing? And on the other hand, why should they abandon such signal gains in the struggle against hostile nature? Would not such defeatism be an even worse human retrogression? And in any case is there really so much evidence that Nomads and Eskimos are really so unadaptable? After all, neither group is monocultural and neither lives in a uniform environment. The classical igloo and the classical 'pure' nomad cultures were always restricted and are now dwindling; and that the changes in cultures implied by this have come by outside contacts is not to the point, since it needs no Diffusionist bias to recognize that such contacts have been among the primary factors of cultural change in practically all societies that have ever existed. A reading of Codring-

---

15 193-97/III. 154.174.
16 197/III. 172.
17 533/VI. 175.
18 327/III. 79-88.

ton and Febvre[19] suggests that for the Nomads at least it is Toynbee's view of them, and not their own way of life, which is single-track; and this despite the very real contribution which Toynbee makes in his long analysis of the great Nomadic incursions, their causes and their affects.

Yet Toynbee on occasion can be completely mechanist: 'On Marxian principles we must expect that, if a Russian peasant is taught to live as an American mechanic, he will learn to think as the mechanic thinks.'[20] About the works of his tractor, yes; but who proposes that he shall lead such a life? The tractors on a *kolkhoz* may be the same as those on a mid-West farm mortgaged to the local bank. Are the social life and organization the same? One does not need to be a Marxist to regard this an an over-simplification; the aim of the Five Year Plans was not just 'to transform the old Russia into a new America.' Of course Toynbee admits this verbally, but he regards—or regarded!—any ulterior motives as 'a strange dream to be dreamed by statesmen for whom a materialist interpretation of history is an article of faith.' But here he sees *only* technique, and not the whole socio-economic situation: the very ground on which he elsewhere disposes of economic determinism. Thus he rather unnecessarily asserts that the abandonment of Roman roads was not a cause of the break-down of the Roman Empire (but who is so simple-minded as to think it was?) and cites with approval Rostovtzeff's rejection of the economic explanation of the decline.[21] This was due to 'the failure of administration and the ruin of the middle class'; but if the latter is not economic (as well as social), what is?

The elasticity of the English language is not infrequently stretched to breaking-point. One ambiguity—the use of the word 'break-down' for the initial false step which sets a civilization *on the road* to breaking down—evokes a spirited defence from Somervell, from which 'it will be seen that, when the term is used in this sense, some of the most fruitful, illuminating, and celebrated achievements in the history of a civilization may come after the break-down, and, indeed, in consequence of it.'[22] Quite: one sees (with altogether undue effort) what is meant, but what would we say to a student who used plain English words with this Humpty-Dumptyish licence? And why not find some term, however

---

[19]See K. de B. Codrington, "A Geographical Introduction to the History of Central Asia', *Geographical Journal*, civ (1944), pp. 27-40, 73-91; L. Febvre, *A Geographical Introduction to History*, pp. 261-86.

[20]205-06/III. 200-02. 'On Marxian principles' is put in as a supplementary *argumentum ad hominem*, and not by antithesis to Toynbee's own view in this context.

[21] 256/IV. 41-42.

[22]274.

clumsy, which means what it says? But indeed Toynbee often indulges a penchant for Pickwickian usage:

> When in connection with Western civilization one sees a *pax oecumenica* assigned to the years 1797-1814 and 1528-1918, one is inclined to ask if words have the same meaning for professor Toynbee as for the rest of us.[23]

This wresting of language is sometimes combined with a wresting of the actual historical sequence to make it square with the formula; this is perhaps most strikingly seen in the discussion of England's 'withdrawal' from continental entanglements after the failure of the medieval adventures in France and the defeat of the Armada.[24] This has been faithfully dealt with by Geyl: 'The Glorious Revolution is indeed a fine example of the great deed which England was able to achieve by her seclusion! Have William the Third and his Dutchmen been forgotten?' Apparently so: there was indeed 'a partial and temporary return to the continental arena, under the brilliant leadership of Marlborough' (who doubtless commanded at Minden, Fontenoy, Vittoria, Waterloo, and the Crimea), but on the whole from 1588 to 1914 'the avoidance of continental entanglements was accepted, without further question, as one of the fundamental and perpetual aims of British foreign policy.'[25] One wonders what the elder and the younger Pitt thought they were doing. The aim may have been at times accepted, but rarely without question, and more often as a meaningless slogan which would go down well, though British statesmen (as distinct from the leader-writers of the *Daily Express* and their forbears) knew it for an impossibility in fact. On the few occasions when we did hold more or less aloof our isolation was not very splendid and at times perhaps enforced rather than sought; 'non-intervention' had an ugly ring long before the Spanish Civil War, in 1863-64 for instance, or in relation to James I and the Palatinate. In fact we avoided continental entanglements by the not very indirect method of intervening in nearly every major crisis and not a few minor ones; once more there seems a decidedly Pickwickian sense to be attached to the phrase 'withdrawal from the general life of Europe' or from 'the trammels of a regional society'. This holds for arts as for arms: can anyone really see the age of Dryden (or indeed of Shakespeare) as fitly summed up in such terms?

The recurrent Toynbeean device of shooting-up an Aunt Sally

---

[23]Geyl, *loc. cit.*

[24]235-39/III. 350-63 and 366-68.

[25]'This statement requires some qualification in regard to English foreign policy during the period A.D. 1689-1815' (Toynbee's footnote)—over a third of the total span. And, on a point of detail, why not twenty years earlier, the period of the Triple Alliance and its reversal?

is well illustrated, notably by his treatment of 'British' Diffusionism: the iteration of the adjective fits in with the general polemic against a narrowly occidental view of history (in itself absolutely correct) and is perhaps a little prejudicial. Toynbee's general refutation of Diffusionism is unexceptionable, and indeed common form; but the materialist bias ascribed to the Diffusionists is surely gratuitous. It is of course perfectly true that civilizations are not built up—solely—of such bricks as sewing-machines and rifles; nor is it the Diffusionist view that they are. Further, one cannot but feel that Toynbee's antithesis between the ease of exporting Western material techniques, as against the incommunicability of the spiritual flame of the Western poet or saint, is a little too facile. Has it not often been just the abstractions of thought and feeling which have most easily made the rounds? —goods undoubtedly of minimal bulk and possibly of highest value, to use the cliché of economic geography. One thinks of the rock of Tangtse, beside the hidden Tibetan lake Panggong, with its medley of Buddhist and Nestorian inscriptions attesting that faiths, more than merchandise, have been the traffic of these savage mountain ways. In our own day there is the wide acceptance of Aldous Huxley (for instance) in the East, or of Tagore in the West; and if these are thought rather dubious 'goods', is it not a commonplace that the true mystics, wherever found, speak like unto like, just because they are largely divorced if not from local colour at least from local mundane reality? *Ex Oriente Lux;* and conversely the greatest Tamil statesman of our day perhaps takes no less pride in his translation of Plato's *Apology* than in his place in the councils of his country. The ideologies suffer their mutations, of course, but so do the techniques; and in any case this is hardly the right end of the stick with which to beat the Diffusionists.

Finally, there is a fine promiscuity in the selection of authorities in fields other than Toynbee's own—and not necessarily subsidiary fields, since geography at least lies at the heart of much argument on the genesis of civilizations. The results are at times diverting. We find Mr. Gerald Heard described as 'a modern anthropologist', in what Toynbeean sense is difficult to determine since the passage cited[26] is an odd mixture of sociology and archaeology, though it contains, as Toynbee says, 'a finely imaginative touch' in describing Anglo-Saxon dykes as the frontiers of the Iceni. Mr. Heard turns up again as a sort of palaeo-biologist, suggesting (in Toynbee's words) that the 'armour which saved the primitive mammals *vis-a-vis* the dinosaurs 'was not physical but psychic.'[27] The truth in Heard's arguments is surely a common-

[26] 199/III. 183-4.
[27] 329/IV. 427.

place of evolutionary theory, but that it may not be the whole truth is suggested by the cloudy rhetoric in which it is embedded: the antitheses seem to be too pat to be more than half-truths. It is difficult to take entirely seriously 'the principle that life evolves by sensitiveness and awareness; by being exposed, not by being protected; by nakedness, not by strength; by smallness, not by size.'[28] Certainly these are elements to be reckoned with; yet if the development of a spinal cord and a brain is to be considered of any importance, we cannot entirely overlook the connection between increase of size in terrestrial animals and the strong vertebral framework which it called for. The dinosaurs, like the Eskimos and the Nomads, doubtless did stray into 'the blind alley of over-specialization'. One certainly cannot accuse Toynbee of ending in this particular *cul-de-sac,* but some of the addresses whence he gets information are in dubious streets, and he rivals the dinosaurs in bulk.

After Mr. Heard as a representative of almost everything, we have M. Demolins as the representative, presumably, of modern geography. His narrow determinism, which is probably subscribed to by no geographer of repute in his own country, by hardly any in Britain, and by very few in America, provides ample ammunition for a short annihilation of environmentalism.[29] But there are few modern geographers who have not played this same game, which has now become too easy; and Toynbee's failure to notice, let alone to understand, the outlook of modern students of physical environment[30] vitiates a part at least of the discussion of Challenge-and-Response, which cannot but rest largely upon a consideration of geographical factors. To these we may now turn.

III. TOYNBEE'S GEOGRAPHICAL CONCEPTS

At least 75 pages—about 13 per cent—of the abridgement are taken up by essentially geographical matter: the question of the relation between human societies and their physical environments. A general caveat might well be entered against Toynbee's cavalier approach: environmental questions have been studied in a scientific spirit for at least 150 years, since Humboldt; it is thus something of a shock to find as the chosen spokesman of environmentalism a Greek of the fifth century B.C.[31] Remarkable as the work of Hippocrates is, it is surely absurd to test the validity of a concept by analysis not of its developed forms but of one of the earliest

---

[28]What's wrong with earthworms?
[29]199/200/III. 193-4.
[30]Exception must be made for Ellsworth Huntington.
[31]In the writer's opinion this repudiation has gone too far, but there can be no doubt of its existence.

known statements of it, some 2,400 years old; we do not go to Lucretius for our views on atomic structure. Demolins has hardly enough weight to be worth citing as a witness; Huntington is more to the point, but his views are very largely repudiated by the present generation of geographers.[32] But in any case, as Gourou remarks, putting the questions as if environment created a human society is quite beside the point:

> Comment une civilisation supérieure, qui est un
> ensemble complexe de faits humains, pourrait-elle
> être produit par un milieu naturel qui est un
> ensemble complexe de faites physiques?[33]

We are invited to reject 'the popular assumption that civilization emerge when environments offer unusually easy conditions of life.'[34] Nothing is easier; very few, if any, serious students of environment would subscribe to so simple a view, which incidentally involves the assumption that 'easy' and 'favourable' are complete synonyms. The emphasis of modern geography is no opportunity and stimulus; nor are even the surviving determinists immune from this tendency. It is less easy to follow Toynbee in favour of 'exactly the opposite view'; hence 'stimulus' rather than 'challenge', though this is admittedly a mere matter of verbal emphasis. At the same time Toynbee's paradox itself leans rather far in a determinist direction:

> Le déterminisme des conditions défavorables au lieu de
> déterminisme des conditions favorables, est-ce un progres?[35]

In practice, of course, common sense breaks in, and Toynbee shrinks from his own extreme formulation: 'there is a mean range of severity at which the stimulus is at its highest, and we shall call this degree the optimum, as distinct from the maximum' severity.[36] Exactly; but does it really need these pages and pages of intellectual travail to produce so meagre a mouse? As Geyl puts it, a blow on the head may stimulate one to fisticuffs, but it may be so hard as to knock one right out; 'this has a less impressive sound, but does it not convey precisely the same meaning?'[37] It is fairly clear, without much research, that on an ice-cap or in a rainless desert no civilization is likely to arise since no human beings can permanently live there (on their own resources at least); and that if there were ever a Lotus-land which offered food and drink for the

---

[32] 55-6/I. 251-2.
[33] P. Gourou, 'Civilisations et Malchance Geographique', *Annales Economies Sociétés Civilisations* iv (1949), pp. 445-50, reference at p. 449.
[34] 80/II. 1.
[35] Gourou, *loc. cit.*, p. 446.
[36] 146/II. 260, 290-1.
[37] Geyl, *loc. cit.*, pp. 101-2.

asking (there never has been out of Eden) there would be no point in taking the not inconsiderable trouble of building a civilization.

Nevertheless, though the result be so jejune it may be that the way to it, if rather roundabout, is in itself worthwhile. And indeed it often is; the concept of 'old and new ground', for example, is most stimulating and admirably presented. But also the track lies through a tangle of misrepresentations of the physical facts on which, after all, the argument is based: misinterpretations serious enough to throw doubt on the validity of the conclusions, not mere slips. Fundamentally Toynbee is here writing as a geographer; without grasping the fact that a hundred square miles of marsh is not, from a human point of view, merely ten times ten square miles, but is qualitatively different, it is impossible to reach a right evaluation of the challenge provided and the response required. This sense, as fundamental to the geographer as the 'placing oneself in the movement' is to the historian Toynbee quite simply lacks. Moreover his view of the physical environment is a rule too narrow, confining itself in a given case to but one or two of the complex factors, climate, soil, location and the rest, which make up an environment. And he sees entirely non-existent uniformities, as when he speaks of the Eurasian Steppe as extending to the Arctic Circle.[38]

The treatment of the crucial case of the early Afrasian civilizations is not untypical. To establish the thesis that 'the special environment offered by the Nile in Egypt is the positive factor to which the genesis of the Egyptiac civilization is due' we must show that 'in every other separate area in which an environment of the Nilotic type is offered, a similar civilization has independently emerged.'[39] We might suggest that 'every' and 'independently' leave out important matters of location and timing, and indeed beg a lot of questions; but more decisive is the comparability (or even implied identity) of various riverine environments. The environmental theory is valid in the Euphrates-Tigris region, 'but it breaks down completely in the case of the much smaller but similar Jordan valley, which has never been the seat of a civilizazation.' In part probably simply because it *is* much smaller, not offering (were it otherwise favourable) the minimum base for the production of the large surplus necessary for the development of a civilization. But in fact the Jordan is far indeed from being just the miniature Nile which Toynbee thinks it. It rises in the lee of Lebanon, in an area with a rainfall of some 25 inches a year; but

---

[38]I. 254.
[39]58/I. 256.

this area is very limited, and Tiberias has only 18, while evaporation in the lower valley is equivalent to about 180 inches. It has only 1 per cent as much discharge as the Nile; the stream itself is sunk nearly everywhere between steep banks; the terraces above are in the lower half largely formed of disintegrated limestone, fertile soil but terribly thirsty; and (according to Zionist sources!) at least a third of the valley is 'ridged . . . entirely unsuitable for cultivation', while the soils in the lower third are highly saline. The contrast with the Nile flood-plain, enriched by the basaltic silts of Ethiopia, could hardly be more complete. Irrigation has been and is practised on a small scale here and there, mostly at the debouchments of tributary valleys; but the grandiose schemes for a Jordan Valley Authority rely on water from Syria or even the Mediterranean.[40] Above all, there is nothing in the least comparable to the annual Nile flood. Yet Toynbee can speak of the Jordan environment as 'the same' as that of the Nile, or as one 'in which the required conditions are fulfilled equally well on a miniature scale'![41] As a matter of fact, even the Euphrates-Tigris environment is only generically, not specifically, kin to the Nilotic.

Again we are told that 'the most captious critics cannot deny that the environmental conditions offered by Egypt and Mesopotamia are also offered by the valleys of the Rio Grande and the Colorado.'[42] One does not really have to be very captious. To begin with, hardly any of the basin of the 1,750 miles long Colorado has over 20 inches of rain; contrast this with the 40-80 inches of the Blue and White Nile catchments in Abyssinia and Uganda. The topography of the Nile and the Colorado basins is different in the extreme; the Colorado is much more broken, but there is nothing like the staggered series of tributaries above Khartoum, with the Blue Nile ponding back the White and prolonging the period of high water. The vegetation cover of the more humid parts of the Nile basin, and its lakes and marshes, are far more efficient regulators of run-off than the vegetation of the Colorado. In the Nile basin rainfall is either almost non-existent or falls fairly steadily in well-defined seasons; in the Colorado as a whole there is more rain than on the lower Nile, but much of it falls in irregular violent downpours, and erosion is intense. The Rio Grande approximates more nearly to the Colorado than to the

---

[40]'Whereas Egypt has 5,000 cubic metres of Nile water per inhabitant . . . Palestine has about 1,000 cubic metres from all its streams, springs, and water torrents, many of which are quite unusable.' (E. C. Willatts, 'Some Geographical Factors in the Palestine Problem', *Geographical Journal* cviii (1947), pp. 145-79: reference at p. 166). And in 1947 the population of Egypt was nearly 10 times that of Palestine.
[41]I. 257.
[42]58/I. 258.

Nile, though it is not a very close approximation. Neither the Colorado (obviously) nor the Rio Grande offers anything like the potentialities for navigation which are found on the Nile, with its peculiar advantage of the Etesian winds blowing upstream; and the role of the river as a highway (which Toynbee does not so much as mention) was only second to its value for irrigation in the development of Egyptian civilization. In both the Colorado and the Rio Grande there are doubtless some broad and general analogies to the Nile; but they are far from 'offering the environmental conditions' of Egypt, and the differences are very significant from the cultural point of view. The most fundamental are that the Nile has a unique advantage in its flood-régime, and that in its Nile basin 'the coarse stuff is caught in the sunken fault-block depressions into which the upper Nile flows' (the fine and fertile basaltic silt of the Blue Niles passes on) while 'the Tigris and the Colorado, fresh from the canyon, are ditch-chokers,'[43]

It may even be suggested that on the human side also Toynbee's comparison breaks down. The history of modern development in the Rio Grande and Colorado valleys is not one of 'miracles' but rather a melancholy story (until very recently) of reckless exploitation and bad planning, made worse by the violent changes of channel, from which the Nile is almost immune, owing to its peculiar physiography. The full irrigation possibilities of these American rivers have not yet been developed, and in places there has been actual abandonment of irrigated areas owing to silting and erosion consequent on overgrazing on the watersheds. And, even if the Pueblo culture was not autochthonous,[44] it had at least taken the first steps to civilization: 40 of the 150 miles of ancient canals in the Salt River valley are incorporated in the modern system, and the bold massing of the pueblo has been an influence, and not a bad one, on modern building in Arizona and New Mexico.

But it is in the attempt to reconstruct the primitive environment of the lower Nile that the lack of a sense of scale and the neglect of all the factors of environment except terrain (in a most limited sense) and vegetation are perhaps most strikingly shown. The reconstruction assumes that the lower Nile floodplain closely resembled the present condition of the great Sudd swamps of the White Nile around the Bahr-al-Ghazal.[45] With a remarkable

---

[43]J. Russell Smith and M. Ogden Phillips, *North America*, 1942 ed., p. 599, f.n. 16. The writer apologises for the technical detail in this section, but it seemed better to examine the evidence which Toynbee neglects rather than to offer a mere flat denial.

[44]I. 258. f.n.

[45]1/I. 302-15.

heroism the founders of the Egyptiac civilization met the challenge of desiccation by 'plunging into the forbidden Sudd'. Ecologically the marshes of Lower Egypt and the Delta may well have been similar to those of the Bahr-al-Ghazal today; but there was indubitably one difference of fundamental importance: size. The Nile flood-plain is only some 10-12 miles wide, and has firm sites as bases for settlement on either side; nor would it have been unknown to a fishing, hunting, and fowling ground to the inhabitants of the little valleys on the uplands which, as desiccation set in, became oases and perhaps thereby fostered the beginnings of settled agriculture. In any case, you can see right over it from the scarped valley-sides. On the other hand the vast marshes of the Sudd are 100 to 150 miles across in any direction. Obviously there is a difference in tractability between the two; on Toynbee's 'determinism by unfavourable conditions' one might expect the Egyptiac civilization to emerge from the Sudd proper. Moreover, the narrow view of environment which Toynbee takes leaves out of sight such an important factor as the presence of the Lower Nile, and the absence of the Sudd, of ample and excellent tool- and building-stone; not to mention, at a later stage, the readily accessible copper and other minerals of Sinai. Without these things it seems unlikely that there would have been an Egyptiac civilization.

Things are little better when we turn to the less debatable (because less ambiguously documented) North American continent in the colonial phase. Victory in the competition for exploiting rights went to the New Englanders, who had the hardest environment.[46] It is arguable, to be sure, that the victors were first Virginians and later New Yorkers, and in any case a whole host of factors is left out, among others the sort of support from and links with the metropolitan base, and the social factors involved in this. But the matter here is the environment. 'Taking all in all—soil, climate, transport facilities, and the rest—it is impossible to deny that the original colonial home of the New Englanders was the hardest of all.'[47] Once more, denial is a duty rather than a right. The climate of Lower Canada is far harsher than that of New England: open to polar air masses over the land, away from the moderating influences of the sea, the agricultural base of French colonization has January mean temperatures of 10-13° F., against 25-28° in New England. Summer temperatures are more relevant to agriculture: they are 64-68°, but the growing season is shorter: 120-150 frost-free days against 150-180. The amount of useful soil is more limited, and soils on the whole poorer than in New Eng-

[46]96/II. 65-73.

[47]99; cf. II. 70. The formulation is Somervell's rather than Toynbee's but it is warranted by II.70.

land. As for transport, it is true that the St. Lawrence is navigable for ocean-going vessels for 1,000 miles, as far as Montreal, but for four or five months of the year it is ice-bound; and above Montreal there are eight sets of rapids with a total fall of 226 feet before Lake Ontario is reached; and beyond lies Niagara. Climate, soil, transport: in every aspect the claim fails. But it is not even consistent: later[48] we find that New England is actually within the optimum climatic area of the eastern seaboard; in Maine we have diminishing returns, and the Maritime Provinces of Canada are worse still! This can hardly be squared with the preceding arguments; and if the Maritimes are themselves worse than southern New England, what are we to say of Quebec, with its far more extreme climate and relatively less good soil than New Brunswick and Nova Scotia.

It is hardly necessary to go into further detail. Throughout these geographical pages we find repeated failures to take into account the elementary findings of the study on whose subject-matter the argument rests. Locational factors, for instance, vital as they are, are often neglected; mere shapes on the map are married to the standard formulae: for instance, 'the challenge of the sea' in Japan, where in fact the sea was a moat defensive, opportunity, food, riches, almost anything rather than a challenge in the Toynbeean sense.[49] Again, it is consistently assumed that a landscape exploited and then abandoned by man simply reverts to its original condition: the 'latter-day wilderness' of the Roman Campagna 'has reproduced the pristine state of the forbidding landscape which was once transformed by Latin and Volscian pioneers into a cultivated and populous countryside.'[50] But the state of the Campagna in Livy's day or in ours is not evidence as to its state before it was settled by agriculturists; it is not very likely that it was any more 'dour' than most areas of central Italy. Within the time-span of civilized societies it is only rarely that anything like the original vegetation cover would succeed by reversion to natural processes after the balance of the natural climax vegetation has been destroyed; and indeed one might almost hazard the generalization that the last state of an area once tamed and then abandoned is more often than not worse than the first, for human occupancy.

Admittedly this is a specialist view, and it would be the height of unreason to expect all the arguments in so immense and wide-

---

[48] 147/II. 294.
[49] It may be noted that while the discussion of the culturally 'stimulating effect of a sea-crossing . . . in the course of a *Völkerwanderung*' is valuable, generally valid, and very well worked out, Toynbee can think of only six examples (104/II. 86-87). It is, perhaps, fairly clear why his six examples do not include one of the most obvious: the Vandals . . .
[50] 84/II. 17.

ranging a study to have equal weight of documentation and equal validity. But it can hardly be maintained that a discussion of environment is marginal to the problem of the origins of civilizations or to such themes as 'Challenge-and-Response'. In a matter so germane to so much of Toynbee's initial argument it is surely legitimate to suggest that more acquaintance should be shown with the work of those who have sought to unravel the complicated strands which link man to his home, the earth. Such geographers as he does quote—they number five—belong mainly to the determinist school whose findings are definitely not accepted by the great majority of modern geographers; yet the subject is not an esoteric one, nor are Humboldt, Reclus, Vidal de la Blache, Febvre, Mackinder entirely obscure names. Huntington, Hippocrates, and Strabo are essentially Toynbee's geographical authorities; is it too harsh to suggest that this is a lapse from the standards of scholarship?[51]

IV. Conclusion

It would be unfair to suggest that his exceedingly shaky geographical foundations invalidate Toynbee's general conclusions, dependent as these often are on sheer psychological analysis of impressively documented human situations. Yet it is perhaps symptomatic of a certain looseness or even recklessness of thought, displayed also in the too frequent reliance on argument from analogy.

To examine the psychological and philosophical bases of *A Study of History* would lead the writer into metaphysical heavens where his footing would be as unsure as is Toynbee's on the physical earth. But one may at least draw attention to the lapse from detachment when Toynbee considers the chance of survival for Western civilization. There is a conflict here between the demands of the seemingly inexorable pattern and the natural desire for a way out; in so far as *A Study* is scientific, all the marks of breakdown seem glaringly displayed, but by an act of faith there may be reprieve. But this act of faith, while certainly not insincere nor merely verbal, yet seems constrained: it is significant that even in the abridgement its discussion is couched in a rhetorical, almost apocalyptic, tone; eloquent prose, but one has an uneasy feeling that the structure is as stable as a house of cards. The more sober

---

[51]According to the index, Huntington has 26 citations, Owen Lattimore and Griffith Taylor 3, Demolins 2, Isiah Bowman 1. Of these Demolins hardly counts, Taylor is usually regarded as far too rigid a determinist, and Huntington as little better; though this is perhaps unjust. The index, though not quite complete, is remarkably thorough, even including passing quotations from Gray's *Elegy* and from *The Ancient Mariner*.

estimate of Geyl's concluding section seems infinitely preferable, offering a surer basis for action and unity.

It is, indeed, not very easy to discover what Toynbee really does believe in: in progress, but not in 'the superstition of Progress'; in reason, but not in rationalism; he blows hot and cold on liberalism; he is avowedly anti-determinist, and yet the general cast of his work is a necessitarian one; he stands perhaps for so nice a calculation of the golden mean, so careful a looking before and after, that the springs of action are relaxed. Really, it would be only fair to tell us what, finally, is his message; that he has one we can hardly doubt, or his massive work would be only a melancholy monument to nothingness, and it is assuredly not that. But doubtless this is to be the theme of the concluding volumes, though one may think it is already forshadowed in the sixth; and as for that, *credo, quia impossible.*

To those who cannot do this, who cannot accept brooding on myth and seductive analogy as substitutes for objective weighing of fact, Toynbee offers—and they are no trifling gifts—the sheer pleasure of reading him, an inexhaustible treasury of historic situations which as units are often magnificently analysed, an irritant stimulus to rethinking their own postulates. For these we must be grateful. But on the whole *A Study of History* appears to one reader, and perhaps to more than one, a house of many mansions, all imposing, many beautiful; but builded upon sand.

TOYNBEE AND SUPER-HISTORY*

WALTER KAUFMANN

Judged by low standards, *A Study of History* is an impressive
and often interesting work. Judged by the standards which color
Toynbee's judgment and have molded his performance, it is super-
colossal: a cast of thousands, ranging from churches and civilizations to the author and his family; ten volumes compared to Spengler's two; and forty-eight pages of "Contents," no more analytic
than the text but mystifying and titillating. Here is, as it were, a
screen larger than Cinemascope, and above all, entertainment
coupled with religious significance based on lots of research. This
research, to be sure, does not preclude amazing oversights and
errors, but the author is not writing for the historians who have
by now roundly condemned his work.[1]

For whom does he write? He writes for posterity, for generations centuries hence who will read him after all the other writers
of our time have long been forgotten. Again and again he takes
posterity into his confidence with words like these: "As for the
writer's use of the traditional language . . . he might say, for his
readers' information, that his regular and deliberate practice was
to continue to employ traditional language unless and until he could
find new words that seemed to him to express his meaning more
clearly and more exactly. In the writer's day the resources of
language were still utterly inadequate" (VIII, 421). But can the
inadequacies of Toynbee's style really be blamed on "the writer's
day"?

Sir Ernest Barker judges that Toynbee "writes English almost
as if it were a foreign language, in long periodic sentences, with
one relative clause piled on, or dovetailed into, another"; and he
adds: "The reviewer found himself tempted, again and again, to
break up and re-write the long rolling cryptic sentences: in particular he found himself anxious to banish . . . the 'ornate alias,'
and to substitute, for instance, the words 'St. Paul' for 'the Tarsian
Jewish apostle of Christianity *in partibus infedelium.*'" And A. J.
P. Taylor, the Oxford historian, remarks that "adjectives are piled
on with all the ruthlessness which the Egyptians used when building the pyramids."

Partisan Review, vol. 22, no. 4, Fall 1955, pp. 531-541.
[1]Pieter Geyl in *Journal of the History of Ideas*, January 1948 and April
1955; A. J. P. Taylor in *The New Statesman*, Oct. 16, 1954; Sir Ernest Barker
in *International Affairs*, January 1955; and *The Times Literary Supplement*,
Oct. 22, 1954, among others.

If we considered Toynbee as in the main a poet, such criticisms of his style would certainly be pertinent; but is he not really a historian? The enormous difficulty of doing justice to Toynbee is due to his determination to mix genres. If you find fault with him as a historian you are likely to be told that he is really a social scientist who is a pioneer in a new field and out to discover hitherto unknown laws; and it is only when his method has been shown to be a travesty of science that apologists are apt to say that he is a poet.

Today "integration" is popular, and its many spokesmen in our colleges sometimes overlook, as Toynbee does, that there is no special virtue whatever in a fusion of fanciful history with unsound science and poor poetry, even if it is spiced with ever so frequent references to God. The fallacy here is exactly the same which leads some people to suppose that five invalid proofs of God's existence are better than one valid proof. The answer to this infatuation with quantity has been given long ago in one of Aesop's fables: when a vixen boasted of the size of her litter and asked the lioness about the size of her's, the lioness replied: *hen alla leonta*, one, but a lion.

Let us then consider Toynbee first as a historian. I shall give two examples of his inadequacy, which could be multiplied at random; both are selected to obviate the objection that I am merely pitting my view against his or dealing with abstruse and remote incidents about which it is easy to make some small mistake. In both cases the author is dealing with material that is well known to millions of his contemporaries; and both demonstrate that he lacks the conscience of the sound historian.

The first example concerns Part X, which deals with "Contacts between Civilizations in Time" and is subtitled "Renaissances." On the first five pages we are told, with a wealth of metaphor, analogy, and simple repetition, that "in using the word *renaissance* as a proper name, we have been allowing ourselves to fall into the error of seeing a unique occurrence in an event which in reality was no more than one particular instance of a recurrent historical phenomenon. The evocation of a dead culture by the living representatives of a civilization that is still a going concern proves to be a species of historical event for which the proper label is, not 'the Renaissance,' but 'renaissances.' " There follows a Survey of Renaissances" in which these turn out to be a particularly repulsive form of necromancy—a word that is used scores of times, together with the metaphors which it invites. After Toynbee's indictment has taken up "Renaissances of Political Ideas, Ideals, and Institutions"; "Renaissances of Systems of Law"; "Renaissances of Philosophies" (five and a half pages of China and two and a half on Aristotle); and "Renaissances of Languages and Literatures" we finally do get to "Renaissances of Visual Arts" and *our* Renaissance. At this point I wonder how Toynbee will make good his indictment. You want to see what Toynbee will have to say about Leonardo, Michaelangelo, Titian, and a dozen others. But he can't quite spare five pages for "Renaissances of Visual Arts"; and though he indicts the Italian Renaissance, he simply does not mention Leonardo, Michaelangelo, Titian, or the other great painters and sculptors of the period.

I should not dream of challenging Toynbee's right to dislike these artists and should certainly find an intelligent critique much more to my liking than a conventional appreciation. As it happens, Toynbee is not at all interested in them, and in his whole ten volumes he has absolutely nothing to say about any of them. This too is his privilege, though it certainly diminishes his competence as a student of Western Civilization and raises grave doubts about his critique of renaissances—especially "of visual arts." But what is irresponsible and unjustifiable to my mind is that he should support his indictment of the Italian Renaissance by passing over in silence what does not readily fit his case.

The second example of Toynbee's lack of the historical conscience may be found in his discussion of "Contacts between Civilizations in Space (Encounters between Contemporaries)" which constitutes Part IX of his work. I shall confine myself to section 5: "The Modern West and the Jews." He begins not with the modern West but with antiquity, and after that spends some time on the Jews in Spain after the Visgoths and later under Muslim rule. This discussion should be most interesting, seeing that Toynbee has committed himself to all sorts of implausible theses in his earlier volumes: we must make civilizations the unit of study, he has said, because unlike nations they can be studied in isolation from each other; Western Civilization and Islam are two civilizations which are autonomous in this sense, and the Jews are a fossil (the word is his) of a third, so-called Syriac, civilization. What, then, will Toynbee make of the apparent fusion of these three civilizations? What will he say about Jehuda ben Halevy, Gabirol, and Maimonides' relation to scholasticsm? Alas, he does not so much as mention any of them. He might, of course, plead that he is mainly concerned with "The Modern West and the Jews," though in view of his implausible theses he ought to say something about events which seem to refute them so clearly. What, then, does he have to say about Spinoza? Again, not a single reference in 334 pages of indices. Perhaps Spinoza is not modern enough. What happens when we come to the nineteenth and twentieth centuries? What will Toynbee say about the remarkable behavior of this fossil after the emancipation, about the scores of Jewish scientists and thinkers, about the way in which the Jews suddenly entered into Western Civilization and made major contributions? Nothing, absolutely nothing. If medieval Spain does not fit his scheme, he ignores it; and if the Jews are a living refutation of his theories, attack is the best defense.

Toynbee tries to establish the word "Judaical," mainly by using it in this fashion, as a synonym of "fanatical" (by way of contrast with "the gentle and unaggressive ethos of Christianity"), as when he speaks, for example, of "a series of anti-Jewish enactments of a Judaically fanatical ferocity"—enacted by Christians, of course. Toynbee likes to use the epithet "Judaical" for elements of Christianity which he does not approve. If this prejudice, however unworthy of a historian among all people, is at least common, Toynbee also suggests, again and again that "Jew" and "businessman" —not to use a less polite term—are synonymous. This, coupled with his failure to mention in this context a single Jewish scholar, scientist, poet, philosopher, or artist, amount to a grotesque falsification of history and a complete perversion of the relations between "The Modern West and the Jews."

When he finally comes to "The Fate of the European Jews and the Palestine Arabs, A.D. 1933-48" and his thesis that "On the Day of Judgment the gravest crime standing to the German National Socialists' account might be, not that they had exterminated the majority of the Western Jews, but that they had caused the surviving remnant of Jewry to stumble," he shows as much contempt for history as any Hollywood director ever did. It is not the merits of Zionism that are at issue here. An intelligent and honest indictment always deserves a hearing, though what one has a right to expect from a historian is first of all an honest account of what happened. Such an account should make us understand what we previously failed to understand; it should enlarge our horizon and affect our prejudices and valuations.

Does Toynbee explain the origin of Zionism, with which he deals at great length? Decidedly not! But it is one of the great oddities of his work that he prints, in footnotes and appendices, critical comments by scholars who have read parts of his manuscript—and again and again these comments invalidate the text but are left standing without any reply by the author. In the present instance, James Parkes, a Gentile student of anti-Semitism, throws more light on the origins of Zionism in three lines on page 294, not to speak of his two-page "Annex," than does Toynbee in his daydreams and sermons in the text.

There is no reason why Toynbee should know a great deal about Zionism or Judaism; but as long as he does not, why does he insist on writing about both at such great length? The indices of volumes VI and X (which take care, between them, of all but the first three volumes) contain over four columns of references to the Jews, and a column apiece about "Judaism"—but not a single reference to Hillel or Akiba, not to speak of lesser men or such contemporary representatives as, for example, Buber.

Actually, the name of Hillel is mentioned once in Toynbee's indictment of Zionism: "The image and superscription of this new human coinage was not Hillel's but Caesar's." But a few sentences later, on the same page (311), he pontificates: "This mystical feeling for an historical Eretz Israel, which inspired the Zionist pioneers with the spiritual power to move mountains, was entirely derived from a diasporan orthodox theology that convicted the Zionists of an importunity which verged upon impiety in their attempt to take out of God's hands the fulfillment of God's promise to restore Israel to Palestine on God's own initiative." Clearly, Toynbee does not know one of Hillel's most celebrated dicta: "If I am not for myself, who will be? And if I am for myself only, what am I? And if not now, when?" Nor does Toynbee see the weakness of his own conception of religion, which would indeed turn it into a mere opiate by so unhesitatingly divorcing God's initiative from man's.

What is most unjustifiable is surely Toynbee's report to posterity about what happened in Palestine after the British left. In the text he gives the impression that the Jews did to the Arabs precisely what the Nazis had done to the Jews. In a footnote he belatedly admits that "the cold-blooded systematic 'genocide' of several million human beings . . . had no parallel at all in the Jews' illtreatment of the Palestinian Arabs." But they deprived of "their homes and property" and reduced to the status of "displaced persons" some 684,000 Arabs. In a note this figure is qualified and the Jews are blamed only for 284,000; but these "expulsions," we are told, "were on the heads of all Israel." Did they occur during a war or in the midst of peace? Toynbee does not say, but throughout he gives the consistent, if fantastic, impression that the Jews attacked innocent Arabs to vent the aggressive feelings acculated during their own persecution by the Nazis. That any Arab had ever fired a shot at a Jew in Palestine before 1948, or that the Arab states had declared war on Israel the moment the British had left their former mandate, and that the Jews were fighting a war in self-defense against armies pledged to exterminate them to the last man, woman, and child—all that is not only mentioned but brazenly denied by implication.

Judged by high standards, what the Israelis did may well deserve censure, as does, perhaps, our systematic bombing of civilians toward the end of World War II, not to speak of Hiroshima or, worse, Nagasaki. But those who are fighting for their life and liberty can at least plead extenuating circumstances. What can the historian plead who wilfully falsifies the history of events with which no man required him to deal?

So much for the historian. Surely, A. J. P. Taylor is too kind when he says: "Professor Toynbee's method is not that of scholarship, but of the lucky dip, with emphasis on the luck." But in a recent note on "What I Am Trying to Do," in the same issue of *International Affairs* in which Sir Ernest Barker offers his strictures, Toynbee tells us: "One of my aims in *A Study of History* has been to try out the scientific approach to human affairs and to test how far it will carry us."

What he proposes to show, as is well known by now, is that some twenty-odd civilizations exemplify certain patterns in their development. Taylor has suggested that Toynbee's scheme was, in fact, a generalization from classical antiquity: "If other civilizations failed to fit into this pattern, they were dismissed as abortive, ossified, or achieving a wrong-headed *tour de force*." This criticism is valid as far as it goes, but it does not bring out the full enormity of Toynbee's method.

In the first place, Toynbee's anthropomorphic conception of civilizations is superstitious: the question how many civilizations there are is like asking how many sciences there are, and the question when a particular civilization originated is on a level with the query when art began. Worse still, the conceit that civilizations are not only individual entities but the only units which can be studied historically one at a time, without referring beyond them, is the height of naiveté. Only a few completely isolated societies can be studied thoroughly without reference to other societies; but any unit whatever, whether a civilization, a nation, a city, a university, or a railroad, can be made the object of a historical study in which outside entities are introduced as sparingly as possible. Specifically, no "Syriac Civilization," for example, ever existed, though it may possibly be convenient in some contexts to lump together the many kingdoms that existed between ancient Egypt and Mesopotamia and to give them some such name as this; but this fictitious civilization could hardly be studied very fully without reference to its two mighty neighbors. It should be added that the untenable thesis that civilizations are the only self-contained "intelligible field of historical study," which Toynbee had argued with much rhetoric and little logic in the first fifty pages of volume I, is quickly, though not pointedly, abandoned at the beginning of volume VII.

Secondly, if you want to verify the presence of a certain pattern in the geneses, growths, breakdowns, and disintegrations of twenty-odd civilizations, the scientific approach would seem obvious. You have to consider your twenty-odd items in turn, admitting frankly where we either lack sufficient evidence or find what does not fit our pattern. But Toynbee spurns this approach. He finds his illustrations in nations and individuals, in Goethe's *Faust* and the New Testament; and he is not beyond illustrating the genesis or growth of a civilization from the fate of a nation, or even a small part of a nation, such as New England, during a period when the civilization to which it belonged was, according to Toynbee, breaking down and incapable of any further growth in any of its parts. His procedure, in short, is unsystematic and inconsistent in the extreme. In this manner no historical laws could possibly be established, even if there were any.

Toynbee's delight at finding several examples of this sort which fit, or seem to him to fit, into his scheme is generally increased by their waywardness. Thus he shows for some seventy pages how civilizations grow, by finding examples of "withdrawal and return" in the lives of Philopoemen, Leo Syrus, Ollivier, Clarendon, Ibn Khaldun, Kant, Hamlet, among many others. This sort of thing pleases him so much that he forgets altogether that, to take a single example, Kant, who perhaps lived a withdrawn life, never returned. That students went to Königsberg, which he had never left, is hardly a return; and even if it were, what would this prove about the pattern of the growth of civilizations?

That illustrations of this kind could be adduced at random for any theory of pattern whatsoever, Toynbee does not realize any more than that a truly scientific approach would require him to go out of his way to deal specifically with (1) evidence which on the face of it appears to contradict his theories, and (2) rival constructions of that evidence which, as *he* construes it, does fit.

Consider Part VI, on "Universal States," with which the last four-volume batch begins. It contains a lot of miscellaneous data, but no survey at all of Toynbee's twenty-odd civilizations. Instead of taking them up one by one, Toynbee offers such chapter headings as "The Doom of Tithonus" and "The Price of Euthanasia." To be sure, in this case he also offers a "Table" of "Universal States," reprinted without change from Volume VI. Now this table was criticized some years ago by Pieter Geyl in a brilliant essay on the fatal flaws of "Toynbee's System of Civilizations"—an essay which was reprinted in a book, *The Pattern of the Past*, together with the text of a debate between Toynbee and Geyl. Geyl is passed over in silence in the last four volumes. The only major critic with whom Toynbee deals at length, in a very amusing "Annex" which, however, shows no understanding at all of his critic's position, is R. G. Collingwood. But to return to the fatal Table:

Geyl had called attention not only to the triteness and vagueness of Toynbee's so-called laws but also to the startling fact that, according to this Table, there was universal peace in Western Europe from "A.D. 1797-1814," and in the area of "The Danubian Hapsburg Monarchy A.D. 1526-1918." Yet Toynbee did not see fit to revise these claims; his system takes precedence.

Confronted with this sort of thing, it has become customary to say that Toynbee is really a poet. But is that not rather like saying that Cecil B. De Mille is a poet? The Napoleonic wars don't fit, so Toynbee rewrites history. And how much De Mille there is in such a sentence as this: "In the field of encounters in the Time-dimension an Antaean rebound that wins from Necromancy an anticipatory communion with the Future has its antithesis in an Atlantean stance in which a Necromancer who has yielded to the legendary Epimethean impulse of Lot's wife is petrified by the hypnotic stare of a resuscitated corpse's Medusan countenance into the rigidity of a pillar of salt pinned down by the incubus of the Past" (LX, 363).

Is Toynbee really a poet? Toynbee himself says: "As a consequence of his fifteenth-century Italian education, the writer's spiritual home was, not a post-Christian Western World, but a pre-Christian Hellas; and, whenever he was moved to put his deeper and more intimate feelings into words, they found expression in Greek or Latin verse, and not in the English vernacular that happened to be his mother tongue" (IX, 411). Indeed, Volume I and VII begin with two long poems written, respectively, in Greek and Latin; but "intimate feelings" are also expressed frequently in the vernacular of the text, in which the author feels less at home. But is it poetry when the author informs us, after giving a reference in a footnote: "My aunt Gertrude's copy, with my name written in it in her handwriting, dated 'September 1906', is here on my desk in May 1951"? Or doesn't it seem to come straight out of a movie? And there are a great many similar passages.

Surely, people begin to think of Toynbee as a poet only where he has raised other expectations and then failed to fulfill them. At the end of Part XI, for example, after well over 200 pages on "Law and Freedom in History," one expects some resolution of the conflict between those who affirm and those who deny the presence of laws in history. But Toynbee concludes:

> Since the God who is Love is also Omnipotence, a soul that loves is liberated by the maker and master of all laws from a bondage to the laws of the Subconscious Psyche which Babylonian souls used to project on to inexorable stars in their courses and which Hellenic souls used to personify as malignant *kêres* and daimones; and a liberating truth which had once proved

potent to set free (John VIII. 32) fast-fettered Hellenes and Babylonians might once again be taken to heart by the children of a post-Christian World which had been vainly seeking to ban those dread psychic principalities and powers (Rom. VIII. 38; Eph. III. 10 and VI. 12) in the name of a Science that was impotent to exorcise them as any pre-Christian magic.

I have moved the footnotes into parentheses and might add that probably more than half of Toynbee's footnotes are of this nature. But is this poetry or merely murky?

It might be suggested that Toynbee is really a theologian. In this capacity, however, I should rank him with the friends of Job. To vindicate the justice of God, he regularly infers, as they did, that misfortune is a proof of a prior moral transgression. From the destruction, apparently by external force, of the Central American Indian civilizations, Toynbee infers that they deserved their fate. Evidence to the contrary does not deter Toynbee. Thus he speaks, for example, of churches which "committed spiritual suicide by going into politics" and forfeited the chance of "playing a church's authentic role"; and he continues: "Cases in point were the syncretistic Egyptiac Church . . . Zoroastrianism, Judaism, Nestorianism, and Monophysitism, which had allowed themselves to be used by a submerged Syriac Civilization as weapons in its warfare against a dominant Hellenism." Elsewhere, too, Toynbee sharply condemns the Jewish uprisings of 135 A.D. But, I wonder, did not Islam and Christianity go into politics and wage wars—and not merely to defend a threatened way of life, but aggressive wars? No, says Toynbee in the very same passage from which I have just quoted: "Islam alone had partially succeeded in retrieving a false step into which it had been led in its infancy by its Founder." (VIII, 532) Islam has flourished; so Toynbee infers, after the manner of Job's friends, it must have been virtuous. And when our gentle scholar comes to the Crusades, only thirty-five pages after his indictment of the Zionists, he develops all the enthusiasm of a Sunday-morning quarterback as he pictures the victories that might have been, if only the Crusaders had followed his strategy.

In his footnotes Toynbee carries on a prolonged theological discussion with one Martin Wight, a Christian, who eventually draws from our author an admission that he is no longer a Christian. Toynbee's position is developed in an "Annex" on "On Higher Religions and Psychological Types." The types are those of Jung (Freud is not listed in any of the indices), and the "higher" religions are the four with the largest following. Toynbee's religious outlook also finds expression at the end of Part XIII (the last Part of his work) when, after piling up quotations in different languages for several pages, he concludes with a long prayer of his own which alternates between Latin and English. I quote two of its twenty stanzas:

> Sancta Dei Genetrix, intercede pro nobis.
> *Mother Mary, Mother Isis, Mother Cybele, Mother Ishtar,*
> *Mother Kwanyin, have compassion on us, by whatsoever name*
> *we bless thee for bringing Our Savior into the World.*

It would be hard to guess whom this will offend more: Catholics or Protestants? But if hitherto syncretism usually meant an attempt to offend no religion, consider Toynbee's bow to Islam:

> Sancte Petre, intercede pro nobis.
> *Tender-hearted Muhammad, who art also one of the weaker*
> *vessels of God's grace, pray that His grace may inspire us . .*

For any who might wish to commemorate the event, Toynbee finished this prayer in "London, 1951, June 15, 6:25 p.m., after looking once more, this afternoon, at Fra Angelico's picture of the Beatific Vision."

Immediately before this prayer, Toynbee refers the reader twice to the New Testament, but understandably not to those words in the Sermon on the Mount: "But thou, when thou prayest, enter into thy closet, and when thou hast shut thy door, pray to thy Father which is in secret. . . . But when ye pray, use not vain repetitions, as the heathen do: for they think that they shall be heard for their much speaking."

Toynbee's religiousness, like the rest of his work, has something of Hollywood in it: it is spectacular, has a huge cast, and is, for all its ostentatious humility, charged with self-importance. And his conceit is essentially different from the self-stylization of Socrates in his Apology or of Nietzsche or Shaw. It is more like that of a movie star: there is neither sarcasm in it nor any discrimination between what is representative and what is trivial. In the first two indices, little space was given to the author, and hardly more to God. In the new index both have attained to two whole columns, and many references to "Toynbee, Arnold Joseph" are on the level of "walking, liking for."

There are of course many good things in these volumes, including not only some of the contributions of Toynbee's critics, which he had the good grace to print, but also occasional thought-provoking judgments, many fascinating quotations and observations, and several good anecdotes. More's the pity that it all does not add up to a great work. Far from being more scientific than Spengler, whom he calls a "pontifical-minded man of genius," Toynbee is more pontifical, less original, and endowed with an essentially eclectic and digressive mind. What suggests the possibility of greatness in Toynbee's case is mainly the lavish expenditure and sheer size of his undertaking. Beyond that, the fashionable taste for a mixture of almost any kind of religion with erudition has helped to make Toynbee one of the idols of our new illiteracy.

This illiteracy does not know the distinction between erudition and scholarship, between irresponsibility and poetry, between assurance and evidence. One reads Toynbee's indictments and is impressed by the wealth of footnotes, and one does not notice that they sometimes refer to nothing but other passages in which the same unfounded claim is made, supported by similar cross-references—or that a spectacular figure is cut down to less than half its size in a note; or that a splashy fifty-page claim is unostentatiously dropped in a few sentences, much later. In an age in which similar techniques beset us so sorely, the scholar bears a greater responsibility than ever. I have no quarrel with the virtues Toynbee advocates. "The voice is the voice of Jacob, but the hands are the hands of Esau."

THE PROFESSOR AND THE FOSSIL*

FREDERICK E. ROBIN

Ask the literate man-on-the-street to name a famous psychologist and he might answer, Freud. Asked to name a physicist, he might choose Einstein.

Ask him a year or two hence to name a famous world historian and he might well reply, Toynbee. For the sixty-six-year-old English historian, Arnold Toynbee, resembles those two great system-builders to this extent: He shares their talent for capturing public imagination with a system whose dazzling complexity is admittedly too much for most of its admirers.

Few historians devote twenty-seven years to creating a ten-volume *Study of History* that seeks, in the author's own words, "to use our knowledge of history as a telescope-lens for taking a look at the universe as a whole." Even fewer historians have known the distinction of having such an opus—while still uncompleted—popularized as a one-volume best seller—an event that occurred in 1947 to Toynbee.

This exploit has its significance. Public acclaim of Einstein, and to a lesser degree, Freud, came as a result of their tremendous impact upon their professional colleagues. Toynbee, paradoxically, is vaulting over a rather cool reception from his fellow historians to enjoy the adulation of influential American liberals and intellectuals. His overpowering erudition is conceded by even his severest opponents, who envy his wealth of knowledge while rejecting his conclusions. One such critic wrote: "I could not help feeling an admiration . . . bordering on amazement or awe, for the tremendous intellectual energy . . . juggling with the events, the crises, wars, revolutions, state-formations, religious manifestations of all centuries and races . . ." Yet Toynbee is no mere academician. His views have been featured in *The New York Times Magazine* and reprinted in the forceful medium of *Reader's Digest*. He was saluted as "The Master, if not the Father of Universal History," by Lewis Mumford last year in *The New Republic*. "One of the greatest living historians," editorialized *The Saturday Review*. *Time* and *Life* have delivered similar eulogies.

In his massive superstructure of twenty-one civilizations and six major religions, what image of Jews and Judaism does he forge for future generations to read?

Committee Reporter (New York), vol. 12, no. 6, Oct.-Nov. 1955, pp. 1, 7-8.

Four arresting concepts are the key to Toynbee's views:

Judaism is "a fossil."

Bigotry is essentially a Jewish invention introduced into Christianity and Islam. Christianity was "betrayed" into bigotry by "Judaic fanaticism" or "intolerance."

The creation of Israel is an "act of impiety," by the standards of the Jewish religion itself; a "dangerous archaism" by historical standards.

Arab-Israel conflicts are "a perversely predestined catastrophe," a "supreme tragedy" wherein the Jewish fall from grace exceeded the "moral nadir of Nazism."

Those recurring themes run through the ten volumes. They form a small but potent aspect of Toynbee's vast system. But in a 41-page section of Volume 8, Toynbee rivets them into one structure with a blinding display of curiously selected incidents, and unproved assertions.

Toynbee sees Judaism as a "fossilized relic of a civilization that was extinct in every other shape." Jews managed "to survive the loss of their state and their country . . . by improvising a new social cement." This was developed out of "their heritage of religious law." Thus evolved the Jewish ethos—"a meticulous devotion to Mosaic law and a consummate virtuosity in commerce and finance."

Having reduced a living religion to a "fossil," Toynbee finds that Judaism has made unique contributions to Western civilization. He pays tribute to "its discovering of a single Divine Being" and "concepts of Love and Charity." But then Toynbee the professional historian is engulfed by Toynbee the zealous prophet. His indictment of Judaism, delivered with the prestige of a man rated by some widely read American magazines as among the greatest historians of the 20th century, refurbishes an ancient dogma for the condemnation of Jews. As "a student of history," he makes this theological judgment:

> The error of the Jews is exposed in the New Testament . . .
> a fatal error of looking upon a momentary spiritual eminence as
> a privilege conferred upon them by God in an ever-lasting
> covenant.

His most singular charge is that the Jews launched bigotry.

> The abuse of political power for the inhuman purpose of imposing on a subject minority a choice between abandonment of its
> ancestral religion and the extreme penalty of banishment or even
> death had been practiced by the Jews against their Gentile neighbours in Syria seven hundred years before they themselves had
> been confronted with the same choice by the Visgoths in the

Iberian Peninsula. The earliest known instance of 'bigotry' is the compulsory conversion of the conquered Gentiles of Galilee to Judaism by their Maccabean Jewish conquerer Alexander Jannaeus in the first quarter of the last century B.C. . . . . and the Maccabean temper was inherited by Christendom from a Jewry that came to be the principal victim of this Jewish vein in the Christian religion.

The fact that the charge against the Maccabeans rests on a single reference—Joseph Flavius (1st century A.D.), and even if true, was preceded by similar tragedies in Near Eastern history does not deter Toynbee from insistently characterizing such treatment as "Judaically inspired." For example, certain Visgothic laws, in the 6-7th century Spain, are called "anti-Jewish enactments of a Judaically fanatical ferocity." A temporary decline in the mutual persecution of Protestants and Catholics is called the "damping of a Judaic flame of religious fanaticism."

In a published reply to one of his critics, Toynbee condensed his astonishing thesis into this blunt sentence:

> The irony of Jewish history surely is that the Jews have been the chief sufferers from a spirit which they themselves originally kindled.

Toynbee views with horror the State of Israel and the Zionism out of which it was born. A measure of his attitude toward the former lies in this characterization of the average Israeli:

> the child of the diaspora was no longer recognizable. The image and superscription on the new human coinage was not Hillel's but Caesar's. The Janus-figure—part American farmer-technician, part Nazi *sicarius* [Latin: a dagger-wielding assassin]—was of a characteristically Western stamp.

For all his careful efforts to depict the creation of Israel as "an act of impiety," Toynbee's real argument against it stems from his deep-seated conviction that nationalism is baneful. Thus Israel "in its diminuitiveness, its fanaticism and its Ishamelitish enmity with its neighbours"—was a faithful reproduction verging on parody, "of the Modern Western national state." He puts the blame for its creation primarily upon England but also America, specifically on American Jews. The latter, he says, were fearful lest their own security might be jeopardized by the admission of many Jewish DP's to America.

It was a misfortune, for both Jewry and the World, Toynbee concludes,

> that this statement . . . should have seen the light at a moment when it might be hoped that the species of community of which this was the youngest member was at last approaching its eclipse.

This passage indicates how a prophet's mantle can become a blindfold. Israel is but one of more than a dozen new states that have been born since World War II. Far from facing an imminent demise, in the last decade modern nationalism has brought a measure of independence to more than 625,000,000 people—about a fourth of the world's population—in these nations: Lebanon, Syria, Laos, Vietnam, Cambodia, Jordan, Philippine Republic, Indian Union, Korea, Indonesia, Libya. And while nationalism has certainly not been free of much evil and bloodshed, surely it has given to many millions in recent years—and will give to many more—their first taste of freedom, dignity and human-rights.

Toynbee's remaining judgment about the Arab-Israel conflict is almost startling in its unrelieved severity. There are no shades of gray, no references to the United Nations' role or to Arab declarations of war against Israel, no balancing of claims. Toynbee declares that it was the Jews' "supreme tragedy . . . to imitate some of the evil deeds that the Nazis had committed against the Jews." In this and similar extraordinary declarations, Toynbee, as a moralist, equates 850,000 Arabs existing, to be sure, in squalor among their own kinsmen, but nevertheless alive, with the 6,000,000 Jews who died in crematoria and gas chambers in the cruelest episode of all history. He recognizes the guilt of the Nazis was solely and irrefutably theirs. Yet as a historian, he closes his eyes to the verifiable fact that at least a portion of the misfortune of the Arab refugees is caused by Arab leaders who exploit that plight.

To paraphrase Shakespeare, the evil that ideas do lives after them. Our immigration laws bear the racist stamp of the 19th century Frenchman, de Gobineau. In Germany, Nietzsche's rejection of Judeo-Christianity's "slave ethic" was blended with the pseudo-scientific racial theories of de Gobineau's student, Houston Stewart Chamberlain—"the Kaiser's anthropologist." This brew, fortified by Sombart's economics, was the intellectual yeast of Nazism.

There could be another dark legacy if the pronouncements of Toynbee the theologian-prophet should pass unscrutinized, accepted as carefully measured historical truths. Should his stigmatizing treatment of Jews gain credence, it may become transmuted from a theoretical anti-Judaism into an intellectually rarified anti-Semitism, however abhorrent anti-Semitism undoubtedly is to Toynbee. It may gain standing, if unchecked, because of Toynbee's preeminence—because it is interwoven with a liberal Christian theology, a scorn of nationalism and an earnest desire for the true brotherhood of Man, all set forth with an erudition that may prove vastly appealing. If, for want of critical review and discernment, these views become popularized and distorted in the course of ever-widening spread, they may be cultivated assiduously by coarser hands, ultimately to be reaped as a terrible new hate.

THE TOYNBEE HERESY*

Abba Eban

I come before you tonight not in any diplomatic capacity but rather as a student of history and letters, seeking a brief respite from the claims of contemporary affairs. The subject before us is however not unrelated to the urgent issues of Israel's destiny; and I do not feel that I am deserting the immediate arena in favor of an ivory tower of academic detachment. The place which Israel occupies in the pride and love of our generation has not been won solely by the achievements of this decade. It is an eminence earned largely by historic repute. The emergence of modern Israel is an event conceived in the highest dimensions of history. It is the result of one of the most tenacious passions in the records of human action. It marks a triumph of faith and will over the calculations of rational chance. It symbolises the survival, and perhaps the renewed fluorescence of mankind's oldest culture. More than any other national revival in modern times, it has been a primary theme in the moral history of a whole generation, sharply contested, agitated, and discussed as a theme of conscience, as well as of international politics.

Thus if the bright image of Israel's resurgence is distorted, if this historic process is held up to ridicule, if the stature of this event is degraded—if our new birth of freedom is portrayed as a squalid and bloodthirsty conspiracy, then Israel loses a priceless asset of her security and honor. There is no state in the modern world whose progress has been more dependent on idealistic and moral postulates. A response to an assault upon Israel's historic repute is thus not a mere exercise in academic controversy. It affects the very essence of Israel's destiny in life and thought.

It is against this background that I come to discuss a view of Israel's history which has recently been proclaimed with the authority of an impressive name in contemporary scholarship.

In order to define and rebut the heresy, it is necessary to recall the orthodox historiography from which the heresy deviates.

The Traditional View

The writers of Jewish history portray the national experience of a people in a continuous narrative of four thousand years. The

---

*This is the full text of an address delivered by Ambassador Abba Eban at the Israel Institute-Yeshiva University (Amsterdam Ave. & 187th St., New York City) on January 18, 1955.

experience in antiquity is well-documented and preserved, clad in the raiment of superb literary artistry, articulate and coherent in all its parts, and drawing substantive confirmation from the recent discoveries of archaeology. At the center of this experience stands the revelation to Israel of a concept of history in terms of progress. This people of shepherds and farmers, in a small country on the shores of the eastern Mediterranean, evolved ideas of startling originality which have remained an unattainable standard for mankind across the gulf of generations. First came the doctrine of the moral choice. The pre-Jewish civilizations were gripped by religions of fatalism, determinism and resignation. They saw human life in relentless cycles coming back to a starting point in darkness and chaos. They denied the concept that the will and conscience of man governed the world's future. Mysterious and inscrutable forces of Nature or of Supernature disposed of human destiny by arbitrary and superstitious laws. Man was the passive object, not the conscious agent of historic processes.

Against this determinism and resignation there arose the revolutionary concept of Judaism in the realm of the individual conscience: בחור בטוב ומאוס ברע. The capacity of choice between good and evil could determine the destiny of human life, in accordance with a coherent system of moral thought. This concept of the power of moral choice was the authentic and original contribution of Judaism to the question of purpose in individual life.

The societies which preceded the Jewish Kingdoms were dominated by concepts of permissible exploitation. Man was helpless against the adverse forces of Nature and against the cruelties of his innate avarice. Against the doctrine of social resignation, there arose the Hebrew idea of social justice. The primary theme was Thou shalt love they neighbor as thyself ואהבת לרעך כמוך. From this notion of solidarity in human relations came the concept of moral law applicable to societies, as well as to individuals.

Spreading out into its third circle of influence, the Hebrew ideal attacked the prevailing concept of war as a natural state of the universe, a part of mankind's very nature and character. Three thousand years ago the Prophets proclaimed the doctrine of universal peace. Nation shall not lift up the sword against nation, neither shall they learn war any more.

These were the triple foundations of the Hebrew ideal: individual morality, social justice, universal peace. Historians have portrayed their development as illustrated in the experience of a people who, believing themselves to be the responsible custodians of these ideals, conserved their integrity and union even against the disparate forces of dispersion and exile. They conserved this union and identity not for their own sake, but in order to maintain trusteeship over these revolutionary ideals. The narrative goes on to describe the break-up of the Jewish Kingdoms, the dispersion of its citizens, and the subsequent struggle to preserve a sense of nationality and spiritual mission without the political and territorial attributes of statehood.

THE DOCTRINE OF RESTORATION

In every appraisal of Jewish history particular attention has been devoted to the doctrine of Restoration. With unique tenacity this people maintained the theory of its exile as a temporary state to be succeeded by a reunion between the people, the land and the language out of whose original coalescence the Hebrew revelation was born. True, the Jewish people continued its creative course in many scenes and capacities after the loss of national independence. But the fact remains that it was in conditions of separate national independence in Israel that the Hebrew mind rose to levels of creativeness which it never subsequently attained.

The restoration is described by Jewish historians both as a Divine will and as a human duty. The Divine promise decreed that this people should be restored; it was, therefore, its own duty not only to dream but also labor for that redemption. As Jewish history enters the eighteenth and nineteenth century, the doctrine of the Restoration assumes concrete form as a response to homelessness. The absence of an independent physical center for the Jewish people results in the danger both of physical extinction and of spiritual assimilation. The problem of survival is seen as a function of Israel's capacity to emerge from the handicap and reproach of homelessness. This theme dominates Jewish history at the turn of the century, when Zionism becomes the central collective purpose of the Jewish people. Finally there comes the great crescendo, a symphonic climax with overtones of tragedy and grandeur, of horror and salvation. The deepest agony is succeeded by the sudden illumination of hope. The massacre of Jewish communities in Europe is followed, within a single decade, by an act of salvation through the restoration of Israel's sovereignty, the salvage of its authentic personality and the assurance of its national and cultural survival. This last climax, a fantastic transition from the depths of paralyzing weakness to new peaks of sovereign opportunity, is played out on a broad universal canvas with the international conscience actively engaged. Twice within a single decade the world tribunal recognises the right of the Jewish people to the restoration of its homeland. The recognition itself creates new incentives for the renaissance.

The themes which I have described in very broad and, therefore, approximate strokes, do not vary considerably between the work of one historian and another. Jewish historians naturally stress the undying validity of the original Jewish heritage, while Christian scholars see their own civilization evolving in progress from the Judaic ideal. But even the writings of most Christian historians pay pious tribute to the affirmative qualities of the Hebrew spirit and to the unique achievement of Jewish survival. They, too, revere the Hebrew tradition as the parent source of their own Christian civilization. As apostles of faith and opponents of determinism, they rely upon Israel's resurgence as a striking lesson in the potency of the human will. A dream which had no ostensible prospect of realisation was carried to fulfilment against all calculations of material chance. There had seemed to be no historical prospect a few decades ago that this people could establish its sovereignty in a land coveted by more powerful nationalisms and imperialisms; that it could overcome the diversive factors of its exile in a measure sufficient to restore national unity; that it could revive the original medium of its culture; or that it could secure international recognition of the link between the Jewish people and its ancient homeland —a concept which a short time ago had no place in the jurisprudence of nations. In these circumstances, any historian of unprejudiced insight would see Israel's rise as a vindication of the spiritual impulse in human history, a crushing argument in the eternal discussion between the advocates of faith and the adherents of materialistic or deterministic doctrines of history which deny the human will any status as a governing factor in human destiny.

I have stated some of the orthodox attitudes in Jewish historiography. They are not free from challenge or controversy. It is not difficult to find moments, or even whole generations, in which this people fell short of its elevated standards. There are those who argue that other current of human thought overtook and broadened the original insights of the Hebrew mind. It is possible to advocate but not possible to prove this theory of improvement. But a generally affirmative approach to the history of the Jewish people can be discerned in all but the most eccentric historical writing until Toynbee. Indeed, the attempts to discredit the Jewish historic process have, until this year, been confined to those who have sought an academic rationalisation for religious or political hostility.

SIGNIFICANCE OF TOYNBEE'S REVOLT

We cannot, therefore, fail to regard Professor Toynbee's analysis as a significant event in contemporary scholarship. Here we have no partial or selective criticism of the Jewish historic performance. We have an almost total negation of anything affirmative in the entire record. The attack is not alone upon the credit of contemporary Israel. There is a vehement assault on the antecedents of modern Israel reaching back into the mists of antiquity. Rising up in revolt against orthodox history, Professor Toynbee, in a grandiose framework of a study of the rise and fall of civilizations, presents the story of Israel over thousands of years as a grotesque psychic aberration leading to a squalid tragedy of historic injustice.

THE FOSSIL THEORY

The Toynbee thesis begins with the picture of a "Syriac community" which recognizes the supremacy of "a provincial and jealous god" marked by fanatical vengefulness and exclusiveness. There is something in this provincial and jealous god, perhaps the very ferocity of his exclusiveness and fanaticism which gives him supremacy in his contemporary world of ideas. But soon, everything which is of affirmative value in the Hebrew concept of divinity is inherited by the higher religion of Christianity, thus leaving the Jewish mission fulfilled and exhausted.

In this part of Professor Toynbee's writing there is a marked reluctance to recognise any ideas as authentically Jewish, except the quality of fanaticism. This is singled out as the most typical of all the Hebrew qualities. Indeed, the Jewish people is awarded the original copyright. Whenever there is a description of extreme brutality, it is described as being "Judaic" in character. The persecutions of the Visigoths are portrayed as being of typically "Judaic" fanaticism, and Professor Toynbee finds no records of religious persecution before the Maccabees, who thus became the historical parents of forcible proselytism.

There is a reluctance, if not a refusal, to recognise divine and human love as indispensable and central themes of the Hebrew tradition. The domination of love is represented as a spectacular deviation achieved by Christianity from the original concept of the provincial and jealous god. The three circles of Hebrew morality—individual conscience, social justice and universal peace—would not present themselves at all to any reader dependent on Toynbee for his insight into the essence of the Hebrew ideal.

From this provincialism and tribalism the Jewish people, having outlived its mission almost in its infancy, lingers on in Toynbee's world of history as "a fossil remnant." The word "fossil" fascinates this writer. He rolls it lovingly over his tongue with the complacent air of one who has coined an immortal aphorism. Statisticians will be delighted to count the number of occasions in which the Jewish people is descirbed as a "fossil" remnant in the eight volumes. Dr. Toynbee will not tell us what he means. The concept is never defined. It is indeed a basic weakness of his work that it evades the definition of its fundamental terms. But the word "fossil" has a scientific definition. It denotes something petrified which retains its original shape and semblance without the breath of life. The mollusc or shell lingers on eternally, while the spirit which once gave it the glory of animation has long since departed.

Now, the doctrine of the fossil is the very core of the Toynbee heresy. If Israel was a fossil centuries ago, then its survival is certainly an archaism and its restoration is a grotesque paradox. On the other hand, if the concept of Judaism as something petrified and embalmed cannot be sustained, then it is difficult to challenge the right of a sentient living spirit to seek survival and restoration. Prof. Toynbee fails, indeed declines, to substantiate the fossil theory, despite the fact that it is the absolute premise and starting point of all his subsequent judgments.

But the fossil, not having read Dr. Toynbee's eight volumes, is unaware of its own petrefaction. It clings to its sense of mission, and even strives for national restoration. For Toynbee, this is a rebellion against the orthodox Jewish tradition which decrees that the restoration, if it comes at all, must proceed exclusively from the Divine initiative. Toynbee portrays the movement for the restoration of Jewish nationhood as a usurpation by human beings of a destiny which can only be righteously envisaged as the work of the Creator. The fossil remnant, instead of accepting what is called the doctrine of "political quietism" and waiting in resignation for the Divine purpose to unfold itself, has presumed impiously to take the law into its own hands and to conceive Jewish restoration as a process of human activity. In attributing political quietism and resignation to orthodox Judaism, Professor Toynbee becomes an unexpected and explicit adherent of *Agudath Israel*. This movement is mentioned with a straight face several times as the embodiment of the authentic tradition; Orthodox Judaism, decrees Prof. Toynbee, in a mood of Rabbinical dogmatism, requires acceptance of Diaspora until, in God's good time, if at all, a Divine initiative, unsupported by human revolt, will bring about the restoration together with Messianic redemption. The natural Jewishness is the condition of Diaspora. The return is an archaism, a paradox, an impiety, and an injustice.

Direct quotation will prove that the principles of this heresy have not been stated by Professor Toynbee in terms less drastic than those which I have ascribed to him. Moreover, the story is told with a vehemence, a moral passion, a subjective indignation, rare in historical writing and indeed without parallel elsewhere in Toynbee's work. The adjectives are those of journalism, of political polemics. The writer is not content to describe. He insists also on the capacity to judge and condemn. It seems vitally important to him that the reader should despise many of the processes and the most striking recent results of the immemorial Jewish story. In the end, Professor Toynbee too takes his story to a climax—but not to a climax of chivalrous triumph, of incredible recuperation of will power vanquishing material obstacles and impediments. His is a climax full of tragedy, pathos and paradox. The torment of Jewry under Nazism is described in terms of violent and vehement indignation. But this indignation forms the bridge to the blasphemous conclusion that the immeasurable torment of Jewry under Nazism is "less tragic" than the circumstances in which 750,000 Arabs are homeless, though alive, upon the soil and the territory of the independent Arab States. Finally, the State of Israel is portrayed as a caricature of all the imperfections of society, a squalid little Ghetto without grace or meaning, the abode of "an Janus figure, part American farmer technician, part Nazi sicarius". With this chivalrous pat on our shoulder we are sent on our way down the road to damnation on Judgment Day,

THE HEBREW DIVINITY

Let me vindicate the accuracy of my summary in Professor Toynbee's own words. Here is how he begins with a description of the Jewish concept of Divinity:

> It is not, of course, surprising to find these two traits of provincialism and exclusiveness displayed by Yahveh simultaneously. A God who keeps to his own domain may be expected to warn other Gods off it. What is surprising, and even repellent, at any rate at first sight, is to see Yahveh continuing to exhibit an unabated intolerance towards the rivals with whom he courts a conflict when, after the overthrow of the Kingdoms of Isreal and Judah, and the establishment of the Syriac universal state, this God of two highland principalities steps out into the wider world and aspires like his neighbors to win for himself the worship of all mankind.

Provincialism and exclusiveness, then, rather than Oneness, love and justice are the dominant characteristics of the Hebrew God. Provincialism is diagnosed by Professor Toynbee in his attack on the doctrine of the chosen people. This concept is described as the arrogation of a privilege, not as the acceptance of responsibility and obligation. It is, in fact, defined by Professor Toynbee in terms of a narcissistic self-idealization. He writes:

> The most notorious historical example of this idealization of an ephemeral self is the error of the Jews which is exposed in the New Testament. In the period of their history, which began in the infancy of the Syriac civilization and which culminated in the age of the Prophets, the people of Israel and Judah raised themselves head and shoulders above the Syriac peoples by

rising to a monotheistic conception of religion. Keenly conscious of their spiritual treasure, they allowed themselves to be betrayed into an idealization of this notable but transitory stage in their spiritual growth. They had indeed been gifted with unparalleled spiritual insight but after having divined a truth which was absolute and eternal they allowed themselves to be captivated by a relative and temporary half-truth. They persuaded themselves that Israel's discovery of the one true God had revealed Israel itself to be God's chosen people; and this half-truth inveigled them into a fatal error of looking upon a momentary spiritual eminence as a privilege conferred upon them by God in an everlasting covenant. Brooding on a talent which they had perversely sterilized by hiding it in the earth, they rejected the still greater treasure which God offered them in the coming of Jesus of Nazareth.

My criticism of this passage is directed not, of course, against Toynbee's reverence for the Christian revelation, but against his invidious definition of a Jewish doctrine for the sake of its debasement. He states without proof that the doctrine of Israel's selection is the assertion of exclusive membership in a restricted club. He ignores the true essence of this idea, which is the acceptance of a burden of obligation heavier than that carried by other peoples who were not the original custodians of the inspired revelation. The concept of Israel's choice is one of humility, not of arrogance. The selection is a burden, not a grace. There is a vast exegesis on this theme in Rabbincal literature. But Professor Toynbee need not have gone beyond the first documents which expound the theme of Israel's selection: "You only have I known of all the families of the earth; *therefore* I will visit upon you all your iniquities."

THE FOSSIL AGAIN

From this description of a provincial self-idealisation and the assertion of a privileged status, Professor Toynbee goes on to grapple with the mystery of Jewish survival. He has no device except the metaphor of the fossil:

> The Jews and the Pharisees are fossils of the Syriac society as it was before the Hellenic intrusion upon the Syriac world,

and again,

> A number of fossils in Diaspora have preserved their identity through a devotion to religious rights and a proficiency in commerce and finance.

This doctrine of Jewish survival as a result of an excessive ritualism and of financial astuteness is disturbingly akin to the diagnosis of anti-Semitic historians, from whom Toynbee would justly claim dissociation. The economic history of the Jewish people is in fact a poignant record, with a ghastly volume of starvation and poverty. The legendary proficiency in commerce and finance is a characteristic which modern Israel has still failed to discover. But for Dr. Toynbee it is sufficient to assert these time-worn platitudes. It is not necessary to prove them. He rules by negative implication against any idea that Jewish survival is the result of an affirmative spiritual dedication. It is by commercial shrewdness and rigid ceremonial orthodoxy, that the fossil survives. There is more of Shylock than of Isaiah or Maimonides in this prototype.

> At the present moment they survive as a mere Diaspora; and the petrified religion, which still so potently holds the scattered members of these communities together, has lost its message to mankind and has hardened into a fossil of the extinct Syriac society.

A fossil cannot create or even interpret original ideas. Thus by his very definition Professor Toynbee disposes negatively of the entire post-Biblical Jewish culture, through medieval Hebrew philosophy and poetry, right up to the achievements and insights of Hebrew literature and scholarship in the present day. It is doubtful whether Professor Toynbee is equipped, linguistically or otherwise, to deny the breath of life or the spark of inspiration to this vast literature. But the beloved slogan of the fossil is, in fact, judgment on the ideas and writings of these many generations.

The Sanctity of Diaspora

That the natural state of the fossil is the Diaspora is another central theme in Professor Toynbee's heresy. Hear it in his own words:

> The historic Jewry was the Diaspora and the distinctively Jewish gethos and institutions . . . *A meticulous devotion to the Mosaic Law and a consummate virtuosity in the commerce and finance* were those which the Diaspora in the course of ages had wrought into social talismans endowing this geographically scattered community with a magic capacity for survival.

All would have been well, then, if this people had patiently accepted its petrified status. Unfortunately, however, the fossil revolted against its petrified nature, and this is the source of the paradox and the tragedy.

> So long as the Jewish Diaspora was content, *bona fide,* to leave the future of Palestine in the hands of God, the existing Christian and Moslem inhabitants of the promised land could afford to do likewise. And when the orthodox Jewish doctrine of an eventual repatriation of Jewry to Palestine through an act of God was thus accompanied by a traditional Jewish practice

of political quietism, the doctrine, like a derivate Christian doctrine, of the second coming of Christ, could be interpreted in
crude Machievelian or Marxian terms as a psychological device,
not for bringing to pass a far-off Divine event to which the
whole creation moves, but for maintaining en attendant and ad
infinitum the social confusion of a mundane community in
Diaspora.

If you will allow me to translate that last passage into English,
Prof. Toynbee says this: So long as the doctrine of the Restoration
was held as a pious abstraction, with nothing done to fulfil it, the
idea could exist harmlessly. But any attempt to put it into practice
was bound to reveal its inherent contradictions and to lead to a
climax of tragedy.

The Attack on the Restoration

It is a far cry from a fossil in diaspora to a robust modern nation in its original home. Professor Toynbee feels that the transition needs much explanation. He finds the explanation in a catch-
word. It is "archaism".

Archaism, as we have seen in another context, is always a
perilous pursuit. But it is most perilous of all when it is taken up
by members of a community that is a fossil relic of a dead civilization, since the past to which the archaists have it in their
power to cast back in such a case may be more sharply at vari-
ance with present realities than even the remotest past state of
the society belonging to the living generations of the species.

Now, it is amply clear at this stage that Professor Toynbee har-
bors a fierce resentment against Jewish survival and still more
against Jewish national restoration. The fossil whose lack of animation he has so authoritatively diagnosed keeps getting up and
biting him in the ankle. All he can say is that the entire phenomenon is against the proper theory. His answer is not that the theory
is wrong, but that the phenomenon is reprehensible. Thus, the
tenacity with which the Jewish people worked for the Restoration
invites Professor Toynbee's greatest indignation. It is here that he
attacks the Restoration as a usurpation of the Divine Will. For a
truly Divine objective must be carried out by the Almighty alone;
and any effort to advance it by human effort is an impious rebellion against the Divine prerogative. Man may not busy himself in
the reform of the world into the Kingdom of God.

To establish this analogy in another sphere, we might say that if
social justice is a God-given ideal, then any human being who
strives for social justice through political or economic organization
is guilty of impious revolt against God's purpose, for he is denying
the capacity of the Almighty, unaided by human agencies, especi-

ally fossilized ones, to bring about the realization of the ideal. Lest you think that this is an exaggeration, this very *reduction ad absurdum* actually occurs in Professor Toynbee's thesis:

> A Western-inspired archaism carried the twentieth century Zionist faction of a Jewish Diaspora back to the aims and ethos of the generation of Joshua. The consequent replacement of the traditional Jewish hope of an eventual Restoration of Israel to Palestine on God's initiative through the agency of a divinely inspired Messiah, by a Zionist movement working to establish a Jewish national state in Palestine on Jewry's initiative by mundane political and military means, had the same explosive effect as the contemporary replacement of the Christian hope of social justice to be inaugurated at the second coming of Christ, by a communist movement working to establish a mundane new dispensation by means of a world revolution.

This is too wonderful to be true. But it is there in black and white. Just as the human efforts to achieve Jewish restoration lead to the "impiety" of Zionism, so any attempt to achieve a social milennia by human struggle is a distortion of Christianity and may lead to such aberrations as Communism. It is faith to cherish a Divine vision; it is "impiety" to stumble forwards towards its fulfillment.

We can see how the love of slick analogy, the most perilous occupational hazard of a historian, has gripped Prof. Toynbee. Having related the dream of Jewish Restoration to a usurpation akin to Communism, he goes on to prove that traditional attachment of Israel to its original soil is a form of Fascism. Observe how this record *tour de force* is accomplished. First, it is stated that the Jewish people's title to the soil of Eretz Israel is based "on the physical grounds that they are a master race in virtue of having Abraham for their father." This definition of the theory of the link between land and people in terms of "master race" is stated as a fact. The attachment is not a cultural tradition, it is not a spiritual link, it is not a mystic unity of the mind between the people of Israel and the physical conditions in which it underwent the immortal Biblical experience. It is the concept of blood and soil and herrenvolk. This is the basis of our claim, and by this "the Zionist is unwittingly testifying that he has been ensnared by the lure of a post-modern Western Gentile racialism in which a late modern Western Gentile nationalism had denounced itself through the self-exposure of self-caricature as being the naked neo-paganism that it was."

In simpler language, (for Toynbee's turgidity of language is one of the most unprepossessing features of his study), Zionists claim Eretz Israel on the grounds that they are a master race descended from Abraham: This shows that they are ensnared by the Nazi theory of the herrenvolk: Therefore Zionism is kindred to Nazism. There is a little difficulty about anachronism here, since the Jewish teaching on the relationship of Israel to Eretz Israel has been fully and sublimely developed for twenty centuries before Nazism existed to ensnare anybody. But if it is convenient to portray this link as the derivative of the Blood and Soil concept of the Nazi ideologists, let convenience prevail.

The passion for analogies between events and ideas separated by centuries and continents marks Toynbee's greatest weakness as a historian. Dr. Talmon has pointed out that there is nothing in his work of that particular intimacy which marks the authentic historians, who select a small sector of the scene, a single period or a single land, and immerse themselves in that specialized realm until they become a part of its very breath. Here the canvas is vast and broad. The aim is to say something about everything but not to know everything about anything. The effect is secured by grandiose dimensions. It is as though a painter in search of fame and repute were to seek it not by the intrinsic quality of his work, but by painting upon a canvas physically vaster than any work of art before. The absence of specialization, and the insistence upon generalized slogans is a primary weakness of Toynbee's scholarship. Nowhere does the superficiality become as unattractive as in these glib and invidious analogies which relate the Jewish dream of restoration to Communism and Nazism in turn.

Toynbee on Modern Israel

Against this background it is easy to predict how Dr. Toynbee will proceed from his historical premises to his contemporary appraisals of modern Israel. There is no purpose in discussing his modern picture, except by reference to his definitions of pre-Israel Jewish history. Never has the Hebrew tradition been described by any historian in terms of such profound disrespect. The rejection of Israel's rebirth is an organic consequence of his theories concerning the "fossilised relic", the "exhausted mission" and the impiety of any revolt against the "natural state of diaspora" or the duty of "political quietism."

If Zionism is a usurpation of the Divine province, then there is nothing more that need be said against it.

> The mystical feeling convicted the Zionists of an importunity which verged upon impiety in their attempt to take out of God's hands the fulfilment of God's promise to restore Israel to Palestine upon God's own initiative.

Note that here again, the basic premise is stated without proof.

It is affirmed *ex cathedra* to be the Jewish orthodox doctrine that the Restoration must proceed from the Divine initiative without human aid. There are, of course, countless refutations of that premise in orthodox Hebrew literature. It is true that the Hebrew doctrine of history describes the restoration as a Divine purpose. But it also describes it as a purpose which human effort should strive to accelerate. Indeed, Judaism rejects Dr. Toynbee's persistent division between the Divine Will and human action. He constantly sees these two concepts in terms of antithesis. In Judaism, except for the mystical heresies, it is deemed that if something is willed by God, then it is the duty of man in his material life to strive for its fulfilment.

Toynbee's theory of "importunity" brings him smoothly to the events of 1948 and the description of the processes which gave birth to the State of Israel. The Zionists had jogged the Divine elbow to the brink of great events.

Three causes are cited by Prof. Toynbee for this event which he admits to be unusual.

First, the strength of American Jewry. You may be fossils but you are very formidable fossils and despite your petrified character, you have the rights of franchise and political influence.

Second, the genocide committed by Nazism of which he writes with deep qualified indignation; Third, the cold war. These are the three components of Israel's rebirth. By them, and by them alone, does Dr. Toynbee seek to explain the inopportune revival of the fossil, its emergence from its "natural state of diaspora," its advance through "archaism" and "usurpation" to its present tragic lease of nationhood.

Instead of discussing what Toynbee says about modern Israel, it would be instructive to recount what he omits. He omits any treatment of the theme in terms of international equity. The rise of Jewish independence, side by side with a far broader Arab emancipation, is the essence of this problem from the viewpoint of comparative international equity. This is ignored. The historical material is dealt with in terms of British and American Realpolitik; and in the British and American pro-Zionist traditions he allows for no ethical or moral consideration at all. The British promise of 1917 was the product of a mistaken expediency; a bid for Jewish support in America and in the countries of the Central Powers. Similarly, domestic pressures, the reluctance of American Jews to allow Jews to immigrate to the United States for fear of anti-Semitism, and plain ignorance are the impulses behind American support. The Zionist theme in the idealistic literature of both Anglo-Saxon countries is not mentioned. There is no indication that there ever took place in the United Nations a discussion of Palestine from the viewpoint of self-determination. The judgment ruled that even as it is right for the Arabs to possess their empire, so it cannot be wrong for the Jewish people to enjoy the tranquil possession of its modest home. To all of us who took any part in that turbulent international controversy, it was clear that this contrast between the continental opportunities of Arab nationalism and the Jewish people's lack of any free domain determined the character of the discussion and its eventual outcome. Statesmen were simple-minded enough to believe that it would not be a cosmic tragedy if the Arab world made do with nine sovereign States, covering two million square miles; and that it would be a more authentic tragedy if every people were to be established in national freedom amongst those which had suffered the Nazi onslaught—except the people which had suffered the most. In ascribing to the United States and to Britain the responsibility for a blind tragedy of error, Toynbee entirely ignores these high themes, just as he ignores the part which small nations played in the judgments which helped Israel's rebirth. The fact that the first serious proposal for Jewish state-hood came from a group of eight small countries against Great Power scepticism is not considered at all.

CARDINAL OMISSIONS OF FACT

I do not dispute Professor Toynbee's right to argue with these international judgments, to deplore or regret them; but I cannot understand what concept of historical scholarship allows their complete suppression, the absence of any allusion to the chief milestones which led up to the results which he describes. And there is an even greater sensation in store. There is no war. Neither the Arab declaration of unofficial war on November 30, nor the historic document whereby, on May 15, the Arab States informed the United Nations of their intention to embark upon military intervention, is even mentioned. Since every residual problem affecting Arab-Israel relations is a function of the military clash of 1948, it is startling to find no record of the fact that the Arab rejection of Israel was put to the test of the sword. I could respect a historian who published these actions and then exonerated them; who said that the Arab States were justified morally or emotionally or historically in attempting by force to prevent Israel's emergence. But you would really have to look to George Orwell in his morbid vision of totalitarianism to find such a successful suppression of extant historical evidence. It is as though an historian of the first World War were not even to mention the assassination at Sarejevo and the invasion of Belguim, or if the chronicler of the Second World War were to mention neither the assault on Danzig and Poland in 1939, nor the bombing of Pearl Harbor in 1941. Even the more honest amongst the Nazi apologists do not attempt to deny these military facts. They may ascribe to them a legitimacy or a righteousness of motive, but they operate with the same material as the rest of us. Here the most explosive dramatic fact in recent Arab-Israel relations, namely the convergence of Arab armies on Israel and their repulse, is not even accorded the courtesy of record.

From this massive suppression we are bound to reach strange results. All of a sudden the Jews, a petrified fossil, without any international authority, usurping Divine purpose and rebelling against their own orthodoxy, launched themselves like a barbarian invasion upon a Holy Land with which they had nothing to do, wilfully drove out all the inhabitants and thereby committed an act of cruelty in the image of those of which they had been victims. The reason for this is that the Great Powers did not know of the existence of the Arab world. For example:

> President Truman's personal susceptibility to this popular American confusion of mind and mixture of motives (it is an axiom of the Toynbee theory that the American mind is covered by large areas of generous imbecility—A.E.) might go far to explain presidential interventions in the Palestinian imbroglio which would have been utterly cynical if they had not been partially innocent-minded. The Missourian politician philanthropist's eagerness to combine expediency with charity by assisting the wronged and suffering Jews would have appeared to have been untempered by any awareness of the existence of wrongs and sufferings inflicted upon the Arabs.

The picture then is that in 1947, the United States was unaware of the existence of an Arab world, and therefore made a unilateral award of self-determination, never attempting to balance the Jewish claims against those of a sated Arab nationalism. The fact is that the State Department was almost as aware as Professor Toynbee of the existence of Arab interests. Nevertheless the determination was made: the eight or nine sovereignties for the Arabs, the single little home for the Jews. I do not quarrel with Professor Toynbee for not accepting this award, but I am puzzled by his disdainful refusal to discuss it.

Apart from its origins in Great Power politics, Israel, according to Toynbee, derived its statehood from the incentives, the compassion, the yearnings evoked by the Hitler persecution. The Nazi extermination of six million Jews was an evil thing, and Professor Toynbee uses some of his most violent adjectives in describing this tragedy. But it is not the greatest tragedy. The Nazi gentile's fall was less tragic than the Zionist Jew's.

> On the Day of Judgment the gravest crime standing to the German National Socialist's account might be not that they had exterminated a majority of Western Jews, but that they had caused the surviving remnant of Jewry to stumble.

Now, this is one of the most extraordinary sentences in literature. First, let us note the reference to the Day of Judgment. This occurs more than once. Professor Toynbee is not merely the historian of the twentieth century; he is the Attorney-General of the Almighty upon the Day of Judgment. He knows already how the matter will appear in the eternal perspectives of history. And what is the "lesser tragedy?" The lesser tragedy is that six and a half million Jews including one million children, were exterminated and obliterated with all their life and institutions. They were butchered as cattle, cut off from their inheritance of life. A ghastly silence broods over these obscene ditches and incinerators. The shrieks of agony have died away; they are no problem for the United Nations. The potentialities within those millions, whatever they were, are lost to human destiny. This is, for Toynbee, a "lesser tragedy" than the fact that Arab governments have not yet been persuaded to give their kinsmen, on their own soil, the opportunities of liberty and progress which lie within their gift.

Ponder first upon the arithmetical equity. Assume that Arab refugees had undergone the fate of extermination and massacre of our own brethren in Europe. Why even then would the 750,000 killed have been a greater tragedy than the six million? But the true comparison is not of arithmetic. It is between death and life. The six million are dead. The 750,000, with all their suffering, are alive. But their aliveness is for Toynbee a greater tragedy than those irrevocable deaths. Moreover, they are alive on the soil of their kinsmen, on Arab lands, not in captivity; in countries which are free, emancipated, entitled — even exhorted — to give them homes, Arabic environment, Arabic national loyalty and sentiment. A broad future stretches before them if their own people will open the door of its heart. That is "more tragic" than the burning of our children in incinerators and the extermination of their parents in gas chambers!

The passion for analogy can never have run riot with more insidious or irreverent results. A writer of Christian faith stands before the most unfathomable agony of all generations and compares it with what is an admittedly grave hardship in a totally different and infinitely less tragic dimension. The one disaster is irrevocable, the other entirely within human alleviation; yet the former is "less tragic" than the latter. The death of many is "less tragic" than the hardship, in survival, of the relatively few. The Nazi sum of deliberate massacre is not more heinous than the injury inflicted by Israel in a war for the defence of hearth and home. I am no authority, as Toynbee is, on the verdicts of Judgment Day but I cannot see how his cruel observations on the "lesser tragedy" can ever win forgiveness in a compassion less than Divine.

But when all is said and written, the State of Israel stands firm, and the pride of exaltation has come into the tents of Jacob everywhere. All that Professor Toynbee can do is to wish us ill. He genially sees American Jews and Israel becoming "progressively alienated" from each other. Your nourishment of Israel, the most remarkable outpouring of a voluntary public spirit, is written off in a niggardly spirit with a suggestion that you are being duped into submission "to taxation without representation" and will soon wake up to a more prudent and egocentric parsimony. After two thousand years the only people whose continuous historic memory comprehends all the cycles of civilization which Toynbee records, is reunited with its original inheritance. And Dr. Toynbee can only celebrate this wondrous consummation with the following tirade of invective:—

> In its diminutiveness, its fanaticism, and its Ishmaelitish enmity with its neighbors, the new Zionist Israel in Palestine was a reproduction of the Modern Western national State that, in its faithfulness, verged on being a parody.

TOYNBEE ON NATIONALISM

If there is any consolation, it is in the knowledge that we are being castigated in the name of all nation states. For Professor Toynbee regards national sovereignty as obsolete, and hankers after the more perfect system in which national identities were suppressed under the millet system of the Ottoman Empire.

This is a typical confusion between historical fact and a Toynbeesque wish. The eclipse of nationalism by some supra-national federalism has been predicted so often that it is one of the platitudes of twentieth century writing. But, in fact, this very century is the triumphant epoch of the nation state, and the burial ground of broader associations and groupings. At least twenty separate nationhoods have been founded in the past few decades, mostly in Asia. It is all very well to fulminate against "the antiquated patchwork of ghetto-like nation States," and to talk of an irresistible tide sweeping us back towards the Syriac institution of the millet, which is Toynbee's institutional ideal. But has the tide antiquated patchwork of ghetto-like nation States," and to talk of an irresistible tide sweeping us back towards the Syriac institution of the millet, which is Toynbee's institutional ideal. But has the tide been so irresistible after all, in a generation in which "the species of community of which (Israel) was the youngest member" has been fruitful and multiplied to a degree which seemed inconceivable a few decades ago? Perhaps, it is because in our small way we disprove the great sweeping thesis about the "institutional future" not belonging "to the western institution of the national State" that we are called upon to bear these unfaithful wounds, inflicted without love. I doubt whether an analysis in which an inaccurate and hostile passion smothers any spark of human sympathy will supersede the traditional appraisal of Israel's history, including its modern resurgence, as one of the most exhilarating testimonies to the eternal gallantry of the unconquered human spirit.

TOYNBEE AND RELIGION
A CATHOLIC VIEW*

Linus Walker, O.P.

The writings of Professor Arnold Toynbee have received a warm welcome in America since the last war. Perhaps this is because the intensifying world crisis has made us all wonder whether our civilization may not also perish, like all the others known to history. Perhaps it is also because Professor Toynbee stresses the importance of freedom and activity in history, and because he points to an unending natural, spiritual progress in a religion without creeds.

Toynbee's view of history is universal, comprising all known ages and places on earth. His aim is 'to throw some light on the mysterious unfolding of human life through time-space." (*Civilization on Trial,* N.Y.: Oxford, 1948, preface). For him the smallest intelligible unit of history is a whole civilization, not a national state like England. Toynbee's key to the riddle of history is his hypothesis of challenge and response. According to this theory, the rise and fall of civilizations result from the successful or unsuccessful response of a society to a physical or moral challenge, usually physical, coming from the geographical environment, is met; 2) Growth, in which material obstacles are overcome and there is a progress in meeting spiritual (moral) challenges; 3) Breakdown, which is caused by the failure to meet a moral challenge; 4) and finally Disintegration. The last is characterized by three conflicting classes: a dominant minority, which establishes a universal state, like the Roman Empire; an internal proletariat, which produces barbarian war bands and attacks the dying civilization from without. There is a rhythm of dissolution in a dying civilization, following a pattern of rout-rally-rout, as rebellions are put down or as various invasions are repelled only to occur again.

Toynbee tells of the genesis of his hypothesis in the first chapter of *Civilization on Trial* and in his *Study,* vol. I, pp. 272-99. Finding race and environment inadequate explanations of the rise and fall of civilizations, and Spengler's theory too rigid and deterministic, he turned to mythology and received his inspiration from Goethe's *Faust.* In the prologue of this poem, the heavenly choirs are praising the works of God, which are so perfect that there is no room for His further creative activity. Fortunately, however, God is freed from his impasse by the Devil, who challenges God to

The Thomist, vol. 18, 1955, pp. 292-299.

allow him to spoil the perfection of one of His noblest creatures. God's response is to accept the challenge and thus gain the opportunity of continuing and advancing His creative activity.

Toynbee's challenge and response are closely related to Hegel's thesis and antithesis. He considers Hegel's account of creation an "academic abstract of the living truth," which "makes nonsense of it" by reducing it to the purely logical process of the absolute intellect (*Study*, IX, 395). Hegel's idealistic, pantheistic evolution is a dialectical process. It is dialectical because its dynamic force is a conflict of opposites—being and non-being, thesis and antithesis—which are resolved in a higher synthesis, becoming. When opposed by its negation, this synthesis results in a new ascent in the evolutionary spiral. Hegel's philosophy is pantheistic because the absolute spirit (Hegel's "God") is in each and all things. It is idealistic because this evolutionary process is the purely logical workings of the absolute spirit.

Toynbee, in asserting the reality of matter and spirit, drops the idealism of Hegel, and denies the pantheism, though he seems unable to avoid it entirely. He keeps the dialectical evolution but rejects the determinism of Hegel, for the will of man is free, being determinable by an infinite number of possible objects. Although he does not claim to have discovered any absolute, universal laws of history, he does find some apparently constant patterns according to which men freely work out their destiny. The most universal one is challenge and response. All progress results from a static condition (a thesis in Hegelian terms) being challenged by some dynamic force (antithesis). The resulting response gives genesis and growth (synthesis, becoming). Such was the beginning, for example, of the Egyptian civilization, which resulted from a double challenge and response: 1) There was a static condition when primitive men lived in the grasslands of North Africa. Then there was a challenge when these lands became a desert at the end of the ice age. Men responded by moving. 2) Some moved to the Nile delta, were challenged again by the marshy land there, and responded by draining it and founding a great civilization.

In 1953 Toynbee gave a series of radio lectures which were published under the title of *The World and the West*. He viewed the present world crisis as a result of a response by the rest of the world (Russia and the Orient) to the challenge of continued Western aggression. Drawing a parallel between Western and the declining Roman Civilization, he thought it likely that the West would be converted to a new religion coming from the East, as Rome had been converted to Christianity. He hoped that this new religion would retain the Christian belief in a God of Love but would drop Christian dogmatic exclusiveness for the more tolerant attitude of India. (Letter to *The Times Literary Supplement*, Apr. 16, 1954).

Mr. Douglas Jerrold, an English Catholic historian, has written his response to Professor Toynbee's challenge.[1] His first response is to challenge Toynbee's facts. The West, he says, has not been continually aggressive. On the contrary, it was on the defensive for a thousand years against the Northmen, the Magyars, and against Islam. The East has been aggressive too. Islam was a threat to Christendom from 700-1600 A.D. The Russian hegemony has steadily expanded from 1480 to the present, except for a brief setback in 1918. Nor was Rome consistently aggressive. She was on the defensive for centuries against barbarian hordes on her north and east.

Mr. Jerrold also challenges Toynbee's logic. Because of his dialectical theory of history, Jerrold thinks he too often forces historical facts into preconceived patterns. He creates an entity, "the West," which he does not clearly define, then treats it as though it were a real unity, like one man or one government, with a continual life and consistent policy. He makes it appear to have such a policy by identifying any single aggressive Western power with the entire West—for example, Germany in 1918 and 1941. But in both wars the other Western powers were on Russia's side.

Finally Jerrold accuses Toynbee of treason against the faith of the West. Christianity was not one of many Oriental, exotic religions imported to Rome. It was preached by a Roman citizen. It was based on historical fact and is therefore unique and binding. By questioning the unique value of our Christian faith, our political institutions, our economic freedom, our independent families, Toynbee spreads doubt against all the basic values which the West has derived from Graeco-Roman civilization and from Christianity. And by spreading doubt, he promotes the downfall of our world.

By hurling the pebble of his little book at Goliath, Mr. Jerrold has scored a hit, but has not slain his enemy. In the first place, his book is an answer to Toynbee's series of lectures, not to the ten volume *Study*. In the second place, it is indignant and polemical in tone; consequently, *The Lie About the West* will not appeal to professional historians because its language is not restrained and scholarly. In the third place, some of Jerrold's arguments are not convincing, for example, that Christianity was preached by a Roman citizen, arose within the Roman Empire, and was therefore not a foreign importation into Rome. For St. Paul was a Roman

---

[1]*The Lie About the West*, Douglas Jerrold, Sheed & Ward, New York, 1954, pp. 85.

only *de jure*: the Jews were a conquered people; and Jewish and Christian beliefs were alien to Roman culture. Finally, Jerrold seems a little too patriotic in his defence of the West, a little too unwilling to allow a modicum of truth to Toynbee's arguments. He tends to identify the West with Christianity and to ignore the apostasy of the Western powers. He "gasps" (p. 66) because Toynbee says that "the spiritual initiative . . . has now passed, at any rate for the moment, from the Western to the Russian side." But this is true enough to make the reader weep, not gasp. Toynbee is referring to the ability of Communism to inspire men to sacrifice for a cause. As he says (*Times Literary Supplement, Apr 16, 1954*), *"Leviathan-Juggernaut* has over-triumped our little idol— *homunculus."* He means that the false common good and diaboli-cal world society of Communism have made a greater appeal to many men than the goal of a secular, capitalistic individualism— wealth, utility, and pleasure for every man.

Fundamental to Toynbee's way of thinking are his ideas on re-ligion. The section on "Universal Churches," therefore, is the most important one in the new volumes of the *Study* and will be the principal source of what is said below. Toynbee gives a relig-ious interpretation to history, seeing spiritual meaning and purpose in it. Religion is the end of civilization, which exists to promote it. Toynbee has no naive belief in a steady and inevitable material progress. His standard of progress is spiritual, not bigness or technical efficiency. All this we can applaud.

In some places Toynbee seems at first glance to be sympathetic to the Catholic view of things. For him the historic Church is the Catholic Church, which is united by two great institutions: the Sacrifice of the Mass and the hierarchy (*Civilization on Trial*, p. 242) The Catholic Church was the animating principle of Western Civilization, not a mere cocoon for its genesis. The pope, "the Vicar of Christ," is its spiritual leader. (*Study* IV, 583) The Renaissance and Reformation were symptoms of cultural sickness. The saints are our models for religious conduct.

But the context of such statements reveals that in using the language of the Church, Toynbee does not mean what the Church means at all. His theory of religion is naturalistic and evolution-ary. It is influenced by Modernism, which Toynbee praises. (VII, 456). Much of what St. Pius X said in the first part of *Pascendi* is applicable to Toynbee. As we have said above, Hegel seems to be his father: the evolutionary spiral of religious progress moves on as a result of the conflict of opposites. Man is naturally religious. As he progresses materially, however, he tends to idolize the things which serve him—the forces of nature, a deified leader, or a totali-tarian state. He does so because each spiritual advance causes its opposite. The spiritual flowering under St. Benedict, for example, brought great wealth and power to the monasteries which caused a spiritual decline and eventually the suppression of the monasteries. The monks failed to meet the challenge posed by their prosperity. On the other hand, the tribulations of the Jews (a challenge) during the Babylonian captivity inspired "Deutero-Isiah" to write the canticles of the suffering servant (a response).

Toynbee finds antithesis at the core of all religious belief, causing new beliefs in old religions and sometimes entirely new religions. The "feminine epiphany of the Godhead" as Mother is opposed to the "masculine epiphany" as Father. The "forbidding aspect" of God as a jealous judge is opposed to and difficult to reconcile with the "consoling aspect" as a forgiving "loving Saviour." Religion as social worship under a priest is opposed to individual, intimate communion with God. And so on. (cf. VII, 716) These conflicts are facile and misleading. First God is neither masculine nor feminine; the masculine gender is used in referring to Him because it expresses greater perfection. Second, He is a terrible judge only if we place ourselves outside His mercy by sin. Third, it is a fact that some saints have been most intimate with God in ecstasy during Mass.

Toynbee recognizes four "higher religions" or "universal churches," each of which emphasizes one or the other pole of an antithesis: Christianity, Islam, Hinduism, and Mahayana Buddhism. Each corresponds to, is caused by, and serves some psychological characteristic of man. Following Jung, Toynbee classifies Christianity and Islam as extrovert religions, tending to God as outside, transcendent; whereas Hinduism and Buddhism are introvert religions, tending to God as within, immanent. He describes the four according to Jung's four functions of the mind. Christianity emphasizes *feeling* in the doctrine that God is Love. Hinduism stresses *thinking* in seeing God as omnipresent. Islam, following *sensation,* teaches that religion is a fact and that Allah is Power. Buddhism by *intuition* has discovered that the desire for existence is the cause of evil and that escape lies in the extinction of desire— Nirvana.

This classification depends on the reduction of the living religions to four, which does not seem to be consistent with fact. It also depends on the psychology of Jung, which is not entirely satisfactory. It might be possible to reconcile thinking, feeling, and sensation with the Thomistic psychology, but what is intuition? Is it instinct or an unscientific use of reason? One must also ask, are not all faculties of the mind and all character types represented in those who follow each of Toynbee's four religions? Were the founders of these religions of the type corresponding to their religion? Did Christ "feel" only and suppress thinking into His subconscious, while Buddha made an "intuition" and suppressed sensation?

Toynbee professes belief in a transcendent God, but his God is apparently finite and subject to limitations. (I, 279-280) It is difficult to see how Toynbee can escape the charge of pantheism, or at least andratheism, to coin a word from the Greek, for God is the "Dweller in the Innermost," that is, in the subconscious depths of the soul. (VII, 501) Perhaps like the Modernists Toynbee confuses the action of God and the action of human nature, thus confounding man's being and God's being, the natural and the supernatural. (cf. *Pascendi,* 19) It need hardly be said that Toynbee tacitly assumes the impossibility and inappropriateness of a special, supernatural revelation through the external signs of miracles and prophecy and through an internal, supernaturally infused prophetic light. Miracles and special revelations are classed by him as "myths" and "legends." Our Lady in his hands becomes an "etherealized" pagan goddess, her Annunciation a universal myth "transfigured." (I, 272) Christ too is a "transfigured" Mithras or Adonis. (VII, 437) Here Toynbee seems to be using the modernist notion of "transfiguration"—the elevating of a historical fact above its true historical conditions so that by faith it becomes clothed with "religious truth." (cf. *Pascendi,* 9)

In developing his parallel between Christ and the pagan fertility gods, Toynbee refers to Christ's "divesting" Himself of divine power in the Incarnation and quotes Philippians 2:7, where St. Paul speaks of Christ's "emptying Himself." But the context of this passage belies such an interpretation, as do many other passages of the gospels and epistles, for example, Colossians 2:9, where we are told that in Christ "dwells all the fullness of the Godhead bodily. . . ." St. Thomas explains that Christ emptied Himself not in putting off the divine nature but in taking up a human nature. (*Super Philippenses,* II, i, #57)

Consequently, there is no parallel between the Word Incarnate, who suffered and dies *as Man* through an assumed human nature, and a pagan fertility god, who by nature dies and is reborn again, as the greenness of the earth dies in the autumn and is reborn in the spring. The evolution of Our Lord and Lady out of pagan divinities is not a demonstrated fact, nor is it even demonstrable.

Toynbee exalts flux, change, and becoming because of his hypothesis of progressive evolution in history. Consequently a closed body of divine revelation is an abomination to him, for religion, which evolves from within man, must be constantly changing, adapting itself to changing human needs. Fixed creeds only thwart this development. Our response to this is that any progression is a movement towards an end. Objective revelation has reached its end, having been completed with the death of St. John. It therefore need not develop further. But subjective religion can and must progress, for we must constantly advance in our penetration and practice of objective revelation.

Consequently, it is evident that Toynbee reads something that is not there into the Gospels which he quotes so often in support of his thesis and into George Herbert's *Pulley*. (VII, 462) Herbert did not say that we must give up our old beliefs for new as the price of advancing, but only that as long as we are wayfarers towards God we cannot rest. Toynbee quotes the process of canonization of St. Thomas Aquinas to illustrate his argument. (VII 484, n.) St. Thomas, however, did not change his beliefs when after his ecstasy he could no longer write and considered all his writings merely straw. For the process of canonization also tells of St. Thomas' magnificent profession of faith in the Blessed Sacrament and his submission of all his writings to the Church when he received Holy Viaticum.

Behind Toynbee's religious relativism is his false dichotomy of man's faculties into the reason and the unconscious and of truth into the truth of science and the truth of religion. Following the Modernists, Toynbee classifies historical facts as pertaining to science and reason and religious doctrines to faith and the unconscious. (cf. *Pascendi,* 16, 30) As a result he makes religion something sub-rational, anti-rational. He unjustly accuses St. Pius X of condemning Modernism for holding "that there is no ground for collision between Faith and Science." (VII, 485, n.) Actually the condemnation was of the *reasons* of the Modernists in holding this, as the context of the passage will show. (*Pascendi,* 16) It is a commonplace of Catholic teaching that there can be no real conflict between true science and true religion, because Truth, which is one, embraces both. Truth consists in the correspondence of the mind to the objective reality. Therefore, it cannot be true by faith that God is a Trinity and that Jesus Christ is true God and true Man, while at the same time according to science these statements are not true.

Sister doctrines to the theory of the double truth in Toynbee's writings are the equivalence of all philosophical systems and the futility of theology. Philosophies are the by-products of civilizations such as the Hellenic or Indic and are all ephemeral. At best theology makes only a verbal reconciliation between "scientific truth and prophetic truth." (VII, 474-476). Creeds, we are told, are the product of theology. This is an egregious error. Creeds pertain to faith and need not use theological language at all. The deducing of conclusions from the creeds is the work of theology.

Toynbee accuses theologians of a refined form of anthropomorphism in conceiving of God in terms of feeling, will, and intellect. They worship an idol—"God the Reason." (VII, 467-68) But Toynbee overlooks the role of analogy in theology. Theologians do not place God and creatures in the same species. They speak of God and creatures analogically, by a remote similarity in which there is more unlikeness than likeness. God is said to be intelligent because He knows Himself and other things. His intelligence is infinitely above ours; but by denying all imperfection in God's knowledge, we can say that the relation of His mind to its objects is similar to the relation of our mind to its objects. If as Toynbee says, there is *no* ground for comparison between the infinite and finite, then God cannot be known in any way. He becomes completely unintelligible. Yet Toynbee holds that God exists and that he is Love. Surely these predications of God are no more adequate than the predication that God is intelligent. We can know God's existence and love only by comparison with the existence and love that we know already. If we are to love God, we must also know that He is good, perfect, holy, intelligent, wise, living, merciful, and in possession of all beatitude. But although we know these and many other essential attributes of God, no theologian would claim that our analogical knowledge of God is adequate to comprehend Him. St. Thomas was certainly well aware of the limitations of theology long before his ecstacies. He was aware of them when he wrote the first question of the *Summa* and when in the prologue to the third he said that we do not know *what* God is but rather what he is *not*.

Toynbee's notion that the Christian God is a God of Love but not of Justice, that there is an incongruity between the God of Josue and Jesus is not supported by the facts. Christians have always praised God by singing the Psalms, where the power, majesty, and justice of God are extolled as well as His love and mercy. And Christ, said, "He that is not with me is against me," (Matthew 12:30) proclaiming Himself as jealous as when He gave the Decalogue. He warned, "He that believeth not shall be condemned," (Mark 16:16) and showed Himself as just as He was merciful in promising mercy to those who believe and are baptized.

It should be noted that Toynbee's own beliefs are almost all entirely Christian in inspiration. He speaks of the sacrifice of the Incarnate God, of grace, original sin, salvation, eternal life, the kingdom of heaven. Christianity is superior to all other religions in its "intuition" that God is Love. But it is still dogmatic, and the broad tolerance of Hinduism is in advance of Christianity. (VII, 735) This "charity" towards all other revelations is the only inspiration which Toynbee has derived from the Orient. The new religion which he hopes for as a result of a more universal outlook, of the reconciliation of heart and head, of East and West, would be a syncretistic stew, a dogmatic cipher. He leaves the reader with no positive idea of what it might be, except a monstrous blasphemy, if the sentimental, incongruous travesty of the Litany of the Saints in volume X, p. 143, be a sample of the new "religion." Begging "Christ Tammuz" and other "Christs" to hear us, invoking "Mother Isis" and "Mother Cybele" in the same breath with Our Lady suggests that it might be a reversion to polytheism, which Toynbee abhors.

There is much more that could and should be said. It is regrettable that nearly all that has been said in this review has had to be negative. It is even more regrettable that such a devoted historian of genius as Professor Toynbee has sought to be a prophet and preacher as well.

REASON OR RELIGION
AN OLD DISPUTE RENEWED*

Jan Romein

In the years following the appearance of the first three volumes of *A Study of History,* that is to say since 1934 when the author was 45 years old, up to the present time when he has completed his life-work and approaches his seventieth year (which will be in 1959), many a criticism has been made against many parts of that tremendous work, which he is so proudly entitled to call his own. There will not even be any field of historical research, against which some or other of its representatives will not have some objection as to the manner in which it has been treated by Toynbee. Some of these objections may be valid—the range of my own knowledge is not vast enough to judge them all—but nevertheless I am of the opinion that most of them are not as important as the critics themselves generally seem to suppose. As far as I am able to judge, more often than not misunderstanding has played a large role in the criticisms brought against Toynbee by specialists from within the narrow bounds of their special fields. More often than not these specialists appear not to have understood the real nature and function of theory in general, and have therefore misjudged the theories concerning history set up by Toynbee.

What, generally speaking, is a theory? Let us attempt to answer that fundamental question.

We experience reality with our senses, but our senses are all but mechanical instruments, apart from the mind that thinks, forms opinions, explains. Therefore, all our impressions from the outer world of phenomena are at the same time thought, judgment, explanation. That holds good for the natural world around us, but even more so for the historical world, which we can only estimate by the impressions of other people. We may, then, conclude that every detailed historical description, let alone a summarizing theory concerning an historical process, never quite renders reality in its fulness. Every theory is simplifying and contracting, because it is its function to simplify and to contract. In the words of the greatest sociologist of this century, Max Weber: to grasp the real context we have to construct an unreal one. The function of theories is to experience new contexts on the basis of known facts in order to suggest the existence of unknown ones, which in their

---

*Introductory remarks of the chairman at a lecture given by Professor Toynbee at the Hague 28 September 1954.

turn may give rise to conjectures concerning new contexts, and so on for the years to come.

In addition to intuition and sagacity, knowledge and experience, the devising and setting up of theories needs a rare flexibility of mind. For the mind must not only be able to construct as many theories as will be necessary to demonstrate these contexts, but must as well be prepared to drop them at the instant they have fulfilled their function.

In my opinion it will be very difficult to show that Toynbee, in his *A Study of History*, has not conformed to these conditions. No one can deny him either knowledge or experience, and no one can deny him a rather uncommon, even somewhat uncanny, intuition and acuteness.

Does my general defence of Toynbee's theory of history, against most of his critics, mean that I have myself no objections whatever to make against it? Of course not. I, too, have objections to make, and it would seem to be part of my duty to explain them to you—at least, the most important of them. It is my profound conviction that not even a sketch of one's work can have any value if all criticism is omitted, for it is only when one is acquainted with another person's limits that the content of what is within these limits may be known.

For one thing, I cannot subscribe to his belief that a Christian renaissance could help us escape the dangers with which our Western civilization is at the present time beset. That is to say, I do not object to Toynbee's belief as such, for there is no meaning in objecting to beliefs as such. No scientific argument can convince a believer that his belief is wrong. That is of the nature of faith. For the personal consciousness faith transcends science. All that I can say concerning the religious renaissance for which Toynbee hopes, is that from my viewpoint all religious phenomena are part of the social whole, a product, an important product no doubt, perhaps the most important, but nevertheless a product only of society itself. And I can see no possibility of a product of a certain entity regenerating that entity.

More important still than this objection is the related one: If I understand him correctly, Toynbee has no confidence in our scientific accomplishments as a possible means of overcoming the social crisis in which we find ourselves. It seems to me a type case that Toynbee, analyzing the possible mental attitudes prevailing during a critical period of a civilization—at least up to the present time—appears to overlook the mental attitudes of those who, against all odds, are trying to find the progressive response to the challenge of dissolution. That is to say, such persons, among whom I should desire to be numbered, as are endeavoring to keep the future open by continuing that tradition, are neglected by Toynbee in his *Study,* but are most essential to me: I mean that most original and most typical Western contribution to the civilization of mankind, at least since the Renaissance, the tradition of rational science and technology.

With the assistance of science and technology it is the hope, of some of us at least, that mankind may yet achieve rational control and regulation of our social relations. It is my opinion that it is in the lack of that control that the kernel of our crisis is to be found. I am fully aware that Toynbee can reply to this objection that what I have said is as much an act of faith as is his. I even admit that while a religious renaissance may perhaps be harmless, a further scientific and technological development has its own dangers. Nevertheless, I am convinced that the only possible solution—quite another thing from the warranted solution—is the further development of the natural and social sciences, notwithstanding the possible dangers.

Faith in science, to be sure, is not the kind of faith that moves mountains, but a kind of faith that moves minds, which is perhaps rather more pertinent to the human situation. Toynbee may object that science, too, is only a product of our civilization. This is, of course, true. But the difference between science and religion seems to be that the former is able to develop itself to an always higher stage, whereas religion in its essence, is what it is and always has been. Moreover, whereas religion speaks the language of the civilization in which it was born, science speaks only the one language of reason all over the world. Religion, therefore, is a dividing force, whereas science is a binding force. I therefore cannot see that religion can perform in the future what it has failed to perform in the past. Science, however, possibly can.

But now let us suppose for a moment that all the critics of Toynbee are right, and let us also accept for a moment the possibility that even my objections are sound. Nothing of this alters in the least the fact that Toynbee *is* and will remain *for years to come* the man who made the profoundest analysis of human civilization ever made. And more: that he gave us with his life-work a contribution to history not only of the past but of the future as well. In his work there are two trends which make it of immediate and of lasting importance. I mean this. Toynbee is not the first to have stated that Europe does not represent the nucleus and the apogee of the history of mankind—many have said this before him, and even more or less attempted to write world-history in a world-wide spirit. But Toynbee's enduring merit lies in the fact that he was the first whose knowledge was wide enough, and whose spirit was detached enough, to give us a history in which a real world-view could be taken seriously. Fundamentally this is because Toynbee is wholly and rightly, I think, convinced that the *unity* of the world is in the making. On almost every occasion Toynbee speaks of this coming unity. It might even be said this is his gospel. But in this, his gospel is more than faith alone. Hard facts teach us that the history of the last eighty years cannot be interpreted in any other sense, all objection and opposition to the contrary.

Some years ago I was in Indonesia, and being in Central Java I of course paid a visit to the old temple-complex of Lara Djong-grang, commonly called Prambanan. The chief temple there is con-secrated to the Hindu-deity Shiva, the god of flowering and destruc-tion, of life and death, in which the old sages of India symbolized the cosmic energy, which is as horrible in its destructive aspects as it is holy in its beneficent aspects. The conception behind the idea of Shiva is this: that all antitheses are only the opposing appearances of an unnamed unity. It seems to me that Toynbee has been one of the first to penetrate once more the secret of that old wisdom of Shiva. He saw that, as in all oppositions, that be-tween East and West is only a relative one, and that insight is the first condition with which to master that opposition. This insight is growing among us, and it is in my opinion the imperishable service rendered by Toynbee to have helped mankind, morally and scientifically, in mastering this opposition between East and West. In this connexion science and action are becoming one.

The first condition in mastering the antithesis between East and West, which threatens to split the world, is to make that anti-thesis relative rather than absolute. The second condition, follow-ing naturally from the first, is to secure peace. The real danger by which we are confronted is not the A-bomb, nor even the H-bomb, and not even the cobalt-bomb. They are only the symptoms and symbols of the tension between what is at the present called East and West. The real danger lies in that tension itself. The real danger lies in the world being divided into two camps. One World or None is a slogan of the UNO, but at the same time it is more than that, it is the truth. It is as Masaryk, the first president of Czechoslovakia, put it many years ago: We are on the threshold of a new era in which the human race feels its unity. In principle the unity of mankind already exists. This unity is not created, by the way, by religion, and this is the core of my original objection, but by the technicians' feat of annihilating distances. It is our task and the task of the generation to come to lift this unity into reality. We have to help to bridge over the tension between East and West, until the time when a better world may come, in which that funda-mental unity no longer has to be defended convulsively, but in which it will be a matter of course.

FAITH AND VISION OF
· A UNIVERSAL WORLD*

HANS KOHN

Professor Arnold Toynbee has now published the four concluding volumes of the ten which form his magnum opus, *A Study of
History*. These last four volumes alone are a monumental achievement. They contain more than 2,500 pages and cover in a panoramic sweep all ages from early historic times to the present day,
and all civilizations, even the least familiar ones. A vast, and
today probably unparalleled, learning and an earnest dedication
have gone into the writing of these volumes, and a somewhat old-
fashioned but delightful urbanity of style and mind enhances the
pleasure of reading them. This pleasure is not so much based on
an agreement with Mr. Toynbee's fundamental position as on the
wealth of fascinating details and new vistas with which the author
presents us. Toynbee's work is not clothed in the cool garb of the
detached scholar. It is an intensely personal document, the profession of faith of a great scholar and a universal mind, and as
such it deserves our respect in spite of doubts and disagreements.
Many years have elapsed since the publication of the first six
volumes; they were years of fateful historical events—the initial
triumph of National Socialism, the Second World War, the emergence of Communist Russia as a leading world power, and finally
the Asian revival with its passionate nationalism and imperialism.
These events have understandably impressed Mr. Toynbee. His
work bears their traces to such a degree that the *Study of History*
is also a tract for our own age and its predicament. Therein lies
part of its value as a human document, as a witness to the time of
our life and its problems, and as such it will remain of enduring
interest to all future historians. Yet it is with the tract for our
"predicament" that I find myself in disagreement, a disagreement
not only with Mr. Toynbee but with the whole and recently rapidly
growing school of writers who lament the decay of modern Western civilization and call for a "return to God". Of all these innumerable mournful or gleeful prophets, Mr. Toynbee is by far
the most serious and reasonable one. For his approach is distinguished by a broad tolerance and a reasonable empiricism, which
belong to the best characteristics of modern Western civilization
and which are so sorely missing in the Russian Danilevsky and
the German Spengler.

---

*The Christian Register, Vol. 134, 1955, pp. 9-12.

As a student of nationalism, I agree with Mr. Toynbee's position that nationalism in the twentieth century has often degenerated, politically and spiritually, into a danger to individual liberty and international peace, to the human mind and man's wellbeing. In my first essay on nationalism, which I wrote in 1919, at the end of the First World War, I drew the parallel to which Mr. Toynbee also refers, between the religious wars and intolerance of the seventeenth century and the nationalist wars and intolerance of our time. I then expressed the hope that we might return to an age of Enlightenment which would control the political passions of nationalism as the Enlightenment which started with Locke ended the similar passions of religion. The experiences of the Second World War have led other historians toward a similar hope. In his last work, *Geschonden Wereld,* the Dutch historian J. Huizinga wrote in 1943 that "nationalism, the exaggerated and unjustified tendency to emphasize national interests, has produced in our time the abominable fruit of hyper-nationalism, the curse of this century".

In his sweeping condemnation of nationalism, Toynbee disregards, however, the fact that nationalism began in eighteenth century Western society as a striving for the protection of the rights of the individual citizens against the power of government and the dogmatism of religion. In the atmosphere of Enlightenment it was a liberating movement from the fetters of a deadening tradition. From Milton and Locke to Jefferson and Condorcet, this early nationalism helped the growth of man's stature. But in the course of the nineteenth century, when nationalism spread from the shores of the Atlantic eastward, into lands with an entirely different political and cultural tradition and social structure, nationalism turned more and more into a desire for collective power and self-assertion and tended to subject the individual to the political, intellectual, and moral authority of the collectivity.

Professor Toynbee's insistence that the units of history are not nations or continents, not political or geographic areas but civilizations, has always impressed me as a fertile proposition. Asia for the Asians or Europe for the Europeans makes little sense, for where are the boundaries of these continents? Do they end at the Ural mountains, the Straits of Constantinople, or the Suez Canal? Are Egypt or Tunisia part of the same Africa as the Congo? What is the unifying link between two Asian lands like Islamic Saudi Arabia and Buddhist Burma? Asia is the home of several great civilizations, Islamic, Hindu, Chinese, which have nothing in common but borders which have given rise, and may give rise again, to violent conflicts. Nor is Europe a cultural unit. The European settlements in North America have been throughout their brief history infinitely closer to Western Europe than has Moscow or Constantinople. We should be grateful to Mr. Toynbee for putting civilization and not nations in the foreground of history. Whereas nations have played a very great role in the events of the last centuries, civilization has been a determining factor for human life and history throughout all ages.

But Mr. Toynbee's approach to civilization demands on our part two reservations. Why does he emphasize so much the fact that Western civilization is not the only one, that it does not tower as the fulfillment over all others, and that no civilization is final or immortal? The Chinese or the medieval Christian might have felt certain about the unique superiority and finality of his own civilization, and modern Western common man might have shared this feeling around 1910 about his own civilization. But I doubt whether any serious thinker in the contemporary West holds such a position. The modern Western intellectual on the whole does not overestimate, he rather underestimates his civilization. And Mr. Toynbee does, too. We shall always respect and even envy him for the ecumenical breadth of his thought, vision and knowledge. In that respect he is the foremost and most representative historian of the twentieth century, in which for the first time all issues have become world-wide and demand an ecumenical understanding.

Personally I have always stressed the need for an ecumenical understanding too. Forty years ago I published an essay "Der Geist des Orrents", and a quarter of a century ago a book *A History of Nationalism in the East*. In both I paid my respect to non-Western civilizations. I have been fully aware of the existence, and the right to exist, of other civilizations, of their greatness in the past, their importance in the present, and their potential promise for the future. Yet I do not share Mr. Toynbee's over-critical attitude to modern Western civilization. I admire the glory that was Greece and the beauty of thirteenth century Western Christianity, the practical sagacity of Islam and the mysticism of the Sufi poets, the depth of the Upanishads and wisdom of Chinese sages, but modern Western civilization, inferior in other ways, has set new and probably higher standards of respect for the individual, of social responsibility, of critical inquiry, than any preceding civilization. Though all civilizations are a product of history and enmeshed in temporality, and though each one has its virtues and foibles, there is in modern Western civilization a vital spiritual force which in the nineteenth and twentieth centuries has helped to revitalize other civilizations and to enhance their self-awareness.

Toynbee accepts the fundamental faith of the Judeo-Christian religious tradition that history is God's path—a course from God, its source, toward God, its goal. This faith presupposes an encompassing vision of the unity, the rationality, and the purposefulness of all history, a religious vision secularized in Hegel and Marx, which the scholar as scholar cannot accept. He remains ignorant of the final aims, if any, of the Divine in and through history. A meaning and a fulfillment of history are postulates for the emotional and aesthetic satisfaction of Western man. They are not the subject of historical scholarship. History has no answers concerning its ultimate course and goal; faith alone can supply them. Mr. Toynbee has a strong religious faith and he believes that only a religious revival can save civilization. But Mr. Toynbee shows much greater moral earnestness and historical awareness than the other prophets who call for "a return to God". He sees in the return to institutional orthodoxy a symptom of spiritual cowardice.

> A post-Christian Western Society's temptation to seek refuge from the consequences of its own technological handiwork by begging for readmittance into the fold of a conventional Christian orthodoxy was neither morally nor intellectualy defensible. . . . Souls that have once had the experience of intellectual enlightenment can never thereafter find spiritual salvation by commiting intellectual suicide . . . for the progressive decay of a belief in, and an allegiance to, an ancestral religion, which had been the note of a Western Society's spiritual history since the latter decades of the seventeenth century of the Christian era, had not been due solely to Modern Western Man's perversity nor even solely to his bewitchment by his intellect's entrancing scientific discovery . . . [but to the Western Christian Church having] alienated its long-suffering votaries by its grievous sins of both heart and head.

There would be more respect for all the new seekers of God today if they would, like Mr. Toynbee, take a courageous stand not only against the insufficiences of the prevailing civilization but against the moral iniquities of all institutionalized religion, west and east. In that respect Mr. Toynbee's humanitarian and rationalist Christianity recalls that of other great moral teachers of our time, of Count Leo Tolstoi and of Albert Schweitzer. A teacher of tolerance, free of all dogmatic exclusiveness, Toynbee even resembles the great mind of the German Enlightenment, Gotthold Ephraim Lessing, who in his play "Nathan the Wise" told eighteenth century Europe that man's religious beliefs and dogmas are unimportant compared with his action and his ethical spirit. As Lessing saw in Judaism, Christianity, and Islam variations on a single theme, so Mr. Toynbee, on the enlarged and world-wide scale of the twentieth century, no longer regards Christianity as the only possible true religion, but sees all universal religions—Christianity, Islam, Hinduism, and Buddhism—as equally sharing in their great message to mankind, the message of unity beyond all ethnic divisions.

In spite of his broad tolerance and his critical insight, Mr. Toynbee seems to overestimate the moral beauty of the ages of faith and to underestimate the vigor of modern Western civilization. To quote Huizinga's last book again, written while he himself suffered from the effects of the Second World War, "Has Christianity ever, even in the period when it found most passionate and general adherence, made the average man better and wiser?" The Middle Ages was the time not only of great and sublime piety but also of unsurpassed cruelty and excessive immorality. Nor did the poets and writers of the time speak of it without that critical bitterness which reminds us of some writers of our own day. In the fourteenth century Eustache Deschamps wrote of

> Temps de doleur et de temptacion,
> Aages de plour, d'envie et de tourment,
> Temps de langour et de dampnacion,
> Aages meneur près du definement,
> Temps plain d'orreur qui tout fait faussement,
> Aage menteur, plain d'orgeuil et d'envie,
> Temps sanz honeur et sanz vray jugement,
> Aage en tristesse qui abrege la vie.

And his British contemporary Langland was equally bitter:

> Loud laughed Life . . . .
> And armed him in haste — with words of harlotry
> And held Holiness for a jest — and
>   Courtesy for a waster,
> And Loyalty a churl — and Liar a gentleman,
>   Conscience and Counsel — he counted it a folly.

Two centuries earlier John of Salisbury, in discussing Caesar's times in his "Policraticus", a treatise on court vanities, wrote words familiar to readers today:

> The picture of that time often comes to mind, when subjects see their every act determined by a tyrant's nod, and however their minds rebel, are forced to condemn themselves to exile or to death. . . . So priests are forced to deny the precepts of divine law, old men forget their wisdom, the judge is ignorant of justice . . . . the free citizen despises liberty, and the whole people at last scorn peace and quiet. For when all are at the mercy of the ruler's nod, one and all are deprived of the exercize of free will.

Mr. Toynbee is not the only one to lament the follies, misery, and insecurity of twentieth century Western man. Therein he follows only a broad and fashionable trend among intellectuals today, especially on the European continent. But the outstanding student of history which Mr. Toynbee is knows well that there have been few ages not suffering from the same predicament. There were, of course, exceptions, but only two come immediately to one's mind, the Mediterranean world of the second century of our era, led by Rome, and the Western world of the nineteenth century, led by Britain. A century ago man and people lived in an unusual feeling of security, yet even then sensitive minds felt approaching earthquakes. In any case, the twentieth century Western man was rudely awakened to a realization of the general human condition. This awakening gave him the feeling of an unprecedented crisis. Arthur Koestler has, intentionally or not, caricatured this crisis feeling of an approaching total catastrophe in his novel *The Age of Longing*. In it the crowds accompanying a funeral in the streets of Paris, sometime in the early 1950's, are seized by excitement at the sounding of air-raid sirens. "The siren wailed, but nobody was sure if it could have meant the Last Judgement, or just another air-raid exercise". The American heroine of the novel thought, observing the panic-stricken faces, "Thus must medieval crowds have stared at the sky Anno Domini 999, waiting for the Comet to appear". In the age of faith the crowds waited in vain — not only in 999 but also on several later occasions — and the Parisian crowds in Koestler's age of longing waited certainly in vain too. Koestler is not the only one to admire the alleged youth and strength of the new age of faith which has dawned in Eastern Europe. It is being contrasted, to the latter's disadvantage, with a sceptical, insecure, decaying, and obsolete West.

This message is not new. We have heard it many times from German romanticists and historicists, from Russian Slavophils, from Hindu spiritualists and nationalists. Mr. Toynbee is too great a historian and too deeply steeped in the spirit of liberty and tolerance of the modern West to accept this over-simplified version of the "apocalyptic" and "crisis" thinkers of our time. Yet he, too, regards modern Western civilization as an apostasy from Christian Western civilization, as a desertion of modern man from faith into the barren grounds of secularism. He dates the beginning of the modern West from the fifteenth century Portuguese and Spanish discoveries. In reality, it began in the seventeenth century, in England and Holland. Mr. Toynbee regards "an elimination of religion, not an introduction of science" as the essence "of the seventeenth century Western cultural revolution". But modern Western civilization was not a negative phenomenon, an elimination of religion, it was an entirely new civilization, a new moral, spiritual, and practical attitude, which can be called post-Christian only in the same sense as Western Christian civilization from the eighth to the seventeenth century can be called a post-Greco-Roman civilization.

What happened in the seventeenth century, in the great crisis of the birth of a new Western consciousness, was the rise of a new civilization. It was affiliated, both historically and in its content, to the Western Christian civilization of the Middle Ages, as the latter was affiliated to the Greco-Roman civilization of Antiquity. Religion was in no way "eliminated". On the contrary, it lost only its dominant and all-encompassing function which it had exercised during the Middle Ages and in the first part of the seventeenth century. Not only a new spirit of scientific inquiry but a new respect for liberty under law, for individual dignity, for freedom of thought, for political and intellectual tolerance, a new concept of human relationship in society and of the rights of the citizen in face of his government were born then. Modern Western civilization is not "old", it is "young", barely three centuries in existence even on the shores of the North Atlantic. Communism and fascism are not the fruit or result of this modern civilization. They are a rejection of it and of its spirit, though eager to take over its technology and material results. Communism and fascism gained hold only in countries where modern Western civilization had not taken firm root. They were a "return" to the "Middle Ages", in Russia and Italy, Germany, and Spain.

Mr. Toynbee underrates the newness and greatness of modern Western civilization. He overstresses, and therein he again follows a fashionable trend, the need for a political unification of the world. Such a demand was understandable in the naive and hopeful belief, only a few years ago, in the universality of Western civilization. Many people believed then that Western civilization would spread all over the earth and become the only civilization. The Russian Marxists, heirs of this over-confident self-estimation of the bourgeois West, are today convinced that their Communism will establish on the basis of its one civilization a unified world. We are less inclined to disregard the diversity of civilizations and historical traditions. Their diversity and even their antagonism add to the richness of human experience. Several "worlds" can live together provided that they follow Mr. Toynbee's "unflamboyant virtues" of fortitude and reasonableness, which are in the best Western tradition. What is needed is not the—at least at present— impossible unity of the world which can be based only on at present non-existent common attitudes to liberty and law, but the unity of the nations of modern Western civilization, their outgrowing of nationalism and parochial loyalties into a loyalty to their common civilization, which is for them the spiritual source of their life, as Christianity was for thirteenth century Western man. Such a Western or Atlantic unity in diversity was not needed before 1914. It is essential now when modern Western civilization has found itself under severe attack from non-Western civilizations and from anti-Western movements like fascism and communism.

Mr. Toynbee is too keen and too broad-minded to emphasize differences between Western Europe and the United States. The United States certainly differs in many ways from Britain, but so does Britain from France or Switzerland. The present crisis is a common phenomenon of the whole of modern Western civilization. "Any contemporary critic of American *mores* could silence the carping West European visitor", Mr. Toynbee writes, "with a crushing *De te fabula narratur*". Yet even Mr. Toynbee seems to believe in a "third way" followed by Britain and Scandinavia between the apparently dogmatic capitalism of the United States and the communism of the Soviet orbit. Rightly he praises the trial and error method followed by Britain since the Glorious Revolution. But the heritage of the Glorious Revolution is common to Britain and the United States, and John Locke has been rightly called the "American philosopher". The New Deal of 1933 was as much a peaceful domestic revolution as Britain's reforms under the Labor government of 1945. Nor is American isolationism so different from British insularity. The wealth of diversity, the acceptance of contradiction and criticism, the incessant quest for new frontiers of truth, a profound spiritual mobility, a permanent social and intellectual revolution—these are characteristic traits which distinguish modern Western civilization. Naturally they produce a feeling of crisis, insecurity, and change unknown to other civilizations, but they also form the modern West's strength and glory.

No short essay can exhaust the riches of Mr. Toynbee's massive volumes nor note the many points of admiration or of disagreement which every reader will encounter. The details in Mr. Toynbee's work are much more important than the general framework, for history, the totality of human life and experience, is not a surveyable whole. It is, however, at least in the West, a continuous chain of tradition. Modern Western man knows, and gratefully acknowledges, how much he owes to medieval Christianity. But he owes a debt to the ancient world, too. Two great Germans who still lived in the community of Western tradition—before some Germans adumbrated, with their interpretations of the struggle against the French, the "war against the West"—Goethe and Schiller, seeking a crisis of Western man for healing forces, turned not to the Christian Middle Ages but to Greek antiquity.

Und die Sonne Homers, siehe, sie leuchtet auch uns.

Modern Western civilization is a new civilization, neither is it an apostasy from Christianity nor from Greece. The cosmos of the thirteenth century is as distant from us as Homer's nature or as Periclean Athens. But in them, and their continuous life in us, we are rooted. Today we are confronted by the danger that this chain of tradition is being broken. Mr. Toynbee, for whom the Old and the New Testament, the Greek and the Roman classics are a living reality, recalls us to a continuity without which the creativity of our modern civilization must wither. At the same time, however, he does not confine us to our own civilization. He broadens the horizon, as no other historian has done, to include the whole panorama of past and contemporary civilizations. History feeds on the diversity and contrariety of men and civilizations. But the Old Testament tells us at the very beginning that all men descend from Adam and Eve and that they share dreams of a lost past and hopes for salvation from the human predicament. To have stressed, beyond the confines of history, the fundamental oneness of mankind and of the human condition, will be a lasting merit of Mr. Toynbee's work and vision.

TOYNBEE AS PROPHET*

PIETER GEYL

The last four volumes of Arnold Toynbee's great work have been issued from the press. I confess that at the sight of those 2500 closely-printed pages, duly provided with diagrams and tables, my heart sank. But it was inevitable that I should have to find my way through that strange and yet familiar country. Everybody seemed to expect it of me, and I could not refuse reviewing the volumes.

Once I had overcome my initial reluctance, I found myself fascinated. The system of the six volumes which I tried to analyze eight years ago[1] is now practically discarded, but the new system springs naturally from it, and if the pretence of a scientific argument leading up to a rationally irrefutable conclusion has by the change been rendered patently absurd, I was never taken in by that pretence so that the spectacle of this subtle mind deceiving itself in so naive a manner was nothing new to me. In spite of that, my weariness was shot through with feelings stronger than irritation this time, but also (again familiar!) I could not help feeling an admiration, bordering on amazement or awe, for the tremendous intellectual energy which has not flagged under the crushing task of 27 years and which goes on throughout this long and sustained argument juggling with the events, the crises, wars, revolutions, state-formations, religious manifestations, of all the centuries and all the races, drawing effortlessly (or so it seems) on libraries of books in I don't quite know how many languages. If one could only accept the work as a collection of stories and glimpses of life, and dissertations on aspects and problems from the history of the world, what a mine of curious and out-of-the-way information (I know that by that word "out-of-the-way" I betray myself as the confirmed "parochial" Westerner I am), what flashes of insight, what instructive juxtapositions even—what learning, what brilliance!

But in the author's mind it is all subordinated, and intended to contribute to a system, a message. It is on the relation that the details bear to the system and the message, and on the system and the message themselves, that the work must be judged. The change which these have undergone (as I already hinted) only brings out their nature more clearly. Reading these volumes has confirmed

*Debates With Historians, Philosophical Library, New York, 1956, pp. 158-178.
[1]"Toynbee's System of Civilizations."

360

me in the views expressed in my earlier criticisms; it is all as I said it was, only more so.

Toynbee's thinking is revolutionary, "metaphysical" in the sense in which Burke used that word, abstract. To my view, this is as much as to say, *unhistorical*. For all his wealth of detail, and although the spectacle of the particular obviously interests him in some detached part of his far from simple mind, he is never for one moment captivated by it; not for one moment does it free him from the obsession of his dream. His dream is the unity of mankind in the love of God. Or rather, his dream is to participate in that loving vision and to see it approach realization. He has pretended to "investigate" the phenomena of communal life, within the framework of "civilizations," throughout the course of history. In reality he is the prophet revealing that one, to him all-meaning, idea and trying by his revelation, accompanied by warnings and denunciations, to contribute to its glorious and blessed consummation.

As for me, I am not speaking against the love of God, although I have no doubt that to Toynbee I must appear to be doing so. What I criticize and oppose is, first of all, the pretence of an empirical investigation.

When I wrote my earlier criticisms on the strength of the incompleted work, this was the aspect that thrust itself most prominently upon the attention and that is why I still give it pride of place. Yet after my exposure of "fallacious arguments and spurious demonstrations"[2] in the first six volumes, it will be hardly necessary to examine particular passages from the four new ones for the purpose of showing up their insufficiency from the point of view of "scientific" (as Toynbee loves to say), or simply rational, argument. It is enough to say that these new volumes are, when considered from this angle, a further installment of the same maddening profusion of vastly learned examples, stated in an attractive or impressive, but frequently slipshod, fashion, and *proving* exactly nothing. It is enough—and yet I shall give three instances, which will at the same time serve me to make a transition to the second objection I have to offer to the work as a whole.

In describing the plight of contemporary Western civilization (post-Modern, in his jargon), Toynbee mentions the trade-unions. They were, he says, an outcome of the spirit of Freedom, intended to resist the regimentation consequent upon the new industrial conditions; unfortunately the trade-unions led to the workers regimenting themselves and so we are left with a self-defeating contra-

---

[2]*From Ranke to Toynbee, Five Lectures on Historians and Historiographical Problems;* Smith College Historical Studies, Northampton, Mass., 1952.

diction. I shall not deny that there is a grain of truth in this observation, but if the matter is left there it is no more than a half-
truth like the many forming the stock-in-trade of the cheapest
political clap-trap. Yet Toynbee, without saying a word on the
improvement of material conditions nor on the building up of
political power, does leave the matter there and imagines that he
has now presented us with another fact by which to judge, and of
course to condemn, the present state of our civilization.

Extraordinary (but one learns, when reading these brilliant and
self-assured dissertations on everything under the sun, to be surprised at nothing) is Toynbee's appreciation of the extermination
of the Jews by the National-Socialist regime. Of course he abhors
it. Yet he places the policy of evicting Palestinian Arabs from
their homes, to which the Government of Israel resorted in 1948,
on a par with it; at least he describes this as a more heinous sin
than that committed against the Jews, at divers times in the past, by
Nebuchadnezzar and Titus and Hadrian and the Spanish and Portuguese Inquisition, for these were not sinning against the light
that God had vouchsafed them.

As for the Nationalist-Socialist Germans, "on the Day of Judgment the gravest crime standing to their account might be not
that they had exterminated a majority of the Western Jews, but
that they had caused the surviving remnant of Jews to stumble."[3]

I have personally always regarded the Zionist adventure with
misgivings, but is it possible to discuss the unfortunate consequences with a more complete lack of balance or with less sense
of proportion? And what is it that has moved the writer to this
amazing outburst against the Jews? It is neither the love of God
nor a scientific survey of the world's history as a whole. It is his
hatred against nationalism in every shape and form, because nationalism, even when it means no more than the recognition of the
fact of nationality, a basic fact in the life of civilizations, is to him
merely a stumbling block on the road to his idolized unity.

My third instance has to do with a question even more directly
connected with the view taken of Western civilization at this
moment.

"It will be seen," says Toynbee,[4]

> that Hitler's eventual failure to impose peace on the World by
> force of arms was due, not to any flaw in his thesis that the
> World was ripe for conquest, but to an accidental combination
> of incidental errors in his measures for putting into execution a
> nefarious grand design that, in itself, was a feasible scheme for
> profiting by a correctly diagnosed psychological situation. A

---

[3]VIII, 290/1.
[4]IX, 502.

twentieth-century World, that had thus, in A.D. 1933-45, been reprieved, thanks only to a chapter of lucky accidents, from a fate which Mankind's patently increasing defeatism and submissiveness had almost provocatively invited, could hardly count upon any future would-be world-conqueror's being so clumsy as to let the same easy prey escape for the second time . . . .

"It will be seen." This refers to the preceding two pages in which the Hitlerian attempt and its failure had been described, and it is, as usual, a gratuitous assertion that this description must carry conviction to the mind of the average unbiased reader, for, also as usual, the facts had been marshalled in accordance with the writer's pre-conceived conclusion. "Thanks only," "patently," it all comes out of the bag of tricks, not of the scholar, but of the orator out to persuade or, if need be, to bluff. Toynbee *will* have it that we were ripe for conquest and he *will* have it that we are more so now. He *will* have it that Western civilization is doomed, and indeed, why should he care? Western civilization means nothing to him.

I know the weakenesses of the position of the West as well as anybody. I shall not prophesy that it will be able to beat off another attempt to overthrow its badly-organized independence. Toynbee is sure that in any case a World Government will be forced upon us by the dangers inherent in atomic warfare. I shall not dispute the possibility, not even the likelihood, of a development in that direction, but the tone of indifference in which Toynbee discusses the future fate of the "parochial states" under a world dispensation is significant. He only remarks in passing that these *peritura regna* (their doom is a matter of certainty) "might be ostensibly preserved instead of being overtly liquidated."[5]

I should have thought that from the point of view of Western civilization, the alternative here stated is one of vital importance, nor is it fully or fairly stated unless a third possibility is added: preserved for more limited purposes.

But there is to me one dominant conviction to be affirmed when viewing these large possibilities hidden in the impenetrable future, namely that even in the worst case of a direct overthrow by some world-conqueror on the Hitler or Stalin pattern, Western civilization will prove to have sufficient moral and intellectual reserves to continue the struggle for existence and will survive.

I know that I am not speaking as a historian, although my reading of history comes comfortably to my support. I am speaking as a son of that Western civilization in which I believe and which I

---

[5] IX, 409.

love, and I should consider it base treason to accept with acquiescence the sentence of ignominious extinction which Toynbee, wrapt in his dream of world unity, passes on it with so light a heart. Here come into play feelings which Toynbee has throughout his immense work ignored, and of which—as he now gives more patent evidence than ever—he is constitutionally unable to recognize the existence.

They do exist nevertheless. I remember the summer of 1940, when Holland had just been occupied by the National-Socialists and when after the defeat of France the war seemed to hold out very little prospect for the one ally still holding out. There were many Dutchmen then who urged us to judge the facts coldly and realistically and to draw the inevitable conclusion, however unpalatable, that we were in for a period in which Germany would rule Europe if not the world. "We shall have to come to terms," they said; "the Dutch people must live." And at the same time many Frenchmen were saying the same. But there were many others who refused to accept the evidence because they were judging the situation by a faith. And these men felt that they must so judge, that this was the sacred duty laid upon them by the hour. Why should not there be such men again, in every country of the West, if the trial came to be imposed upon our world once more?" "Mankind's increasing submissiveness and defeatism" may be patent to Toynbee, and indeed he sets an example of these weaknesses by so blatantly proclaiming them. But there will be resisters upheld by a more manly faith, and as long as there are, it will be premature to talk about the dissolution of Western civilization.

This, then, is the second reason why, after my initial reluctance, I feel an irrepressible urge to testify against this false witness and indeed to criticize and oppose a system productive of such pernicious counsels.

Western civilization, I said, means nothing to Toynbee. This is a new development (although by no means a new departure) in his mental attitude towards his subject, and it must be more closely examined.

The preface to the 7th volume, the first of the four now published, is illuminating on the point. According to the scheme drawn up as long ago as 1927-9, this volume deals with Universal States, and in a second part with Universal Churches. When he was at liberty to resume his interrupted task in 1946, the writer—so he tells us—felt constrained to recast his notes.

"The world around me and within me had, indeed, met with a number of challenging and transforming experiences in the course of the nineteen years and more that, by the summer of A.D. 1946, had already passed since the first of the original notes for the book had been written." He then mentions "further discoveries in the field of Archaeology," but also "the horrifying practical demonstrations of the moral depths to which the heirs of a Christian civilization were capable of dragging themselves down"; besides, there was the work of the psychologists and that of the atomic physicists. "An Einstein and a Rutherford, a Freud and a Jung, and a Marshall and a Woolley, as well as a Gandhi, a Stalin, a Hitler, a Churchill and a Roosevelt, had been changing the face of the Macrocosm." But moreover: "my inner world had been undergoing changes which, on the miniature scale of an individual life, were, for me, of proportionate magnitude."

We shall see in a moment that the resultant change in the structure of the system was a momentous one; the whole view of the significance of civilizations is modified. First, however, a somewhat disturbing reflection, but one which does not seem to disturb Toynbee, imposes itself. Does it not follow that the empirical investigation as set out in the first six volumes had not, after all, led to any reliable conclusions about the laws of mankind's historic life, with the help of which the future might be forecast? This was the purpose for which we were assured that investigation was undertaken. Toynbee is still convinced that he can tell us something about the future. He admits the speculative nature of all predictions, he is careful not to be dogmatic either about the period needed for the process or about the exact modalities. Yet the twenty years between 1929 and 1950, so he repeats when starting, in part 12, to deal with the Prospects of Western Civilization,[6] make it possible for the historian to speak with much greater confidence about the inevitable merging of parochialism into universality. The Wall Street collapse, the break-down of France, on the whole "the experience of twenty-one sinisterly illuminating years" makes "relatively sure prediction"[7] possible. It is startling to see with how little ado the author himself brushes the labor devoted to his first six volumes aside and in effect bases his concluding wisdom on his observations of the world's vicissitudes during the last twenty years, observations such as are indeed the source of innumerable pronouncements on our condition and our prospects in newspaper articles, political speeches and sermons.

To these experiences common to his generation must, in Toynbee's case, be added—to explain the views he is now expounding—changes in his own inner world. So he admits in this same preface to volume VII. *Hebemus reum confitentum.* I said eight years ago that the study of history cannot supply us with fore-

[6] IX, 406. seq.
[7] IX, 409.

casts having universal validity. Toynbee's refreshingly frank confession now implies agreement with that view. I say "implies" for, in spite of his refreshing frankness, he does not go so far as to admit that his work is not really the scientific investigation for which he has all along tried, and is in the face of his change of front still trying, to pass it off.

What does this change in the writer's inner world amount to? Martin Wight, who read the chapter on Universal Churches before publication, and whose remarks, printed in the book, sometimes but not always caused the author to modify his text, expresses in an Annex his profound gratitude as a Christian critic to Toynbee for having "abandoned [his] original judgment that all civilizations are philosophically equivalent and for having found that 'civilizations . . . have ceased to constitute intelligible fields of study for us and have forfeited their historical significance except in so far as they minister to the progress of religion.' "[8] But although grateful, Mr. Wight is not entirely satisfied. Toynbee, while distinguishing religions into higher and lower, is not prepared to grant to the Christian religion a unique place of preeminence.

> The writer of this study [as he puts it, for he always uses the third person to describe himself] ventures to express his personal belief that the four higher religions that were alive in the age in which he was living were four variations on a single theme, and that, if all the four components of this heavenly music of the spheres could be audible on Earth simultaneously, and with equal clarity, to one pair of human ears, the happy hearer would find himself listening, not to a discord, but to a harmony.[9]

Mr. Wight would be completely satisfied only if Toynbee had come to the conclusion "that the higher religions in their turn cease to be intelligible fields of study and forfeit their historical significance except insofar as they are related to Christianity." It is instructive to see that the admiring critic wants to confine the concept of "historical significance" within still narrower bounds than Toynbee in his changed state of mind is willing to do. Even to him, nevertheless, civilizations are no more than "the handmaids of religion,"[10] and he writes, for instance, that

> we have to think of the civilizations, of the second generation [i.e., the Babylonic, the Syriac, the Hellenic, the Indic and the Sinic] as having come into existence, not in order to perform achievements of their own, and not in order to reproduce their kind in a third generation, but in order to provide an opportunity for fully-fledged higher religions to come to birth; and, since

[8]VIII, 748.
[9]VII, 428.
[10]VII, 445.

the genesis of these higher religions was a consequence of the breakdowns and disintegrations of the secondary civilizations' histories—breakdowns which, from their standpoint spell failure—as being their justification for existence and their title to significance.[11]

The consequences for Toynbee's appreciations of Western civilization are set forth uncompromisingly in volume IX. When after the change of heart subsequent upon the completion of the first six volumes he discovered that the civilizations, between which he had until then assumed a philosophical parity, were unequal—as he puts it: when he found them to be unequal *as a matter of historical fact* on the evidence of an assay in which the touchstone had been the part played . . . in the history of Religion" (Can anything be more obvious than that the selection of that touchstone was an arbitrary decision, governed by personal or subjective feeling, and that the slipping in of the words "historical fact" is therefore an act of naive, but very characteristic, presumption?)—when the civilizations were (on the test!) found to be unequal, "the result was," says Toynbee, "not to re-exalt the Western civilization to the pinnacle on which it had once been placed by a naively vulgar native Western egocentric prejudice." By comparison with, for instance, the Indic and the Hellenic civilizations which had given rise to, respectively, Hinduism and Christianity, "the Western civilization and its contemporaries of the third generation had been 'vain repetitions of the heathen' (Matth., VI, 7)," and this time he has the grace to add: "from the standpoint of an observer who saw the guide-line of History in a progressive increase in the provision of spiritual opportunities for human souls in transit through This World."[12]

Western civilization does not, it will now be realized, interest Toynbee; I should perhaps add "any more." It is for this reason that he is ready with so much complacency to insist on its defects and weaknesses. He proves to himself, by doing so, his freedom from that "blight of egocentricity" which "had been the nemesis of an act of hybris"; from that "intellectual effect of Original Sin." What he seems to overlook entirely is that it is *his* civilization, and *our* civilization, and that he and we can work and think to any purpose only on the lines issuing from it. This is no reason to ignore what has been or is being wrought and thought outside it (in fact no civilization has been so catholic in its interests as this Western civilization which Toynbee singles out for the reproach of egocentricity); it is no reason either to exalt it above others (and in so far as we are apt to indulge in that somewhat sterile habit

[11]VII, 422.
[12]IX, 411.

it is good to be reminded of the special virtues of other civilizations); but it *is* a reason why we are perfectly justified in giving it special and loving, though not uncritical, attention; indeed, this is one of the conditions for creative work in the present, and one of the tasks of history as I understand it is to entertain a living sense of tradition.

Toynbee, however, tries to escape into a non-existing world unity, which he sees as God's idea and purpose. The energy with which that concept has inspired him is impressive; it is indeed almost superhuman. But his vast, global knowledge of history has tempted him into what strikes me as a prideful and sinful, an inhuman and at times slightly ridiculous, ostentation of detachment from his own heritage, to which his work nevertheless owes so many of its most admirable traits.

Often one cannot help suspecting that the detachment is actually spite masquerading as detachment, so incredibly biased is his treatment of Western civilization when he comes to discuss its prospects. Every sign of crisis or of decadence, every flaw, every incidental infidelity to its professed principles, is by him eagerly displayed as evidence of its approaching dissolution. On the other hand there is hardly more than a grudging word, now and then, about its positive achievements. And indeed, how can one make much of these when the last four centuries at least are regarded as "a vain repetition of the heathen"? The great European thinkers and poets and artists and scholars serve Toynbee to decorate his pages or to strengthen his ideas; but as far as his estimation of Western civilization is concerned they might as well never have existed. The scientists, of whose contribution he makes so much use in his explanation and interpretations, are never valued for what they helped to make of Western civilization; the atom bomb seems at times to outweigh all their merits.[13] The great advance made during that period in the countries of our civilization in the matter of social security and material prosperity (which also have their importance when it comes to "spiritual opportunities"), in humanity coupled with more stable order and more equitable law —it weighs as nothing in his scales. The deficiencies in these respects of the centuries when civilization had in Toynbee's view a more real significance are ignored or condoned. The study of history is not to concern itself with men as they lived and strove. The system requires that it should all be viewed and "assayed" by the one test which Mr. Arnold J. Toynbee discovered a few years ago: religion.

---

[13]He has, it is true, a passage where he distinguishes between the beneficent possibilities inherent in a knowledge of the laws of nature and the destructive effects due to human sin: IX, 172.

Western civilization can hardly expect to pass with honors when it is called before an examiner to whom neo-paganism, beginning with the Renaissance and suddenly blossoming out in the 18th century, has no other than the negative significance of a departure from the one vital principle of the West, Christianity. Toynbee consistently refuses to it any value or any strength of its own, except for evil. A highpowered enormity, the Abomination of Desolation, are some of his names for it and he holds it responsible for the deadly menace of a third world war waged with atomic weapons. "But this appalling prospect was merely the unveiling of a goal towards which a secularized Western Society had been heading ever since it had erupted out of a medieval *Respublica Christiana.*" Can the simplification, and one might say distortion, of history be carried farther? *The Respublica Christiana* was never more than an aspiration. The people of the Middle Ages waged war, without atomic means it is true, but with no less ferocity for that, every day of their lives. And Neo-Paganism has as little to do with the atom bomb as has Christianity or Buddhism or Mohammedanism. A world in which all these spiritual states are mingled together is striving to avert the disaster with which the purely mechanical intrusion of this wonderful as well as awful invention is threatening it; more cannot be said "A.D. 1955" any more than in "A.D. 1950."

But neo-paganism is Toynbee's butt. Occasionally, in so far as he can represent it as a pale reflection of the religion which is denied, he will condescend to say something for it. As to admitting that among its adherents, too, there may be allies for the building up of a firm defense against the deadly dangers with which he sees our civilization threatened—never! In this single-minded judge of the civilizations' view, it would be absurd to look for moral strength in any principle divorced from positive religion.

Toynbee loves to talk about humility; "a contrite humility the first of the Christian virtues," he reminds us on the very last page of his Part on the Prospects.[14] He had rejected Mr. Wight's plea for a recognition of the Christian religion as (to use Toynbee's own words) "possessing a monopoly of the Divine Light," and he rejected it on the ground that in making such a claim, "a church seems to me guilty of hybris."[15] But in making the claim on behalf of the four higher religions collectively, or on behalf of his own personal conviction supported by ten volumes of eloquent and biased interpretation of history, it seems to me that he makes himself guilty of hybris no less.

---

[14]IX, 644.
[15]VIII, 428, footnote.

I give one instance of the demagogic fashion in which the impression of Western civilization being undermined by neo-paganism is supported. Toynbee quotes a long passage from Frazer's *Golden Bough,* in which the Renaissance is described as the period marking the weakening of "the obsession" with "a future life" and "the return of Europe to native ideals of life and conduct, to saner, manlier views of the world. The long halt in the march of civilization was over. The tide of Oriental invasion had turned at last. It is ebbing still."[16] It is a passage which bears the mark of the time when it was written, fifty years ago. But now listen to Toynbee's comment:

> It was indeed still ebbing when the present lines were being written on the 4th of March 1948, and, in fact, the present writer was wondering what the gentle scholar would have had to say if he had lived to see some of the ways in which Europe's 'return to native ways of life and conduct' had manifested itself since.

Frazer, Toynbee asserts, has been proved to belong to

> the last generation of Western neo-pagans of a rational, unenthusiastic, tolerant school . . . . By A.D. 1952 they had been swept off the field by demonic, emotional, violent-handed successors who had suddenly emerged, unheralded, out of the unplumbed depths of a secularized Western society. The words of Frazer had been re-uttered by the voice of Alfred Rosenberg with a different ring.

But is Alfred Rosenberg now in occupation of the field off which he has swept these gentle scholars? Is Western civilization really dominated by National-Socialist theories of race and culture? One might also ask: Has no non-secularized civilization ever known outbursts of human devilry?—and recall the Crusade against the Albigeois, or the Inquisition (which when he wanted to belabor Jewish nationalism was excused by Toynbee because the Inquisitors naively believed themselves to be carrying out the behests of religion), or the Anabaptists, or the burnings of the witches. But the point I want to make here is that once again we see Toynbee making capital out of the National-Socialist aberration at the expense of Western civilization. To me it seems the height of irresponsibility to speak as if in the Western world at large the spirit of Frazer had been ousted by that of Rosenberg. But it is all grist to Toynbee's mill.

Once one has grasped the spirit and purpose of the last instalment of the great work, one feels that demonstrations of fallacious arguments, of perversions of the significance of historical data, or

---

[16]VIII, 384.

of their complete irrelevance for the thesis, demonstrations which seemed worth attempting in connection with the first six volumes, have indeed become utterly superfluous. These volumes, especially VII and VIII, again testify to the enormous learning of the writer. Only, learning, even when assisted by an acute mind and a sensitive as well as a powerful imagination, is not enough to produce history. What is needed, unless all the rest is to go for nothing, is an attitude of mind, from which Toynbee's is as far removed as it can be.

The historian should take an interest in his subject for its own sake, he should try to get into contact with things as they were, the men and their vicissitudes should mean something to him in themselves. I do not mean that the historian should not have a point of view, that he should be indifferent to the problems of his own time; nor that he, having a point of view, and caring about the present and the future, should try to tell about past events as if they bore no relation to either. But if a man comes to the past with a compelling vision, a principle, or dogma, of such magnitude or emotional potence as Toynbee's unity in the love of God; with a system which causes him to reduce the multitudinous movement of history to one single, divinely-inspired current, and to judge civilizations and generations by one single criterion, rejecting most of them, and incidentally his own, as unimportant; *that* man can write a work full of color and striking theories, glowing with conviction and eloquence, but no history. The *Study of History* is no history. The Student of History, as Toynbee calls himself, may know more of history than I ever shall, but he is no historian. He is a prophet.

There has never been any love lost between prophets and historians. Toynbee devotes a paragraph of 46 pages of a chapter on Law and Freedom in History (vol. IX) to criticizing and ridiculing Modern Historians as a class, and as the air resounds with the scornful reviews that historians are writing of his last volumes[17] (I was the first in the field in 1946, but I have long lost the feeling of doing something adventurous or audacious), it might seem that we are quits. Historians, however—I believe that, although an interested party, I am stating an objective truth—have a better understanding of the rules of the game of polemics than prophets. And at any rate, Toynbee's attack on the Modern Historians and

---

[17]I have read the front page article (anonymous) of the *Times Literary Supplement,* 22 October, 1954; articles by A. J. P. Taylor in *The New Statesman,* 16 Oct; Geoffrey Barraclough in *The Listener,* 14 Oct.; Hugh Trevor-Roper in *The Sunday Times,* 17 Oct. Only Noel Annan in *The Manchester Guardian Weekly,* 21 Oct., takes the work seriously and seems to regard the strictures passed on it by "the academic" or "professional" historians with distrust.

their Antinomianism is a piece of very spirited, but at the same time very questionable, polemics.

Toynbee in this chapter maintains, not only that the course of history is governed by laws, but that these laws can, and therefore should, be discovered and defined. He had of course long been aware that modern historians regard this thesis with suspicion and are on the contrary accustomed to stress the infinite complexity and intangibility of the factors of the historical process; and he had also found that they were inclined to criticize his practical attempts in the *Study of History* as utterly unconvincing. So he now denounces them wholesale as purblind worshippers of technique and *minutiae,* indifferent to the great problems of the present and the future, and deaf to the call to action, which is the essence of life.[18]

There are no doubt and always have been historians whom this description fits. But when applied to the profession as a whole it is no more than a caricature. Because we do not swallow Toynbee's generalizations and systematizations, are we to be charged with lack of interest for the meaning of the facts of history? Because we try to solve problems of less world-wide proportions on the basis of a close attention to the sources, do we bury ourselves in technique? I need only point to the work of the three English critics of Toynbee mentioned in footnote 17 to confound that ill-directed counter-attack. Are we not interested in the world around us? Are we not aware that our scholarship has a function to civilization or society at large to fulfill? The very criticisms levelled against Toynbee are often inspired by that feeling: the gradiose and impassioned, wrong-headed and one-sided prophesyings and pronouncements offend against the spirit of scholarship which the scholar must feel it to be his first duty by the community to uphold.

The real truth of the matter is, of course, that there is an incompatibility between Toynbee's mental attitude towards the past and that of "the historians." They would not care if he wrote as a prophet, but they feel that the best traditions of their profession are insulted when the prophet poses as a historian. I have already indicated the difference. It is not only, not in the first place even, the looking for laws, the generalizations, even the faulty reasonings, that offend; it is the vision itself in which every age and every civilization is judged by a standard foreign to it, and its importance restricted to what it contributed to the progress of an arbitrarily chosen principle. The historian believes that history can enrich the civilization of his own age especially by trying to enter into the habits of thought and the relationships of past generations and

---

[18]X, 35.

that only thus can these be understood. He believes, too, that the discipline of transferring oneself into strange surroundings and states of mind has in itself an educative, a broadening, a moderating influence, which should be a valuable component in the spiritual life of his own community. To see a self-styled historian reducing the whole of the wonderful and mysterious movement of history to one single motif, rejecting whole centuries as uninteresting, forcing it all into the scheme of a presumptuous construction, strikes him as going against all that history stands for. This spate of moral judgments, too, this highly-strung sense of impending disaster and contempt for vital currents of thought, it does not seem to the historian to be "humble," it denotes a hectoring and censorious attitude towards the social phenomena which to him seem an integral part of life, to be explained, but, with life, to be accepted first of all. The modern historian, in other words, is intellectually the descendant of Burke[19] rather than of Rousseau. With Toynbee it is the reverse. His speaking of modern historians as taking refuge from larger views in the sands of technique is therefore doing less than justice to the far-reaching philosophic difference involved.

In his more direct defense of his thesis about historical laws Toynbee is little more to the point. Here too he follows a well-known, though far from admirable method of debate. The only professional historians whom he permits to state the case which he intends to demolish, do so in a way which few of us will accept as a fair representation of the position. (One marvels, by the way, at the insularity, or parochialism, of Toynbee's reading on the subject: both the historians quoted are British, and so are most of the other modern writers mentioned in this chapter either in support or for refutation. No notice is taken of the important German contribution to the theory of history.)

H. A. L. Fisher's saying that there can be no generalizations, and that the main thing is to recognize in the development of human destinies the play of the contingent and the unforseen, is patently an overstatement. E. L. Woodward, on the other hand, took up a somewhat too apologetic attitude when he argued that for "a final synthesis . . . the difficulty at present is that the *data* are insufficient." The real and permanent difficulty is rather that the *data* are so unmanageably abundant. The chance is too good for Toynbee to be missed and he pokes fun at adversaries who excuse themselves with two diametrically opposed pleas. But in the meantime he fails to advance any effective arguments against the really serious objection.

---

[19]One might, of course, also mention Ranke and his famous dictum about every epoch being immediate to God.

It is true that he deals with it at some length, but the argument, when examined, turns out to consist of an assertion, endlessly repeated in that inexhaustible wealth of language and of metaphor which he has at all times at his disposal, and enveloped in scientific and biblical and mythological allusions and parallels. The assertion is, that the complexity by which historians allow themselves to be paralyzed, is of their own making; it is the result of their own nihilistic technique. "While the shivered splinters had become unmanageably numerous and complicated, the intact bones remained intelligibly few and simple. . . . The significant known integral events in the history of Man in Process of Civilization were, not awkwardly abundant, but awkwardly scarce."[20] (until new archaeological finds added to their number).

An amazing statement! There is, to begin with, the familiar confusion in Toynbee's mind as to what constitutes a historical fact. He qualifies his "known events" in this passage by the words "significant" and "integral," but apparently without realizing that he thereby introduces a speculative or subjective element, which must make all generalization on the basis of these *data,* not valueless, but uncertain and hypothetical. And the bones of the structure of history are simple! If any work is apt to make the reader doubt the truth of that bold assertion, it is Toynbee's *Study of History.* For the feeling created in the mind of the beholder of the picture drawn even by this "terrible simplificateur,"[21] is one of bewilderment. One searches one's way desperately through the jungle of arguments, metaphors, digressions, hypotheses; one tries to follow the eloquent (at times one is tempted to say, loquacious) demonstrator, but inevitably one loses the thread. The non-sequiturs and the contradictions, the far-fetched comparisons, the dizzying assumptions, are too confusing. And if conclusions are all along drawn with the glowing conviction, with that unshakeable self-confidence, one feels that they spring from another source altogether than that of the preceding exposition, which has seldom succeeded in covering up the unruly and indomitable complexity of historical reality.

The simplifications are at their most "terrible" in the tables (at least they are nowhere so glaringly patent). One of Toynbee's laws is the recurrence in history of a War-and-Peace Cycle in so many phases. In a table on p. 255 of volume IX he shows these phases—"Premonitory Wars (the Prelude), the General War, The Breathing-space, Supplementary Wars (the Epilogue), The General Peace"—in an Overture and four Regular Cycles between 1494

20IX, 210.
21Jacob Burckhardt, *Weltgeschictliche Betrachtungen.*

and 1935. It looks beautifully "simple." I shall say no more than that I have rarely seen a more arbitrary juggling with the known facts of history.

Toynbee, meanwhile, also holds up to the historians the example of the sociologists and economists, and twits the former somewhat laboriously for ignoring the activities of these searchers for laws in human affairs. He never mentions the fundamental difference presented by history, which deals, not with one more or less confined and homogeneous sphere of man's communal life, but with the whole of it. It is not only the large number of data (all this talk about the "shivering" or "splintering" effect of "technique" and archival research is largely beside the point), but their belonging to the most diverse and mutually incomparable spheres, including that of events, which makes it so difficult to embrace them all in one fixed and balanced survey. In fact even the sociologists in their more restricted sphere, are not finding it so easy and have grown more cautious.

Toynbee's indictment of the historians, then, is a disappointing performance. But the worst remains to be said of this chapter in which he tries to dispose of them. It is that, while obviously seething with resentment, he limits his counterattack to this more spectacular than solid exposition in the field of theory and avoids coming to grips with the concrete criticisms made against his earlier volumes. The proof of the pudding is in the eating. These theoretical discussions have their importance, but after all the theory in the world I should try to preserve an open mind when someone comes along with a work of even suspiciously large synthesis, and judge it on its merits. It is what I did with Toynbee's six volumes in 1946, and if in the end I rejected them, it is not because they offended me in any dogmatically held theory, but because I had found them wanting.

Toynbee makes an allusion to the essay I then wrote, when he says that "these distracted latter-day Western historians were appalled" by "the novel universe of an incomprehensible complexity," which they had conjured up themselves, and which "made the sheltering sands of technique look like the only practicable refuge from the mental hell of being compelled to play an eternal game of croquet with the unmanageable implements prescribed for the luckless players of the game in Lewis Carroll's fantasy *Alice Through the Looking-glass.*" It was indeed to that game with continually changing and unexpectedly moving implements (the description occurs, by the way, in *Alice in Wonderland*) that I had compared the method of *A Study of History,* and the comparison still seems to me a very apt one. But no other reference to my criticisms is to be found in Toynbee's defense, and I am not alone in thinking that his position is untenable unless he refutes a good many of my precise demonstrations of the fallacies and inconsistencies and misinterpretations to be found in his "empirical investigation."

This is a good deal more than a question of "technique." If the historical foundations which Toynbee assures us securely support his theories about the destinies of civilizations are proved to be unsound, as I believe that I have proved them to be, the whole imposing structure becomes a dream-like fantasy—not unlike (since Toynbee has reminded me of that parallel) the Wonderland through which Alice wandered, with, I must say (and in so far the parallel seems to be defective), her critical faculties very much awake.

But I am afraid that it is too late in the day to issue an express challenge to Toynbee to prove that, for instance, his reading of 19th century Italian history, which according to my demonstrations (*The Pattern of the Past*, p. 41-50) did not warrant the conclusions he built upon it, was right after all; or to do the same for his reading of North American history, which I argued was hopelessly wrong, so that his laws and large theories fell to the ground (*From Ranke to Toynbee: Five Lectures on Historians and Historical Problems*, Smith College, Mass., p. 71-75). He has missed the opportunity afforded him by his chapter in volume IX to respond to the challenge implicit in my earlier essays, and he is less likely to respond to it now than before. He dwells in a world of his own imagining, where the challenges of rationally thinking mortals cannot reach him. Prophets will at most traduce and scoff at their critics. As to showing that their critics are wrong, why should they? They know in their inmost hearts that it is themselves who are right.

And indeed, prophets have experiences which more earth-bound scholars cannot hope to share. In the little intellectual autobiography which is to be found in volume X (and which is from more than one point of view absorbingly interesting) Toynbee relates how on seven occasions, all carefully dated and located, he was momentarily "transported" or "rapt into communion" with historic events or historic personages, generally connected with the outlandish place where he happened to find himself. One of these memorable experiences stands out from the rest.

> In London, in the southern section of the Buckingham Palace Road, walking southward along the pavement, skirting the west wall of Victoria Station, the writer, once, one afternoon not long after the First World War . . . found himself in communion, not just with this or that episode in History, but with all that had been, and was, and was to come. In that instant he

was directly aware of the passage of History flowing through him in a mighty current, and of his own life welling like a wave in the flow of this vast tide.[22]

The book and the man have an importance altogether apart from achievement or failure in the realm of history or of scholarship. I suppose that a later student of history will regard them and their immense, though unevenly distributed, popularity as a curious portent of our times. Is it not highly remarkable, for instance, that Toynbee's admirers are to be found, not only among Christians, like Mr. Wight, but among typically "neo-pagan" and at the same time neo-Marxist scholars like Professor Romein of Amsterdam, who took the chair when Toynbee delivered at The Hague the lecture on "World Unity and World History" which I had shortly before heard him deliver in London. The religious garb can apparently be quietly removed and the preaching of the idol Unity, which is Moloch-like, to devour national traditions, attract a man stricken with a craving for what his friend, the Amsterdam philosopher Pos, has dubbed "universalist solidarism."[23]

If I have in this essay, almost wholly confined myself to destructive criticism, the reason is not only that, as I put it before, there is no love lost between prophets and historians. The prophet can be to the historian an exciting and a moving subject. The reason is rather, not only that this prophet usurps the name of historian, but especially that I regard his prophecy as a blasphemy against Western Civilization.[24]

---

[22]X, 139.

[23]A shrewd remark on Romein and the mentality that comes under the spell of *A Study of History* will be found in J. G. Renier, *History, Its Purpose and Method* (1950), 218.

[24]Since writing this article I received from a friend in England an advertisement page cut from the *New York Times Book Review*. "Have you seen what they're saying about Arnold Toynbee?" I quote some of the headings of the seventeen extracts from reviews (among which I spotted only one written by a trained historian): "Amazing and monumental" . . . "An important masterpiece" . . . "The greatest work of our time" . . . "A literary and intellectual phenomenon" . . . "Probably the greatest historical work ever written" . . . "A landmark, perhaps even a turning point."
This chorus of praise is a chastening reminder of the very restricted influence exercised by professional criticism. The effect it had on me was nevertheless a heartening one. I have sometimes felt the uncomfortable thought stirring: "Is it still worth while?" Apparently it *is* still worth while. For we must never abdicate before misdirected popular enthusiasm.

TOYNBEE AS POET*

Edward Fiess

The first three volumes of Toynbee's *Study of History* appeared in 1934, the next three in 1939, and four more in 1954. D. C. Somervell's one-volume abridgement of the first six volumes, which had been preceded by some signs of wide interest in Toynbee's ideas, appeared in 1947 and created a new and popular interest.[1] Both popular and scholarly periodicals featured articles by historians, theologians, critics, and Toynbee himself. At times public interest approached the fashionable, and it was not always easy for friend, foe, or neutral to discuss *A Study of History* without the devices of controversial defense and attack. Certainly it has never been easy to discuss the unity of the work rather than its separate parts.

Now, when we still await the concluding installments of this huge work and when the merely fashionable interest in Toynbee as a prophet has had a chance to subside, it may be fitting to take a new approach to the many volumes, one that will not solve the problems of confronting the historian and the critic but that will perhaps put these problems in a new light. This approach is to Toynbee as a literary artist. There seems little reason why the form-content dichotomy or complex should not in this case be seen occasionally from the side of form. All discourse is in some sense a simplification; but an emphasis on the formal, provided that we keep its partial nature in mind, is no more simplistic than the stress on content found, understandably, in most discussions of *A Study of History*.

The oftentimes haphazard way in which observations about formal structure and texture, for example, are made about prose out-

---

Journal of the History of Ideas, vol. 16, 1955, pp. 275-280.
[1]The appearance in 1954 of Vols. VII-X does not alter the central thesis of this easy written earlier. The popularity of the one-volume abridgment by D. C. Somervell is both fortunate and unfortunate, unfortunate partly because popularity is no substitute for understanding and partly because the short form obscures the literary nature of the work—a quality which is at the center of the critical problem. Of some thirty articles and extended reviews that I have seen in general and scholarly periodicals I should mention three as representative of different kinds of excellence: P. Geyl, "Toynbee's System of Civilizations," *Journal of the History of Ideas,* IX (1948), 93-124; Granville Hicks, "The Boldest Historian," *Harper's,* 194 (1947) 116-124; Lewis Mumford, "Transfiguration or Renewal?" *Pacific Spectator,* I (1947), 391-398. It is curious that very few reviews of the one-volume abridgment showed any acquaintance with the original and still fewer suggested any kind of comparison.

side the realm of *belles-lettres* can be illustrated by the treatment of Gibbon's *Decline and Fall*. Surely it is the one work of history in English to be admitted to the title of work of art, if any is; yet it is represented in most histories of literature by a few comments on the sentence structure and the function of the irony. In the nineteenth century the term *style* often meant whatever the writer made it mean, so that it sometimes covered almost everything from Gibbon's indecent footnotes to his anti-Christian bias. Some writers in that century and more in ours have used the word precisely, to cover imagery, diction, sentence structure, rhythm, balance, and similar elements. Yet few of them seek to indicate the connection between the style and the content, between Gibbon's manner of expression and his angle of vision.[2] In fact, some who dislike the style, seem to intimate that the work would have been better if written in another!

The structure of Gibbon's masterpiece is less often discussed than the texture. When the plan, organization, or design comes in for treatment, it is usually on the basis of a few unsupported, even if sound, generalizations. Not many writers, indeed, go on, like Elton, to exemplify what they mean by the larger and smaller patterns of the *Decline*.[3] And when we look for comment on the relationship between the style and the design, we are almost always disappointed. Likewise, the relationship is scanted between either or both of these on the one hand and historical accuracy on the other. It is as if the historian and the literary critic were afraid of each other.

A Study of History obviously multiplies the difficulties of the literary critic. It is contemporary; being the product of a living writer, it does not permit us the safety of perspective. Whereas Gibbon dealt with a chapter in history that was closed, Toynbee chooses also to deal with many that are still open. The literary critic, confronted with Toynbee, has reason to be timid not only before historians, but also theologians, linguists, natural scientists, economists, and many others.

If the parts still to come follow the pre-established plan, even the most crabbed critic will have to admit that the work has design. Of the five parts into which these six volumes are divided, the first takes up the method of the entire work, and the remaining ones take up respectively the geneses, growths, breakdowns, and disintegrations of civilizations. Toynbee, like Gibbon, has meticu-

---

[2]See, as an exception, Thomas Seccombe, *The Age of Johnson* (London, 1914; reprinted from 1899).

[3]See Oliver Elton, *A Survey of English Literature*, 1730-1780 (London: Arnold, 1928) and J. B. Black, *The Art of History: A Study of the Four Great Historians of the Eighteenth Century* (London, 1926).

lously plotted out his *magnum opus* beforehand. But this very fact raises perplexities, for the work is profusely empirical in method, and empirical studies can hardly have their conclusions outlined in advance. Has the method been sacrificed to the design or are we, as I believe, dealing with a deeper question?

Furthermore, the entire structure, in many senses of the word, rests upon an analysis of the Graeco-Roman or Hellenic civilization. To the pattern that Toynbee discerns in the ancient world the careers of twenty other societies are found in various ways to conform. This raises two problems, both of which have been widely discussed. First, does the analysis of antiquity fit the facts? Second, is this analysis applied flexibly enough to civilizations as diverse as the Mayan and Far Eastern? Yet there is another side to the coin. This "paradigm", as Granville Hicks has called it, of the Hellenic civilization is the backbone of the work and more besides. For its persuades as it pervades, having functions analogous to the plots of certain dramas and pieces of fiction, with its own kinds of foreshadowing, complication, and suspense.

There are other difficulties in method. Consider "the mythological clue." Toynbee arrives at his famous theory of challenge-and-response partly through an examination of myths involving an "encounter between two superhuman personalities"—Yahweh and Serpent in the Garden of Eden, the Lord and Satan in Job, God and Mephistopheles in *Faust*. Yet the work never really makes clear to what extent these mythical patterns merely confirm what has been discovered by other means and to what extent they are themselves taken as evidence. Thus, ironically enough, the historian-reader is ill at ease precisely because Toynbee uses myth organically and structurally, like Joyce and Mann, and not as mere adornment. Again, is the historian's loss the poet's gain?

Among other elements of design, Toynbee employs with the greatest success the devices of climax, contrast, and comparison. His climaxes are likely to come early, and his denouements have a tendency to be long; in fact, the larger rhythms throughout have a "dying fall," as might be expected in the writing of a man who admires Gibbon and Spengler. The contrasts so frequently found in these pages lend lucidity and force, but many of them—like the archaism-futurism division in art—are suspiciously neat. Of comparison Toynbee is a master. In many a brilliant expository *tour de force* he compares from three to ten historical movements with sustained clarity and vigor. Yet the reader notes with a sigh that the very comparability of civilizations is in dispute among historians, to say nothing of the comparability of events.

This technical virtuosity in contrast and comparison is involved with what many a historian would call the weaknesses of *A Study of History*. What other author has dared, or would dare, to draw comparisons between movements, periods, and nations discussed in separate parts of the text, sometimes parts with hundreds, even thousands, of pages intervening? Or, to put the real question, what other author could achieve clarity as often as Toynbee does, and at what price? He has evolved a technique that can make the Roman legions march for us again in the midst of a dependent clause while we are reading about events centuries later and on the other side of the world. To this ability to use words evocatively much is due. But two less obvious effects of the technique deserve comment. One is its necessary iteration of key words, phrases, and statements selected from an originally fuller context. An unwitting oversimplification may thus creep in. Another effect comes from the conviction which sheer repetition, unobtrusive because it is secondary to the main term of the comparison, may carry with it; after the fourth or fifth repetition of some particular interpretation we may find it more acceptable than in its first formulation, especially when the environing statements are more persuasive to us. Similar phenomena are in operation upon reader (and writer) in most cases of protracted exposition; this is the tendency to accept all because we accept some. The scope and scale of this *magnum opus* yield huge returns.

The texture of Toynbee's prose is closely allied with the structure of the work. Comparison, contrast, and climax can also be seen within the sentences, which may sometimes exhibit balances like those of Gibbon, sometimes long cadences like those of De Quincey. True, some sentences are clogged by the mass of material that they contain. And other sentences drag their slow lengths along because of the very qualifications that a historian's scruples make necessary. But at their best the long sentences of Toynbee's style have rhythm, often the rhythms of the King James Bible. His most characteristic type is a partly periodic one; the meaning is suspended for several lines until the pivotal words are reached and then the sentence slides to a close through one or more dependent clauses—"when . . . where. . . ." At times the rhythm is subtly reinforced by alliteration; at other times the alliteration may become excessive, as in "the moral malady of Militarism."

A long but profitable study could be made of the key terms in Toynbee's vocabulary. Some of them, never defined too precisely, acquire their meanings through the accretion of successive contexts, as Matthew Arnold's "culture" does; others reflect the Hellenic civilization — mimesis, hubris, nemesis; still others, grouped in pairs and triads, help to define each other; they reflect the polar organization of parts of the work—*abandon,* self-control; withdrawal, return. Some, like "apparentation" and "affiliation," partake of the persuasive force of the metaphors behind them. The semantic exploration of technical or semi-technical vocabularies has been too seldom pursued; certainly in Toynbee's case it is too large a subject to go into here.

The allusiveness of the style is plain to the casual reader. But again the scope and scale of the work cause the allusions to operate in a different way, much as we found that the more formal comparisons did. When Milton refers to the "wealth of Ormus or of Ind" we recall the associations of our past reading in other authors. When Toynbee refers to the Garden of Eden, like as not we recall our reading of other parts of *A Study of History* itself. The allusiveness thus has a reflexive quality; it is a binder.

The hortatory conclusion (IV, 583f.), too long for quotation here, to a seventy-page discussion of the Papacy illustrates this function of allusions. "The Apostle of Rome," "Servus Servorum Dei," and "Vicar of Christ" are used not as elegant variants but as terms evocative of various stages in the preceding exposition. In asking for a "second Hildebrand" with "the wisdom that is born of suffering," Toynbee recalls to us not only his discussion of Hildebrand but also in the following phrases from Aeschylus a theme which occurs again and again in other sections. And the entire peroration is shot through with Biblical quotation, paraphrase, and allusion. (It is true that in some sections of the text the allusiveness seems to make the passage more opaque rather than evocative and lucid.)

Simile, metaphor, and analogy inform the structure as well as the texture, the plan as well as the manner. Analogies and figurative comparisons are found not only in passing sentences but also in passages extending over whole pages and recurring throughout, like the master-image or leit-motif of the climbers (I, 192-194, 196, 298; III, 2f., 373, 390; IV, 5; V, 165), and the analogy of the interlocking searchlights (III, 227-230), the latter being certainly the most elaborate figure in contemporary English prose. Here again, no longer to our surprise, there is a reverse side to the coin, for the ambiguity between analogy used as illustration and analogy used as argument is bothersome to the judicious reader. Metaphore illuminates, but should it be used to persuade and control? And Toynbee's central method is in a sense analogical.

We find, then, that the rhythm, vocabulary, allusiveness, and figurativeness of individual sentences and passages are part and parcel of the rhythm, vocabulary, allusiveness, and figurativeness of the whole. And we find also, if we are candid, that the form and the content are organically related.

Thus, every esthetic aspect of the work involves the question of

truth. Setting aside the complexities of definition, we should dis-
criminate at least three different levels of that truth. One is that
of particular facts and observations; here the critics have had little
quarrel, for Toynbee does not misplace his dates or misrepresent
events. But the second level, that of interpretation, depends on the
selection and emphasis given to these events; here the minimizing
of material progress is indeed bizarre. The third concerns the
truth of the system taken as a whole; on the one hand, a system
that perversely identifies scientific method with mere technology
is open to question; on the other, we remember that the invalidity
of systems, from Aristotle's to Hegel's, need not vitiate the individual insights of their creators. Piecemeal criticism by specialists
—necessary as it was, is, and will be—has thus far blinded us to
the real character of *A Study of History*. In the first place, it is not
a work of history; Gibbon was the last single man to paint the vast
canvas of a whole civilization, and Toynbee deals with twenty-one
fully developed societies. In the second place, it is, *a fortiori,* not
a work of archaeology, sociology, philosophy, theology, or even
of all these combined; it enters each one of these fields, but no man
can be an authority in all of them. Taken as a whole, it is a huge
theological poem in prose. By so describing it, I do not make it
either superior or inferior to the simple work of history. Nor when
I suggest that it is, or is going to be, a work close to the genres of
imaginative literature, do I imply any use of such disparaging
phrases as *"just* a poem," *"merely* a poem." *Paradise Lost* remains,
but who can mention a work of history contemporary with it?

All this is not to urge that ambitious literary critics should now
concentrate on finding examples of tension, paradox, and ambiguity in *A Study of History* so as to lend luster to Toynbee's name and
their own—although that may well happen—but rather to suggest
that this work is closer to the realm of *belles-lettres* than we realize,
that the non-creative genres may approach creative literature or
recede from it with the changes of time(consider the sermon), and
that the special nature of this work poses unique problems for the
specialist and the literary critic.

A comparison to John Milton may illuminate the point. In
Milton's day such erudition as Toynbee possesses could still find
an outlet in poetry, which has now largely been displaced by prose.
Toynbee combines with his learning a moral force drawn from
Hellenic and Christian sources and, still like Milton, displays architectonic structure, manifold allusiveness, artistry in the use of
proper names, long cadences extending through sentences, paragraphs, and pages, and a most pervasive use of simile, metaphor,
and analogy. Unlike Milton, he has the resources of quotation and
anecdote, the latter sometimes humorous. Even those who would

point to esthetic deficiencies and difficulties can find analogues in *Paradise Lost*.

A Study of History could have appeared only at this particular point in time when events have made the collapse of societies more real, when the world has been brought closer together by the technology that Toynbee so often disparages, when scholarship has shown the interrelations between myths, history, and religion, and, finally, when a sometimes too eager hunger for transcendental faith has prepared the ground in various ways. (The last two conditions did not obtain in the same degree for Spengler.) *A Study of History* comes from the pen of a prose Milton dominated by the conception of St. Augustine's *City of God*. To view it simply as a work of history is as inadequate as it would be to consider Joyce's *Finnegan's Wake* simply as a novel.

COMMENT*

ARNOLD J. TOYNBEE

What struck me in reading the two reviews of my book by Professor Fiess and by my old friend Professor Geyl is that they agree with one another, and that I agree with them, in their view of what I am trying to do. I am trying to use our knowledge of history as a telescope-lens for taking a look at the universe as a whole. I do not see why one should not use historical knowledge in this way, besides using it as a microscope-lens for looking at particular pieces of the universe. Either way, we shall be seeing through a glass, darkly; for that is the limitation under which human minds have to work.

I agree with Professor Geyl that being interested in history, and knowing some, does not automatically make one an historian. If writing history means writing historical narrative, I may be an historian among other things, as I have written and published historical work in that perhaps uncontroversial sense. But, in choosing a name for the book under review, I deliberately called it not a history, but a study of history. If someone wrote a study of Shakespeare, and a critic objected "This isn't Shakespeare," the writer could, I think, reasonably reply: "I never said it was Shakespeare; I said it was a study of him." When one is studying history, one is examining history, not narrating it (except, of course, incidentally, by way of illustration).

Professor Geyl says that historians would not care if I wrote as a prophet. One can write just as well without writing as historian, prophet, or anything else in particular; and to think of oneself as a prophet would be to make a fool of oneself. One would feel still more foolish if the label were seriously meant when it is ironical. On the other hand, to be taken as a poet is agreeable; and I am very grateful to Professor Fiess for presenting me in this light. As far as I can judge about my own work, I should think that Professor Fiess' word describes me better than Professor Geyl's does. Anyway, I would rather be called minor poet than minor prophet. I do not mind being called minor historian, so long as it is understood that I am not renouncing the right to study history and to write some, too, when I choose. I have this right, like anyone else. It is one of our human freedoms.

*Journal of the History of Ideas, vol. 16, 1955, p. 421.

DATE DUE

SEP 20 '67			
NOV 7 '67			
NOV 21 '67			
APR 29 70			
APR 9 '71			
GAYLORD			PRINTED IN U.S.A.

Copyright © 1982 by

University Press of America,™ Inc.

**4720 Boston Way
Lanham, MD 20706**

**3 Henrietta Street
London WC2E 8LU England**

ISBN:0-8191-2026-X(Perfect)
0-8191-2025-1(Case)

Library of Congress Number:81-40162

ARNOLD TOYNBEE AND THE CRISIS OF THE WEST

Marvin Perry

UNIVERSITY
PRESS OF
AMERICA

LANHAM • NEW YORK • LONDON